Alan Palmer first trekked in Morocco 25 years ago. This adventure began serendipitously when he jumped aboard a shared taxi outside Bab er Robb, bound for the trailhead town of Asni, simply to escape the August heat of Marrakech. Once there he decided to climb Mt Toubkal, at 13,670ft the highest mountain in North Africa, and made it to the top wearing nothing on his feet but a pair of flimsy lounge shoes.

Since then he has travelled widely in Europe and Asia, often combining his trips with work as an archaeologist. He has trekked through some of the most spectacular mountainous regions of the Himalaya, Karakorum and Hindu Kush, and has contributed to two other guidebooks, *Pakistan* and *The Silk Road*, both by Insight Guides.

Alan returns to Morocco as often as possible and his latest project is to trek the entire length of the spine of the High Atlas Mountains. He is a Fellow of the Royal Geographical Society and a member of the British Moroccan Society.

Moroccan Atlas – the Trekking Guide
First edition: October 2010

Publisher
Trailblazer Publications
The Old Manse, Tower Rd, Hindhead, Surrey, GU26 6SU, UK
Fax (+44) 01428-607571, info@trailblazer-guides.com
www.trailblazer-guides.com

British Library Cataloguing in Publication Data
A catalogue record for this book is available from the British Library

ISBN 978-1-873756-77-5

Editor: Jim Manthorpe
Series editor: Bryn Thomas
Layout: Nick Hill
Proof-reading: Anna Jacomb-Hood
Cartography and line drawings (pp61-4): Nick Hill
Index: Anna Jacomb-Hood

Front cover photo: On the Toubkal Circular Trek: the steep ascent to Tizi-n-Likemt (3555m) (Photo © Alan Palmer)

Warning: mountain walking can be dangerous
Please read the notes on when to go (pp21-3), mountain safety (pp40-1) and health (p42 & pp257-63). Every effort has been made by the author and publisher to ensure that the information contained herein is as accurate and up to date as possible. However, they are unable to accept responsibility for any inconvenience, loss or injury sustained by anyone as a result of the advice and information given in this guide.

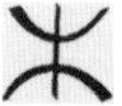

Symbol of the Berbers, *Imazighen*, the 'Free People'.

Printed on chlorine-free paper by
D'Print (☎ +65-6581 3832), Singapore

Moroccan Atlas
THE TREKKING GUIDE

ALAN PALMER

Developed and expanded from
Trekking in the Moroccan Atlas **by Richard Knight**

TRAILBLAZER PUBLICATIONS

Acknowledgements

This project would never have been started without inspiration from countless quarters, still less without the help of a hundred acts of kindness. If its beginning can be attributed to a single experience, then I thank Lynda Corry for suggesting a return to Morocco following far too long an absence. The writing of the route guide for the Jbel Toubkal Circular trek was shared with her. Thank you also to her son, Matthew, for understanding our need to travel together. I would like to thank Ian Wood for agreeing to undertaking two treks, the Mgoun Traverse and the ascent of Sirwa, rather later in the season than was good for anyone, least of all for his wife, Sas, and their children, Laetitia, Ella and Sebastien, whom he temporarily abandoned. He would like to acknowledge the support of Pascal Perron, Hafida Hdoubane and Mohamed Mezine in the completion of his treks.

Whether or not they are aware that they have helped in the shaping of this book, I would like to thank those who have trekked with me – notably Lars, who accompanied me on my first excursion into the Atlas, and Bob Mackenzie, who came to the summit of Sirwa – and the many gracious people who offered hospitality as I passed through their lands. Paramount, however, are the guides and muleteers without whose knowledge and expertise, fortitude and good humour I would never have even considered clambering over half as many mountain passes.

My experience of Moroccan guides began with Hamou, who, plucked from his carpentry workshop in Tighza, led two desperate trekkers across the Mgoun Traverse. Others I would like to thank are guide Mohamed Abouhssen and muleteer/cuisinier Mohamed Alahyan, whose good humour on my first Jbel Sahro Traverse I still remember fondly; guide Jamal Idhamou, muleteer Aigle, and two willing aides-de-camp, Aziz – whose decaying tooth tortured him throughout – and the pious Hassim, for the ascent of Jbel Sirwa. For surviving the trek to Erg Chegaga, I have Mustafa and Idir, both fine *chemeliers* (camel drivers) with warm hearts, to thank, along with my son, Bill, who dared to come, too. I thank Hamid Bahassou for guiding me with enthusiasm around the Mgoun Circular and Lahcen Bahassou for his quiet, thorough work as muleteer/cuisinier; guide Abdou Aït Tadrart and muleteer/cuisinier Lahcen Id Bleaid Bien Mohamed for my second ascent of Jbel Toubkal; guide Youssef Alami, who brought so much colour and interest to the Jbel Sahro Circular through his excellent knowledge of the meaning of place names, along with the most dependable Elhoucine Echourouk, cuisinier, and Kamal Ben Hssini, muleteer. For my second Jbel Sahro Traverse I am grateful to the very experienced, yet unassuming and hospitable guide, Hamou Aït Lhou, and muleteer Hsain Chatter. One further guide to whom I owe many thanks is Jamal Imerhane, based at the Bureau des Guides in Imlil. Although I have not yet had the good fortune to trek with him, he has kindly answered more questions to help with the writing of this book than was ever reasonable for me to ask of him.

Finally, sincere thanks are also due to the Trailblazer team: in particular to Richard Knight whose original *Trekking in the Moroccan Atlas* provided a solid framework for this guide, to Monty Menon, to publisher Bryn Thomas, to Jim Manthorpe for his patient editing, to Nick Hill for his careful cartography, and to Anna Jacomb-Hood for her thorough proofreading. For acknowledgements for the quotations used in the text see p264.

A request

The author and publisher have tried to ensure that this guide is as accurate and up to date as possible. Nevertheless things change. If you notice any changes or omissions that should be included in the next edition of this book, please write to Alan Palmer at Trailblazer (address on p2) or email him at alan.palmer@trailblazer-guides.com. A free copy of the next edition will be sent to persons making a significant contribution.

Updated information will be available at
www.trailblazer-guides.com

CONTENTS

INTRODUCTION

Morocco – 'le pays lointain le plus proche'

Morocco is a fascinating world of extremes. There are few places on earth where you can journey with such ease from the comfort of exotic cities, only ever imagined in an Arabian Nights fantasy, into a remote wilderness with extraordinary contrasts of stark mountains, green valleys and harsh deserts, of colourful, hospitable peoples and isolated, picturesque settlements.

The Moroccan Atlas is a mountain range of exceptional beauty and cultural interest but it is still relatively little visited, a fact which makes the Atlas, to my mind, a far more exciting proposition than the European ranges. Add to that the wonderful hospitality of the local Berber people, the rich texture of North African life and the dazzling allure of Marrakech and other Moroccan centres, and you will begin to see why a growing number of trekkers are choosing to explore this great range which the ancient Greeks thought to be the home of Atlas.

Why Morocco? On the one hand, it can be quickly and easily reached by most Western travellers; yet, on the other, Morocco calls us to step into a fantastic, often surreal world that, in so many aspects, is so very, very far from our own. As was once explained to me long ago, Morocco surpasses all other destinations because it is quite simply 'le pays lointain le plus proche' (the nearest far away country).

About this book

This guidebook has been written with both the experienced and novice trekker in mind. The routes described are challenging but accessible. Regular hikers might find they cover ground more quickly than the route notes suggest but the book has been designed to allow readers to tackle as much or as little as they please at any one time. It also contains detailed information on Marrakech, an exploration of which is a fascinating part of the Atlas experience, and on all other relevant towns and trailheads. There's practical information on every aspect of planning, arranging and enjoying an Atlas trek – from what to pack to what to say in French, Arabic and Berber. There are also sections on the fauna of the Atlas, a guide to bird life and a section on minimum impact trekking.

The routes

This book can include only a fraction of the treks available in the Atlas mountains, a range which spans some 1200 miles across Morocco, Algeria and Tunisia. But the routes reported here form a

representative selection and each offers some distinct or unique draw which qualifies it for inclusion in the guide: the Toubkal area is the highest in the Atlas; Mgoun is arguably the most classically beautiful; Sirwa is remote and challenging; and Sahro is the Atlas at its weird and striking best.

❑ Why trek?

Here's an early experience, shared with Lynda in the Central High Atlas Mountains when, travelling blind, having first blundered naively into danger we were transported deep into the heart of Berber hospitality. This chance encounter helped to open up to us the enchanted world to which we continue to feel compelled to return.

Perhaps he emerged from out of the ground. Perhaps he was a boulder gifted the breath of life or perhaps he was a trick of the light.

As we stood on the crest of a barren hillside and stared into the darkening gloom now enveloping the mountains, our hopes of finding a resting place for the night were fading. It was then that he moved. He must have heard us for a mile or so before he saw us, for no other life stirred that night. So unlikely was life amongst those fields of dust that at first I believed my eyes were being fooled. Not a word was spoken between us but we immediately felt his warmth and he our need. Without a moment's hesitation, he led and we followed.

Only the sense of the ground falling beneath our feet and the occasional ink blue glimmer of Bou Guemez below told us that we were descending. We continued to place our trust in the hands of this stranger and to follow him along ever-narrowing pathways, rather like following the boughs, then branches, then twigs of the indigenous argan tree, into the valley below until, quite without warning, he turned into a courtyard. Only moments before there had been no houses. Yet, rather as had our guardian, just at that point when we had begun to wonder whether fortune had deserted us, houses leaped up, not one or two, but a whole village of sun-baked bricks, out of the blackness of the night.

The glow of a paraffin lamp within drew us like moths to an almost bare room. Boots flicked to one side at the threshold, we were seated cross-legged on the floor around a silver teapot and a copper kettle which, through their very simplicity, assumed magical proportions.

Muffled tones of female voices could be heard from somewhere along unlit passages leading to further recesses within the house, voices which sometimes unexpectedly rose into animated exchanges, yet still we waited, uncertain as to what would unfold, whether we would be permitted to meet them, even in the half-light of the burner. They were active, and we sensed that our arrival had stirred that activity. But though we sometimes glimpsed shadows and silhouetted female forms, no woman came to our room.

When the door finally reopened, a young man entered bearing yet-unripe walnuts and fresh mint tea. They were spread before us across the geometric patterns of deep red hand-knotted rugs. Only when our host was assured that we were satisfied did he withdraw to leave us to our privacy, privacy in this, the prime room of his house, which now, without thought for his family or himself, he gave over to us.

Later that night we looked into each other's eyes and smiled, each mirroring peace and happiness to the other. We had forgotten all about the darkness which had by now quite engulfed the barren hillside outside. And we, though cocooned in our sleeping bags, felt so elated it seemed we were flying. **© Alan Palmer**

PLANNING YOUR TRIP 1

With a group or on your own?

He must be a dog, he goes on foot. **Arab proverb**

In comparison with European ranges such as the Alps or the Pyrenees, tourism in the Atlas Mountains is relatively undeveloped, so trekkers seeking solitude need not explore far beyond the more established routes; 'established' is a comparative word and indeed one meets few fellow trekkers even on the better-known routes. An exception is the Toubkal Circular Trek, although even here you may meet no more than a handful of trekkers once you have left behind the summit of Toubkal and the Aït Mizane Valley. There is a choice to be made, however: trekking with an organised group, with a guide, or completely alone.

INDEPENDENT TREKKING

Kipling said, 'He travels the fastest who travels alone,' but he had never navigated his way across the Atlas Mountains. It's not easy. There are no route markers and the trails themselves can be very indistinct. All but the most competent trekkers and map readers well-versed in the use of a compass should seriously consider employing a local guide rather than travelling solo.

TREKKING WITH A GUIDE AND MULETEER

Guides

It is relatively inexpensive and easy to arrange to employ a guide and muleteer once you arrive at your chosen trailhead. An official guide will cost from about £25/US$37.50/300dh per day, while a muleteer, along with his mule, will cost around £10/US$15/120dh per day or perhaps £20/US$30/250dh if he agrees to double up as your *cuisinier* (cook; see p11). There are some very good reasons for using a guide:

- **Safety** A guide will help prevent you from getting lost and will be ready to help find a way out of the mountains in an emergency.
- **Communication** Atlas Berbers have only recently begun to welcome visitors to their previously hidden world. Few speak French and fewer still know English. A guide will act as an interpreter so that you can talk to local people; apart from the cultural insight that such an exchange might offer, this could be critical in an emergency.

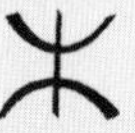

• **Understanding** If you form a good relationship with your guide, which is likely over the course of a trek, you'll benefit enormously from the chance this gives to learn more about Moroccan life and the land through which you pass.
• **Enjoyment** Finding your own way through the mountains will take some effort. Admittedly, it is this very challenge which appeals to some. However, if your guide is leading the way, you are free to concentrate on trekking rather than map-reading.

Morocco has a well-organised programme for training mountain guides. Would-be guides must pass a demanding three-day selection test before even being accepted on to the course. They are then given six months' training at the Centre de Formation aux Métiers de Montagne (CFAMM) just outside Tabant before qualifying. As official guides usually live at trailheads, finding one is simple. They can be identified by the personalised *guide de montagne* card which bears their name and photograph as well as by the set of documents they are given upon qualification. You should always ask to see these before agreeing to employ a guide.

Although there are only about 400 officially trained guides in the country, it is important that you employ one rather than a '*faux guide*' (unofficial guide). First and foremost, their profession is a proper one and they deserve to be taken seriously. They have undertaken a long and rigorous training which calls for respect. A guide who leads a trek into the mountains undertakes a big responsibility for your personal safety. Not only is a '*faux guide*' untrained to cope with unforeseen circumstances, he works illegally and faces prison should you have an accident. He may be able to offer his services for a lower price than an official guide, but he is able to do this because he neither declares his earnings nor pays tax.

There are likely to be times when employment of a guide will bring its own difficulties. To minimise the chance of this, do not engage the first official guide you find simply because he is qualified. It is important to employ a guide with whom you can develop a friendly, working relationship. First, drink tea, talk together and try to gauge whether you will get on well in the mountains. Clearly a shared language is important, especially if you are to learn from your guide. Most guides speak Berber and French and, increasingly, English, too.

Mules and *muleteers*

In districts like the Atlas, mules are more serviceable than any horse, and on the mountain roads will perform almost a third longer journey in a day.

R B Cunninghame Graham, *Mogreb-el-Acksa*, 1898

It is the custom in the Atlas for mules to carry baggage; locals will think it bizarre should you wish to carry your own. You should employ a muleteer as by so doing you not only respect local tradition but also you put money straight into local pockets. This even makes your trek safer since evacuation by mule is often the fastest way out of the Atlas in an emergency (see Mountain rescue, p41). Your guide will almost certainly expect to take responsibility for finding a muleteer for you, who will often be a family member or family friend.

The muleteer will stack what appears to be an enormous amount of baggage onto his mule but, if you fear for its safety, remember that this animal is a very expensive asset to him and he will not risk its health. In fact each mule carries about 100kg which usually equates to only about four rucksacks.

Despite his burden, do not even think about setting your pace against that of your mule. Your muleteer will set his own variable pace, his reasons often only truly understood by himself. In the morning he will usually be last to set off, so as to shut down camp after you have started to walk, but then race ahead of you to set up the next, often taking a different, more mule-friendly route.

For these reasons alone, never make the mistake of employing a muleteer as a cheap form of guide: it is not his job to walk with you and his choice of route will sometimes be restricted to less interesting, lower-level paths with gentler inclines. Indeed, while it is certainly true that most muleteers know their way round the mountains as well as guides, attempting to use a muleteer as a guide would be heavily frowned upon. Equally, never suggest paying a little extra for your guide to carry your pack as he would find such a proposal insulting.

Cuisinier

You will need to plan your food and water carefully before you depart from the trailhead. Whereas on some treks it would be quite possible on most days to eat meals prepared in *refuges* and *gîtes* along the way, notably around Toubkal, on other days and on other treks, such as in Jbel Sahro, this would be quite impossible and buying even basic provisions en route in mountain villages to prepare your own meals would be very problematic (see Eating in the Atlas, pp82-3).

It is the custom that you should pay for the food of your guide and muleteer while on the trek. Usually this involves employing your muleteer to double up as a *cuisinier* (cook), although you could employ a separate cuisinier. The cuisinier, usually with the help of your guide who has a vested interest in overseeing what will be eaten on the trip, will help you budget and buy food for the entire trip (see Budgeting and costs, pp19-21). If you negotiate a price *tout compris* (everything included), you will not even have to concern yourself with shopping for the food. It might sound rather indulgent to employ a cook but this is the accepted way of doing things.

Gîtes d'étape, refuges and camping

In summer the prospect of sleeping under the stars becomes a very tempting proposition, although on the higher slopes nights can become very cold even on still nights. Moreover, the weather can be very unpredictable and a tent (see What to take pp28-9) is strongly recommended as insurance. In winter, overnight temperatures plummet well below freezing in the High Atlas and, on the trail in the more southerly Sahro and Sirwa areas, nights can become very cold, too, even in spring and autumn (see When to go, pp21-3), so good-quality camping equipment is advised.

Remember to ask permission to camp whenever possible and always tidy up afterwards (see Environmental Impact, pp88-9). You will enjoy greater freedom if you take a tent and at times camping will be the only option open to you.

The Atlas is more populated than might be expected so, if camping is not your preferred option, you will often, but not always, find a village to stay in overnight. A large number provide simple accommodation in a basic gîte d'étape, which typically costs £4/US$6/50dh per night. Alternatively, the nature of Berber hospitality is such that, if you find yourself in a village with no gîte, or if it is full, there's a good chance you will be offered accommodation by a local family in a private house. Many trekkers prefer to take such opportunities to gain an insight into daily Berber life. Clearly, there is no set rate for such hospitality, but you should not expect to pay more than the price of a gîte.

There are also a few scattered refuges (mountain huts) in the High Atlas, some managed by Club Alpin Français (CAF), which can cost as little as £3/US$4.50/35dh for a bed in a dormitory . Both gîtes and refuges will often provide drinks, meals and even hot showers for an extra charge; refuges may also offer cooking facilities. Don't, however, expect five-star luxury. Even the better Atlas accommodation can be quite uncomfortable by European standards. The locations of refuges and gîtes are included in the route descriptions in Part 6.

GROUP TOURS

People join organised treks mainly because it is convenient but there are other advantages: there is a greater chance that your guide will speak your language and you might find yourself in a group of friendly, like-minded people. Certainly, this is one way of avoiding trekking solo. Many agencies combine trekking with other Moroccan 'highlights', such as the 'Kasbah Trail' or 'Imperial Cities', or other mountain activities. If you are looking for a higher level of comfort on your trek, the better agencies are likely to be able to provide this. Also, if you book through a company in your own country, you will probably find a representative on hand in Morocco to ensure that all runs smoothly.

On the downside, group tours are relatively expensive. Expect to pay about £600/US$900 for a one-week trek as part of a group in the Toubkal region excluding flights or about £800/US$1200 including flights. Also on the downside, group tours tend to follow a fixed itinerary. You might find that a group trek proceeds at a different pace to yours, typically adopting a mean speed which can be rather slow. What is more, trekking with a large group of the same nationality can put up barriers between you and the very local culture that you went to Morocco to experience.

If you do decide to take the group option, however, an internet search will quickly throw up a bewildering choice of both international adventure travel companies and Moroccan specialists offering a range of Atlas itineraries. You will also find a host of Moroccan-based trekking agencies and even freelance guides. These local agencies tend to be cheaper than their overseas competitors and, with the advent of the internet and email, are now much easier to make arrangements with than they were even in recent years. Ironically, the overseas-based agencies tend in any case to sub-contract to these Moroccan-based agencies to carry out their work for them, in the process draining potential revenue away from Morocco and into their own pockets. If you want local people to gain most benefit from your visit, employ local people directly.

TREKKING AGENCIES

In Britain

There are several British-based travel companies which offer treks in the Atlas Mountains.

- **Discover Ltd** (☎ 01883-744392; 🖳 www.discover.ltd.uk)
- **Best of Morocco** (☎ 0845-0264 585, ☎ 01249-467165, mob ☎ 07809-506787; 🖳 www.morocco-travel.com)
- **Guerba Expeditions** (☎ 01373-826611; 🖳 www.guerba.co.uk)
- **Exodus** (☎ 0845-863 9600; 🖳 www.exodus.co.uk)
- **Explore** (☎ 0845-013 1537; 🖳 www.explore.co.uk)
- **Great Walks of the World** (☎ 01935-810820; 🖳 www.greatwalks.net)
- **KE Adventure Travel** (☎ 017687-73966; 🖳 www.keadventure.com)
- **Sherpa Expeditions** (☎ 020-8577 2717; 🖳 www.sherpa-walking-holidays.co.uk)
- **Mountain Kingdoms** (☎ 01453-844400, ☎ 0845-330 8579; 🖳 www.mountainkingdoms.com)
- **Icicle Mountaineering** (☎ 0845-058 9878; 🖳 www.icicle-mountaineering.ltd.uk)
- **Pebbles Adventure Travel** (☎ 01392-427212; 🖳 www.pebblestravel.com)
- **Treks and Trails** (☎ 01539-567477, mob ☎ 07971-244907; 🖳 www.treksandtrails.co.uk)

Women who would prefer to trek with an all-female group should try **Walking Women** (☎ 0845-644 5335, ☎ 01926-313321; 🖳 www.walkingwomen.com). However, they do not operate treks to Morocco every year.

In continental Europe

Austria **El Mundo Reisen** (☎ 316-810 698, 🖳 www.elmundo.at).

Belgium **Allibert** (☎ 02 526 92 90, 🖳 www.allibert-trekking.com); **Boundless Adventures** (☎ 015-407 520; 🖳 www.joker.be); **Trek Aventure** (☎ 061-24 04 10; 🖳 www.trekaventure.com).

France **Icicle Mountaineering** (☎ 06-75 56 21 55; 🖳 www.icicle-mountaineering.ltd.uk); **Allibert** (☎ 08-25 09 01 90, Paris office ☎ 01 44 59 35 35; 🖳 www.allibert-trekking.com); **Atalante** (☎ 01-55 42 81 00, ☎ 04-72 53 24 80; 🖳 www.atlante.fr); **Terres d'Aventure** (☎ 08-25 70 08 25; 🖳 www.terdav.com).

Germany **Wikinger Reisen** (☎ 0 23 31/90 46, 🖳 www.trekking.de).

Netherlands **Flach Travel Company** (☎ 03-43 59 26 59; 🖳 www.flachtravel.com).

Switzerland **Allibert** (☎ 022-849 85 51; 🖳 www.allibert-trekking.com); **Acapa Reisen Mutschellen GMBH** (☎ 056-631 86 64; 🖳 www.acapa.ch).

Trekking agencies in North America
- **Explore** (☎ 1-800 486 9096; 💻 www.explore.co.uk)
- **Wilderness Travel** (☎ 1-800 368 2794; 💻 www.wildernesstravel.com)
- **Trek Escapes** (☎ 1-780 439 0024, 1-800 387 3574; 💻 www.trekescapes.com)

Trekking agencies in Australia
- **Intrepid Travel** (☎ 03-9473 2626; 💻 www.intrepidtravel.com)
- **Peregrine Adventures** (☎ 03-8601 4444; 💻 www.peregrineadventures.com)

Trekking agencies in New Zealand
- **House of Travel** (☎ 0800-838747; 💻 www.houseoftravel.co.nz)

Trekking agencies in South Africa
- **Mask Expeditions** (☎ 011-807 3333, 💻 www.maskexpeditions.co.za)

Trekking agencies in Morocco
For Marrakech see p101; for Ouarzazate see p127; see also entries for individual trailheads in Part 6: Route guides.

Getting to Morocco

Morocco can be reached from Britain by air, road and rail and from Europe by air, road, rail and sea. Information in this section is particularly vulnerable to change and you would be wise to confirm that the following details remain accurate at the time of planning your trip.

BY AIR

The best way of reaching Morocco, from anywhere other than from southern Spain, is by air. Despite rises in world oil prices, the cost of air flights into Morocco from Europe remains relatively low.

A return flight from London or Paris to Marrakech, for example, using one of the listed carriers below, can still cost as little as £150/US$225/€170. Your chances of securing such a low fare improve if you have the flexibility to select either early morning or late night midweek flights.

Note, however, that prices can rise significantly for weekend flights and at peak times, particularly around Christmas and New Year, and in school holidays, notably the summer months of July and August, when prices can rise to as much as £600/US$900 return. Fares are all the more unpredictable because of the pricing policies of the 'low-cost' airline companies that serve Morocco. In general, prices rise closer to your departure date and you would therefore be well advised to book your ticket as far in advance as possible.

Morocco is served by a number of international airports. Of these, Marrakech and Ouarzazate are the most convenient for reaching the High Atlas Mountains, while Ouarzazate and Agadir are the most convenient for the Sirwa region and Jbel Sahro.

From Britain

At the time of writing, the following airlines have direct flights to Morocco; fares start at around £150 return. **Easyjet** (☎ 0871-244 2366, 💻 www.easyjet.com) operates daily flights between Gatwick and Marrakech; twice daily on Tuesdays, Thursdays and Saturdays. Flights also operate between Manchester and Marrakech (3/week), and between Gatwick and Agadir (2/week). **Ryanair** (☎ 0871-246 0000, 💻 www.ryanair.com) operates flights between London Luton and Marrakech (4/week), and from Bristol, East Midlands and Edinburgh to Marrakech (2/week). Flights also operate between Liverpool and Agadir (2/week) and between Stansted and Fes (3/week).

Royal Air Maroc (☎ 020-7307 5800, 💻 www.royalairmaroc.com) flies from both Heathrow and Gatwick airports to Marrakech, Fes, Agadir, Ouarzazate and Casablanca; Casablanca serves as its hub airport in Morocco. **Atlas Blue** (a subsidiary of RAM; ☎ 020-7307 5803; 💻 www.atlas-blue.com) fly regularly between London Gatwick and both Marrakech and Fes, and between London Heathrow and Tangier. **Thomson** (☎ 0871 231 4787, 💻 www.thomson.co.uk) fly to Marrakech (2/week) from both London Gatwick and Manchester; **Thomas Cook** (☎ 0871 230 2406, 💻 www.thomascook.com) fly weekly to Agadir from London Gatwick and from Manchester.

From Continental Europe

Easyjet (💻 www.easyjet.com) flies from Paris CDG, Lyon, Madrid and Milan Malpensa to Casablanca, as well as from Madrid and Paris CDG to Tangier. In addition, Marrakech can be reached from Madrid, Geneva, Milan Malpensa, Lyon, Paris CDG and Basel-Mulhouse-Freiburg, and Agadir from Paris CDG and Milan Milapensa. **Ryanair** (💻 www.ryanair.com) flies to Marrakech from: Madrid, Barcelona Girona, Barcelona Reus, Seville, Alicante, Brussels Charleroi, Frankfurt-Hahn, Dusseldorf Weeze, Bremen, Milan Bergano and Pisa. In addition, Agadir can now be reached from Dusseldorf Weeze, Brussels Charleroi and Frankfurt-Hahn; Tangier from Brussels Charleroi, Milan Bergamo, Marseille and Madrid; and Nador from Brussels Charleroi and Madrid.

Royal Air Maroc (💻 www.royalairmaroc.com) flies from Paris to Marrakech and Ouarzazate daily, as well as to Tangier and Casablanca. **Atlas Blue** (💻 www.atlas-blue.com) operates regular flights between Marrakech and Barcelona, Bordeaux, Brussels, Geneva, Lille, Lyon, Madrid, Marseille, Milan, Nantes, Nice, Paris (Orly) and Toulouse, as well as between Tangier and Brussels, Barcelona, Madrid, Paris (CDG and Orly) and Amsterdam. Additional flights connect Fes with Lyon and Marseilles. **Air France** (France ☎ 0820-320 820; 💻 www.airfrance.fr) flies from Paris Charles de Gaulle to Casablanca four times daily and into Rabat twice daily, fares starting at about €200/US$270/£180.

From USA and Canada

Royal Air Maroc (💻 www.royalairmaroc.com) flies several times per week from New York (fares from US$1100) and Montreal (fares from US$1000/CAN$1200) to Casablanca in just over seven hours from where there are connecting flights both to Marrakech and Ouarzazate, amongst other Moroccan cities. The alternative would be to take a flight from North America to Europe with a European airline and from there a connecting flight to Morocco.

From New Zealand and Australia

As there are no direct flights between Australasia and Morocco, travellers would need to fly first to either the Middle East or Europe, perhaps with **Emirates** (NZ ☎ 050 836 4728, Australia ☎ 0130 030 3777; 💻 www.emirates .com) or a European carrier, before taking a connecting plane.

BY ROAD

Morocco can be reached from Britain by road, supported by a ferry crossing (see below), either by private car or by coach. **Eurolines UK** (☎ 08717-818181, 💻 www.eurolines.co.uk) runs air-conditioned coaches to Marrakech out of London Victoria coach station on Mondays and Fridays, departing at 10pm and arriving at the *gare routière* in Marrakech at 8am on day four.

The return journey departs Marrakech on Tuesdays and Fridays at 8pm arriving at Victoria coach station at 6am on day four. A single journey costs £144 and a return journey £246. The 58-hour journey includes a lengthy stop in Paris in both directions where additional passengers are picked up.

BY RAIL

It is equally possible to go by train (and ferry) from London to Marrakech. The quickest route takes about 48 hours: take the **Eurostar** (☎ 08705-186186; 💻 www.eurostar.com) from London to Paris and then a sleeper train (called train-hotel) to Madrid. The Altaria train goes from Madrid to Algeciras where the ferry (see below) crosses to Tangier-Med. There is another train service from here to Marrakech, with the option of taking an overnight sleeper. The cheapest way of completing this journey would cost around £350/US$475 return (second class).

Details of this and various other permutations, including instructions on how to book each of these stages, are explained at 💻 www.seat61.com. Alternatively, for a truly comprehensive consideration of all possibilities consult the *Thomas Cook European Timetable*, updated monthly, which has train, bus and ferry times for every country in Europe, and the *Thomas Cook Overseas Timetable,* updated bi-monthly, which contains the same for the rest of the world, including Morocco. These timetables are available from Thomas Cook (☎ 01733-416477; 💻 www. thomascookpublishing.com) and most bookshops.

BY FERRY

European road and rail users will need to cross to Africa by ferry. Two companies operating ferries to Morocco are **SNCM** and **Comanav**. Tickets for both can be bought in Britain through **Southern Ferries Travel Limited** (☎ 0844-815 7785; 💻 www.southernferries.co.uk), based at 30 Churton St, Victoria, London SW1V 2LP.

The most commonly used and cheapest route is from Algeciras to Tangier-Med, about 40 km east of Tangier, completed in as little as an hour (from £53/US$70/€60 return for a foot passenger or £200/US$300/€229 return for a single passenger with a small car), although there are alternatives from Spain including the shorter crossing from Algeciras to Ceuta (45 mins; from £60/US$90/€65 return for a foot passenger or £200/US$300/ €231 for a single passenger with a small car), Málaga to the Spanish enclave of Melilla (8hrs from £53/US$70/€60 return for a foot passenger or £310/US$415/€350 for a single passenger with a small car) and Almería to Melilla (10hrs, also £53/US$70/€60 return for a foot passenger or £310/US$415/€350 for a single passenger with a small car). Comanav run a ferry service from Sète in southern France to Tangier in 36 hours. This last ferry, however, is expected to transfer to Tangier-Med, along with a number of other services, from October 2010 onwards.

Another good source for bookings is **Direct Ferries** (☎ 0871-222 3312; 💻 www.directferries.co.uk) which can book ferries through Balearia, Transmediterranea, FRS and Grandi Navi Veloci into Tangier, Ceuta, Al Hocemia, Melilla and Nador. Perhaps the most interesting route on offer is the weekly 45-hour crossing from Genoa, Italy, into Tangier.

Visas and documents

All visitors to Morocco require a passport which must be valid for at least six months from the date of entry into the country. In exceptional circumstances, some European Union citizens forming part of a tour group might be permitted to use an identity card. Nationals of the United States, Canada, Australia, Japan,

❑ Moroccan embassies and consulates

Australia Embassy (☎ 061-262 900 755/766; 💻 www.moroccoembassy.org.au) PO Box 3531, Manuka, ACT 2603, Canberra; **Canada** Embassy (☎ 1 613-236 7391/2/3; 💻 sifamaot@bellnet.ca) 38 Range Rd, Suite 1510, Ottawa, Ontario, K1N 8J4; **Canada** Consulate General (☎ 01-51 42 88 50/69 51; 📠 01-51 42 88 48 59; 💻 www.consulatdumaroc.ca) 2192, Boulevard Levesque, Ouest Montreal, Quebec, H3H 1R6; **France** Embassy (☎ 01-45 20 69 35; 💻 www.amb-maroc.fr) 5 rue le Tasse, Paris 75016; **Spain** Embassy (☎ 915-63 1090; 💻 www.embajada-marruecos.es) Calle Serrano 179, 28002 Madrid; **UK** Embassy (☎ 020-7581 5001/2/3/4; 💻 consmorocco.uk@lycos.co.uk) 49 Queen's Gate Gardens, London SW7 5NE; **UK** Consulate General (☎ 020-7724 0624/ 0719; 💻 consmorocco.uk@lycos.co.uk) Diamond House, 97-99 Praed St, London W2 1NT; **USA** Embassy (☎ 202-462 7979; 📠 202-462 76 43/62 35 77/62 13 27/62 65 01; 💻 www.themoroccanembassy.com) 1601 21st St NW, Washington DC 20009; **USA** Consulate General (☎ 01-212 213 96 44; 💻 www.moroccanconsulate.com) 10 East 40th St, 24th Floor, New York, NY10016.

For a full list of all Moroccan embassies and consulates, visit the Ministry of Foreign Affairs and Co-operation (💻 www.maec.gov.ma).

Ireland, Britain and other EU countries require neither a visa nor a return ticket to stay in Morocco for up to 90 days. Nationals of South Africa, New Zealand, Norway, Switzerland and Turkey, amongst others, require a visa valid for three months. They should apply to their nearest Moroccan embassy or consulate well before their planned date of travel.

Application forms for all types of visa can be downloaded from the **Moroccan Embassy** homepage (💻 www.morocco.embassyhomepage.com) and from the **Ministry of Foreign Affairs and Co-operation** website (💻 www.maec.gov.ma). Visitors can apply for an extension to their stay. However, this is a fairly protracted procedure and would necessitate a visit to a *Bureau des Étrangers*, located in main police stations of large towns, at least 15 days before your 90 days are due to expire.

Be aware that the Moroccan Embassy homepage clearly warns, 'Embassy rules and regulations can and do, very occasionally change overnight. We accept no responsibility for any such changes'. All travellers to Morocco, therefore, should check that the information above remains current.

❑ FURTHER SOURCES OF INFORMATION

Travel advice

For up-to-date advice on travel in Morocco or, indeed, anywhere in the world, contact:

- **The Foreign & Commonwealth Office** (UK) ☎ 020-7008 1500; 💻 www.fco.gov.uk
- **Department of State** (USA) ☎ 1 888-407 4747 (from the USA), ☎ +1 202-501 4444 (from abroad); 💻 www.travel.state.gov
- **Department of Foreign Affairs and International Trade** (Canada) ☎ 1 800-267 8376 (toll-free in Canada) or ☎ 613-944 4000 (outside Canada); 💻 www.international.gc.ca
- **Department of Foreign Affairs and Trade** (Australia) ☎ +61 2-6261 1111; 💻 www.dfat.gov.au.

National tourist information offices

Moroccan tourism information offices (ONMT, Office National Marocain du Tourisme) are located in numerous capital cities around the world.

Australia (☎ 02-9922 4999) 11 West St North, Sydney, NSW 2060; **Canada** (☎ 514-842 8111; 💻 onmt@qc.aira.com) 1800 McGill College, Suite 2450, Montreal, Quebec H3A 3J6; **France** (☎ 01 42 60 63 50 ; 💻 tourisme.maroc@wanadoo.fr) 161, rue Saint-Honoré, 75001 Paris; **Italy** (☎ 02-5830 3633; 💻 info@turismomarocco.it) 23 Via Larga, 1-20122 Milano; **Spain** (☎ 91-542 7431; 💻 informacion@turismomarruecos.com) Ventura Rodriguez 24, 1-IZQ28008 Madrid; **UK** (☎ 020-7437 0073; 💻 www.tourism-in-morocco.com) 205 Regent St, 2nd Floor, London W1R 7DE; **USA** (☎ 347-791 5640; 💻 info@mnto-usa.org) 104 West 40th St, Suite 1820, Manhattan, New York.

For information on other ONMT offices visit 💻 **www.visitmorocco.com**.

Most major Moroccan towns have an ONMT which can provide basic information such as town maps and accommodation lists. See p100 for details of the Marrakech office and pp126-7 for that in Ouarzazate. The office in Rabat is at 31 rue Oued Fes (at the junction with avenue Al Abtal), Agdal, Rabat (☎ 0537-68 15 31/32/33, 68 15 41/42; 💻 visitmorocco@onmt.org.ma).

Before formal entry into Morocco, all visitors are required to complete a disembarkation form. Travellers' folklore advises all to keep answers simple to minimise the risk of attracting unwanted attention from officials.

There are reports that some tourists have experienced difficulties leaving the country at the end of their stay because their passports bore no entry stamp. It is worth making absolutely sure that your passport is provided with an entry stamp at passport control each time you enter Morocco and that this stamp is legible.

No certificate of vaccination is required for travellers coming from Europe or America although a cholera vaccination may be required for travellers coming into Morocco from an infected area. No trekking permits are required for any of the routes described in this guide nor, indeed, for any other part of the Moroccan Atlas.

Budgeting and costs

ACCOMMODATION AND MEALS

Western travellers will find Morocco to be a fairly inexpensive destination. **Accommodation** is plentiful and can be very cheap. Only in August are you likely to experience difficulties in finding a bed, and even then only in busy tourist destinations, such as Marrakech. In the Medina of Marrakech, prices typically start at around £5/US$7.50/60dh per person for a room in a small unclassified, bottom-of-the-range hotel, although even for as little as £25/US$35/300dh you could be provided with a double room in one of the city's larger, main street hotels. Prices in smaller towns and villages can be lower still. A bed in a rural *gîte d'étape*, for example, normally costs £4/US$6/50dh while some hotels in small towns like Azilal might charge as little as £2.50/US$4/30dh. In the mountains, CAF huts typically charge around £4/US$6/50dh to £8/US$12/100dh in summer per person for a bed in a dormitory, dependent upon your membership status, though their rates can double in winter.

On the other hand, there are many opportunities, particularly in and around Marrakech, to stay in much more expensive, luxury accommodation, where the top prices can match anything you might pay in Europe (see Marrakech, Where to Stay pp108-11). Between the two extremes is a growing number of chic *riads* and *maisons d'hôtes,* renovated, historic town houses built around a central, classically-tiled courtyard or garden, often with a small, splashing fountain adding to its beauty. Particularly common in Marrakech, they are also becoming increasingly prevalent in other towns and cities across Morocco. One of their main benefits can be their roof terrace, often affording memorable views across a medina. Maisons d'hôtes begin at around €50 (£45/US$65/500dh); riads tend to be more expensive, sometimes much more expensive.

Like its accommodation, **food** in Morocco can also be very cheap; a full meal in a simple café might cost as little as £2.50/US$3.50/30dh or 40dh and even in a rural gîte, where transport costs might slightly push up the price, it might cost only £4/US$6/50dh. There are excellent restaurants, too, although the top recommendations, again often in Marrakech, are usually less expensive than their European counterparts (see Where to eat, p111-13).

GUIDES AND TRANSPORT

There are few expenses to be incurred in the Atlas Mountains. Once your trek is underway, even if you feel you want to spend money, there will be few opportunities. Your biggest outlay will be for your guide, muleteer, *cuisinier* and food.

The cost of hiring an official guide starts at £25/US$37.50/250dh per day, rising to perhaps £33/US$50/400dh, particularly for an English-speaker. A muleteer and his mule will cost around £10/US$15/120dh per day, or perhaps £20/US$30/250dh if he agrees to double up as your cook, otherwise a specialist cook will cost about £12/US$18/150dh. Whichever option you take, food will cost a further £8-12/US$12-18/100-150dh per trekker per day, depending on the meals to be prepared. The price for food should include breakfast, lunch, evening meal and small mid-morning snacks, such as nuts and fruit (see Eating in the Atlas, pp82-3). Mineral water and soft drinks are not normally included. It is the responsibility of your muleteer to provide for the needs of his mule, including the mule's food, from his own wages. In the unlikely event that you decide to buy your own mule, count on paying between £400/US$600/5000dh and £800/US$1200/10,000dh.

Clearly, these costs are reduced per head when two or more trekkers combine to form a team: the cost of the guide can be shared and one muleteer/*cuisinier* will normally suffice for two or even three trekkers.

On the other hand, organised treks can be much more expensive. Expect to pay about £600/US$900 for a one-week trek as part of a group in the Toubkal region excluding flights or about £800/US$1200 including flights, bearing in mind that prices vary with the level of comfort offered and the route selected.

The cost of transport in Morocco is substantially lower than in Europe. A second-class train ticket for the three-hour-and-ten-minute journey from Tangier to Marrakech will cost £15/US$22.50/190dh, while a seven-hour bus journey from Marrakech to Taliwine costs just £5/US$7.50/65dh. *Grands taxis*, which can cover ground much more quickly, are more expensive but still very good value: a single seat from Marrakech to Azilal costs £6/US$9/70dh while to book the whole taxi to cover the same two-hour journey would cost £40/US$60/500dh. Shorter journeys by grands taxis, however, while still good value, do become proportionately more expensive. (See relevant town sections for details of specific fares). Cheapest of all is a hitched ride on the back of a *camion* (lorry).

OTHER EXPENSES ON THE TRAIL

The price of everyday goods bought in the Atlas can be double that which you might pay in a town. The standard charge for many small items in the mountains seems, for now, to have settled at £1/US$1.50/10dh, whether this is for a large bottle of mineral water, a small Coca-Cola, a Mars bar or even a toilet roll. There

❑ Prices for everyday goods in the mountains

Item	Price
Large bottle of water	£1/US$1.50/12dh
Small bottle of Coca-Cola	£1/US$1.50/12dh
Box of matches	10p/15cents/1dh
Bread	12p/18cents/1.50dh
Half a litre of milk	30p/45cents/4dh
One egg	12p/18cents/1.50dh
Toilet roll	£1/US$1.50/12dh
AA batteries	£1/£1.50/12dh
Film	£2.50/US$4/30dh
Tin of tuna	£1/US$1.50/12dh
Sunscreen	£5/US$7.50/60dh
Chocolate bar	£1/US$1.50/12dh

is little point in haggling: any savings that you might make are going to be small, yet any good will that you might lose could be substantial. Similarly, why soil the atmosphere of your night in a Berber house by haggling?

At the end of the trek, your guide and muleteer/*cuisinier* will hope for a tip. Normally this might be the equivalent of an extra day's wages. While keeping the size of your tip to sensible proportions (see Tipping, p76), you should regard this as an opportunity to show them your respect, to acknowledge the skill and expertise of those who have brought you safely over the mountains, who have shared their world with you, thereby adding much richness to your experience. One of my finest memories is that of a triumphant march into Nkoub, at the end of a beautiful trek across the Jbel Sahro, made all the more special by the relationships that had formed on the trek. Language barriers had partly inhibited my guide's understanding of how much he was appreciated: the tip he received removed all such doubts.

When to go

CLIMATE

Marrakech sits in the foothills of the High Atlas but shares the predominantly Mediterranean climate of north-east Morocco. Summers are usually very hot and dry with little rainfall and temperatures soar to 40°C and higher. Winter temperatures hover around 20°C with rainfall seldom much above 25mm in any one month, although the influence of the Sahara can make nights cold.

The **Central High Atlas** can be trekked all year, although winters are cold, wet and snowy. The highest peaks can be under snow from as early as November to as late as June, when both inexperienced and ill-equipped trekkers are limited to walking below the snow-line. This period is overlapped by the rainy

AVERAGE MAX/MIN TEMPS

AVERAGE RAINFALL

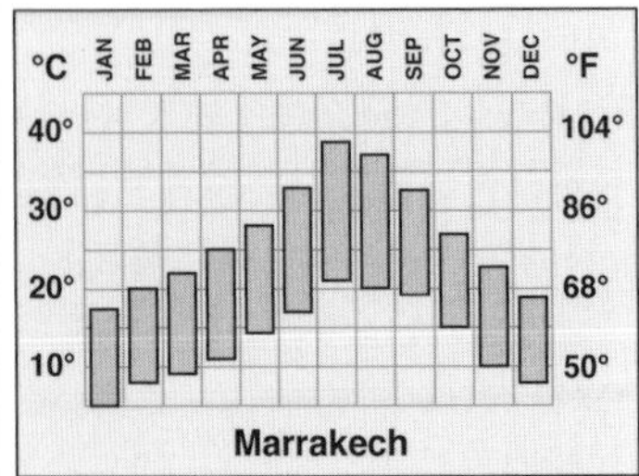

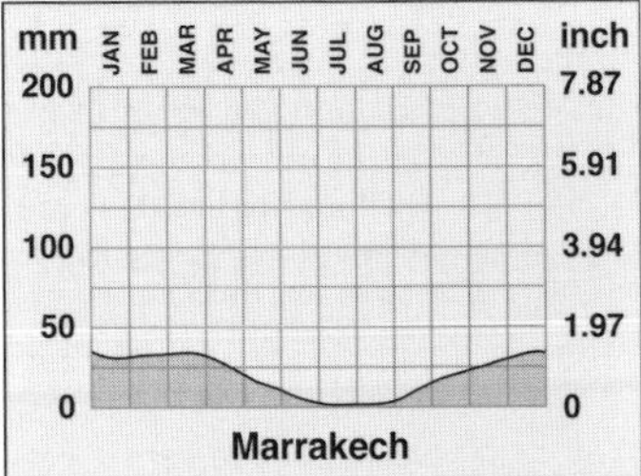

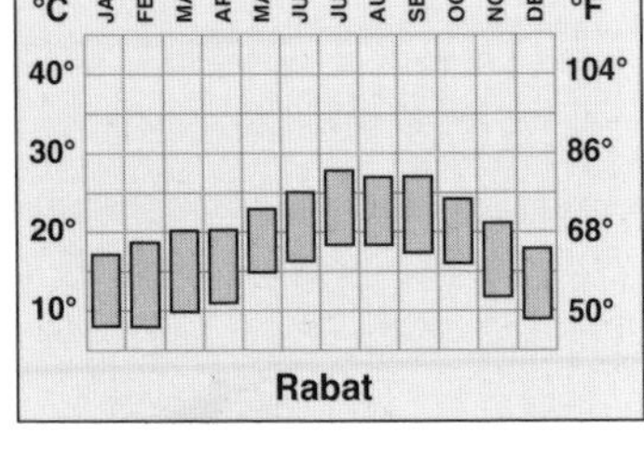

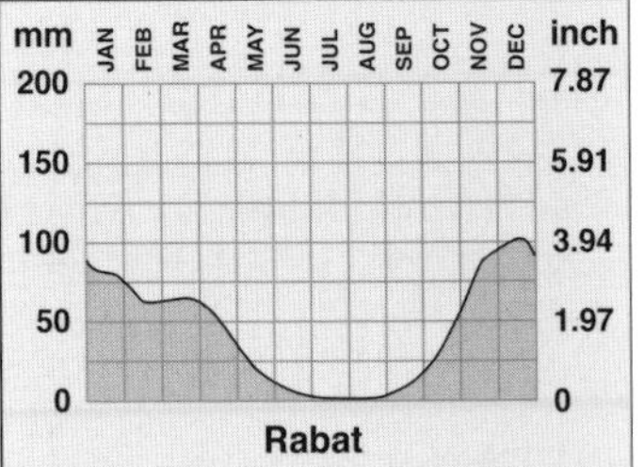

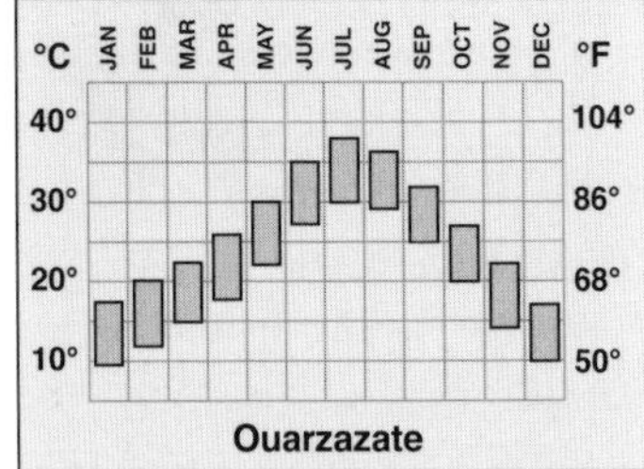

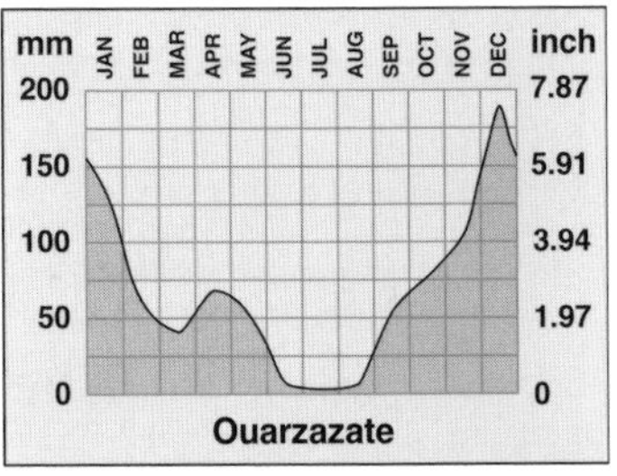

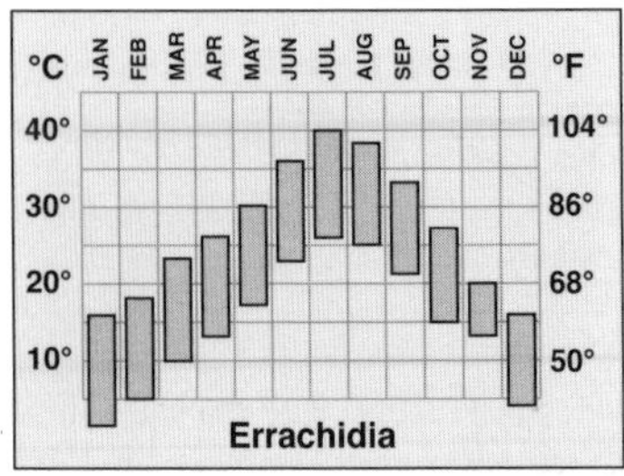

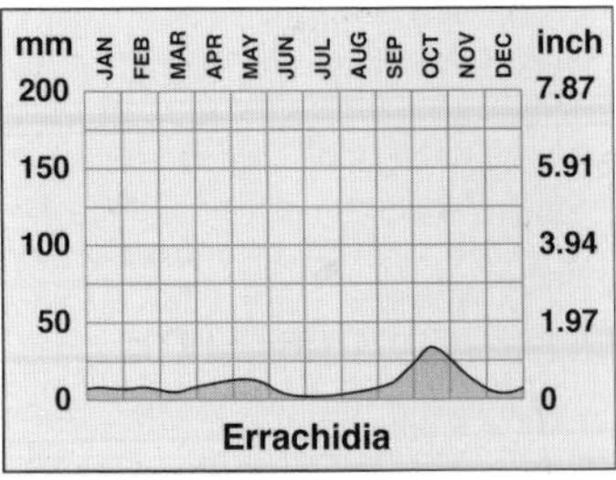

season which lasts from October to April. During these months the mountains can become very wet, with swollen rivers even flooding their banks.

In summer, once you climb out of the often searing heat of the valleys, temperatures are generally fairly comfortable, although it can be very cold on the higher peaks at night. Rivers and other sources of water, plentiful in winter, become trickles or even disappear completely. In general, the better time to go is between April and November; within this, the quiet, low season months of May and June are probably the best of all.

The **Anti-Atlas** are best trekked between October and April when the temperatures during the day are very pleasant, although nights can be very cold at altitude, even at the beginning and the end of this period. Temperatures outside these months can climb to very uncomfortable heights which would remind you of the region's close proximity to the Sahara.

At all times, be mindful of the possibility of flash floods.

RAMADAN

While trekking in Morocco during Ramadan would provide a fascinating cultural insight into the Muslim world, your experience might be complicated by the reluctance of some guides and muleteers to work during this holy month (see p74). Of course, the very practicality of abstaining from food and water, especially in years when Ramadan falls during hot summer months, makes their job more difficult. You too might feel uncomfortable eating or drinking at such times and may even decide to join them in their fasting. On the whole, however, despite commonly repeated views to the contrary, it is not unduly difficult to trek during this period as many guides, given the opportunity, do choose to continue working.

Route options

The Atlas Mountains form one of the world's great trekking ranges. Beauty and adventure, diversity and challenge are all to be found here. The route you choose, however, will depend upon a number of factors. These will include not only the season but also your level of fitness. You should also think carefully about your reasons for visiting the Atlas. If you wish to reach the roof of North Africa, make for Toubkal; if you want to drink tea in a traditional Berber village, go to Mgoun. Trekkers hoping to find solitude will meet few other travellers on the ascent of Jbel Sirwa, while the Sahro region offers striking landscapes and isolated, semi-nomadic communities.

PLANNING YOUR ROUTE

In whichever part of the Atlas you decide to trek, make sure that you allow enough time to comfortably complete your route; the most rewarding treks are those taken leisurely enough to allow you to enjoy the world through which you are passing. You should also ensure that you leave sufficient time to get to and from your trailhead, allowing for any unforeseen delays in public transport.

Finally, no matter how many times you have visited Morocco, try to build in a couple of days both at the beginning and at the end of your trek – first to acquire a sense of place on arrival as well as giving you time to find a guide and afterwards to give an opportunity to reflect upon your experiences. There should be no pressure to get into your trek, nor any to leave it behind.

JBEL TOUBKAL (see pp138-51)

The Toubkal region of the Central High Atlas is by far the most frequented area of the whole of the Atlas, chiefly on account of the attraction of Mount Toubkal (4167m/13,667ft), the highest summit in North Africa. Indeed, many visitors, particularly at weekends, settle for a rapid ascent and a hasty retreat to the plains in as little as two days.

Circular trek

The classic circuit described here, however, which incorporates the climb to the summit, requires six or seven days' trekking. Both this and the two-day option involve setting out from and returning to the lively, upbeat market town of Imlil.

Pros and cons The views, not only from the summit of Toubkal, but also from the two major passes of Tizi-n-Ouanoums (3664m/12,017ft) and Tizi-n-Ouraï (3109m/10,200ft), are quite stunning. A swim in Lac d'Ifni would never be forgotten. The significant presence of fellow trekkers on this route, however, particularly in the Aït Mizane Valley, will be seen as a blessing by some and a distraction by others. Toubkal is a beautiful but stark and uncompromising landscape which often surprises visitors. In 1986, during the course of my first unplanned and poorly prepared visit, the shoes that I wore were cut right from my feet by sharp scree, almost omnipresent on mountain slopes in this region. What is more, the Toubkal trail involves both significant ascents and steep descents which, apart from being very arduous, all too often cause some trekkers to experience serious altitude-related difficulties (see p42).

MGOUN MASSIF (see pp151-88)

Also in the Central High Atlas, the Mgoun massif is the second most popular trekking destination in Morocco. The area is distinguished by Ighil Mgoun (4068m/13,343ft), the only peak above 4000m outside the Toubkal area. Two six-day routes in the area are described here, both departing from the pleasant, relaxed market town of Tabant in the fertile Aït Bou Guemez Valley.

Circular trek

This trail climbs up over the Tizi n'Oumskiyq (2909m/9541ft) and the Aghouri Est (3400m/11,152ft) passes to the glorious Tarkeddid Plateau (2900m/9512ft) and then higher again to the exposed summit of Ighil Mgoun before finally descending to the Oulilimt Valley and on to a series of charming Berber villages. From here the route climbs once more to cross the Tizi-n-Aït Imi (2905m/9528ft) then finally descends back into Tabant.

Pros and cons The picturesque villages and green valleys of the lower reaches of this trek contrast wonderfully with the remoteness of its dramatic passes and the approach to the summit of Mgoun from where spectacular views are to be enjoyed. For better or for worse, it is almost inevitable that other trekkers will be met along the way, especially on the final ascent of Mgoun but also before crossing the Tizi-n-Aït Imi where groups are likely to be met coming over in the opposite direction from Tabant towards the Valley of the Roses (see box p224).

Traverse

This relatively easy route, which leads from one picturesque village to the next, largely following successive river valleys, nevertheless includes the challenging pass of Tizi-n-Rougelt (2960m/9380ft).

Pros and cons More than any other route described in this book, this trek is likely to offer opportunities to experience warm Berber hospitality, even to seek overnight accommodation in traditional homes and gain an insight into a way of life which has largely remained unchanged for centuries. The gentleness of the trek will allow you to appreciate the beauty of the villages all the more: Megdaz is often referred to as the most picturesque village in the Atlas. On the other hand, some might feel dissatisfied by the trek's lack of strenuous challenge.

JBEL SIRWA (see pp188-203)

The challenge of the volcanic Jbel Sirwa (3305m/10,840ft), lying between the High Atlas and Anti-Atlas ranges, provides a natural focus in this arid landscape of wonderful rock formations and remote villages. Although one of the most popular and inspiring destinations in Morocco, trekkers are relatively scarce and certainly much less common than in the High Atlas range to the north. A trek in the Jbel Sirwa consequently can offer a much greater sense of isolation.

Circular trek

The six-day trek described in this book, allowing for a start and finish in Taliwine, is the classic circuit of Jbel Sirwa. Climbing steadily through a succession of villages, the summit is reached in four strenuous days.

Pros and cons The final ascent of Sirwa makes this a fairly difficult trek, but the approach, through unspoiled picturesque villages with the ultimate reward of stunning 360° views from the summit across a deserted landscape, lifts the spirits and soothes aching muscles.

JBEL SAHRO (see pp203-46)

A trek in the Jbel Sahro offers the opportunity for a lower level, less physically demanding hike than others covered in this guide whilst still presenting its own set of challenges. For one, the region is less frequented by trekkers than even

Sirwa and consequently there is almost no infrastructure to support your trek. Also, navigation through this area is particularly difficult (see the introduction to this region on pp203-4) so, even if you only take a guide with you once in Morocco, seriously consider taking one here.

The rewards for your efforts will be considerable. The landscape is mostly dry and is only really occupied by transient, semi-nomadic goatherds. The fascinating rock formations that punctuate the terrain can leave a sense of walking on a different planet.

Traverse

The desolate but fascinating southern town of Nkoub, the town of the 40 kasbahs, is the trailhead for this 4- to 5-day trek through the heart of Jbel Sahro. It allows for a finish either in Boumalne du Dades or Qalaa't Mgouna, both in the green valley of the River Dades.

Pros and cons The very act of traversing this wild landscape alone provides a fine sense of achievement. The route itself threads a path through some of the most wonderful and unusual rock formations that the region has to offer while

❑ AFTER YOUR TREK

Trekking through the Atlas Mountains may have been your motive for travelling to Morocco but it would be a great pity to leave the country without tasting some of its other delights. Indeed, a broader experience of Morocco, culturally so rich and diverse, is not only desirable in its own right, but will provide a context that will add depth, meaning and understanding to those very mountain experiences that you initially sought.

The Imperial Cities

Whereas Marrakech, the imperial capital of the south, has long captivated the imagination of travellers, writers, artists and all others who, through the ages, have passed through her walls, the twin imperial cities of the north, Fes and Meknes, rival her for our attention. An exploration of one or all of these cultural centres, each steeped in its own history and tradition, would make an excellent finale to a stay in Morocco. Through their souks and their palaces, their gardens and their medinas, the trekker is offered a final stimulus to the senses, whilst the sanctity of a hidden riad gives the chance to enjoy some of the finest hospitality to be found anywhere on earth – and a final opportunity to reflect upon your adventure before your journey home.

Aït Benhaddou and the Draa Valley to M'hamid and Erg Chegaga

To experience a cross-section of southern Morocco, hire a car in Marrakech (see Car hire, p98) and drive to the oasis town of M'hamid via Ouarzazate, the gateway to the south. The winding road will take you up and over the dizzy heights of the Tizi-n-Tichka and across the spine of the Central High Atlas, before dropping to the kasbah-strewn, sandy floor of the Draa Valley. From there, it continues through Zagora towards the desert itself. Where the road ends in M'hamid, just 40km from the disputed Algerian border, it is a simple matter to make arrangements for a camel trek west across the desert to Erg Chegaga, the most spectacular sand dunes in Morocco (see opposite). On your return north, try to visit the fascinating kasbah of Aït Benhaddou, about 30km beyond Ouarzazate. As a result of its restoration for use in such epic films as *Lawrence of Arabia*, this is surely the best-maintained kasbah anywhere in the Atlas.

affording an opportunity to pass through small, isolated villages and semi-nomadic encampments.

It is hard to think of any drawbacks to this trek. At times the going can be quite strenuous and the lack of infrastructure requires a fair degree of self-reliance, but for many these factors will only add to the sense of adventure.

Circular trek

This 5- or 6-day trek, beginning and ending in the Dades Valley, involves traversing large areas of flat floodplain both at the beginning and at the end, between times rising to cross a series of moderate but quite beautiful passes, the highest being Tizi-n-Tagmout (1913m/6276ft) and Tizi n'Tmircht (2378m/7799ft).

Pros and cons Here is an opportunity to leave much of the world behind, especially during the summer months when the transhumance farmers quit the region to head north for the cooler climes and higher pastures of the High Atlas. Moreover, the rugged beauty of the isolated pastures of Tafoughalt and the colourful primeval gorges of Irhissi will long live in the memory.

Erg Chegaga and the Saharan Dunes

I came into contact with camels on three occasions, and each occasion ended tragically. **Elias Canetti**, *Encounters with Camels*, from *The Voices of Marrakech,* 1967

It doesn't have to be this way. Any number of agencies, whose representatives quickly approach you in the central square in M'hamid, might be capable of putting together a successful camel trek for you. Indeed there has been quite a growth in the number of organisations offering desert trekking experiences in recent years. Do take some care over your selection, however, as not all have the necessary knowledge or experience to perform the job adequately. The poor organisation of my trek as recently as March 2008 proved a huge disappointment. As with a trek into the Atlas, do not rush into choosing a guide. Talk to others who have recently finished a trek or try the long-established **Sahara Services** (GSM ☎ 0661-77 67 66; 🖳 www.saharaservices.info) based in the centre of M'hamid.

The 40m-high dunes of Erg Chegaga lie three punishing days to the west across a flat, stony landscape, punctuated by lesser dunes with occasional shade provided by a rare acacia tree, all set against the backdrop of the smoky blue Bani Mountains away to the north. Once at Erg Chegaga, however, the rewards are considerable: from the crest of the higher dunes, the views across the sea of sand stretch all the way to Algeria, giving a beautiful insight into the wonder of the true Sahara. Alternatively, you could hire a 4x4 and reach Erg Chegaga in a matter of hours.

Essaouira and the Atlantic coast

If the dust of Marrakech gets too much, or you need a rest after your exertions in the Atlas, head for Essaouira on the Atlantic coast. Although becoming increasingly popular as a resort, frequented even by day trippers from Marrakech, the town retains its laid-back reputation and certainly provides a coastal calm which stands in stark contrast to the bustle of Marrakech.

What to take

During the day the men on foot resorted to a curious expedient for diminishing the effect of the heat, by thrusting a stick down the back between the skin and their scanty woollen garment, and thus securing ventilation.
Joseph D Hooker & John Ball, *Journal of a Tour in Marocco and the Great Atlas*, 1878

Trekking in the Atlas Mountains is physically demanding and its demands need to be taken seriously. It is imperative that you are properly equipped. What you decide to pack will, however, depend on how and when you decide to travel. If you travel in a tour group, for example, tents and accommodation should be organised for you. If you hire a mule, you will be able to transport more than you would on your back. Remember that it can get very cold at altitude at any time of year, particularly at night, while the sun can be strong during the day, even in winter (see pp21-3). Remember, too, that if you trek without the help of a guide you will not always be able to find overnight shelter; the routes suggested in this guide assume that you have your own tent.

The following list of kit and equipment is fairly extensive and it will need to be tailored to the needs of your particular trek. Availability of both kit and equipment is very limited in the Atlas Mountains and even Marrakech has very little to offer, so you will need to organise all your gear before travelling to Morocco. Also, keep some clothes back to change into when you have finished the trek so that you will then be able to relax and enjoy the sensation of being clean again. After an arduous trek to Erg Chegaga (see box pp26-7), my son once asked of me, 'Is this the only reason that you trek – so that you can feel good at the end?'!

TENT

Of all your equipment, you must be able to rely upon your tent. If you are trekking with an organised group, a tent should be included in the equipment that is provided by your agency. Similarly, if you hire a local guide, it is very likely that he, too, will be able to provide you with one. However, unless you are sure of this before you set out from home, it would be sensible to take a tent with you. All treks outlined in this book assume that you have a tent.

There are lots of expedition-quality tents on the market; they are available from a good number of excellent specialist retailers. Consult, for example, Ellis Brigham (💻 www.ellis-brigham.com) who stock a range of top makes of tent, including North Face, Terra Nova, Marmot and Trango. Top models can easily cost £400-500/US$600-750. Depending upon the nature of your trek, you may feel that you do not need a top-of-the-range model. However, you would always be wise to select a model which is waterproof and resilient to strong winds. At times you will be a long way from the nearest village and you will need to be self-sufficient. You should make sure that your tent has enough storage space for your pack. Also, as the terrain in the Atlas can be very hard and stony, choose one that has a tough groundsheet and ensure that your fly sheet has elastic loops to allow you to pitch your tent using rocks.

REHYDRATION SYSTEMS

At the most basic level, you will need at least one tough one-litre **water bottle**, such as manufactured by Sigg or Camelbak (around £12/US$18). However, there's an increasing number of sophisticated rehydration systems on the market (from around £40/US$60) which can be carried in or clipped on to a day pack. This allows you to drink as frequently as required, through a tube and mouthpiece

❑ Water purification systems

You should never drink or even clean your teeth in water which has not been purified. A pure-looking mountain stream can be tempting to drink from, particularly when you watch your guide or muleteer take long, luxurious gulps, but the chances are it will have been polluted by bacteria from animals or higher human habitation. This might not adversely affect your guide or muleteer, but it will certainly affect you. Even if you spend a lot of time in Morocco or in the mountains, do not make the mistake of assuming that your immune system will adapt like theirs: it won't. Of course, natural water sources usually provide the safest water, besides bottled water, to drink and trekkers should replenish their bottles whenever such opportunities arise. Nonetheless, always err on the side of caution and treat even source water before drinking it.

- **Boiling** Even though water boils at lower temperatures at altitude, this is still one of the most effective ways to kill bugs, making hot drinks and soups safe to drink in the mountains. However, it is not practical to boil all the water you need to drink to prevent dehydration while trekking, so alternative methods should be used in conjunction.
- **Chemical purification** Chlorine tablets are not sufficient to kill harmful bugs. Preferably use iodine which can be applied to water in two forms; liquid tincture, which is more widely used, or tablets. If using tincture, follow the instructions on the label carefully. Normally you will need to let the iodinised water stand for 10 minutes before drinking it. If using tablets, one tablet normally purifies one litre of water. These have the advantage of being cheap; a bottle of 50 tablets will cost around £7/US$10. However, iodine is bad for you if drunk regularly over long periods and pregnant women should avoid it completely. What is more, it adds a distinctly unpleasant taste to your water; if you decide to opt for iodine tablets, make sure that you also buy neutralising tablets to remove the taste.
- **Filtering** Quality portable filter pumps are extremely effective and are strongly recommended. It has been said that they are very expensive (from around £80/US$120), but compare the emotional, physical and financial cost of your trek being ruined by a bout of giardia against the cost of the pump. What is more, a quality pump will bring you peace of mind, enjoyable drinking water in the most unlikely of places and years of use. Try, for example an MSR Waterworks EX water filter. Since beginning to use one myself, I have never so much as experienced a minor stomach twinge while in the mountains and I consider my filter pump to be the best item of trekking equipment I have ever bought.
- **SteriPen** Alternatively, try a SteriPen (💻 www.steripen.com), still rather new on the market, which uses ultraviolet light (UV) to destroy waterborne microbes, including viruses, bacteria and protozoa, such as giardia. It costs around £100/US$150.

while on the move, yet keeping your hands free. Many water containers offer some insulation, thereby protecting the water within from the heat of the day and keeping it cooler for longer. However, all this is to no avail if the water that you drink is of poor quality. See the box on water purification systems (p29).

WHAT TO PACK IT ALL IN

A **backpack** is essential: even if your bag is bound for the back of a mule, there will inevitably be occasions when you will need to carry it yourself. There's a vast range of backpacks on the market. The only rule is to choose carefully and make sure that yours is both comfortable and fit for purpose. Some will offer highly air-vented back systems, while others will include facilities to accommodate rehydration systems.

Critically, make sure yours allows full adjustment, familiarise yourself with it and adjust for comfort before leaving home, making sure that the bulk of its weight is supported by your hips, not by your shoulders. Most packs are still designed for men although a number of companies now produce backpacks specifically for women, allowing for a narrower neck, different hip:shoulder ratios and shorter back lengths. It is worth taking a slightly bigger pack than you think you will need because you are almost bound to accumulate items on your travels.

In addition, a small **daypack** is essential during the trek. It should be big enough for your camera, snacks, water and any other items which you would not want to be separated from during the day. When selecting your daypack, be aware of your airline's restrictions on the permitted dimensions of hand luggage. Finally, a **holdall** is also useful for storing any items you do not need on your trek either at the trailhead or back in your hotel in Marrakech.

SLEEPING BAG

Whether camping or not, a sleeping bag is essential. Even where *gîtes d'étape* provide bedding, your own bag is likely to be a better, more sanitised alternative.

You will need to select between a down and a synthetic bag and ideally your decision will be based upon the type of trek you are to undertake. **Down bags**, which are more expensive (a good four-season bag will cost up to £200/US$300), hold the advantage in very cold conditions as they offer better insulation, although recent developments in **synthetic bags** (the best cost around £100/US$150) have led to improvements in the warmth that they can offer. Be aware that down bags lose much of their insulation when wet and can be very difficult to dry out again. On the other hand, they are very compressible in contrast to much bulkier synthetic bags. You might also want to consider the big discrepancies that can exist between the weights of different models of sleeping bag.

Sleeping mat

Animal droppings should provide a warm comfortable mattress for sleeping bags.

Michael Peyron, *Great Atlas Traverse,* Vol 1, 1989

If camping, you will need to take a sleeping mat, not only to help keep you warm, but also to take some of the sting out of the hard, stony ground you are likely to sleep upon at some point. Although a simple **foam mat** might prove adequate, a **self-inflating mat**, such as those produced by Thermarest (💻 www.thermarest.com), from around £65/US$100, is much superior in terms of providing both comfort and warmth. Opinions differ as to whether a three-quarter-length version, which saves a little space in your pack and a little cash in your pocket, is able to provide the same level of comfort.

FOOTWEAR AND FOOT CARE

Probably the most common complaint suffered by any trekker is that of blisters. Although seemingly a minor problem, they could seriously diminish your enjoyment of your trek and even force you to stop walking altogether. It is therefore very important to look after your feet and this begins with having the right boots and socks. Ignore the fact that local muleteers might skip past you in plastic sandals; given that you are relatively unaccustomed to the Atlas terrain, you should make sure that you keep your feet dry, well-supported and blister-free.

Boots

Proper walking boots are essential. The choice is between traditional leather boots and modern fabric or, more recently, a hybrid of the two. Whichever option you make, you are likely to pay over £100/US$150. **Leather boots** are generally more durable and offer better ankle support, but they can also cause more problems. They are considerably heavier and are more likely to cause sores and blisters, particularly if not worn in properly before a trek. They probably hold the advantage when trekking at higher altitude, such as in the Central High Atlas, or in wet conditions, when you might also want to take along Nikwax or some similar product to maintain their waterproof qualities.

Fabric boots generally hold the advantage at lower altitude and in drier conditions, such as might be found at most times of the year in the Jbel Sahro region. Low cut boots, offering better ventilation, if less ankle protection, might also be considered if trekking in such conditions. Ultimately it is a question of personal choice. Whichever type of boot you select, include a pair of spare laces in your pack.

Socks

Good specialist walking socks, such as manufactured by Bridgedale and Thorlo (around £10/US$15 per pair), are important. Select carefully as different socks are on the market to suit particular climates. Make sure you have at least two pairs so that you can change and wash them regularly and so avoid irritants, such as dry sweat or grit, accumulating and causing blisters. Some people advocate wearing thin, silk, inner socks next to the skin under thicker walking socks.

Other footwear

Take an alternative pair of shoes, such as trainers or rafting sandals, to wear in the evenings after you have finished your trek for the day. **Trainers** can also be useful for trekking should your precautions fail and your boots cause you blisters, while **sandals** serve a useful purpose when washing or wading through streams.

Foot care

Keep your feet dry, take your boots and socks off during long breaks, wash your feet regularly and change your socks often. Some trekkers believe in coating their feet and toes with anti-fungal foot powder every morning and evening as a preventative measure.

CLOTHES

It is important to take a sensible range of clothes to deal with the extremes of weather you might encounter on your trek (see When to go, pp21-3). The market in specialist outdoor clothing is expanding rapidly and there are two very good reasons why it is advisable to buy into it. First, specialist clothing brings comfort and the more comfortable you are, the more you can enjoy your trek. Second, specialist clothing prepares you properly for your trek and, in extreme situations, saves lives. Even if you decide not to invest in specialist clothing, remember that several thin layers of clothes will keep you warmer than one or two bulky garments.

Waterproof jacket and trousers

This is another essential piece of equipment at all times of the year, not just to provide protection from the rain but also from wind at altitude and cold at night. Even in summer, you are likely to encounter rain in the Central High Atlas, notably in the afternoons. In winter, particularly during the wet season between October and April, it is important to take waterproof trousers also.

Buy the best quality you can to provide yourself with the best protection. It is important that your jacket is not only waterproof but breathable, allowing perspiration to be drawn from your skin to your outer fabric from where it can evaporate. This process maintains the dryness of your skin and your comfort. All top brands of jacket now include a Gore-Tex membrane between the outer material and the lining which achieves all of these objectives, allowing perspiration to escape while also acting as a barrier to penetration by both external water and wind. Expect to pay around £200/US$300 for a top jacket.

Base layer and intermediate layer

Any benefits you achieve, however, through purchasing a breathable waterproof jacket will largely be lost if the layer of clothing next to your skin, your base layer, or the layer of clothing between your base layer and your jacket, your intermediate layer, do not allow for your perspiration to be wicked away efficiently. This should be given serious consideration when packing other clothing as detailed below.

Fleece

A good quality fleece is very useful for mornings and evenings, as well as during colder moments at altitude. Choose one which will roll up tightly.

Shirts/T-shirts

Take two light trekking shirts, such as those by Mountain Hardware or Lowe Alpine (around £30/US$45), at least one of which should be long-sleeved and with a collar to protect your arms and neck from excess sun (see Sunburn and heatstroke, p263). These are both practical and comfortable on the trail; allow perspiration to wick away quickly, thereby keeping you dry; and are easily washed and dried.

Trousers

Take two pairs of light, full-length trekking trousers (around £50/US$75), such as manufactured by Rohan or North Face. The advantages over other trousers made with more traditional materials are similar to those listed for shirts, above.

Shorts

Do not wear shorts. You will be trekking in a conservative Muslim area and will cause offence to many, including to those who are too polite to tell you. Show respect and keep your legs covered (see Travelling in a Muslim country, p78-9).

Underwear

Loose fitting cotton underwear is best. Thermal underwear can be useful during colder months or, if your sleeping bag is insufficient, to sleep in. Take enough underwear to allow a regular change, so avoiding unnecessary discomfort or skin complaints.

Other items

Take two **hats**: one should be wide brimmed to protect you from the sun and preferably floppy so that it can fit into your daypack. The other should be warm for cold evenings and higher altitudes. Likewise, take **gloves** for cold evenings and higher altitudes. There's an increasingly sophisticated range of gloves on the market which allow your hands to breathe. A **neck-scarf** is a useful item both for sun protection and for wiping perspiration from your brow. Good-quality **sunglasses** capable of blocking out ultra-violet rays, are important at altitude (see Sunburn and heatstroke, p263). Men should wear **swimming shorts** and women should wear one-piece swimsuits. As **towels** can be heavy and bulky, take a small one. Better still, take a specialist lightweight, highly absorbent travel towel, such as produced by Lifeadventure, for as little as £6/US$9/70dh.

TOILETRIES

Basic supplies such as **soap** and **shampoo** are available both in Marrakech and, to a lesser extent, at trailheads, although it is better to bring toiletries from home if you are at all particular about what you use. Take small samples if possible: this not only saves space but also, as washing opportunities are limited, you will use far less than you might normally use at home. You might even consider sharing your toiletries with a friend.

Try to take biodegradable products and avoid contaminating water supplies that locals depend upon. This means avoiding washing and shaving with soaps directly in rivers and streams or, for that matter, in still water such as at Lac d'Ifni on the Toubkal Circular Trek.

Good quality, water-resistant, high-factor **sunscreen**, or even total **sun-block**, for lips, ears and nose, is essential. **Lip-balm** will help prevent chapping from general exposure. **Toilet paper** is on sale in some larger villages but, since locals use only water and their left hand, do not rely on finding any on the trail. Do not forget a **lighter** to burn used paper. You might consider taking **baby wipes** although they will need to be carried back to your trailhead after use.

Tampons, expensive in Morocco, are available in Marrakech and some larger villages but it is wise to bring a supply from home, along with any other essentials which you normally use, including **contraceptives**.

MEDICAL AND FIRST-AID KITS

If you join an organised trek, the leaders should have a well-stocked medical kit so you will only need to take day-to-day personal supplies. If, however, you plan to trek independently, you will clearly need to be better prepared. Even when trekking in those parts of the Atlas which are relatively well populated, do not assume the availability of either medical resources or expertise. On the contrary, trekking in a relatively well-populated part of the Atlas is more likely to lead to local people putting a strain on your own medical resources. Make yourself aware of some of the **potential hazards** of your trek in the Atlas (see Health Appendix, pp257-63) and consider including the following in your pack:

Medical kit

Oral rehydration sachets (such as Dioralyte) in case of diarrhoea, dehydration or simply to restore the balance of sugars and salts in your body after a day's trek. **Antiseptic cream or iodine drops** for immediate treatment of cuts. **Paracetamol** to treat headaches. **Tinidazole/Flagyl** for the treatment of giardia (see Health, p260). **Imodium** for dealing with the symptoms but not the cause of diarrhoea – best used when you have diarrhoea and need to be temporarily blocked up, such as when you have a long trip ahead of you. **Tweezers** for splinter and thorn removal. **Nail clippers** not only to keep your toe nails neat to avoid problems in your boots but also to keep your finger nails short to help keep them clean. **Waterproof plasters** – take a long strip. **Zinc-oxide tape** is excellent for preventing blisters. **Blister plasters** – take more than you think you will ever need. **Vaseline** for sore lips, hands and feet. **Antihistamine tablets** to tackle an allergic reaction. **Anti-fungal foot powder** can help prevent blisters. **Water purification** tablets or drops are necessary only if you have decided not to invest in either a water filter pump or SteriPen (see Water purification systems box p29). **Personal medication** to last the length of your stay.

First-aid kit

The basic components of a first-aid kit should include: **non-adhesive dressing**; **bandages** (one triangular, one crêpe and one medium-sized to large); small **scissors**; **safety pins**; **sterilised needle pack**; winter ice trekkers should consider taking an **inflatable splint**.

GENERAL ITEMS

Consider also the following: a **torch** (flashlight) and spare batteries; **compass**; **lighter**; **plastic backpack liner** to ensure your belongings stay dry; one-litre

❑ **Cooking gear**

If you go on an organised trek or employ a cuisinier to cook for you, you will have no need to take your own cooking gear.

Normally in the mountains the most effective stove is a Trangia. However, it needs methylated spirit to burn which is difficult to find not only in the Atlas but even in Marrakech. A more practical solution, therefore, is to fall in with the locals and use a stove which runs on readily available Butagaz. Wood is sometimes also used, although, on environmental grounds, you will no doubt want to discourage use of this rare commodity.

water bottle; **sewing kit** for running repairs; **biodegradable washing liquid**; **travel games** or a **pack of cards**; **shortwave radio**; **camera** and **batteries** plus **film** or **digital/compact flash cards**; **watch** to gauge progress along routes against times given in route guides; **Swiss Army knife**; **multi-fit sink plug**; **plug adaptor** (three-pin to round two-pin); **pens**, **pencils and journal**; **ice axe and crampons** are necessary only in winter for higher level treks. Crampons can be rented in Imlil for the ascent of Jbel Toubkal.

PROVISIONS

If on an organised trek, there should be little food that you will need to take into the mountains beyond perhaps some dried fruit, nuts and chocolate. Alternatively, if trekking independently, at least within the Toubkal region, it would be possible to plan a route allowing each evening to be spent in a refuge or gîte at which cooked meals might be ordered. Otherwise, all food provisions should be organised before setting out on the trail and carried by your mule (see Eating in the Atlas, pp82-3). Times are changing. Although even a few years ago, trekkers were commonly advised to stock up on provisions in big towns before heading for the mountains, this is increasingly unnecessary. Unless you have a particular penchant for the obscure, you are very likely to find all you need at the trailhead for your trek without even waiting for the weekly souk. This becomes even simpler should you decide to employ a *cuisinier* (see p11) who will carry out the shopping for the whole trek based upon what he intends to cook.

MONEY

Although debit and credit cards are beginning to gain some acceptance in the Atlas Mountains, this is still only in exceptional situations. You would be as well to leave the plains behind presuming that everything in the Atlas Mountains must be paid for in cash with Moroccan dirhams. Even though ATM machines are becoming much more common in towns and cities, they are yet to reach many trailheads (see the relevant trailhead description for your trek), still less mountain villages. Do, therefore, make sure you are carrying enough cash before you begin your trek. Also, when changing money for your trek, ask for small denomination notes. This avoids the risk of causing embarrassment by producing a large note only to find that nobody has sufficient change. (See also Money, pp75-7).

PHOTOGRAPHY AND PHOTOGRAPHIC EQUIPMENT

The Atlas region is an outstanding location for photography, not only because it is full of colourful and exotic people and places, but also because of its wonderful natural light, especially towards the beginning and end of each day. However, be prepared also for the intensity of this light: you should seriously consider taking both a sunlight filter and a lens hood to provide protection from the negative effects that a strong sun can have upon the quality of your pictures.

You will, of course, remember that Morocco is not a museum: you should always ask permission before taking somebody's picture or even a picture of their property or possessions. Many people, on the plains as well as in the mountains, will be reluctant to be photographed which, naturally, should be respected. Their reluctance is culturally based and is very common within the Muslim world, especially in economically developing countries. On the other hand, ironically, you may equally find yourself being approached by someone, typically children but sometimes even women, wishing you to take their photograph in exchange for a fee of a few dirhams (see Photograph with sensitivity, pp90-1).

If using a digital camera, make sure you take a digital card or compact flash card with a large memory. If using film, you would always be wise to take more with you than you think you could possibly use. Take spare camera batteries with you, too, and do not rely upon recharging them in the mountains (see Electricity, p70).

Although film and batteries for standard SLR cameras are readily available in Moroccan cities and large towns, you are unlikely to be able to buy these items at trailheads. Memory cards, compact flash cards and rechargeable batteries for digital cameras are currently only usually available in major cities.

Note that after a cold night on a mountain, you may find that your batteries appear to be flat. Take them out and warm them up in your hands to restore life to them. Some people even keep them in their sleeping bag at night.

RECOMMENDED READING

Literature, in the modern Moorish state, is confined but to the Koran, the sacred books, an occasional Arab poet, and the study of the one book known to be written in the Berber tongue, and called El Maziri, which deals exclusively with the ceremonial of the faith.

R B Cunninghame Graham, *Mogreb-el-Acksa*, 1898

Just as having a good guide can enhance your understanding of Morocco, so too can a good read.

Guidebooks

Rough Guides publish a good practical Morocco guide, as does Lonely Planet. Check the imprint date for whichever guide is the latest.

The *Cadogan Guide to Marrakesh, Fez and Rabat* by Barnaby Rogerson provides excellent in-depth background to those cities.

For further trekking information there are a few options. Michael Peyron (West Col, 1st volume 1989, 2nd volume 1990) is responsible for the most inspirational *Grand Atlas Traverse*, which plots a choice of routes from the

Western High Atlas Mountains, not far from the Atlantic Ocean, right through the Central High Atlas, all the way to Midelt and on to the Middle Atlas.

Though not strictly a guidebook, *The Great Trek through the Moroccan Atlas*, produced by the Moroccan Ministry of Tourism, theoretically available free, is packed full of practical information, including lists of *gîtes* and names of guides, and would be of much greater benefit if only it was reprinted more regularly. In the French language, take a look at Vincent Geus's *Maroc* (Éditions de la Boussole, 2007) for coverage of some of the wider trekking options that Morocco has to offer, including in north Morocco and the Atlantic coast.

If you fancy spending more time in the mountains on wheels rather than feet, Chris Scott's *Morocco Overland*, also published by Trailblazer, is invaluable. It's a comprehensive route and planning guide to 49 easy-to-follow routes for mountain bikes, motorcycles and 4WDs. (See p271).

Birdwatching

A Bird Watcher's Guide to Morocco by Patrick and Fedora Bergier, *Birdwatching Guide to Morocco* by Peter Combridge, Alan Swook and James McCallum, and *Finding Birds* in Northern Morocco by David Gosney are all readily available.

Other books

There are disappointingly few contemporary books in English which focus specifically on the Atlas Mountains. For nineteenth-century perspectives on early exploration of the Atlas, read *Journal of A Tour in Marocco* (sic) *and the Great Atlas* by Joseph D Hooker and John Ball, Joseph Thomson's *Travels in the Atlas and Southern Morocco*, and Walter Harris's *Tafilet: The Narrative of a Journey of Exploration in the Atlas Mountains*. Hamish Brown's *The Mountains Look on Marrakech*, provides a more modern account of his own epic 96-day, 900-mile trek along the entire length of the Atlas. Having recently returned from his 50th visit to Morocco, few are better placed to write such an account.

Elias Canetti's *The Voices of Marrakech*, winner of the Nobel Prize for Literature in 1981, is an outstanding piece of artistic writing which offers a fascinating insight into daily life in the pink city. Set in Casablanca, Tahir Shah's *The Caliph's House* provides a light-hearted and very enjoyable insight into the trials and tribulations of attempting to buy a house and settle in Morocco.

For a glimpse of the art of traditional Moroccan story-telling, a personal favourite is Richard Hughes's *In the Lap of Atlas,* 1979. A series of magical short stories heard in childhood and adapted later in life for publication, sadly only one of these is actually set in the Atlas.

For excellent modern fiction, turn to American Paul Bowles, probably the best-known Western writer on Morocco. Try in particular *The Sheltering Sky*, set in the Moroccan Sahara, *Let it Come Down*, set in Tangier, or *The Spider's House*, which, set in Fes, squares up to the early twentieth-century conflict between Moroccan nationalism and French colonialism.

Perhaps the most exquisite book specifically on the Atlas is the French language, *Un Hiver Berbère* by French-born Karin Huet and Moroccan Titouan Lamazou. The journal of their eight months in the Aït Bou Guemez Valley in the winter of 1981-82, it contains text and sketches that are both beautiful and simple. If you are heading south, particularly to Jbel Sahro, you might want to consult David Hart's account of the socio-political organisation of the celebrated Aït Atta tribe, *Dadda 'Atta and his Forty Grandsons*, though be warned: this is very dry reading. If heading even further south, try *Valley of the Kasbahs*. This is American Jeffrey Tayler's account of his epic camel trek along the entire course of the River Draa from its source in the High Atlas to the Atlantic Ocean near Tan Tan.

Classic books on Morocco to be recommended include: Walter Harris's account of life around the royal court in the late nineteenth and early twentieth centuries, *Morocco That Was*; Gavin Maxwell's telling of the early twentieth century rise and fall of the Berber House of Glaoua in *Lords of the Atlas*; and the nostalgia-inducing *A Year in Marrakech* (previously published under the title *The Alleys of Marrakech* in 1953) by Peter Mayne, one of the earliest Europeans to succeed in buying a house in the Medina. Do not forget also RB Cunninghame Graham's account of his failed late nineteenth-century venture to become the first Christian to set foot in Taroudannt, *Mogreb-el-Acksa A Journey in Morocco*. Less well known, and harder to read, but well worth grappling with, is Englishman Thomas Pellow's account of his 23 years as a slave in Morocco, *The Adventures of Thomas Pellow, of Penryn, Mariner*. For choice excerpts from many of these books, and a good number of other travellers' writings besides, dating as far back as to the 14th-century wanderings of Ibn Battuta, see *Marrakech, the Red City* edited by Barnaby Rogerson and Stephen Lavington.

If you wish to get below the surface to explore the hidden values, traditions and beliefs of Morocco, you would enjoy Ernest Gellner's *Saints of the Atlas*, Nina Epton's *Saints and Sorcerers* and Françoise Legey's *The Folklore of Morocco*. If, however, it is the mysteries of Moroccan cooking that you seek, try Paula Wolfert's *Couscous and Other Good Food from Morocco*.

Finally, if a picture can paint a thousand words, then three photographic records should be consulted. Lisa Lovatt-Smith's *Moroccan Interiors* explores the wonder of the riad; for a pictorial documentation of the changing face of Morocco over the last century, see *The Magic of Morocco* by Tahar ben Jelloun et al; and if this leaves you fearing that Morocco's history is disappearing too quickly, take a look at *Imazighen* by Margaret Courtney-Clarke for an insight into the vanishing traditions of rural Berber women before they, too, disappear.

MAPS

Ride on to the lone tree on the horizon, then bear a little to the right, and if you keep the line, you cannot miss the houses, for the barking dogs will guide you, if it falls dark.

R B Cunninghame Graham, *Mogreb-el-Acksa*, 1898

Several of the series of maps of the Atlas Mountains are on a suitable scale to be of interest to trekkers. Unfortunately, although most of Morocco, including the Atlas Mountains, has been mapped at 1:50,000 by the Division de la Carte as part of the official Morocco Survey, these maps are notoriously difficult to come by. They are likely to remain so unless the survey authorities relax their attitude to their supply. You might, however, try contacting Hamish Brown

(☎/📠 01592-873546), AMIS, 3 Links Place, Burntisland, Fife KY3 9DY, Scotland, who holds an impressive selection.

Most of the Atlas has been mapped both at 1:100,000 (again by the Division de la Carte) and at 1:160,000 (based on Russian military sources, published by EWP). In addition there is a useful 1:100,000 ridge map of the Mgoun Massif (published by West Col) plus two German-language maps, once more at 1:100,000. The latter are based upon the 1:100,000 maps produced by the Division de la Carte but are printed on much inferior paper. One is of the Central High Atlas (*Kultur-Trekking im Zentralen Hohen Atlas*), the other of Jbel Sahro (*Kultur-Trekking im Dschebel Saghro*). Both have recommended trekking routes clearly marked plus gîtes and other accommodation available on the trail.

If you are unable to acquire 1:50,000 maps, the 1:100,000 (Division de la Carte) series is strongly recommended. Granted, these maps are not always wholly accurate, partly because they were last published in the 1970s: sometimes villages are marked without being named, sometimes they will be marked with a different name to that known by your guide and sometimes they are simply not marked at all. (See the introduction to the Jbel Sahro treks, pp203-4).

Recommending these maps is one thing, finding them is another. An excellent source for all these maps is **The Map Shop** (☎ 01684-593146; ☎ 0800-085 4080; 💻 www.themapshop.co.uk) in Upton upon Severn. Their semi-retired Morocco specialist, Tony Atkinson, first pressed the Division de la Cartographie in Rabat for maps in the 1:100,000 series back in 1996. Despite strict controls on their availability, he has returned on numerous occasions and steadily and skilfully built up a collection of maps for most parts of the Moroccan Atlas. **Stanfords** (☎ 020-7836 1321, 💻 www.stanfords.co.uk; 12-14 Long Acre, Covent Garden, London) stock a set of the four 1:100,000 (Division de la Carte) maps covering the area around Toubkal. They have a second branch in Bristol (☎ 0117-929 9966) at 29 Corn St. It has long been held that, should you arrive in Morocco without the necessary maps, you should try to purchase them direct from the Division de la Cartographie in Rabat. I confess that I have never met anyone, apart from Tony Atkinson at The Map Shop, succeeding in this respect. His advice is this:

'*Write in advance of your visit to explain your requirements, although half the time when you get there you will be told that they have not received your letter. Even so, you should politely request, in French or Arabic, the maps you need, then go away, wait an hour or two, and then go back and ask again. You are actually beholden upon the minister in charge to give his authorisation and eventually, with patience and persistence, you may be rewarded, although even then this can take up to three days. Whatever you do, however, do not simply turn up unexpectedly as you really will be wasting your time*'.

The Division de la Cartographie (☎ 0537-29 55 48) is inconveniently located at out-of–the-way 31, avenue Moulay Al Hassan II, Rabat.

❑ GPS

Since most visitors currently trek with a guide in Morocco, GPS usage here is not what it is in parts of the world where independent trekking is more established. GPS waypoints have not, therefore, been included in this guide. They will, however, be included in future editions as GPS usage develops in Morocco.

Mountain safety

All mountains can be dangerous. The Atlas ranges, like all mountain systems, are liable to rapid weather changes. Hailstones are possible in the Jbel Sahro region at Easter; snow is even possible on the summit of Toubkal in August. Consideration for personal safety is therefore paramount. Always ensure that you are fully prepared for extremes of weather at all times of the year (see What to take, pp28-32) and make certain that you keep one reserve set of clothes completely dry. Look after yourself on the trek and ensure that others do likewise. Deal with small issues as they arise so that they do not grow into big problems. Try to avoid covering more distance than you feel comfortable with.

There will always be a degree of pressure to reach a recognised stage at the end of each day and to cover your trek in a designated number of days, but balance this pressure with your own physical needs and those of your group. After all, the real art of trekking is to enjoy the beauty of the surrounding countryside. The best of experiences are missed by those in haste.

TREKKING INDEPENDENTLY

Always consider taking a guide and a muleteer. Quite apart from ensuring that you keep to your route, a guide will help you understand the lands through which you pass and reveal the hidden secrets of the mountains. Your muleteer will deal with the practicalities of mountain-living that will leave you with the

❑ Trekking with children

Trekking in the Atlas is even tougher on children than adults as they are naturally more susceptible to the effects of common complaints such as heatstroke, dehydration and stomach bugs. Depending on their age, children may also be less able to tell you clearly any distress that they might be experiencing, including the effects of altitude. However, rather than letting this put you off taking your young ones, build simple precautions into your planning. Either keep them well-covered with high-factor sun cream or keep their skin well-covered, or both. Take particular care with personal hygiene. Make sure you have read the section on Altitude-related problems (p42) and the Health section (pp257-63) in the Appendix, particularly the box on Acute Mountain Sickness (pp258-9).

There are many benefits to travelling with children who are generally very well received in Morocco and who can even open doors for you which otherwise might well remain closed. In 2007 I met a Swiss family on the slopes of Jbel Sirwa, including four children, all under 10 years of age, who were having the time of their lives. They had devised a shorter, circular trek, allowing them to retain a lower altitude, and had taken extra mules along with them so that their children could ride whenever they grew weary. The joy that they shared was wonderful: never before nor since have I felt jealous of another's experience in the Atlas.

Note that it would be unwise to trek at altitude during the early stages of pregnancy.

freedom and energy to absorb the beauty of your environment (see With a group or on your own, pp9-12). Conventional wisdom decrees that trekkers should always walk in groups, yet the bigger the group, the harder it is to experience the culture. True, it is sensible to operate in a group of three or more, but where possible include your guide and your muleteer within that number. In whatever number you choose to travel, remember that mountain rescue services in the Atlas are very limited (see Mountain rescue below) and you should always inform someone at your trailhead where you are going and how long you intend to take. Arrange to contact them when you have completed your trek so that they will know that you have arrived safely or so that they can act if you do not reach your destination within the expected time.

Unless you plan to tackle one of the higher peaks over the winter months, in which case you will need to know how to trek on ice with crampons, it is not essential to have any specialist knowledge or experience for the treks in this book. You will, however, need to be reasonably physically fit, well-prepared and, unless you take a guide, be able to read a map and/or use a compass.

Additionally, you should seriously consider undertaking first-aid training given the dearth of medical help available in the mountains (see below).

MOUNTAIN RESCUE

Despite the increasing numbers of trekkers in the Atlas, there remains no official mountain rescue service. Although official mountain guides qualify in basic first aid as part of their training, they are only taught how to deal with injuries such as open wounds and broken bones. The best response to a serious accident from most points in the mountains is to **return to the nearest trailhead by mule** and from there to the nearest town by road. If, however, the accident is too serious for your patient to travel in this way, you should call upon the **rescue helicopter** stationed in Marrakech. Unless you have a short-wave radio, this would require first locating someone who has, typically the mayor in a larger village. However, even then the helicopter, which operates over a massive area and is in much demand, should not be relied upon to respond quickly.

❑ FURTHER SOURCES OF ADVICE

• **Morocco** **Centre d'Information sur la Montagne** (☎ 0537-77 06 86; 🖷 0537-77 08 26) 64 Avenue Fal Ould Oumeir, Rabat; **Fédération Royale Marocaine de Ski et de Montagne** (☎ 0522-20 37 98/47 49 79; 🖷 0522-47 49 79) Parc de la Ligue Arabe, Boîte Postale 15899, Casablanca 01; **Club Alpin Français** (☎ 0537-72 72 20) 13 Boulevard de la Résistance, Rabat; and (☎ 0522-27 00 90; 🖷 0522-29 72 92) Boîte Postale 6178, Casablanca 01, Morocco.

Note that the **Fédération National de Guides de Montagne**, previously based at Asni, no longer has an office and now only exists on paper.

• **UK** **Royal Geographical Society (with the Institute of British Geographers)** (☎ 020-759 3000; 💻 www.rgs.org) 1 Kensington Gore, London, SW7 2AR.

Health precautions

Morocco has a reputation for afflicting visitors with stomach upsets. It is true that, like most economically developing countries, Morocco has generally lower standards of hygiene than those typically found in the West. But by being careful and taking some simple precautions the chances of getting any illness can be considerably lessened. Trekking, of course, carries its own inherent risks. But if you are fit before you start, look after yourself and respond promptly to any problems as they occur, there is no reason why your travels should be marred by medical trouble. See pp257-63 for details about **specific health problems** you might have in the Atlas Mountains.

ALTITUDE-RELATED PROBLEMS

Since the highest peak in the Atlas Mountains, Jbel Toubkal (4167m/13,667ft), is well above the height at which the effects of altitude can begin to take hold, **acute mountain sickness** (AMS) is a potential danger. AMS can affect anyone regardless of age, gender or fitness level. By following the advice given in the box on pp258-9, however, trekkers should be able to avoid this hazard. That said, people with chest, heart or blood-pressure problems should seek medical advice before tackling any of the treks described in this book. Particular care should be taken with children (see p40).

INOCULATIONS

Officially, Morocco does not require any inoculations. Travellers to Morocco, however, are advised to make sure that their primary courses and boosters are up to date as recommended for life in Britain. In addition, vaccinations against tetanus and hepatitis A are usually advised, and are sometimes recommended against typhoid, diptheria, hepatitis B, rabies and tuberculosis. Consult your doctor well in advance of travel for up-to-date information and to check that all recommended immunisations have been received. For malaria see p261.

INSURANCE

Good, fit-for-purpose insurance is essential. Make sure that yours covers not only any possible medical treatment you might need but also the full value of any potential loss or damage to your possessions. Be sure that your policy specifically insures you while you are trekking, including the cost of helicopter evacuation. Read and understand your policy before you go, including how to claim and, should the need to make a claim arise, take care to closely follow procedures. Leave a photocopy of your policy with someone at home.

The British Mountaineering Council's (💻 www.thebmc.co.uk) policies have been recommended, although you will first need to join the BMC itself.

MOROCCO

2

Facts about Morocco and the Atlas Mountains

GEOGRAPHY

Mogreb-el-Acksa, though it means Far West, is perhaps as eastern as any country in the world. **R B Cunninghame Graham**, *Mogreb-el-Acksa,* 1898

The Atlas Mountains form the spine of Morocco stretching some 1500 miles (2400km) from close to the Atlantic port of Agadir in the south-west of the country almost as far as the Tunisian capital of Tunis in the north-east. Within Morocco the Atlas Mountains consist of three broadly parallel ranges: the Middle Atlas, the High Atlas and the Anti-Atlas. Together they throw up an enormous physical and cultural barrier, rising between the Sahara and sub-Saharan Africa to the south and the more northerly Atlantic and Mediterranean basins.

Their highest point, indeed the highest point in North Africa, is Jbel Toubkal (4167m/13,677ft), closely followed by the Mgoun massif (4068m/ 13,343ft), both of which nestle within the High Atlas Mountains. The Anti-Atlas Mountains are dominated by the lesser but still extremely impressive peak of Jbel Sirwa (3305m/ 10,840ft), on its northern flanks, and the Jbel Sahro range in the east. The treks chosen for this book focus upon these four areas.

GEOLOGY

The basement rock of most of Africa was formed in the pre-Cambrian era (between 4.5 billion and 550 million years ago), by far predating the Atlas Mountains which were formed subsequently during three separate periods in the earth's history.

The oldest chain in the Atlas, the more southerly Anti-Atlas Mountains, owe their formation to the collision of the continents of Africa and America some 300 million years ago during the Palaeozoic Era. The resulting chain of mountains that was thrown up is believed to have once rivalled the scale of the Himalayas today.

Next, during the Mesozoic Era (more than 65 million years ago), when Africa and America separated again, a series of thick sedimentary basins were formed. Amongst these basins were the very rocks which would come to form the more northerly Middle and High Atlas Mountains. At this time they were deposited under the Atlantic Ocean.

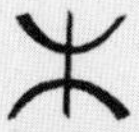

However, they were finally lifted to form the Middle and High Atlas Mountains when Africa collided with Europe during the Tertiary Era (65 million to 1.8 million years ago) which also led to the formation of the Pyrenees and the Alps.

HISTORICAL OUTLINE

Much of Moroccan history is characterised by complex tribal power struggles, religious developments and self-interested European interference. Feudal in outlook until at least the advent of colonial rule, independent in the modern era only since 1956, Morocco is presently undergoing a period of rapid transformation.

From the eighth century until the colonial period, Morocco was governed by a series of sultanates which never succeeded in holding sway over the whole country. It was divided between the *Bled al-Makhzen*, or 'governed lands', and the untamed, uncontrollable, chiefly Berber-populated regions of the deserts and of the Rif and Atlas Mountains, the *Bled al-Siba*. Even today, the Atlas Mountains, which are technically and legally part of the Kingdom of Morocco under government control, form a distinct region with a questionable regard for the authorities in Rabat. The government, perhaps tacitly recognising the de facto independence of the region, appears wary of imposing itself too firmly upon the Atlas.

Earliest inhabitants

The first inhabitants of North Africa were probably **nomadic hunter-gatherers**. They are believed to have arrived in the Sahara, then a very fertile savannah teeming with wildlife, including mammals as large as elephants and zebras, around 1,000,000BC. The earliest known dwellings appeared during the Paleolithic period, around 15,000BC, supported by the first simple pastoral and agricultural farms. Not until the Neolithic period, some time after about 10,000BC, is there evidence of further incursions into the area when finally two successive waves of migration saw new arrivals, one of which is believed to have come from Egypt. It was during this period that the earliest cave and rock drawings appeared in the High Atlas and pre-Sahara.

The Phoenicians

The prehistoric period ended with the arrival of the Phoenicians around 1100BC. Being a seafaring people originating from the Eastern Mediterranean, they established a series of isolated trading posts in defensible positions all along the coast of Morocco from Tingis (Tangier) in the north to Mogador (Essaouira) in the south, but hardly ventured inland. The interior of the country therefore remained in the hands of the indigenous **Barbaroi** (the Berbers). By the fifth century, with the emergence of the Phoenician colony of Carthage (Tunis) as the dominant force in the Mediterranean, the Phoenician trading posts in Morocco themselves were able to develop rapidly into cities of considerable status and influence.

Roman occupation

Out of the lands of the Barbaroi there emerged the Berber Kingdom of Mauritania which gradually grew in strength, especially after it had allied itself with the adjacent Berber state of Numidia (modern-day Algeria).

Soon Morocco was under threat again, however, this time from the Romans who, once having defeated the **Carthaginians** in the last of the Punic Wars in 146 BC, next turned their attention to the annexation of the rest of the Maghreb (the Arab term for North Africa). By 24AD Morocco had been absorbed into their expanding empire; in 42AD the Roman province of Mauritania Tingitana (which largely equates with modern Morocco) was created by the **Emperor Claudius**, its capital established at Tangier and its provincial governor seated at Volubilis.

Although the process of Romanisation of Morocco continued apace, this was not achieved without a struggle. Indeed, wave upon wave of local rebellions in the early years took away any Roman appetite for conquest both of the Rif and of the Atlas Mountains, where, true to the Berber tradition which survives today, independence was retained. Ultimately, the Romans would withdraw from Morocco altogether in 253AD. Even the **Vandals**, who swept across Europe and poured south through Spain, did not advance further into Morocco than the northern coast. In fact, not until the coming of Islam would Moroccan independence be truly challenged.

Coming of Islam

The advance of Islam westwards across the deserts of North Africa, following the flight of Mohammed (*pbuh*; see p256) from Mecca to Medina in 622AD, was unstoppable. So important is his flight in Muslim history that the Muslim world counts its years from this event (see Time and dates, pp71-2).

As early as 652AD, Islam had reached Tunisia. Although it was then slowed down for a while in Algeria by a unified resistance offered up by Berbers, amongst them both Christians and Jews, the new, rising faith was established on the Moroccan plains by the beginning of the eighth century, advanced by a new Arab leader, **Moussa Ibn Nasr**. The Arab Empire had extended into Europe, too: an historic victory over the Visigoths in 711AD had led to much of Spain being over-run by Muslim forces. Only an epic French victory, engineered by **Charles Martel** at Poitiers in 732AD, helped France avoid following suit.

At this point in history, however, Morocco could not be described as an Arab nation, for most of the invading army probably consisted chiefly of Berber converts to Islam. True to type, early attempts by the new lords of Morocco to impose taxes upon the local Berber population resulted in widespread rebellion and once more Morocco fragmented into the hands of local rulers.

Moulay Idriss and the first sultanate dynasty

Following the violent split in the Muslim world which followed the death of Mohammed and the consequent division of Muslims into Sunni and Shia factions, the Shi'ite **Moulay Idriss**, a great grandson of Mohammed, was forced to flee to Morocco and settle in Voloubilis. Here, however, he quickly gained local support and was able to set up an Arab kingdom. Perhaps the most important aspect of this kingdom was his being recognised as *imam*, thereby acquiring both spiritual and temporal power. Though assassinated by Sunnis around 791, his success was such that his son, **Moulay Idriss II**, was eventually able to succeed him in 807 and, with that, the first recognisable Moroccan dynasty, that of the Idrissids, was born.

During his 20-year rule, Moulay Idriss II was able to build upon the foundation provided by his father. He actively encouraged Shi'ite refugees to join him, thereby spreading Arab influence across the north of Morocco. Fes now rose in prominence. Not only did the city develop its own important trade routes, but it also earned distinction through the founding of Kairaouine University, respected throughout the Muslim world as one of the three most important in Islam.

With time, however, the authority of this new dynasty began to fade and once more authority in Morocco fell into the hands of local rulers.

The Almoravids (1062-1145)

The resulting power vacuum was exploited first of all by the Almoravids, emerging from among the Sanhaja Berbers. Based in the deep south, they channelled their growing sense of anger over perceived corruption within Islam across the Maghreb into a *jihad* (holy war) against the alleged perpetrators. By 1062 their area of control spread from Morocco in the north to Ghana in the south. Even more significantly, their leader, **Youssef bin Tachfine**, unified Morocco more than at any time before under a simple and harsh form of Sunni orthodoxy. His authority was such that, when the Spanish city of Toledo fell to Christian crusaders, the Muslim citizens of al-Andalous turned to him for help. He responded by crossing the Straits in 1090 and taking Spain for himself. By the time of his death in 1107, not only had Morocco risen to a position of strength in the Maghreb, but his son, Ali, had seemingly inherited a wonderful legacy. To a point, however, this was illusory, for he had left inherent weaknesses within his empire. Time would soon show that Youssef bin Tachfine had spread his forces too thinly.

The Almohads (1145-1248)

Ironically, having risen on the crest of religious zeal, the Almoravids themselves were to be brought down when their own moral authority came into question. Uncannily, the origins of this challenge again emerged in the south of the country. This time it was the Almohads, a Berber tribe based in the Atlas Mountains, who claimed that the ruling power of the day had become decadent, weakening under the influence of their contact with Andalusians from Spain.

Their leader, **Ibn Toumert**, began his campaign by attacking surrounding Atlas tribes and before long declared that he was 'the chosen one'. Even his death did nothing to halt the ascendancy of the Almohads. Indeed, by the end of 1145, their new leader, **Abd el Moumen**, had not only driven the Almoravids out of both Fes and Marrakech but also had driven them back into Spain. Further success still was gained under his own successor, **Yacoub al-Mansour**. Based upon a new capital at Rabat, built with the wealth gained through war, Morocco expanded to dominate the entire Maghreb with its eastern boundary stretching as far as Tripoli. Only with the simultaneous re-emergence of stronger forces in Europe and the east during the time of Yacoub al-Mansour's successor, **Mohammed en Nasr**, did the power of the Almohad Empire begin to wane and eventually shrink back within the modern boundaries of Morocco.

The Merenids (1248-1465)

Under the succeeding Merenids, the power of Morocco diminished again and even Granada, the last Moorish city in Spain, quickly fell back into Christian hands. Meanwhile, much of the Maghreb gradually fell into the orbit of the new rising star, the Turkish Ottoman Empire. There was, nonetheless, progress in the administration of the country and in the arts. The introduction of a new system of taxation funded the construction of *medersas* (universities) within the imperial cities (see Ali ben Youssef Medersa, p117).

The Wattasids (1465-1554)

The passage of power to the Wattasids, a related but rival dynasty, saw no shift in the fortunes of the country. Indeed central authority continued to shrink; the south fell into the hands of the emerging Saadian dynasty and the north suffered at the hands of a series of Portuguese attacks.

The Saadians (1554-1669)

The Saadians were to become the next, but also the last, Berber tribe from the south to rule Morocco and once again, as descendants of the Prophet, the basis of their power lay in their religious strength. Given the absence of political power in the south, they grew from their capital in Taroudannt to take Marrakech in 1520 and within just a few years were able to consolidate their authority in the north, too. It was with the emergence of **Ahmed al-Mansour Eddahbi**, the 'Golden One', however, that Morocco once more came to a golden age, although his rise to power rests upon a rather bizarre twist of fate. When the successful Saadian sultan, **Mohammed esh Sheikh**, was assassinated by Turkish troops in 1557, no one could have seen how Ahmed al-Mansour, at that time still a fairly unrecognised Saadian prince, would succeed to the throne.

At the **Battle of the Three Kings**, the Portuguese **King Sebastião**, hoping to exploit the latest power vacuum in Morocco, joined forces with the Saadian **Mohammed al-Mutawwakil**, who himself had designs on the throne. Their immediate aim was to overthrow Mohamed al-Mutawwakil's uncle, who had seized the throne with the help of the Turks. The ensuing battle saw all three would-be kings killed and the Portuguese beaten, allowing the almost unnoticed Ahmed al-Mansour to step forward unchallenged. He was able to consolidate his position by demanding such enormous ransoms for the safe return of Portuguese noblemen captured at the Battle of the Three Kings that Portugal was left almost bankrupt. This empowered him to turn his attention both to extending his boundaries in the south and to engaging in European politics to the north. The loyalty he received from many was consolidated when he announced the abolition of taxes. Yet again, however, the power of a dynasty ended with the death of its ruler. When Ahmed al-Mansour died in 1603, none of his sons could gain the necessary support to assert their claim to the throne; civil war ensued and the country again fell into the hands of regional rulers.

The Alaouites (1665 to the present day)

Under the leadership of **Moulay Rashid**, the Alaouites stepped out from their power base in Rissani to take advantage of this latest period of political disarray.

Like others before them, the Alaouites first established their credentials as religious commanders before asserting themselves politically. This strategy paid dividends; once Rashid himself had been assassinated in 1672, within the very walls of his own palace, his son, **Moulay Ismail**, had no difficulty in stepping forward to assume his mantle.

Not only this, during his 55-year reign, Moulay Ismail ushered his country into one of its greatest eras. Still today, his tomb in Meknes draws pilgrims in their thousands. Whilst some commentators point to Ismail's notorious cruelty and ruthlessness, others draw attention to his charismatic and astute leadership. One of his first acts was to stabilise the country by placing an elite guard in kasbahs across the land, allowing him to both police and tax his people. He established Meknes as his capital and there built the greatest palace in the Maghreb.

Arguably his finest achievement was his dealing with European leaders as peers. His son, **Sidi Mohammed**, had watched his father closely. He too would play a prominent role in world politics, being one of the first rulers to recognise the United States of America, and enjoyed military successes against the Portuguese. Following his death in 1790, Morocco once more slipped into decline.

When **Moulay Slimane** came to the throne in 1792 events beyond his control were already conspiring against him. For one, post-Napoleonic Europe was increasingly turning its greedy eyes towards the riches of Africa. Yet, he also added to his own difficulties. Not only did he systematically destroy Morocco's relations with the great European powers, but he also managed to alienate the Berber population, leading to a major rebellion against him in 1818. This critically weakened his authority.

Europe turns to Morocco

Wives, and that sort of thing, he had about three hundred, and was much addicted to their company, and some of them accompanied him on all the journeys which he made.

R B Cunninghame Graham on Moulay al-Hassan, *Mogreb-el-Acksa,* 1898

By the time France and Spain, with their modern, well-organised and well-equipped armies, reached out to take from the Maghreb in the mid-nineteenth century, Morocco was not in a position to offer any serious resistance. Whilst the French, bolstered by their defeat of the Ottomans in 1830, led the European charge by taking Algeria, Spain concentrated on Morocco, taking control of Tetouan. Great Britain also took an interest in Morocco, imposing a free-trade 'agreement' in 1856.

Britain, France and Spain were all able to build a series of industrial centres along the coast which successive sultans were unable to resist. For a while, **Moulay al-Hassan**, who came to power in 1873, was determined to challenge the Europeans, but his resistance was short-lived and his successor, **Moulay Abd al-Aziz** even invited Europeans to his court and himself began to adopt European customs. This had the effect of provoking unrest among his subjects, allowing Bu Hamara to set up an alternative, rival court in Melilla. Ironically, however, this internal division only served to further weaken the country and allow European power to be extended almost unchecked.

Disillusioned by his brother's failure to defend the Muslim faith from 'decadent' European influence, **Moulay Abd al-Hafid** overthrew Moulay Abd al-Aziz in 1907 and launched an attack on French troops in Casablanca. This at least caused the Europeans, if only temporarily, to recognise his authority, but in time his leadership was no more successful in offering resistance to foreign incursions than those sultans who had come before him. Gradually he even lost the support of his own people and had little alternative but to accept a French offer of help. The conditions for their support were harsh: in 1912 Moulay Abd al-Hafid was obliged to sign the Treaty of Fes which turned Morocco into a French Protectorate.

The French Protectorate (1912-1956)

At a certain point in the history of colonialism, the English and French stopped competing, and divided what remained of the earth's surface between them. In return for our taking much of the dark continent, the French were given a free hand in North Africa. We were happy to let them have it. As Lord Salisbury said, 'The Gallic cockerel has acquired a great deal of sand; let him scratch about as he pleases.

Anthony Gladstone-Thompson, *The City in the 1960s*, from *Marrakech, The Red City* ed Barnaby Rogerson & Stephen Lavington, 2003

After the Treaty of Fes, the French government applied to Morocco the model of colonial domination which it had developed in Tunisia and Algeria. However, with its stronger position in Europe, greater strategic importance and a 1000-year history of independence, Morocco would ultimately prove more difficult to dominate than its North African neighbours.

Moreover, France was forced to share Morocco with the Spanish who controlled parts of the northern Atlantic and Mediterranean coasts and the region of Tarfaya in the south. In addition, although the Moroccan government had little power during these years, the French *contrôleurs civils* granted conditional independence to a number of Berber leaders (*caids*) notably in the High Atlas Mountains.

Meanwhile, **General Lyautey**, at the head of the French regime in Morocco, aimed to develop the country into a modern industrial state without destroying its traditional culture and heritage. He established new cities and industrial centres outside the old medinas. The administrative capital was moved to Rabat while Casablanca was developed into a grand French-style port city. Even World War I hardly slowed down this pace of development and regeneration. After 1918 the focus of the French turned to the Atlas Mountains which were eventually brought under control by 1934 (see box p50). However, by this time Lyautey's time in Morocco, which ended in 1926, was over and new challenges to French imperialism were beginning to emerge.

In 1927, one year after Lyautey's departure, **Sidi Mohammed** succeeded to the Moroccan throne, chosen by the French despite their perception of him as a difficult character. He would prove himself to be a strong leader and, after independence, would emerge as King Mohammed V. Sidi Mohammed's rise

Bou Gafer

Greatest resistance to the French occupation came from the Berbers of the Atlas Mountains and above all from the Aït Atta warrior tribe of the Jbel Sahro. Hopelessly outnumbered by the better-equipped French army, they were eventually forced to retreat to their remote, rocky, mountainous stronghold of Bou Gafer in 1933. Here, led by Hassou Ba Salem, around 1000 fighting men, their families and animals beside them, resolved to fight on, despite daily attacks not just on the ground but also from the air. The Battle of Bou Gafer is widely acknowledged as the single toughest battle that the French faced during their entire occupation of Morocco. After more than a month of intense fighting, however, the Aït Atta, by now reduced to half their number and running short of ammunition, were forced to surrender, but not before their heroic defiance had confirmed their place in Moroccan folklore.

to power coincided with an upsurge in **Moroccan nationalism** (see box above), in part fuelled by a disastrous French attempt to exploit Berber and Arab differences. Not even the French expulsion of the Moroccan nationalist leader, **Mohammed Allal al-Fasi**, to French Equatorial Africa, would be enough to completely put out the nationalist flames which would ultimately lead to Moroccan independence in 1956.

World War II and Moroccan Independence

With the outbreak of World War II in 1939, Sidi Mohammed called upon his people to fight alongside the French. Moroccan troops responded by fighting bravely against the Axis forces. Even so, the Moroccan nationalist movement continued to flourish during the war years and, further encouraged by the German occupation of France, saw the emergence of **Istiqlal**, an organised pro-independence party. In 1943, Sidi Mohammed met US President Franklin D Roosevelt and was delighted to hear him denounce French rule in Morocco.

Although the French responded with heavy-handed tactics to Istiqlal's formal request for independence, this led to riots in Fes and it soon became obvious that concessions would have to be made to the nationalists. The news that the French, through their new Resident General **Alphonse Juin**, were prepared to offer elected municipalities in large cities was at first favourably received. Once it became apparent, however, that their intention was to flood French settlers into the municipalities, Sidi Mohammed, whose personal support was growing quickly, at least among the Arab population, refused to countersign the decree.

Sidi Mohammed's Achilles heel remained his lack of Berber support. Juin, aware of this weakness, attempted to exploit it by mobilising powerful Berber *caids*, including **T'hami el Glaoui** (see Marrakech p95 and Ouarzazate, p126), against him. So precarious was Sidi Mohammed's position that he was effectively forced to denounce Istiqlal, though taking care not to directly mention the name of the party itself.

In the short term, however, this was not enough to save him. During 1953 a number of Berber leaders, including T'hami el Glaoui, conspired with the French to orchestrate his removal from office and eventual deportation. In his place was installed **Moulay Ben Arafa**. Nevertheless, by now the march of history was gathering pace. Mohammed's forced departure had the effect of making him a hugely popular figure within Morocco and of enraging Spain, who had not even been consulted by the French. It was now the turn of the colonialists to be divided and the subsequent rift between them allowed Spanish-controlled Morocco to become something of a safe haven for Moroccan nationalists.

Meanwhile, the French grip on Morocco was further weakened by developments beyond her colony's borders. Not only was international opinion against France becoming more vociferous, the wisdom of empire was being challenged on a day to day basis by the strength of nationalist rebellion in neighbouring Algeria. Even the French proposal in 1954 to replace the puppet Sultan Ben Arafa with a crown council supported by Sidi Mohammed was not enough to stem the tide: Moroccan nationalist guerrillas began to attack French units in the north.

Nothing if not a political opportunist, T'hami el Glaoui sealed French fate by transferring his allegiance back to Sultan Sidi Mohammed, who was finally able to return to Rabat. **Moroccan independence** was proclaimed on 2 March 1956 and Sidi Mohammed was crowned King Mohammed V.

The Spanish Zone

Once France had acceded to Moroccan demands for independence, Spain followed suit. In April 1956, Spain relinquished its claim to most of the territories it then held in Morocco, amounting to one-tenth of the country, although still decided to maintain control of the two enclaves of Ceuta, on the Strait of Gibraltar, and Melilla, on the Mediterranean coast.

Morocco since independence

Upon independence, **Mohammed V** inherited an autocratic system of government. He began the process which has steadily led to the democratisation of the country by first introducing a new constitution. This included a cabinet of representatives from various groups of Moroccan society; **Mubarak Bekkai** became the country's first premier. However, Mohammed V retained the right to choose his ministers and controlled both the army and police force, while his son, Moulay Hassan, became chief of staff. His own position was further strengthened when the nationalist movement split into left- and right-wing factions enabling him to claim that he was above party politics. When he died unexpectedly in 1961, his son, Moulay Hassan, succeeded as King Hassan II.

During the early part of his reign, **Hassan II** would need to survive a number of assassination attempts yet, at the time of his death in 1999, he had become the Arab world's longest-serving monarch. He ruled Morocco for almost four decades, initially more as a theocracy, deriding political opponents as heretics and many have questioned his record on human rights.

Towards the end of his reign, however, he moved Morocco back on the track towards constitutional monarchy, even inviting some of his former political opponents into the government. He acquired a reputation as a committed Arab nationalist whilst playing an important behind-the-scenes role in the Middle East peace process and is credited with having played a key role in bringing about the 1979 peace treaty between Egypt and Israel.

He is also renowned for having forced Spain to relinquish control of the phosphate-rich Western Sahara (see Mining, p54) which was then given over to joint Moroccan–Mauritanian control. However, relations between Morocco and Mauritania became strained, not helped by Morocco's claim that Mauritania itself should be absorbed into its kingdom. An independence movement flared up in the Western Sahara, spearheaded by **Polisario**, a group of armed resistance fighters who embarked upon a guerrilla war against Morocco.

Seeing the economic and political opportunities that this conflict afforded, both Algeria and Libya at first sided with Polisario before withdrawing their support. First Morocco was able to reach agreement with Libya in 1984 and then Algeria withdrew having enough internal difficulties of its own to resolve.

Only the intervention of the United Nations was able to bring about a ceasefire agreement between the two sides in 1991 based on the understanding that a referendum would decide the region's fate the following year. However, the referendum has yet to materialise due to a dispute over voting eligibility. Even the appointment of James Baker, a former United States secretary of state, by the then UN secretary-general, Kofi Annan, failed to break the deadlock.

As recently as 2008, the United Nations Security Council called upon the two sides to find a just, lasting and mutually acceptable peace which would allow self-determination for the people of the Western Sahara. Commentators have for the most part criticised Morocco for this failing. Meanwhile, the ceasefire continues to hold, thereby allowing Rabat to maintain its position as de facto ruler of the territory.

MOROCCO TODAY

Upon the death of King Hassan II in 1999, he was succeeded by his son, who was duly crowned **King Mohammed VI**. The rule of the Alaouites, who had risen to prominence in the seventeenth century, was thereby perpetuated. In the twenty-first century, Morocco has generally moved towards greater liberalisation through a number of important social reforms. Many critics argue that these reforms have not gone anywhere near as far as they need.

Shortly after his coronation, Mohammed VI addressed the nation on television, promising to tackle the central problems of poverty, corruption and human rights. Some of his reforms have angered conservatives, particularly some religious groups. Amongst these reforms was the *Mudawana*, a new family code which came into effect in February 2004 and which granted more power to women (see pp79-80).

Mohammed VI also announced the creation of the *Instance Equité et Réconciliation* (IEC), a commission charged with the responsibility of investigating the human rights' abuses which allegedly took place during the reign of his father. However, the limitations of the commission have frustrated many. Not only was the commission forbidden to mention Hassan II, his father, by name, no investigation into claims of abuse since 1999, the year in which he had come to the throne, were permitted.

Whereas some hail the IEC as having moved Morocco towards full democracy, critics are angered that the commission was also prevented from criticising limitations on free speech which many human rights organisations claim are still prevalent today. Unemployment, estimated at around 15% (2008) by some, remains a problem for contemporary Morocco.

Political system

Morocco's political system, ratified in September 1996, is that of a constitutional monarchy, evolving from a strongly centralised monarchy towards a parliamentary system. While the King, Amir Al-Muminin (Defender of the Faithful), retains much of the executive power, Parliament, made up of two Houses, is democratically elected. Members of the lower house, the House of Representatives, are elected for six years by universal suffrage, whilst Members of the upper House of Councillors are elected for nine years through a more complicated system involving electoral colleges: one third of the seats are contested every three years.

Parliamentary elections for the House of Representatives were last held on 7 September 2007. Although the elections were deemed free and fair by international observers, turnout was lower than expected at 37%. No party achieved an overall majority, but the centre-right Istiqlal party won 52 seats and its leader, Abbas El Fassi, was appointed Prime Minister. A coalition government was formed on 14 October, which included seven women.

Elections for the House of Councillors were held on 8 September 2006 as a result of which the governing coalition of the four main parties lost five seats but retained a majority of 169.

Islam remains the official state religion, although freedom of worship is guaranteed. Arabic is the official state language.

Economy

With steady annual growth of around 4.5% since the turn of the millennium, Morocco's economy is today much more robust than it was even a few years ago. One aspect of this has been its increasing diversification. Whilst the service sector now accounts for just over half of GDP and a further quarter is generated by industry, including mining, construction and manufacturing, important developments are also currently taking place in the areas of tourism, telecommunications and textiles. Nevertheless, employment in Morocco is still heavily dependent upon agriculture (see p54).

Average wages in Morocco are below £10/US$15/120dh per day and many unskilled workers earn considerably less than this.

Agriculture

With 40-45% of the population involved in agriculture, Morocco is largely self-sufficient in food production, and is particularly strong in meat, fruit, vegetables and cereals. Major crops include sugar beet, barley, sugar cane, potatoes, tomatoes and oranges. Despite this huge investment of labour, agriculture generates only 14% of GDP. What is more, the stability of its agriculture is heavily reliant upon consistent weather patterns; recent droughts have sorely tested the country's resilience. The drought of 1995, one of the worst in decades, saw grain production drop to one-quarter of its normal level.

Although reforms are being introduced, most Moroccan farmers typically carry out traditional subsistence farming on plots of less than five hectares (12 acres). More than half of this work is carried out by women who not only make the biggest contribution to work with livestock but also make the biggest contribution towards the key tasks of weeding, planting, harvesting and food storage.

Fishing

Morocco is the largest exporter of canned sardines in the world and the leading supplier of sardines to the European market. Fish accounts for almost half of Morocco's food exports and more than 10% of its total exports.

Mining

The mining industry forms one of the major components of Morocco's economy, largely on account of the enormous phosphate reserves that it is able to exploit in the Western Sahara. Morocco is the third largest producer of phosphates in the world, the single largest exporter of phosphates in the world and is said to hold two-thirds of the world's phosphate reserves. Economically less significant, Morocco is also renowned for its silver mines in the Anti-Atlas region, mountains which additionally yield manganese, lead, zinc and cobalt. Significant quantities of copper are found here, too, as well as in central parts of the country.

Other industries

Manufacture of traditional crafts, along with textile production, continues to make up an important part of the country's industrial output with major centres based upon Marrakech and Fes. As Morocco's economy continues to develop, however, newer industries, including construction and tourism, play an increasingly significant role.

Health

Standards of health care in Morocco are far below those of the West. Doctors, for example, are in short supply; currently there is only one doctor for every 2000 Moroccan citizens whilst there is one doctor for every 590 people in Britain, one for every 300 people across Europe as a whole and one for every 180 people in Italy.

There is currently one hospital bed for every 1000 people while in the EU the average is six per 1000; in Britain there are four for every 1000 people.

Meanwhile in Morocco, programmes of mass education in child and parent hygiene, along with the development of government health services in schools and colleges, have recently helped to raise general standards. Even so more than half of health expenditure in the country is accounted for by the private sector. For information on health see pp257-63.

Education

Education was made compulsory in Morocco in 1963 for all children between the ages of seven and 13 and this has had an impact upon both school attendance and education standards. Whereas 5.6 million pupils attended school in 2002, by 2005-6 this figure had risen to 5.9 million. Currently 93% of all school-age children attend school, although this is slightly lower for girls (90%) and for pupils in rural areas (91.6%) where attendance by girls is even lower (87.2%). Understandably, access to schools remains problematic in remote rural locations, but traditionally there has also been less emphasis on the education of girls than of boys. So, despite progress made in the field of education, literacy rates remain low, notably amongst young girls and women, as well as the older generation. National literacy rates have remained at around 50% for some years and at around 70% for school-age children (2002), figures which are even lower in rural areas, including all parts of the Atlas Mountains.

Nonetheless, there is physical evidence that reforms are bringing about change: increasing numbers of small, new pink-coloured schools can be seen on the edges of villages as well as large white tents on the fringes of nomadic communities. Both are made instantly recognisable by the red and green national flag which inevitably flutters above them.

THE PEOPLE

Generally the Moroccan is clean-shaven or wears a small moustache, while the traditionalist wears a full-grown beard, wraps himself in a fine djellaba and winds a turban round his head.
André Launay, *Morocco*, 1976

Morocco is dominated by two races: Berbers, the indigenous people of North Africa (33%), and Arabs (66%), in a total population of about 34 million. Although something of a generalisation, as there is increasing intermingling between these two groups, Berbers have traditionally occupied the areas of the Rif Mountains, the Atlas Mountains and the Sous Valley, whilst Arabs are concentrated chiefly along the Atlantic coast and within the cities. Historically and culturally separate (see Historical outline, pp44-52), tensions continue between Arabs and Berbers to this day, although they share a common religion in Islam (see Religion pp57-8). The official language of Morocco remains Arabic, though many Berbers speak only Berber, of which there are three dialects within Morocco: Tarifit, Tashelhit and Tamazight (see Language pp69-70). Few Moroccan Arabs speak Berber.

The Jewish community has in the past played a significant role in the life of the country although its role is much diminished today. From a population of 227,000 Jews in 1948, at the point of the creation of Israel, this number rapidly fell to around 10,000 by 1989 and currently is only around 7000. Other groups, including French, Spanish, Italian and Algerian nationals living in Morocco make up the remaining 0.7% of the whole population.

Trekking in the Atlas Mountains affords the best opportunity of meeting Berbers. Rightly famed for their hospitality towards strangers, some however, with the increasing numbers of trekkers frequenting trails through their villages, are naturally beginning to recognise the commercial potential that they represent. Nonetheless, traditional Berber friendliness, generosity and helpfulness remain prevalent and a possible invitation to share tea and biscuits with a local family always lies around the next corner. Such occasions present the best opportunity to gain an insight into daily Berber life and will add richness to your trek. In common with many mountain peoples around the world, Berbers are renowned for their pride and spirit of independence. Their historic willingness to defend their territory against waves of invaders (see Historic outline pp44-52) extends

A Berber wedding

The bride could not have been older than 13. She sat in her mother's house surrounded by women from the village. Shyly, she presented her hands and feet to the women to be decorated with henna. As they worked, the women sang mournful songs. The bride then lifted a line of wool, which had been soaking in henna, and wove it between her fingers. Another girl of a similar age, perhaps her sister, gently tied a small bundle of salt around the bride's neck. Over the following two days the women of the village stayed close to the bride, talking to her in hushed tones, decorating her and singing. The men remained in their own group, preparing the marital home and cooking for the entire village.

On the wedding day itself, the bride dressed in an ornate wedding costume which had been made over months by her mother. The mother, crying and singing a lament to her daughter's leaving, arranged the girl's hair, dyed a colourful stripe through it and painted her face brightly. The mother then retreated into the home as the bride's brother lifted her onto his shoulders and carried her to a waiting horse to cheering and singing from the villagers, all of whom were watching.

Bride and brother rode together to the new marital home. A man then passed a live lamb around her head three times and she was given a copy of the Qur'an which she kissed. She then drank a skin of milk passed to her by the groom's mother. Another woman handed the bride an egg which she threw against the door of the new home.

She was then carried on her brother's shoulders to her new bedroom where she was joined by the groom. The bride's brother, joined by his father, waited outside the room while the couple consummated their marriage. After a nervous wait the groom emerged from the room to show his in-laws his bride's soiled wedding gown, proof that she had been a virgin. The groom then retreated to his room to join his bride while the villagers celebrated at the house of the bride's mother. I was told that Berbers attach great importance to virginity; if the girl had been found to have lost her virginity before the marriage, the wedding would probably have been called off.

Richard Knight

to their passion for defending their family honour: a slight on the honour of one demands the unity of all in seeking and then gaining redress. Their historic independence continues in the continued exemption of many from paying tax; the price they have paid has been an historic indifference from central government and, consequently, a limited economic commitment towards them.

The most common form of political structure in High Atlas Berber villages is the *jama'ah* (a variant of the word *djemaa*, meaning assembly or meeting place), where elders from the village meet to direct village life according to the codes of the *kanun* – a set of laws regarding property and personal behaviour. Nomadic Berber tribes normally choose one chief to command the group's movements.

Contrary to common expectations, the High Atlas Mountains are relatively densely populated. A typical High Atlas village will be home to several hundred people housed in steeply terraced houses (see Berber architecture, pp58-9) grouped around a central threshing floor. The surrounding slopes will be divided between different farming families.

The traditional dress for Berber men, still often seen today, is a brown or dark blue full-length smock. Women typically wear colourful, highly decorated dresses with distinctive head-scarves and bright sandals. Women carry out a good deal of the hard work both in the fields (see Agriculture, p54) and in the home. Men, frankly, often appear to do rather little. It's quite common to see an elderly Berber woman struggle past a group of chatting men with a vast sack of crops on her back. The world of business, however, is almost exclusively male. Businessmen and merchants sling a small leather satchel across their chests to signify their position.

RELIGION

The predominant religion of Morocco, followed by about 99% of the population, is Islam. Although both Christianity and Judaism have long histories in Morocco, the numbers following these faiths have greatly declined in recent times. Today there are only about 7000 Jews remaining in Morocco and fewer still Christians (see The People, p55).

Islam, meaning 'surrender to the will of God', was founded in the early seventh century by the prophet Mohammed, born in 570AD. By the time of his death in 632, Islam had extended right across Arabia. Muslims, those who follow Islam, believe the Qur'an to be the word of God as handed down to Mohammed by the archangel Gabriel. It incorporates many teachings of earlier 'revealed books' and is thought by Muslims to replace them.

The Muslim creed focuses on seven articles of faith: belief in one God, belief in angels, belief in holy books including the Qur'an, belief in the prophets, belief in life after death, belief in a judgement day, and belief in God's pre-determination of good and evil. Muslims must abide by the five pillars of Islam to lead a devout life and thereby secure salvation. They are: to speak the profession of faith, 'There is no God but Allah and Mohammed is the prophet of God'; to pray five times a day; to pay *zakat*, or alms, to help the poor; to fast from dawn to sunset during the month of Ramadan; and, for those who can

Magic and Moroccan women

Moroccan women, bound by the strict Muslim Sharia code, live in the shadows of men. Pre-marital sex or infidelity can have appalling consequences for women but Moroccan men can escape imprisonment for rape unless their accuser is able to call two male witnesses.

Magic is one way in which women have attempted to redress this imbalance over the centuries. A surprising number of women claim to practise black magic or to be possessed by djinns, intelligent beings from Muslim mythology, often capable of evil, which can gain complete power over individuals. Witches create spells and potions from ingredients bought from attars (herbalists) in the souqs.

Many of these ancient potions are poisons. So it's no surprise Moroccan men treat the subject of witches seriously. A cheating husband or a man who beats his girlfriend might have every reason to fear a visit from a djinn or being fixed by the 'evil eye'.

Richard Knight

afford it, to perform the *hajj*, a pilgrimage to Mecca, at least once in one's life.

On Mohammed's death, however, a dispute immediately developed about who should succeed him in his leadership, a dispute which continues to split the Islamic world. Whereas Shi'ites believe that Mohammed should have been succeeded by his cousin, Ali, these claims are rejected by Sunnis, who themselves recognise the claims of the first three caliphs.

The vast majority of Moroccan Muslims subscribe to Sunni Islam, more specifically to the Maliki school, one of four schools of Sunni Islam, which is particularly strong across North Africa and perceived as being less strict than the others.

One manifestation of popular religion which you are likely to witness during your trek is the unorthodox practice of venerating the tombs (or *marabouts*) of holy men, particularly, but not exclusively, performed by women. Often in isolated locations, some will travel huge distances to seek saintly intervention in this world to help with matters as diverse as conception, as from Sidi Ifni, and relief from mental suffering, as from Sidi Chamharouch, both to be found on the Toubkal trail (see pp138-51).

The *marabout* can also often serve more earthly functions, such as providing the venue for a weekly *souk*. Even the annual *moussem* (festival in honour of the saint) might also afford the opportunity for a simple social gathering. See also, Travelling in a Muslim country (pp78-9) and Other religious holidays and festivals (pp73-5).

BERBER ARCHITECTURE

Berber architecture is simple and without extravagance, yet somehow all the more beautiful for it. Whole red-brown terraced villages, constructed out of the very earth on which they stand, perched and camouflaged on steep valley sides, often remain invisible to the approaching trekker until the last moment. Only rammed earth, adobe brick, stone and wood were traditionally used because these were the only materials which were readily available. Homes were built closely together, often as terraced houses, partly to economise on the amount of land used, which otherwise might have grown much-needed crops, and partly to bring security to their inhabitants through collectivity. The historic violence experienced by Berber society, even between neighbouring villages, demanded such consideration when they built their homes. Nor is it a coincidence that the prominent secular buildings within a Berber village, the kasbah, the ksar and the agadir, all reflect defensive considerations.

The **kasbah**, an occupied fortress, provided a place of refuge in times of attack. Typically square with turrets at each of its corners, they vary considerably in size from enormous structures, such as the world-famous kasbah found at Aït Benhaddou near Ouarzazate, to quite small buildings, which might only be able to accommodate a single extended family, such as seen at Ti-n-Iddr (see p195) on the Sirwa Circular Trek.

The **ksar** (plural *ksours*) is a self-contained hamlet surrounded by a high wall into which even animals could be brought in times of trouble. A single entrance through the surrounding outer wall leads to a central alley. It contains a labyrinth of houses, mosques and wells which fill all the available space between the main thoroughfare and the outer wall. Like the kasbah, it has corner towers for defence and, like a European medieval town, it has few openings through which unwelcome visitors might enter.

The **agadir** is a large fortified communal granary, often built of stone, which might have been built by a tribe either within a village, such as at Atougha, or outwith, such as at Sidi Moussa, a mile or so outside Tabant in the Aït Bou Guemez Valley. Behind a strong, locked wooden door, it contains an individual lockable store for each family, offering protection not only for grain but also for women and children. The more sophisticated structures might even include a well, an animal enclosure, a mosque or a blacksmith's workshop. Even though agadirs were natural targets for any attackers, you can expect to pass a good number on your trek; many either managed to survive these attacks or else have subsequently been rebuilt.

Contemporary influences

Modern incursions have not as yet, perhaps, affected the Atlas Mountains widely. Nonetheless, as first pistes and, more recently, metalled roads, have cut their way through the mountains to end the isolation of many villages previously connected to the outside world only by mule track, there is evidence that the traditional Berber techniques are increasingly coming under challenge. Modern methods of construction are slowly entering the valleys, including the use of concrete. See, for example, the intrusion of European reinterpretations of Berber architecture in the Aït Bou Guemez Valley at the beginning of the Mgoun Circular trek (see p160).

Fauna and flora

MAMMALS

The number of species of wild mammal in the Atlas Mountains is greater than one might expect. Small mammals include the **North African elephant shrew** and the **Algerian hedgehog**. Elephant shrews, also called Jumping shrews, are so named for their long snouts and large ears. The only primate to live in the Atlas is the **Barbary ape**, actually a terrestrial macaque monkey. These animals, which are also found in Algeria and on the Rock of Gibraltar, are about 60 centimetres long with pale fur and pink faces.

Rabbits, **brown hares** and **Barbary ground squirrels** are common throughout the Atlas up to 4000m (13,120ft). One might also come across the **otter**, **ratel**, **ferret** or **weasel**. A ratel is a honey-loving weasel which looks rather like a badger.

The chance of meeting a large carnivore in the Atlas is slim but there are small populations of **lynx**, **African wildcat**, **common red fox**, **jackal** and **striped hyaena**. African wildcats (also called Caffre cats) are like large, muscular tabby cats. **Leopard** might still inhabit the Atlas but none have been seen for some time. Less threatening are the **Edmi gazelle** and **Barbary sheep** (mouflon) which are present in the Atlas but rarely seen.

REPTILES

The Atlas range, like all of Morocco, is the habitat of a number of different species of **lizard**, **gecko** and **chameleon**. Many of these prefer to live in the walls of houses or on stony ground. Geckoes are essentially nocturnal lizards. Chameleons, of course, are known for their long tongues with which they snap up insects and also by their ability to change colour to disguise themselves against different backgrounds. **Snakes** are prevalent in Morocco but become less common at altitude. Few species present any danger to humans except perhaps those from the viper family, particularly the horned viper. They can be recognised by their triangular-shaped heads and the diamond pattern on their backs.

BIRDS OF THE ATLAS MOUNTAINS

With the exception of a hawk or two, pigeons and partridges, the lesser bustard, the little grey wagtails, and a reddish-brown sparrow, I hardly saw a bird.

R B Cunninghame Graham, *Mogreb-el-Acksa*, 1898

Clearly, Cunninghame Graham was not a natural bird-spotter, for, rare though many of the following birds are, the Atlas supports a wide range of birdlife.

Alpine chough

Both male and female Alpine choughs have a similar all-black plumage with a blue-green tinge. Pale yellow bills provide the easiest way to distinguish an

Alpine chough from a common chough. Alpine choughs also have longer tails. Choughs are noisy, sociable airborne acrobats.
Length: 38cm; **Wingspan**: 75-85cm.

Barbary falcon

BARBARY FALCON

A Barbary falcon is similar to the peregrine but with a longer tail and brown colouring around the nape. The underside is spotted. Females are larger and bolder than males.

The flight of a falcon is fast and powerful with dramatic dives for prey. Barbary falcons often hunt in pairs. **Length**: 45-50cm; **Wingspan**: 95-115cm.

BLACK KITE

Black kite

Both sexes of black kite, despite their name, have dark brown-red plumage with paler heads. Their tails, in common with most kites, are forked. A kite's flight is graceful with slow wing-beats. Kites can sometimes be seen scavenging for food at souqs. **Length**: 55cm; **Wingspan**: 150-165cm.

Black redstart

BLACK REDSTART

The black redstart, from the chat-thrush genus, is a small insect-eating bird. The male has dark wings and back and a chestnut tail with a dark-brown central stripe. Females are similar but with lighter, more grey colouring. Males and females both have black bills and legs. **Length**: 14cm; **Wingspan**: 25cm.

Blue rock thrush

Male blue rock thrushes are all-blue songbirds with darker wings. The female is dark grey with buff spots across her breast and underparts. Young blue rock thrushes resemble the female. These are timid birds with a loud call. **Length**: 20cm; **Wingspan**: 35cm.

BONELLI'S EAGLE

Bonelli's eagle

Adult Bonelli's eagles have pale bodies and are dark underwing. On closer inspection, the wings have contrasting dark and grey sections. There is also a strong, dark grey stripe across the end of the tail. These eagles hunt daily in the same territory and in pairs. **Length**: 70cm; **Wingspan**: 150-170cm.

Booted eagle

The booted eagle in flight has a clear aquiline form but is the smallest eagle found in Europe or North Africa. There are two forms, pale and dark, varying from a pale, yellowish underside with dark flight feathers to an all-dark bird with a slightly paler head. **Length**: 45cm; **Wingspan**: 110-130cm.

Common buzzard

Buzzards, both male and female, are varying shades of brown with darker underparts. Paler buzzards usually have dark flight feathers. Tails are curved. Buzzards often perch in the open. **Length**: 50cm; **Wingspan**: 120-130cm.

DIPPER

Dipper

Both sexes of dipper are similar with dark-brown heads and very dark wings and upper bodies. The breast and throat, in contrast, are striking white. Bills are dark. Dippers reveal white eyelids when they blink. They tend to live near mountain streams. **Length**: 17cm; **Wingspan**: 25-30cm.

EGYPTIAN VULTURE

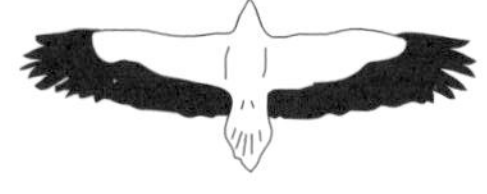

Egyptian vulture

Also called the Pharaoh's Chicken, Egyptian vultures are relatively small and white with black flight feathers and bald heads. Both sexes are similar. Like all vultures, the Egyptian vulture eats carrion but might occasionally prey on small, vulnerable live animals. **Length**: 65-70cm; **Wingspan**: 160-180cm.

Golden eagle

Golden eagles take over five years to grow their adult plumage which, when mature, is a mix of grey and dark-brown which looks dark from below when the birds are in flight. Powerful wings create a seemingly effortless, fast flight and sudden swoops to catch prey. The golden eagle is a much-admired bird which, like other eagles, has often been used as a symbol to represent power and aggression. **Length**: 75-90cm; **Wingspan**: 190-230cm.

GOLDEN EAGLE

Housemartin

Housemartins are common across Europe and North Africa but are most likely to be seen near habitation. They feed on small insects at high altitude and often nest in buildings. Adults have dark blue underparts with white legs and rump. Bills are black. **Length**: 12cm; **Wingspan**: 25-30cm.

Little swift

Little swifts are rare birds which spend almost all their time on the wing. They are dark brown in colour with white rumps and throats with a loud, piercing call. **Length**: 13cm; **Wingspan**: 35cm.

LAMMERGEIER

Lammergeier

The Lammergeier, also known as the bearded vulture, is a giant eagle-like vulture which feeds on carrion. Lammergeiers drop bones from heights of up to 80 metres onto rock in order to break them open to reach the marrow inside. Wings and tail are black, the head orange. **Length**: 105-120cm; **Wingspan**: 270-280cm.

Moussier's redstart

The smallest redstart endemic to north-west Africa, it has a reddish-brown throat, a black and white head, a black back with conspicuous white wing patches. Its song is a warbling sound; its main call 'weet' followed by a rattle rasping. Seen in forests, scrubland and on rocky hillsides. **Length**: 12cm; **Wingspan**: 20cm.

MERLIN

Merlin

Merlins, sometimes described as dashing merlins after their fast flying style, are attractive birds which fly low to hunt smaller birds which they often catch on the wing. The merlin is the smallest bird in the falcon family and capable of impressive aerobatics. Females are larger with brown upper bodies while the males are grey-blue with red-brown underparts. **Length**: 25-30cm; **Wingspan**: 60-65cm.

Red-billed chough (aka chough)

A black bird with red bill and legs. Its call is more like a gull's than a crow's viz 'kyow' or 'k'chuf', hence its name; no song but rarely a subdued chattering like starlings. It both walks and hops and its flight is acrobatic. Found in mountainous areas and round steep cliffs. **Length**: 39-40cm; **Wingspan**: 73-90cm.

Red-rumped swallow

It has a reddish-brown nape and rump, almost black plumage with slightly shorter in-curved tail streamers and slower flight than the swallow. Its song is less musical but its calls are similar. It breeds chiefly near cliffs or bridges, and often in towns. **Length**: 16-17cm; **Wingspan**: 14cm.

Rock thrush

Chunkier than most swallows, the red-rumped swallow has a blue-back upperwing, a black tail and a chestnut stripe across the nape. Underparts are tan with black markings. The bill is black and legs dark. **Length**: 16cm; **Wingspan**: 25-32cm.

Roller

This large bird resembles the crow in shape but displays a bright blue plumage with chestnut back and dark flight feathers. Legs, feet and bill are black. **Length**: 30-32cm; **Wingspan**: 67-72cm.

Tristram's warbler

Male has reddish-brown wings, whiteish rings round the eyes and a whiteish streak under its bill turning to brown underparts; the female's colouring is more muted. Its song is musical; its call a clear 'chit' or 'chit-it'. It breeds and winters in north-west Africa. **Length**: 12-14cm; **Wingspan**: 13-17cm.

FLORA

In summer, the Atlas mountains appear far from lush; barren, perhaps. A closer inspection, however, will reveal a variety of hardy flora including cedar, prickly pear, date palms and juniper trees. Look out for Cupid's Dart (see opposite) and the vivid yellow flowers of woad, the leaves of which, together with 'true indigo', are a source of the deep blue dye used in traditional Berber clothing. At higher altitudes you may also see purple clumps of hedgehog broom, one of the few plants capable of surviving such harsh conditions.

(Colour section (following pages)
• C1 (Opposite) Clockwise from **top left**: Cupid's Darts; Common poppy; Berber hospitality in Assaka; scorpion encountered in the Tislit Gorge. **• C2-3 Sirwa region**: The picturesque village of Atougha on the trail to Jbel Sirwa, (**top left**). The agadir at Tizgui on the descent from Jbel Sirwa, (**btm left**). Snow lies on the ground before the volcanic summit of Jbel Sirwa, 3305m, (**right**). **• C4-5 Mgoun region**: Combatants at the ready for the *fantasia* at Taferlat on the edge of Houaz Plain. **• C6-7 Mgoun region**: The descent from Ighil Mgoun summit along the Assif Ikraween Valley, (**top left**). A contented muleteer approaches the refuge at Aïn Aflafal on the Mgoun Circular trek, (**btm left**). Looking towards Ighil Mgoun from Imelghas in Aït Bou Guemez Valley (**top right**). Approaching the summit of Ighil Mgoun, (**btm right**). **• C8-9 Toubkal region**: The village of Aït Igrane lies ahead, on the Toubkal Circular trek, (**top left**). A mule takes a well-earned rest by the Neltner Refuge and the *gîte* Les Mouflons, (**btm left**). The serene Lac d'Ifni, the largest body of water in the Atlas, (**top right**). Trekkers ascend a ridge at dawn on their way to the summit of Jbel Toubkal (4167m), (**btm right**). **• C10-11 Sahro region**: Spectacular rock formations in the Jbel Sahro, (**top left**). The kasbah of Tigharmet near Qalaa't Mgouna, (**btm left**). The Jbel Sahro Traverse ends at the town of Boumalne du Dades, (**top right**). Sunday souk at Nkoub, (**btm middle**). Approaching *La Tête du Dromedaire* above the oasis of Igli (**btm right**).

C2

C3

C4

C10

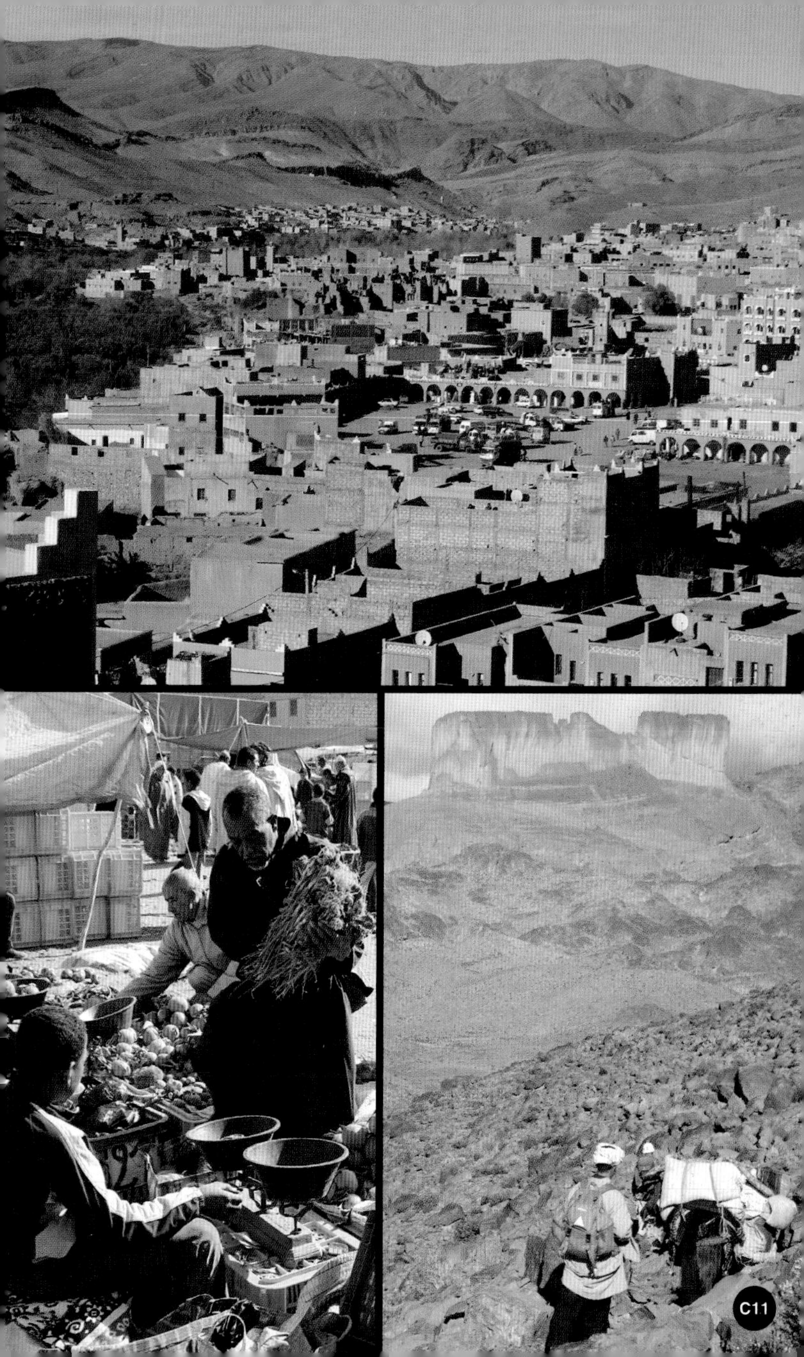

Practical information for the visitor

'But why does he put the coins in his mouth?' 'He always does that,' said the man, as if it had been the most natural thing in the world. He turned away from me and resumed his post behind his oranges.

Elias Canetti, *The Marabout's Saliva*, from *The Voices of Marrakech*, 1967

No matter how hard we try, there will always be aspects of Morocco which we will fail to understand. That, however, is no excuse for failing to try.

LOCAL TRANSPORT

By air

Royal Air Maroc (RAM; ☎ 0522-91 20 00; 💻 www.royalairmaroc.com) is more likely to be of use to those wishing for a change of scenery after their exertions in the Atlas than as a help in getting to the start of their trek. The national airline serves the following Moroccan cities: Agadir, Al Hoceima, Casablanca, Dakhla, Errachidia, Essaouira, Fes, Laayoune, Marrakech, Nador, Ouarzazate, Oujda, Rabat, and Tangier. Flights are relatively cheap: Marrakech to Casablanca, for example, can cost as little as £40/US$60/460dh, although it is quite possible to pay much more depending on when you fly. The major advantage of flying is, of course, time saved and this saving becomes more apparent over longer distances.

Almost all internal flights pass through Casablanca, RAM's hub airport. This causes delays while additional passengers are picked up and effectively adds to the cost of your ticket even though flying via Casablanca might involve taking a very indirect route to your final destination. For example, a flight from Marrakech to Dakhla in the Western Sahara might take around eight hours, including a four-hour stopover in Casablanca, and cost £160/US$320/2000dh, whereas a flight to Dakhla direct from Casablanca might take as little as two hours and 20 minutes and cost only £110/US$165/1400dh. Full timetables are downloadable and tickets can be booked online on the airline's multi-lingual website.

Regional Airlines (☎ 0522-54 34 17/18; 💻 www.regionalmaroc.com) fly to the same airports as RAM with the addition of Goulimine, although they are more expensive than RAM and attract a largely business market.

By bus

All towns in Morocco are readily accessible through an extensive network of inexpensive buses, although departures may be infrequent and journeys can be long and tedious. For example, only one bus leaves Marrakech each day for Taliwine, the trailhead for the Jbel Sirwa trek, taking seven hours.

(Opposite) The heart of Marrakech is its vibrant square, Djemaa al-Fna (see p113) and the 12th century Koutoubia mosque (bottom right; see p114).

There are numerous independent bus companies. Space on board buses is often at a premium. Not only do they quickly become very crowded, often with standing room only available even at the point of departure, most travellers will find that their seat provides less leg room than an economy seat on a budget airline. Furthermore, although Moroccan buses are usually reliable, the quality of the driving and of the bus can at times leave something to be desired.

Most travellers recommend the well-established **Compagnie de Transports Marocains** (CTM; ☎/🖹 0522-43 82 82, 💻 www.ctm.co.ma) which serves the whole country, although both **Supratours** (☎ 0537-77 65 20; 💻 www.supratours.ma), run by the train company ONCF to supplement its train network, and **Satas**, albeit that it serves Morocco only south from Casablanca, also receive good reports. There are cheaper private companies, but with the fares of the better companies being so low and the journey times of the smaller companies often being longer, you have to seriously ask yourself if they are a sensible proposition. By paying £8/US$12/100dh rather than £6.50/US$10/80dh, for example, you could upgrade to the CTM service for your journey from Marrakech to Ouarzazate and benefit from an air-conditioned and altogether much more comfortable journey aboard a faster and more modern coach. (See the relevant town sections in this guide for details of other bus services).

For very long journeys between large towns and cities, you may wish to consider making an overnight journey and, for journeys made during the summer months or in the south at any time of the year, you may want to think about sitting on the side of the bus away from the ferocity of the sun.

By rail

The **Office National des Chemins de Fer** (ONCF; 💻 www.oncf.ma) rail service provides the most efficient way of covering long distances in Morocco by land, providing that the limited network extends towards your intended destination. Trains are quicker and more comfortable than travelling by bus, and fares are competitive with those of the better bus companies. Eight trains per day, for example, cover the three-hour and ten-minute journey from Marrakech to Casablanca; a second-class ticket would cost £7/US$10.50/84dh. Quickest and most comfortable of all, the *Train Navette Rapide*, ONCF's flagship, runs between Casablanca and Rabat.

Trains go no further south in Morocco than Marrakech, and in setting out from Marrakech in any direction, the options are limited. Either head west along branch lines to the coastal towns of Safi and El Jadida, or head north for Casablanca and then onwards following the coastal line to Rabat and Kenitra. From Kenitra, the line turns inland again to the towns and cities of the north and north-east, including Meknes, Fes, Tangier and Oujda. Visit ONCF's website, which operates in Arab, French and English, for fares and downloadable timetables for all of Morocco. Those wishing to head to the south-west from Marrakech, perhaps to Essaouira or even to the Western Sahara, may wish to turn to Supratours, which runs a complimentary bus service designed to link with the train service (see By bus, p65).

By car

There is much pleasure to be derived from driving in Morocco. Roads outside the major cities, especially south of the High Atlas where public transport is often less frequent, are often deserted. A car will allow you the freedom to travel at your own pace and to visit places which might otherwise be difficult to access. It is important, however, to be aware of the risks and to take care. Many Moroccan roads are in poor condition and locals regularly drive unpredictably and dangerously.

Remember to drive on the right-hand side of the road. You will need to be at least 21 years old. Most European driving licences are recognised in Morocco but an International Driving Permit is recommended.

Should you decide to rent a car, third-party insurance might be automatically included, but you might want to pay extra for collision damage waiver and personal insurance to avoid potentially exorbitant charges in case of an accident. Make certain that you properly understand the rental terms, including the mileage allowance, and check that the basic mechanics of the vehicle are sound before you drive it away. Once on the road, take particular care especially if not accustomed to driving on the right-hand side of the road. Remember that speed limits are marked in kilometres and that they vary between 40 and 60km/hr in built up areas, 100km/hr on main roads and 120km/hr on motorways. Police roadblocks, at which you might be asked to produce your documentation, including your passport, are common.

You will find fewer petrol stations than in Europe. In remote areas, fill up whenever possible and take a full jerry can in reserve; your car-hire company should be able to lend you one. If you are setting off for a really long road trip, pack some food, plenty of bottled water and spare clothes in the car as well, remembering that in winter roads in the Atlas can become icy and dangerous.

Car-hire firms are easily found in every major town and city in Morocco (see p98 for information on car hire in Marrakech and pp125-6 for Ouarzazate). Many local car-hire firms offer cheaper prices than international chains and are likely to be open to haggling as most firms will attempt to match their competitors' price. The prices offered by the international dealers vary significantly, but you are likely to pay around 500dh per day for a small, basic car without air conditioning, such as a Peugeot 206, plus 3dh per kilometre and a further 40dh per day for fully comprehensive insurance. A similar car could cost as much as 50 per cent less if you go to a small company and negotiate well. If you're heading for more remote areas or into the mountains, you may choose to pay extra for a 4WD vehicle.

Chris Scott's *Morocco Overland* (Trailblazer, see p271) tells you all you need to know about driving your own car or a hire car in Morocco. For more adventurous trips to the south, the eastern border area with Algeria or across the borders deeper into the Sahara, Chris Scott's *Sahara Overland* (also from Trailblazer) will prove invaluable

One final tip: when parking in towns it's a good idea to appoint a *guardien* (parking attendant) to look after your car. One will probably approach as soon as you park and for a few dirhams will help to make sure that no one breaks in.

By taxi

Morocco is brimming with taxis of which there are two sorts. Shorter journeys within a city are undertaken in yellow *petits taxis*, normally small Fiat Unos, which can be hailed down in the street. They have meters which you might try insisting that your driver uses. Frankly, I have never found a taxi driver prepared to turn on his meter, unless I have had a Moroccan passenger in the car with me, and I believe I have had to haggle over the price of every petit taxi ride I have ever taken. Normally you should expect to pay no more than about £1.30/ US$2/15dh for a ride of a few kilometres across town.

For longer journeys across city or between towns, a *grand taxi*, invariably a large, old beige Mercedes, is required. For journeys across city, although there should be a sticker on the inside of the front windscreen stipulating official prices between set destinations, you will inevitably still need to negotiate the price in advance. Nowhere is this truer than upon arrival at Marrakech-Menara airport where taxi drivers will attempt to charge you an arm and a leg.

For journeys between towns, however, the fare is somehow always less contentious. These taxis are shared and the expectation is that they do not leave until they are full. This means two passengers sharing the front passenger seat and four sharing the back seat. They can be very uncomfortable, especially over very long journeys, but they are considerably quicker than travelling by bus.

It is quite possible to pay your driver for *deux places* (two seats) and effectively reduce the capacity to five. While you might feel that this runs the risk of flaunting your wealth (see p91) it is considered normal when, after a delay, there has been difficulty in finding six passengers. It will even be seen that you are doing everyone a favour and Moroccans are just as likely to offer to do this.

If you want to travel in greater comfort still, it is even possible to book all six places for you and your party. Although the price of '*une place*' in a *grand taxi* is fixed (and no one has ever tried to charge me more than the same rate as locals) the price for the whole taxi suddenly becomes a little more fluid and might typically increase to the cost of six places rounded up to the nearest 50dh. Even so, this still represents very good value for money, especially if you think about the worth of an extra day in the mountains as opposed to a day stuck on a bus.

See the appropriate town sections in this book for information on specific *grand taxi* journeys and prices. For information on taxis in Marrakech, see p97 and p125 for Ouarzazate.

By *camion*

At times in the Atlas, camions (trucks) are the only form of transport available, notably to and from some of the less-accessible parts of the High Atlas. Bouncing around inside or hanging on to the back of a camion, however, can be an extremely uncomfortable, even risky, experience. At least this is a cheap form of transport: the universal charge of 10dh for a trip, regardless of the distance to be covered, still often seems to be adhered to. It is, however, frowned upon to take a camion when taxis are available.

LANGUAGE

What is there in language? What does it conceal? What does it rob one of? During the weeks I spent in Morocco I made no attempt to acquire either Arabic or any of the Berber languages. I wanted to lose none of the force of those foreign-sounding cries. I wanted sounds to affect me as much as lay in their power, unmitigated by deficient and artificial knowledge on my part. **Elias Canetti**, *The Cries of the Blind*, from *The Voices of Marrakech*, 1967

Most trekkers in the mountains, where clear communication is so critical, will want to share a language with the local populace or, at the very least, their guide. Many Moroccans speak French, the language of the colonials, and it would be fairly easy to get by with French alone. Although English is not widely spoken, you are nonetheless likely to find someone who speaks at least a little in all but the most isolated parts of the country.

❑ Weekly souks

Almost before we are aware of it, on going down a slope between some bushes, we found ourselves right in the middle of a crowded market. These country markets are a feature of Morocco, and, I think, of almost every Arab country. Often they are held miles away from any house, but generally on an upland open space with water near.
R B Cunninghame Graham, *Mogreb-el-Acksa*, 1898

One of the most colourful, energy-charged and evocative events you are likely to encounter in the Atlas Mountains is the traditional weekly *souk* (market). Sometimes held in a town, sometimes in a village, sometimes on an open mountain terrace, each souk is staged on a fixed day, established long ago and never questioned, and acts as a magnet for the local population who will travel from miles around to get there for the opportunity to buy and sell their wares and provisions. The souks provide an additional benefit for the trekker: although many would-be traders arrive on either foot, donkey or mule, many others will arrive by taxi or by *camion* (lorry), opening up the possibility of a ride towards a trailhead on the day of the souk, or even the day before, plus the chance of a bonus ride away again afterwards.

Souks north of the main watershed of the High Atlas

Souk	Day
Abachkou (p178)	Saturday
Aït Alla (p186)	Monday
Aït M'hamed	Saturday
Aït Tamlil (p188)	Tuesday
Anargui	Thursday
Asni (p135)	Saturday
Assemsouk	Tuesday
Azilal (p152)	Thursday
Demnat (p188)	Sunday
Ifoulou (p186)	Monday
Imilchil	Saturday
Ouaouizarht	Wednesday
Tabant (p155)	Sunday
Telouet	Sunday
Tilougguit	Saturday
Zawyat Ahançal	Monday

Souks south of the main watershed of the High Atlas

Souk	Day
Asseghmo	Saturday
Boumalne du Dades (p243)	Wednesday
Imi n'Oulaoun	Sunday
Msemrir	Saturday
Nkoub (p205)	Sunday
Ouarzazate (map p128)	Sunday
Qalaa't Mgouna (p225)	Wednesday
Skoura	Monday
Tilmi	Tuesday
Toundout	Thursday

Most Moroccans speak either Arabic or Berber as their first language and both can be difficult to acquire for those unused to their sounds and structure, but in the mountains some knowledge of Berber is useful, if only to show respect. At the very least, try to learn some basic pleasantries. Not only will your efforts be appreciated, you will find people are much better disposed towards you and doors can be opened which might otherwise have remained closed. See the Appendix (pp247-54) for an introduction to some basic Arabic, French and Berber vocabulary with some guidance on pronunciation and also for a glossary (p254-6).

The official language of Morocco is classical Arabic, although Morocco has its own distinct dialect, Moroccan Arabic. The spoken Berber language, of which there are many dialects, extends across at least eleven countries of northern and western Africa, from the Mediterranean to beyond the River Niger, where it is spoken by minority groups. It is also written in several different scripts in different parts of the continent. In Morocco itself, Berber is increasingly written using either Tifinagh script (the traditional Berber script which dates back at least two millennia) or the Latin alphabet.

Within Morocco alone there are numerous **Berber dialects** of which three are more common and, although none are officially used in Morocco, the government radio regularly broadcasts in all three. The first, Tarifit, also known as Riffi, is spoken in the north of the country so you are unlikely to encounter it on your trek. The second, Tamazight, is spoken in central Morocco and has been identified to the east of Marrakech and just north of the Atlas Mountains around Demnat. However, you are most likely to hear the third dialect, Tashelhit, also known as Shilha, which is the language of the High Atlas, Sous and the Anti-Atlas region.

The most accessible of the few English-language resources for the Berber language is EuroTalk's *Learn Tamazight* CD-Rom. Otherwise, try *Méthode de Tachelhit* by Abdallah el Mountassir and Miloud Taïfi which includes a CD.

EMBASSIES AND CONSULATES

Unhelpfully for Atlas trekkers, most foreign embassies are in the capital, Rabat, although happily Marrakech at least provides a home to both a British and a French consulate. For foreign embassies/consulates in Morocco see the box opposite; for Moroccan embassies/consulates around the world, see box p17.

ELECTRICITY

The standard Moroccan electricity supply, like that of Europe, is 220 volts AC, 50 Hz. However, some older buildings still use the older 110-volt supply. Plugs follow the European two-pin round format, so Europeans, Americans and Canadians will need to bring an adaptor in order to use appliances brought from home.

With the installation of increasing numbers of pylons through some of the larger Atlas valleys, electricity is reaching a growing number of villages, but do not depend upon finding a reliable electricity supply on your trek. More remote valleys may have communal generators, but even these are often only used for a few set hours each evening.

❑ **When to bother your embassy**

If you lose your passport, your embassy should be able to help but there are very few other circumstances under which embassy staff can act. It is very rare for an embassy to assist someone who is arrested by the local police; you are, of course, bound by the laws of the country in which you are travelling. In Morocco this advice is particularly pertinent with regard to drugs (see Drugs pp80-1). It is also very unusual for an embassy to help with travel expenses if you find yourself penniless or unable to get home in an emergency.

British Embassy (☎ 0537-63 33 33; 💻 www.britain.org.ma) 28 avenue Sar Sidi Mohammed, Souissi, Rabat; **British Consulate General** (☎ 0522-85 74 00; 📠 0522-83 46 25; 💻 british.consulate@menara.ma) 36 rue de la Loire, Polo, Casablanca; **British Consulate (Marrakech)** (☎ 0524-42 08 06; 📠 0524-43 52 76) 55 boulevard Zerktouni, Residence Taib, Marrakech; **British Consulate (Tangier)** (☎ 0539-93 69 39; 📠 0539-93 68 14) 9 rue Amerique du Sud, Tangier 9000, BP 1203; **Australia (non-resident)** (☎ +33 1-40 59 33 00; 📠 +33 1-40 59 33 10) 4 rue Jean Rey, 75015 Paris, France; **Canadian Embassy** 13 bis rue Jaâfa-as-Sadik, Agdal, Rabat; Visa Services: 31 rue Hamza, Agdal, Rabat; Consular: ☎ 0537-68 74 00; 📠 0537-68 74 30; 💻 rabat@dfait-maeci.gc.ca, 💻 rabat@international.gc.ca; Immigration (visas): ☎ 0537-68 74 01; 📠 0537-68 74 47; rabat.immigration@dfait-maeci.gc.ca; **Embassy of the French Republic** (☎ 0537-68 97 00; 📠 0537-68 97 01; 💻 www.ambafrance-ma.org) 3 rue Sahnoun, Agdal, Rabat; **French Consulate General (Rabat)** (☎ 0537-26 91 81; 📠 0537-26 91 71) 49 avenue Allal Ben Abdellah, BP 139 Rabat; **French Consulate General (Marrakech)** (☎ 0524-38 82 00; 📠 0524-38 82 33) Angles rue Adarissa et El Jahid, Hivernage, BP 538, Marrakech; further French consulates general are to be found at Agadir, Casablanca, Fes and Tangier; **Italian Embassy** (☎ 0537-21 97 30; 📠 0537-70 68 82; 💻 ambassade.rabar@esteri.it) Rue Idriss el Azhar, BP 111 Rabat; **Italian Consulate General** (☎ 0522.27.75.58; 📠 0522.27.71.39) 21 avenue Hassan Souktani, Casablanca; there is also an Italian Vice Consulate in Tangier. **Spanish Embassy** (☎ 0537-63 39 00; 📠 0537-63 06 00; 💻 emb.rabat@mae.es) rue Ain Khalouiya, Route des Zaers, Km 5.300 Souissi, Rabat; **Spanish Consulate General (Rabat)** (☎ 0537-68 74 70; 📠 0537-68 18 56) 1 avenue Ennassr, Rabat; **Spanish Consulate General (Casablanca)** (☎ 0522-22 07 52; 📠 0522-20 50 49) 31 rue d'Alger, 21000 Casablanca; further Spanish consulates general are to be found in Agadir, Larache, Nador, Tangier and Tetouan; **Embassy of the USA** (☎ 0537-76 22 65, after-hours ☎ 0537-76 96 39; 📠 0537-76 56 61; 💻 www.usembassy.ma) 2 avenue Marrakech, Rabat; **Consulate General of the USA** (☎ 0522-26 45 50; 💻 nivcasablanca@state.gov) 8 boulevard Moulay Youssef, Casablanca.

For a fairly comprehensive list of all embassies, consulates general and consulates in Morocco, including countries not detailed above, visit the **Ministry of Foreign Affairs and Co-operation** (💻 www.maec.gov.ma/diplomatic).

MOROCCO

TIME AND DATES

Morocco keeps Greenwich Mean Time (GMT) year-round. In winter (between the last Sunday in October and the last Sunday in March), therefore, there is no difference between British time and Moroccan time, although in summer Britain is one hour ahead.

Also be aware that the two Spanish enclaves of Ceuta and Melilla, like Spain, do not keep GMT; they follow Central European Time (CET) so their clocks are one hour ahead of GMT in winter and two hours ahead in summer.

Morocco, in common with Muslim countries worldwide, operates two co-existing **calendars**. Many key dates are calculated by the Islamic lunar calendar. Although, like the Gregorian calendar, it has 12 months, the Muslim year, having only 354 or 355 days, is 10 or 11 days shorter than a year calculated by the Gregorian calendar, which has 365 or 366. So some dates, for example Islamic New Year, seemingly advance by 10 or 11 days annually when measured by the Gregorian calendar. This is because each new month in the Muslim calendar is counted from the rising of a new moon, which takes place approximately every 28 days, more frequently than the 30 or 31 days that normally make up a Gregorian month. The Muslim calendar has a different set of names for its 12 months; the ninth month is that of Ramadan.

A further difference is caused by the two calendars using quite separate events from which to count their years. Whereas the Gregorian calendar calculates from the birth of Jesus Christ, the Muslim calendar counts from the flight of Mohammed from Mecca (see Coming of Islam, p45), which is reckoned by the Gregorian calendar to have taken place on 13th September in the year 622AD. Years calculated by the Muslim calendar are denoted AH, signifying Anno Hegirae, in the year of the Hijra (the flight of Mohammed). However, the Gregorian calendar is also in common usage and well understood in Morocco, most certainly by those working in business or tourism.

See pp73-4 for calculations of key dates, including religious festivals, by the Muslim calendar.

OPENING HOURS

Bank hours vary with the season. In winter, expect to find them open from 8.15 to 11.30am and from 2.15 to 4.30pm Monday to Thursday, or 4.45pm on Fridays. In summer, banks are typically open only from 8.15am until 2.30pm.

Shops and **souks** stay open longer although many, in keeping with some other businesses, either close early or stay closed altogether on Fridays. In general, expect them to stay open between 8am and 6pm Saturday to Thursday and perhaps even longer in tourist destinations: the souk in Marrakech, for example, now keeps trading until 10pm in summer. In the Ville Nouvelle, shops normally open from Monday to Saturday.

National **museums** close on Tuesdays and those located inside government offices may be closed at weekends. Museum opening hours vary from one museum to another but they are generally open between 8.30 and 9.30am and closed between 5.30 and 6.30pm, with an hour closure for lunch.

All of this information, of course, can radically change during Ramadan (see Holidays and festivals, opposite) when many places are open fewer hours, perhaps 9am to 2pm, and may be further influenced by the time that the fast is broken.

HOLIDAYS AND FESTIVALS

Secular holidays

There are eight secular public holidays (*fêtes nationales*) which are celebrated on the same Gregorian dates every year.

1 January – New Year's Day.

1 May – International Labour Day; this celebrates the efforts of ordinary workers on the same day as many other countries around the world.

23 May – Fête Nationale.

9 July – Youth Day.

30 July – Feast of the Throne; the largest of the secular festivals, commemorates the accession of King Mohammed VI. On this day festivities take place across the country, including fireworks, parades and music in the streets, while receptions are hosted at the Royal Palace.

14 August – Allegiance Day; celebrates the return to Morocco of the Oued Eddahab region in the far south which was formerly held by Mauritania.

21 August – The birthday of King Mohammed VI.

6 November – The anniversary of the Green March (Al-Massira); remembers the day in 1975 when 350,000 unarmed Moroccan civilians, both men and women, marched into the Western Sahara to reclaim this land for Morocco from Spain.

18 November – Independence Day; commemorates the day in 1956 when King Mohammed V returned from exile in Corsica and Madagascar to declare Morocco's independence from France.

Religious holidays

There are also several annual Muslim Festivals, the dates for which are declared by Islamic authorities, based upon the first sighting of the new moon from Mecca (Makkah). Consequently, these dates cannot be precisely predicted in advance with certainty, although it is usually possible to be accurate within a day or two.

Islamic New Year (Achoura/Muharran)
2010 (1432 AH) – 7 December
2011 (1433 AH) – 26 November
2012 (1434 AH) – 15 November
2013 (1435 AH) – 4 November
2014 (1436 AH) – 25 October

The Prophet Mohammed's birthday, is celebrated by **Eid al Mawlid**, **Mouloud** or **Milad-ul Nabi**. Many Muslims attend religious services and enjoy a large feast. Shia Muslims, however, celebrate five days later than Sunni Muslims while some Muslims do not participate at all, regarding this celebration as a religious innovation.

2011 – 15 February
2012 – 4 February
2013 – 24 January
2014 – 13 January

Eid ul-Adha/Aid el Kebir (Feast of the Sacrifice)

Every household must have a sheep of its own for this great festival, and on the eve of the day a faint bleating is to be heard in every home of the city, from sheep tethered in the tiny courts or shut up in some room of the house. But not sheep-dealers alone are busy. In the bazaars which deal with clothes, and, above all, the shops where slippers are sold, customers throng, and the noise of the chaffering rises high.

John Finnemore, *Peeps at Many Lands Morocco*, 1908

Eid ul-Adha marks the end of the annual Muslim pilgrimage to Mecca and is one of the most important feasts in the Islamic calendar.

2010 – 16 November
2011 – 6 November
2012 – 26 October
2013 – 15 October
2014 – 4 October

Ramadan

Ramadan ... is a very strict Fast they observe every twelfth Moon; and during which, if they are known to eat or drink from an Hour before the Breaking of the Day, till the Appearance of the Stars, it is Death by their Law; and they are not only obliged to abstain from all Manner of Food, but likewise from Smoking, washing their Mouths, taking Snuff, smelling Perfumes, or conversing with Women. **Thomas Pellow of Penryn**, *The Adventures of Thomas Pellow, of Penryn, Mariner: Three and Twenty Years in Captivity among the Moors*, 1890

The most important period of all in the Muslim calendar is Ramadan culminating in the celebrations of Eid ul-Fitr/Aid es Seghir (see below). Ramadan, the ninth month in the Muslim calendar, is the period during which devout Muslims fast between dawn and sunset in accordance with the 4th pillar (see Religion, pp57-8) of Islam, abstaining not only from food and drink, but also from smoking and sexual contact. The fast is strictly adhered to by the vast majority of Muslims as it marks the revelation of the Holy Qur'an to Mohammed. Many would even refuse an injection during this period rather than accept any fluids into their body and others would avoid taking part in sport for fear of swallowing their own saliva.

Celebration of Ramadan, however, is for the most part a private, family affair, involving regular participation in feasts within the home after sunset. A notable exception is the sight in Djemaa al-Fna in Marrakech after dusk which, during this month, surpasses even its own high standards for flamboyant entertainment.

Otherwise, the most obvious sign of Ramadan for tourists in Morocco is the universal closure of cafés and restaurants during the hours of the fast itself. Although, as a non-Muslim, you would not be bound to observe the fast, you would, of course, want to be sensitive to those abstaining around you and avoid any obvious public show of consumption.

2011 – 1 August to 30 August
2012 – 20 July to 19 August
2013 – 9 July to 8 August
2014 – 28 June to 28 July

Eid ul-Fitr/Aid es Seghir marks the end of the 30-day fasting period of Ramadan and is a great celebration throughout the Muslim world.

Moussems

And so it is that Saints' tombs stud the land with oven-shaped buildings with a horse-shoe arch, a palmtree growing by, either a date palm or a chamcerops humilis, in which latter case pieces of rag are hung to every leaf-stalk, with running water near; and the place serves as a re-union for pious folk, for women who pray for children, for gossipers, and generally holds a midway place betwixt a church and club.

R B Cunninghame Graham, *Mogreb-el-Acksa*, 1898

A traditional *moussem* is a religious festival staged around a pilgrimage to a *marabout*, the tomb or shrine of a venerated saint. Such festivals are staged all over the country throughout the year, although they are often held in August and September, after the annual harvest but before the new cycle of sowing begins and the rains return in October and November. They are often very small, rural affairs (see Religion, pp57-8) although an exception to this is the spectacular Imilchil marriage *moussem* which takes place during September. It unfailingly draws Berbers from large distances across the Central High Atlas Mountains and tourists in large numbers on package tours from the cities.

Other large *moussems* in the Central High Atlas include that at Setti Fatma in the Ourika Valley in August and that at Qalaa't Mgouna in May when the Festival of Roses is staged (see p223). Note, however, that the term *moussem* has more recently lost some of its original meaning and has grown to encompass almost any celebration, both religious and not.

Music festivals

A growing number of annual music festivals are staged which provide excellent opportunities to enjoy an insight into both traditional and not-so traditional Moroccan music. Perhaps the biggest and the best known is the **Marrakech Festival of Folk and Popular Arts**, involving performances by hundreds of artists, held in early summer. In 2011 it will stage its 46th celebration. Also held in early summer is the **Gnaoua and World Music Festival** at Essaouira at which both traditional Gnaoua and modern jazz artists perform. In late spring or early summer, Fes hosts its own **Festival of World Sacred Music**. Other newer festivals, growing quickly in popularity, include the **Nomads Festival** staged in M'hamid, as well as both the **Casablanca Jazz Festival** and the **Tangier Jazz Festival**.

Dates for all these events vary annually; if you would like to organise the end of your trek to coincide with any one of them you could check dates online either via the Moroccan tourist information website 💻 www.visitmorocco.com or at 💻 www.moroccofestivals.co.uk.

MONEY

The Moroccan currency is the dirham (dh). It is theoretically divided into 100 centimes, although you are unlikely to come across any smaller denomination than a half dirham coin. You cannot officially buy or sell dirhams outside Morocco and, therefore, you will have to buy and sell your Moroccan currency within Morocco itself. This is best done at a bank or exchange counter when you arrive in and ultimately depart from the country. You can take some of your

❑ **Rates of exchange**

With the increasingly volatile nature of world markets the following should be taken as a broad guide only. Prices have been calculated throughout this book by working to a simplified exchange rate of UK£1 = US$1.5 = 12dh. For the latest rates visit 💻 www.xe.com/ucc.

AUS$1	8.06dh
CAN$1	8.40dh
€1	11.05dh
NZ$1	6.33dh
SA Rand1	1.21dh
Swiss Franc1	8.53dh
UK£1	13.35dh
US$1	8.69dh

dirhams home, but current restrictions limit exporting and importing Moroccan currency to 1000dh.

While US dollars, UK sterling and even Swiss francs may be accepted by some of the larger hotels, the number of hotels and businesses that quote prices and accept payment in euros has increased, though they are very much the exception outside tourist destinations. In such cases, however, it seems that the exchange rate is routinely calculated as 10dh:€1, regardless of the official exchange rate.

Travellers' cheques remain a safe way to carry money; however, these cannot be exchanged in the mountains and there can even be difficulties at banks in towns and cities. You should ensure you have enough dirhams in **cash** to cover all expenses for your trek before leaving the nearest big town to your trailhead. **ATMs**, accepting both debit and credit cards from international networks, are now available in most big towns (see Money, p35) so ensure you have at least one tried and trusted **debit or credit card** and the relevant PIN.

International money transfer agents are also readily available in towns. Try either Moneygram (💻 www.moneygram.com), linked to Crédit du Maroc, or Western Union (💻 www.westernunion.com), linked to Attijariwafa Bank and postal offices. Much simpler, however, is to travel with a debit or credit card.

Tipping

Although very much part of life in Morocco, tipping is, of course, discretionary. At times, particularly as a Westerner, you may find yourself under greater pressure than others, but you should not tip unless you are genuinely happy with the service that has been provided, and even then you should not pay over the odds. Waiters in top restaurants might expect to be rewarded with around 10% of your total bill; and those in cafés will probably anticipate the same. Petits taxis drivers would not normally expect a tip at all but will always be appreciative should you offer one, while grands taxis drivers, especially if you have booked the whole taxi for a long journey, will hope that you add a few dirhams to the fare price you have negotiated. Baggage handlers, who load your backpack onto the roof rack of a bus, will often expect 5dh.

Haggling

Bartering is a key ingredient of Moroccan life and you are unlikely to be in Morocco at all long before your negotiating skills have been put to the test, perhaps even before you have left your port of arrival. This can be a very long-drawn out affair: many Moroccans are capable of bartering the hind leg off a donkey.

Restaurant, and most hotel and transport, costs are fixed. Beyond that, however, prices are often established through a long-winded ritual which some travellers hate and others love. Remember to keep a cool head. Stay friendly and cheerful and never bargain for something you don't actually intend to buy. It helps to know how much an item is really worth but, more importantly, decide how much it's worth to you. Keep a fixed upper limit in your mind and don't exceed it. Praise the shopkeeper for his fine goods and then show casual, unenthusiastic interest in whatever it is you hope to buy. It's best to get the shopkeeper to name his price first. Open your bidding at one third of that.

Ignore the shopkeeper's sob stories and bargain hard. He will expect nothing less. Whatever the outcome, shake the salesman's hand and keep the whole transaction friendly. Haggling is, after all, as much about entertainment as it is about buying and selling (see Surviving the souks, p116).

KEEPING IN TOUCH

Post offices

Moroccan post offices can be recognised by their *PTT* or *La Poste* signs. You will need to head here if you wish to post parcels, although, if you only wish to buy stamps, try asking at *tabacs* or even at news stands. Allow at least a week for a letter or postcard to reach Western Europe (7.50dh) and perhaps two weeks to reach North America (10.10dh) or Australia (10.80dh).

Post restante If you do not have a contact address in Morocco, even an intended hotel, but wish for mail to be sent to you, try recommending the *Poste Restante* service provided by some major post offices (Poste Restante, La Poste, place 16 du Novembre, **Marrakech**, Morocco; Poste Restante, La Poste, rue de la Poste, **Ouarzazate**, Morocco) to any would-be senders. Letters could be held here for you for up to a month while you are in the mountains.

Telephones and fax

Often by far the most convenient way to make a telephone call in Morocco is to visit a *téléboutique*, easily found even in small towns. A choice of private, screened booths within allows for a peaceful phone call. Although you will need coins, change is readily available from the supervisor. Many of them also have fax machines. Alternatively, most post offices have a telephone room attached, from where you can also make reverse-charge calls.

All landline numbers are preceded by 05 and all mobile phone (GSM) numbers by 06. Full landline area codes must be dialled even when calling from within the same area. Many European mobile phones work through Morocco's mobile phone network. You should check with your phone provider to see if your roaming agreement covers Morocco. Once in Morocco, you will be charged to receive calls as well as to

❑ Dialling codes

Agadir	☎ 0528
Casablanca	☎ 0522
El Jadida	☎ 0523
Essaouira	☎ 0524
Fes	☎ 0535
Marrakech	☎ 0524
Meknes	☎ 0535
Oujda	☎ 0536
Rabat	☎ 0537
Safi	☎ 0524
Tangier	☎ 0539
Tinerhir	☎ 0524
Zagora	☎ 0524

make them. Alternatively, local SIM cards can be bought (30dh) from Maroc Telecom and from Méditel offices. You will need to show your passport to buy one. Once in the mountains, however, you will usually be without signal.

E-mail

Internet cafés are becoming increasingly common, at least in larger towns. Rates vary but in all cases should cost no more than 5-10dh per hour, although the speed of the internet connection might not be as fast as you are used to at home. Do not, however, expect to find internet access once you are in the mountains.

MEDIA

Newspapers

A good number of Moroccan-based French- and Arabic-language newspapers are published daily, including *Le Matin du Sahara* (💻 www.lematin.ma) and *L'Opinion* (💻 www.lopinion.ma). Many newspapers, including some in English, are available online and can be searched by visiting 💻 www.onlinenewspapers .com/morocco.htm. In addition, a number of European newspapers and magazines are readily available in the major cities, usually arriving just one day late, many of which are also accessible online through their own websites.

Radio

The **BBC World Service** can no longer be listened to on shortwave radio in Morocco but can be picked up 24 hours a day via Hot Bird Satellite English (Europe) in the north of the country, such as in Fes or Tangier, or via Worldspace (Africa West) in much of the rest of the country, including Marrakech, Casablanca and Rabat. You would be wise to plan ahead by consulting programme listings at 💻 www.bbc.co.uk/worldservice before you head into the mountains. **Voice of America** can also be picked up in Morocco from 3am till 10pm daily although its frequencies are subject to change. Programme listings and up-to-date frequencies are available at 💻 www.voa.gov.

Television

Increasingly some of the more expensive hotels receive satellite TV, typically CNN, the French TV5, and occasionally the UK Sky channels. Additionally, in the north of Morocco, it is possible to pick up Spanish TV stations and, in Tangier, the English-language Gibraltar TV, as well as radio broadcasts. In cafés you are likely to encounter the popular Al Jazeera channel; this provides the largest and possibly the most controversial broadcast of Arabic news in the Middle East claiming over 40 million viewers in the Arab world alone. Morocco's TV channels are for the most part broadcast in Arabic, but also include some French programmes and news bulletins in French, Spanish and, more recently, Berber.

TRAVELLING IN A MUSLIM COUNTRY

All visitors to Morocco would want to show respect towards local people and to avoid causing unnecessary offence. This can be achieved by observing some basic Muslim cultural norms.

- Avoid eating or offering gifts with your left hand as this is the hand used for washing private parts after going to the toilet and is considered unclean.
- Wash your hands and lower arms before eating if water is available.
- Remove your shoes before entering anyone's house, certainly before their main reception room, before entering a tent or a building of religious significance.
- Avoid pointing bare feet towards anyone; if sitting on the floor, tuck them under yourself or sit cross-legged.
- Never ask for alcohol unless it's clearly available; it's considered un-Islamic.
- Never ask for pork which is considered unclean.
- Only three mosques and few religious buildings of any description in Morocco are open to non-Muslims and you should make absolutely sure that you are allowed inside before you enter. The three mosques which are open to non-Muslims are the partially restored Tin Mal on the approaches to the Tizi n-Test in the High Atlas, the remains of the Great Mosque at Smara in the Western Sahara, and the modern Hassan II Mosque in Casablanca.
- The exposure of flesh is considered highly offensive. At all times dress should be modest, particularly for women, and shorts, even in the mountains, should be avoided. This is imperative around religious buildings where particular effort should be made to cover legs, shoulders, arms and, for women, hair.

WOMEN IN ISLAM

There are many misconceptions about the position of women in Moroccan society and non-Muslims make too many generalisations about the impact of Islam upon them when in fact the degree of independence experienced by women varies from one Islamic country to the next and even from one region of Morocco to another. Nonetheless it is very true to say that Islamic values underpin Moroccan society and have a huge bearing upon the lives of its women, even while Morocco officially remains a secular state.

Negative Western press tends to focus upon the perception of inequalities between men and women. Contrast is often made between the support given to the practice of polygamy by the Qur'an, providing that the man is in a position to provide for all his wives, against the cultural requirement of women to be virgins until the night of their marriage (see A Berber wedding, p56). It is also true that women in Morocco have traditionally carried the burden of responsibility not only for running the family home and caring for young children, but also for performing most of the back-breaking hard physical labour traditionally required in the fields (see Agriculture, p54).

While all this remains true, nonetheless, there are signs of change. For instance, the advent of King Mohammed VI's Mudawana reforms in 2004 has enshrined rights for women in the areas of custody, divorce, property ownership and child support, while levels of female literacy, too, are on the increase (but see Education, p55). Today more Moroccan women are seen on the street, especially in towns and cities, than could have been seen even 20 years ago and women are steadily redefining their role in the labour market. Although the very first female Moroccan MP was only elected in 1993, 34 women MPs were elected to the 325-seat parliament in the 2007 election of whom seven were invited into the coalition government.

WOMEN TRAVELLERS AND SEXUAL MORES

Sadly, Western women will almost certainly find that they become the subject of unwanted attention from Moroccan men. This is for a number of reasons, not least of which is that many Moroccans hold dear ambitions of living in the more affluent West and hope that its women might provide them with a passport to this new life. Another is that, living in a world in which social restrictions still make it difficult for them to meet Moroccan women, Moroccan men see Western women as much easier to approach; that Western women are generally believed to be promiscuous only adds additional incentive.

All this can make travel in Morocco for single Western women difficult. Think carefully about the signals which you give off which may be open to misinterpretation. Undoubtedly, you will receive less hassle if you dress modestly. This means covering your whole body, including arms and legs and perhaps even choosing to wear a headscarf. You will attract less attention by travelling with one or more men. It has even been suggested that women travellers might wear a wedding ring, whether married or not, to indicate that they are not available. Smoking cigarettes and drinking alcohol by women was seen until recently as the preserve of prostitutes: in some parts of Morocco these beliefs are still held.

HOMOSEXUALITY

Sexual activity between men is illegal in Morocco and punishable by imprisonment. Do not be deceived by the sight of men openly holding hands in public which, as in many Muslim countries, is a common gesture of friendship without sexual connotation. Curiously, there is no legal stance on lesbianism which is not even officially acknowledged.

DRUGS

Morocco has a notorious reputation for the production of cannabis both in the form of *kif* (or marijuana, dried cannabis leaves) and hashish (cannabis resin). Its consumption has a very long tradition, especially in the north of the country, considerably predating the hippy days of the 1960s and 1970s. Today its distribution continues to be widespread, not only within Morocco but well beyond via a worldwide export network. However, you should be under no illusions: whereas its cultivation may be legal, the possession, offer, distribution, purchase, sale or transportation, including exportation, of cannabis in any form is most certainly not and penalties can range widely from a fine of between 2400dh and 240,000dh and/or a jail sentence of between three months and five years.

Much advice abounds as to how to secure cannabis most safely and how best to cope with being caught afterwards, yet the best advice of all is surely to avoid becoming involved altogether: in Morocco the risks far outweigh the benefits.

As production is centred in the northern Rif Mountains, notably in the region around Katama, you might decide not to visit this part of the country at all.

Yet wherever you go in Morocco, if you are perceived by dealers as someone who might be interested, you are likely to be approached by them, often quite openly, with offers of 'chocolate' or 'shit'. This is all the more of a problem as some dealers are believed to collude with unscrupulous policemen to set up Westerners, who can then coerce them into paying heavy bribes to avoid a visit to the law courts. Although such behaviour is said to be particularly common in Tangier and Tetouan, similar tales come out of numerous larger towns, including Marrakech. Stay strong to any pressure from dealers and make it clear that you do not smoke.

FOOD

To my mind four things are necessary before a nation can develop a great cuisine. The first is an abundance of fine ingredients, a rich land. The second is a variety of cultural influences: the history of the nation, including its domination by foreign powers, and the culinary secrets it has brought back from its own imperialist adventures. Third, a great civilisation; if a country has not had its day in the sun, its cuisine will probably not be great; great food and great civilisations go together. Last, the existence of a refined palace life; without royal kitchens, without a Versailles or a Forbidden City in Peking, without, in short, the demands of a cultivated court, the imaginations of a nation's cooks will not be challenged. Morocco, fortunately, is blessed with all four. **Paula Wolfert** *Couscous and Other Good Food from Morocco*, 1973

MOROCCO

Moroccan food

Morocco's cuisine is a reflection of its great history. Being at the crossroads of so many civilisations, each, through time, has brought its special influence and left its individual legacy. From the ancient foundations laid down by the Berbers, most evident today through the omnipresent national dishes of couscous and tagine, through to the most recent twist of sophistication provided by the French colonialists, each migration of people has added diversity to the Moroccan menu. From Middle Eastern cuisine, involving the use of ingredients such as honey, sesame, chick peas and mint, spread throughout North Africa by the march of Arab invaders, to Andalusian spices shipped across the Strait of Gibraltar from Spain by the Moriscos, and from the far-reaching influences of the distant Ottoman Turks to the contribution of the local, immigrant Jewish community, each in turn has added to the melting pot of ideas and tastes.

• **Harira** This thick soup can be eaten either as a starter or as an entire meal. It is a rich and filling concoction made from chick peas, vegetables, mutton, the wings, liver and gizzards of poultry, tomatoes, rice or flour, pepper and coriander. It is traditionally with this dish that the daily fast is broken each day at dusk during the holy month of Ramadan (see Ramadan p74).

• **Tagine** It is impossible to visit Morocco without becoming acquainted with this ubiquitous dish. The word 'tagine' actually refers to the earthen pot with a pointed lid in which the meal is cooked. The meal itself is a delicious, thick stew, made with either meat, fish or vegetables, cooked slowly in spices. Reportedly, poor Moroccans sometimes use inexpensive camel meat as a substitute for beef. If you are eating with others, the tagine will traditionally be placed between you and shared. The secret of this dish, always served very hot, is in the long, slow cooking process. If in the mountains, this can have significant implications (see Eating in the Atlas, below).

• **Couscous** To produce this light, scented classic dish, semolina is steamed in the top part of a *couscousier* (a two-tier cooking pot) while a meat or vegetable stew cooks underneath. After several hours, the two are served together and coated in harissa sauce (see below). As with tagines, this dish is traditionally eaten collectively, served in a large dish placed at the centre of your group. Astonishingly, although rightly considered a meal in itself by most, couscous might be served to you at the end of an already copious meal by an over-generous host to ensure that you do not go home hungry.

• **Pastilla** Moroccans consider this to be a luxury speciality. Indeed, at its best, this very sweet, rich pigeon pie, made with light, crispy pastry and covered in sugar, is excellent. The culinary term for the tasty meat required is *squab*. Unsurprisingly, given that this is the meat of young pigeons, usually only around a month old, it is more tender and more moist than most other poultry.

• **Harissa** This spicy sauce, almost always used on couscous, made from chilli peppers, often smoked or dried, and garlic, is a popular addition to many other Moroccan dishes. Test its strength before you pour it on.

• **Mechoui** A mechoui is a whole lamb roasted slowly in a sealed clay oven. This Berber speciality is usually reserved for weddings or feasts, so if you are offered one you should consider it a great kindness. The lamb's heart and liver will be eaten before the main dish. Traditionally, the most succulent parts of the lamb will be offered to the guests first; this could mean the eyes or even the testicles. Refusal will offend. More worldly-wise Berbers will have encountered Western reluctance to eat steaming lamb's gonads before, but if not there's no way out.

Western food

One daily reminder of the French colonial legacy to Morocco is the milky coffee and croissants that you might enjoy for breakfast in cafés. While simple pizzerias are becoming more widespread, even found in smaller towns, genuinely international cuisine, including French, Italian or even Oriental, sometimes with a Moroccan infusion, can often only be found in restaurants in larger cities.

Eating in the Atlas

Once you have embarked upon your trek, food will for the most part be simple fare. If you have hired a cook (see *Cuisinier* p11) you can, nonetheless, expect to eat well. Meals will be largely Moroccan based but are likely to be infused with a little European influence. **Breakfast**, for example, will normally consist of bread with jam and processed cheese, with the option of olive oil, served with mint tea or coffee. **Tea** (see opposite) will also be served with both the lunch and evening meal. Some fruit and a few nuts will probably be provided as a **mid-morning break**. Before your departure you should enquire whether these have been included in your provisions. If they have not, they are easy to buy in the souks and you may wish to buy some yourself. **Lunch** might typically be a freshly prepared salad served with tinned fish, such as sardines or mackerel and bread. In the **evening**, with just a gas stove and a couple of pans, your highly skilled *cuisinier* can be expected to rustle up a tasty three-course meal. There will usually be a soup starter, perhaps using the remains of the salad as the base. The main course is likely to be tagine or couscous, although increasingly staple foods such as rice and pasta are being included in the repertoire; this will be followed by fresh fruit, often oranges. Unless you buy a live goat or chicken along the way, you are likely to eat fresh meat only in the first few days of your trek.

Otherwise, if your route allows, most *gîtes d'étape* or *refuges* could provide you with a hot meal. If relying upon this hospitality, however, you would be well advised to check availability and to book ahead: simply by arriving unannounced, you are at best likely to find yourself with a very lengthy wait before your meal can be prepared.

DRINK

Faithful to tradition, our host rises to prepare the green mint tea ... oh, that odour that touches the throat with an iced finger, which plumbs the depths of the lungs, tells of snow and subtle pepper, wakens the spirits and deludes thirst!

Colette, *A Moroccan Luncheon* from *A Book of Travellers' Tales* by Eric Newby, 1985

Mint tea

The most readily available drink in Morocco is a traditional mint tea (*thé à la menthe* or *whiskey Berbère*) served in a small glass, sweetened by generous amounts of sugar. There is quite an etiquette not only to the serving of the tea but also to its consumption, a reflection of the importance attached to hospitality throughout Moroccan society and the continuing strength of its traditional values today.

Usually served in a silver teapot, presented upon a silver tray, the host should pour into a single glass, usually from a considerable height, not once, not twice, but three times, each time afterwards returning the contents of that glass to the pot, thereby encouraging the infusion of not only the flavour but also the scent of the mint. Only then, the tea considered properly prepared, will the ritual extend to the host pouring into the glasses of all guests in turn.

This done, all should raise their glasses together to a toast of *Bismillah* and drink as one. Glasses should be quickly refilled, but only when all have first been emptied, before being refilled once more and drunk for a third and final time. Each glass should naturally become sweeter and more inviting than the previous, although tradition asserts that once the third glass has been imbibed, guests should politely withdraw, taking care not to overstay their welcome.

Soft drinks

All internationally known brands of carbonated drinks are widely available throughout Morocco and, increasingly, even in the most unexpected places, along trekking routes both in the High Atlas and in the Anti-Atlas Mountains. Also readily available on the plains, though much harder to find on the trail, is a glass of freshly squeezed orange juice which tastes no better anywhere else on earth than in Morocco.

Water

Never drink tap water in Morocco, nor directly from streams. Across most of Morocco there is a healthy selection of readily available, inexpensive bottled mineral water, including Sidi Ali, Sidi Harazem and Ciel. Even on the trail, do not be surprised to find the occasional enterprising goatherd who has converted his *azib* into a small shop. Otherwise, see Water purification systems box p29 for recommended methods of water purification.

Alcohol

Although alcohol is forbidden under Islamic law and it is not generally possible to buy alcohol in the medinas, alcoholic drinks are nonetheless available in some restaurants, bars and hotels of larger towns and cities, especially in Villes Nouvelles. Morocco produces two very acceptable beers of its own, *Stork* and *Flag*, as well as several good wines. Additionally, many well-known labels are imported from the West.

HAMMAMS

In pursuance of our design to 'do' Morocco as thoroughly as possible, we resolved to have 'a wash and brush up' in the native fashion. The hammam in Morocco, as in all Mohammedan countries, is an institution.

Joseph Thomson, *Travels in the Atlas and Southern Morocco*, 1889

For many Moroccans, a weekly visit to the local hammam, traditional Turkish-style communal steam baths found across the length and breadth of Arabia, provides one of the cornerstones of their lives. Their ritual attendance places as much emphasis upon the social opportunity to chat to friends as it does upon washing. Within, men and women are strictly divided, either by having separate entrances which lead into separate chambers, or else by having separate hours of the day or even separate days of the week, when they are permitted to visit.

Although every quarter of the medina has its own community hammam, to which outsiders are normally welcome, they can be hard to find, so you may need to ask even to locate one. Nonetheless, visiting a hammam at the end of a gruelling trek can be a wonderful experience and once there, someone will usually be willing to help you if you do not understand the procedures. To be better prepared, take along your own shampoo, towel and even a *kii* (rough flannel glove) to ensure that you have a good rub-down.

A traditional, local hammam within a medina could cost as little as 8dh, although some will quite openly want to charge you more as a foreigner, and clearly you should expect to pay more still if you choose to visit one of the growing number of hammams within high-class hotels.

TOILETS

With the growth in numbers of Westerners arriving in Morocco, so the number of European-style lavatories to accommodate them has increased. Nonetheless, it remains true to say that in most homes and cafés, especially on the trail, a hole in the ground is more common, with a tap and small bucket provided for washing and flushing. Toilet rolls are rarely provided apart from at more expensive hotels and restaurants. You will need to decide, therefore, whether to adopt the local 'left hand and tap' method of hygiene or to carry acres of loo roll around. Trekkers should burn used toilet paper. (See Travelling in a Muslim Country pp78-9).

THINGS TO BUY

Just as Morocco's culinary traditions are a reflection of the cosmopolitan nature of its society (see Food, pp81-3), so too each of its major component parts, notably Arab, Berber and Jew, have contributed to the country's strong tradition for producing fine arts and crafts. No visit to Morocco could be complete without a visit to a souk to see these wares being created in small workshops before being placed on sale in the bazaar. Be aware, however, that amongst artefacts of genuine quality, cheap imitations designed for the tourist market will also be displayed. This leads some visitors to buy from an *ensemble artisanal*, a government-run emporium found only in larger towns and cities, where prices are higher than in the souks but are fixed and where quality is assured.

Carpets

Moroccan carpet dealers could teach any double-glazing salesman a thing or two about high-pressure sales techniques. However, if you are prepared to take the time to find a good dealer with some genuinely interesting wares, the experience can be rewarding. You will find yourself sitting cross-legged on the floor, plied with mint tea, while an enthusiastic salesman rolls carpets out for your inspection.

Ask him to explain the differences between hand-knotted carpets and woven kilims, and also the regional variations in colours and patterns. Find out the meaning of the carpet's symbols for every carpet tells a story. Take time to look at the back of the carpets to check the quality of the knots: the more knots per square inch, the higher the value. Ask also about the dyes; whereas originally only natural, vegetable dyes were used, increasingly there is reliance upon synthetic substitutes.

Be sure you know what you are buying. Many carpets which look fantastic in a large Moroccan carpet shop can look faintly ridiculous at home. What is more, be careful what you pay. Whereas some antique carpets can justifiably be very expensive, you need to be sure you are not being seduced into paying excessively for an inexpensive version, even a machine-made copy. You should also consider carefully how you propose to get your carpet home. Don't make the mistake of thinking that a carpet will be an investment or the start of a thriving import business; there is no real market for Moroccan carpets in the West and they are seen as inferior to those of the Middle East and of Central Asia. Buy for your own pleasure only.

Of course if you are interested in a Berber carpet, you are in prime position to cut out the middle man altogether whilst on your trek. The Berber carpets you see in the towns and cities were bought by your salesman from the women who made them, often in their own mountain village home. By visiting a local weekly souk (see p69) or even a local women's co-operative, you can ensure that your money goes directly to those who have most earned it.

Clothes

Clothes, like carpets, are usually better left in Morocco. Bright clothing with intricate embroidery, which can look so beautiful under the natural, bright light of a Moroccan sun, can look inappropriate once back home. If you plan to buy Moroccan clothes to wear while in Morocco, however, *jallabahs* (ankle-length outer garments with pointed hoods) are readily available in the souks, as are multi-coloured knitted caps and bright silk scarves.

Ceramics and pottery

Distinctive pottery provides a practical and inexpensive opportunity to buy an evocative souvenir of Morocco. There is an abundance of plates, bowls, even tagine pots, from which to choose, many sporting traditional Islamic geometric patterns, most regions offering their own traditional colours and styles.

Jewellery

Copious amounts of inexpensive jewellery can easily be found in the souks, reflecting the traditional preference of Moroccan craftsmen to work with silver and such semi-precious stones as coral, agate, carnelian and amber. In the Atlas regions, chunky Berber necklaces and bracelets are particularly common, although sadly plastics are sometimes inlaid to imitate the semi-precious stones you might think you are buying. At other times there is no pretence: both cheap beads and low denomination coins are often beautifully combined to dazzling effect.

Semi-precious stones and fossils

Rarely is an Atlas road journey undertaken that is not peppered with road-side stalls located on hair-pin bends selling fossils and semi-precious stones, including amethyst and quartz. Both are naturally profuse in the mountains of Morocco, but again take care that you are being offered the genuine article: there are stories of stones being coloured with dye and 'fossils' emerging from modern plaster casts.

Leather

You will find abundant high-quality leather accessories, including wallets, bags and belts, in every urban souk. Pouffes, bought unstuffed, can easily be transported home. Moroccan leather book-covers are world-famous for their quality; if you plan ahead you might consider taking a treasured book with you from home to be bound after your trek. More practically, however, you may want to purchase a pair of authentic open-heeled *babouches* (slippers), worn by men and women both indoors and out. Available in all the colours of the rainbow, take advice on 'men's' and 'women's' colours before you buy.

Metal

Examples of inexpensive, decorative metalwork, including candlesticks, bowls and lanterns, made from brass, copper and silver, abound, although above all it is perhaps the Moroccan tea-pot that might provide you with the most enduring symbol of your trekking experience.

Spices

A small bag of saffron or cumin makes an interesting gift; explore the spice souks in Marrakech where each stall is laden with colourful, tapered stacks of spices. If unsure of your preference, ask the trader to let you taste samples.

Wood

Evocative of a by-gone age, gorgeously ornate doors and panels are still created from cedar wood to furnish the homes of the rich, as are carved rafters to support their ceilings; the very finest woodworkers are still employed in maintaining and restoring religious buildings, too. Tourists can take a sample of this magnificent craftsmanship home in the form of luxurious, inlaid draughts, chess and backgammon boards, or jewellery boxes, plates and bowls, all made from the wood of evergreen thuja trees. More simply still, you might consider a long-handled *harira* spoon (see Food, p81) carved from beautiful orangewood.

SECURITY, CRIME AND THE POLICE

In addition to the grey-uniformed *Gendarmerie*, who you are most likely to meet at checkpoints on main roads, and the navy-blue uniformed *Sûreté* police, who operate within towns, a *Brigade Touristique* has been established, specifically to deal with the affairs of tourists; Brigade staff are usually in civilian clothing.

Although Morocco is often perceived to be a difficult country in which to travel, the crime rate is in fact low. Muslims are asked through the Qur'an to show kindness and respect towards strangers and, more often than not, travellers remember Moroccan hospitality as one of the highlights of their trip. As in any country, however, wherever tourists swarm in numbers, conmen and thieves operate. This applies to Marrakech, for example, where travellers ought to employ common sense and exercise caution. In the Atlas Mountains crime is almost non-existent. If you do experience trouble, contact the police (see Emergency numbers, below). Remember, however, that the Moroccan police, if rumours are to be believed, are highly corruptible. You will need to employ tact and patience in dealing with them.

In theory it is compulsory to carry an ID card or passport at all times. Although you would be unlucky to be stopped within a town or city, still more so in the mountains, you would be wise to take yours everywhere, especially when travelling between towns.

❑ Emergency numbers

Police (within a town)	☎ 19
Gendarmerie (outside a town)	☎ 177
Fire Service	☎ 15
Ambulance	☎ 15

3 MINIMUM IMPACT

The need for minimum impact trekking

The Atlas Mountains, which Pliny the Elder claimed in the first century AD to have attracted more legends than any other mountains in Africa, are these days proving successful in attracting increasing numbers of trekkers. Yet by the very act of visiting these mountains and their communities, we bring about change to the very thing which we came to admire. Unfortunately, unless we take great care, this change will often be for the worse. It is important, therefore, that we make every effort to minimise our impact by considering how our actions and decisions might affect the physical environment of the Atlas Mountains, the people who live amongst them and their economy.

As yet, environmental pressure groups within Morocco remain unsubstantial although one group striving to raise awareness in the Toubkal area which you may wish to contact is **Amis Toubkal** (GSM ☎ 0673.62.80.17; 💻 as_amistoubkal@yahoo.fr). However, still no comprehensive environmental guidelines have been written with the Atlas trekker in mind. These below have been devised with the help of the British Mountaineering Council's Mountain Tourism Codes and the Himalayan Tourist Code published by the charity **Tourism Concern** (☎ 020-7133 3800; 💻 www.tourismconcern.org.uk).

ENVIRONMENTAL IMPACT

Waste management

Don't pollute the Atlas with waste. All waste has some consequence. Each trekker should play his or her part in disposing of waste or removing it from the mountains.

- **Minimise group size** The bigger the group, the more damaging its impact.
- **Minimise supplies** Don't carry more supplies than you really need.
- **Educate others** With diplomacy and tact, encourage others in your group, including locals, to help manage waste properly.
- **Burnable waste** Food, paper, card and wood waste can be burnt. Carry this waste with you until you have need of a fire.
- **Toxic and non-burnable waste** Metals, plastics, foams, batteries, petrol, paraffin, methylated spirits, oil and medical waste should be carried out of the mountains unless local people can benefit from these things and are interested in relieving you of them.

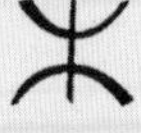

• **Human waste** This should be buried in pits dug downhill of camps and water sources. Don't relieve yourself within 20m (70ft) of a water source. Burn toilet paper.
• **Remove packaging** Get rid of excess packaging before setting off for the mountains. This will also help you to reduce the size and weight of your pack.
• **Don't ignore others' waste** Make the effort to clean up any other waste which you find on your trek, especially waste created by other trekkers.

Limit deforestation

Some local Berbers are guilty of contributing to deforestation but that's no reason why visitors should add to the problem.
• **Avoid open fires** Only make a fire when you really need the warmth. Berbers will almost certainly build fires since it is part of traditional life, but you should at least make sure that they use dead wood. Better still, encourage your group to make the most of heat generated by your paraffin burners during cooking and lanterns after night fall.
• **Avoid asking for boiled water for drinking** There are better, more efficient methods of purifying water (See Water purification systems box p29).
• **Order food at the same time as others and keep it simple** Complicated orders cause problems for remote Atlas cafés which might use wood-burning stoves inefficiently in order to meet your demands. In all cases, ordering a variety of dishes multiplies fuel consumption.
• **Avoid demanding hot water for showers at irregular times**.

Keep water clean

This is crucial. Simple 'green' routines will prevent water contamination which might lead to serious problems for others further downstream.
• **Human waste** See above.
• **Washing** Fill a bucket or bowl if using soap or shampoo and dispose of the dirty water at least 20m (70ft) away from the water source. Use biodegradable products and use them sparingly.

Protect plants

The effect of your removing one mountain flower might appear to be minimal but the Atlas is a fragile environment which will not tolerate large-scale tampering with its flora.
• **Don't pick flowers**.
• **Don't take cuttings** Never remove cuttings, seeds or roots from plants.
• **Avoid trampling plants** Watch where you walk.

Avoid erosion

Take care not to add to erosion any further than you can possibly help.
• **Stay on the trail** Where possible, follow existing trails to avoid creating new paths or shortcuts which might erode the landscape.
• **Respect fields and crops** Pay particular attention when walking near fields and crops to make sure you don't damage the produce or any irrigation system which, while not immediately obvious, might have been built around the field.

ECONOMIC IMPACT

Use local services

Think about where the money you spend will go. Where possible, inject what you've set aside for your holiday directly into the local economy.

• **Use guides and muleteers** Consider employing a local guide, cook and muleteer rather than joining a trek organised by an international tour operator. There are several very good reasons for doing this (see With a group or on your own pp9-12).

• **Gîtes and refuges** Staying in gîtes or refuges rather than camping is one way to invest some money into the Atlas economy. Also, consider offers of hospitality in the homes of locals (see *Gîtes d'étape*, refuges and camping pp11-12).

• **Provisions** Buy in Morocco rather than bringing supplies from home; buy at the trailhead rather than in Marrakech.

Observe standard fees

Remember to keep costs in perspective. Most Atlas Berbers are poor people who live hard lives working in an unforgiving land. Pay a fair price for the goods and services they offer. Haggle for gifts and trinkets – it's the Berber way – but accept standard prices for food, guides, muleteers and accommodation (see Budgeting and costs pp19-21).

• **Don't pay too little** Paying less than the standard price is exploitative and will create difficulties for tourists who follow you.

• **Don't pay too much** Paying too much creates dependency, promotes an inflationary cycle and sets a precedent for future visitors. It might also create resentment in the locality as the beneficiaries of your generosity may become envied by others. Worse still, you will effectively devalue other traditional work which does not attract tourists' money and risk destabilising the local economy, even distorting social values.

• **Tips** Tipping is normally expected (see Tipping, p76) but avoid over-tipping for the same reasons as you should avoid overpaying. Give your tip separately from the payment.

Maintain good relations

Never let business negotiations lead to ill feeling. Be friendly and respectful.

• **Avoid losing your temper** Keep calm when negotiating. Berbers often become very animated when conducting business but are rarely rude.

CULTURAL IMPACT

Photograph with sensitivity

It's all too easy to snap away without realising that your interest might appear voyeuristic, rude or even dangerous. Remember that, to most Berbers, to pose for your photograph is to give you something (see Photography, p36).

• **Ask first** Never take a photograph of a person or their property without asking permission. Many Muslims believe that their souls are captured along with their image in a photograph.

• **Send photographs** Many Berbers in the more remote Atlas villages will never have seen a photograph of themselves. If you photograph someone, ask whether they would like to be sent a copy of the photograph and be sure that you send it; this is a good way to give thanks for their kindness. The reliability of the postal service in remote areas may, of course, present a problem. In this digital age it might be worth asking your guide and others if they have access to email.

Respect holy places

Regardless of your own religious outlook, extreme sensitivity should be shown towards holy people and places. (See Travelling in a Muslim country, pp78-9).

Avoid giving to beggars

You will be pestered with demands for sweets, medicines, pens and money but you should not give in. Encouraging begging fosters a dependent attitude which, in the long run, can be very damaging to the culture and economy. There are genuinely needy people in the Atlas but if you want to help you might do better to contact village leaders, who will apply your gift to where it is most useful, than to hand out money to strangers.

Respect local customs

Pay particular attention when in a public place, visiting a home, eating and drinking or negotiating with local people. (See Travelling in a Muslim country, pp78-9).

Avoid playing doctor

But as all Europeans are supposed not only to know something of medicine and to carry drugs about with them on all occasions, the afflicted fairly besieged me …

R B Cunninghame Graham, *Mogreb-el-Acksa*, 1898

Avoid handing out medicines as this can create a dependency culture and is also potentially harmful. If you treat someone but make them worse, you could justifiably be blamed. It would be better to donate any spare medical supplies to someone in a position of authority, such as a village leader, than to offer treatment to strangers.

Avoid flaunting wealth

No matter how poor you might be by Western standards, to an Atlas Berber you are wealthy. Flaunting wealth is insulting and chips away at local pride. It also creates the impression that Westerners have money to give away and does nothing to help future visitors to form equal relationships based upon mutual respect with local people.

Ask questions but never patronise

You will learn more and foster better relationships with the people if you are genuinely interested in their way of life. Don't behave condescendingly.

Don't expect special privileges

You are one of many thousands who visit the Atlas Mountains. Never expect special treatment because you are from the West or because you are relatively rich.

Paint a realistic picture of the West and encourage local pride

Tell the people you meet what you enjoy about the Atlas Mountains and what you respect about their way of life. Answer questions about the West in a balanced way. If you are asked what you earn, explain that the very high cost of living in the West makes your income rather less impressive than it might at first appear to be. A good example to share is the cost of the mortgage or rent that you pay to live in your home or make other comparisons to which they can relate.

Avoid making 'home from home'

Engage in the local way of life and enjoy it. The opportunity to experience a different culture is, after all, one of the very good reasons for choosing to trek in the Atlas Mountains. If you attempt to create a 'home from home' in your trekking party, you might just as well have stayed at home.

Avoid making promises you can't or won't keep

If you offer to do something for someone, do it. This is particularly pertinent with regard to photographs which you might offer to send (see p91). It's easy to forget promises when you get home, but failing to follow them through can breed resentment and ill-feeling and make it harder for future trekkers to form positive relationships with local people.

Keep your sense of humour

Trekking is hard and uncomfortable and cultural gaps might prove frustrating, especially where there are language barriers. Humour will help everyone. You will notice that Berbers are an exuberant people who enjoy music, jokes and stories. Join in.

MARRAKECH

4

Fes and Rabat, Safrou, Salee and Mogador with Tetuan, Larache, Dar-el-Baida and the rest may have more trade, more art, more beauty, population, importance, industry, rank, faith, architecture, or what you will, but none of them enter into your soul as does this heap of ruins, this sandheap, desert town, metropolis of the fantastic world which stretches from its walls across the mountains through the oases of the Sahara. …

R B Cunninghame Graham, *Mogreb-el-Acksa*, 1898

Arriving in the imperial city of Marrakech is an almost overwhelming experience: the combined assault of sounds, smells and sights will set your senses reeling. Djemaa al-Fna, the city's central square and its cultural pulse, is where the assault is at its most intense. Snake-charmers, story-tellers, street dentists and Berber drummers compete for attention with frenzied enthusiasm. This almost non-stop display is not originally aimed at tourists; look at the crowds around the musicians and fortune-tellers and you will still see mostly Moroccans. Djemaa al-Fna is the single most important feature of the city. There is no other sight quite like it in the Arab world.

Marrakech, the Red City, has another great draw: its low-rise sprawl of red-pink buildings which appear to have grown out of the ground in a moment of blossoming, then baked solid in the scorching African sun. It's hard to see where one house stops and another starts. Indeed, the souks and narrow streets of the old Medina form a beguiling labyrinth. All this is framed by the peaks of the High Atlas which appear to curl around the city. In turn, the mountains are set against a consistently perfect deep blue sky. The effect is quite staggering.

The city is a mix of ancient and modern; in the east the walled Medina suggests time has made only limited progress. The streets, architecture and souks appear to have changed little over hundreds of years. Only television aerials, satellite dishes and the constant roar of taxis and scooters piloted by crazed locals hint that the third millennium has arrived. The west of Marrakech is the *Ville Nouvelle*, or new city, in which modern blocks of apartments and businesses were built during the years of the French Protectorate. But a combination of questionable construction and a faithful dedication to Marrakech's universal colour scheme has left even the Ville Nouvelle looking strangely worn by the Saharan sands of time.

Marrakech is defined by a fascinating blend of Arab and Berber cultures; this is one reason why the city has become such an important centre for arts and crafts. As a fast-growing tourist destination, Marrakech has seen an influx of Western visitors who have to some

extent diluted the city's attitudes. So one might see a Muslim woman veiled in the traditional manner walking alongside a younger Moroccan girl dressed in jeans or even a short skirt. But this is still a deeply religious city. Calls to prayer resonate from the tops of mosques and Koutoubia, the 220ft-high minaret which dominates the city's skyline, is closed to non-Muslims.

For trekkers, Marrakech is above all a sort of base camp. This is where you are most likely to start and finish your Moroccan Atlas trip. Here you will find supplies, advice, telephones, fax machines and the internet. More importantly, perhaps, Marrakech will be ready to welcome you back from the mountains with a warm shower, an extravagant dinner and a long, cold drink. That almost overwhelming assault on the senses with which the Marrakech Medina greets new visitors might cause some to run for cover. Yet travellers have nothing to fear from this colourful theatre: allow several days to explore an extraordinary city.

HISTORY

Although archaeologists have found evidence of an almost continual occupation of the site of Marrakech since Neolithic times, the origins of the current city date back to the decision of **Abu Bekr**, an Almoravid commander, to establish a simple fortress here in 1062. In time, successive dynasties would come in turn to build and thus add on to Marrakech; each dynasty used the very earth of the Houaz plain out of which that first fortress was built and upon which the city still stands. Its strategic position would allow it to grow and to flourish first as a market town, attracting farmers from both plains and mountains, from both near and far. Then its situation at the crossroads of the ancient caravan routes would attract traders from the deep south, from places as distant as Timbouctou and Gao, who crossed the Sahara, with their salt, their gold, and their slaves.

It was, however, under Abu Bekr's cousin and successor, **Yusuf Ibn Tashufin**, that the **Almoravid Empire** was created and Marrakech first began to take its modern, recognisable form. Following rapid expansion through Morocco and a series of conquests abroad, Marrakech quickly became the capital of an empire which stretched from Spain to Senegal. The Medina walls, the irrigation system, and some of Marrakech's finest gardens today, are the clearest enduring signs of that Almoravid legacy.

Marrakech would continue to flower under the Almoravids for 85 years until their defeat at the hands of the **Almohads**, who rose from their base in the Atlas Mountains, in 1145. Their ransacking and vengeful destruction of the city which followed brought Marrakech to its knees, yet the city's demise was short-lived because the Almohads themselves then chose to maintain Marrakech as their own capital and invested heavily in its rebuilding. Their fine work is epitomised by the city's most famous monument, the Koutoubia mosque, built under Sultan **Yacoub al-Mansour** (1184-99): both its size and beauty provided the inspiration for the building of many other minarets across the length of Morocco, and across the waters in Spain, too.

Towards the end of their days, even when all other parts of their empire had fallen into the hands of others, the Almohads clung on to Marrakech. However, once the **Merenids** had wrestled the city from them and decided to establish their own capital at Fes, Marrakech entered a long period of decline under their rule (1248-1465). Worse was to come. With the crumbling of Merenid power, foreign forces, first the Portuguese and then the Ottoman Turks, threatened Marrakech. In addition, the city would suffer a number of famines before ever its fortunes would begin to rise again.

It would be the **Saadians** (1520-1668) who would usher in a new period of prosperity, reviving Marrakech as a major trading and cultural centre and once more establishing it as the capital city of the country. This regeneration of wealth, notably during the sultanate of **Ahmed al-Mansour** (1578-1603), the 'Golden One', provided the means for the creation of both the El-Badi Palace and the Saadian tombs, two of Marrakech's finest pearls.

Yet the fortunes of Marrakech have never been smooth and, with the passage of power to the **Alaouites** in 1668, and their preference for ruling from the northern cities of Meknes and Fes, the status of Marrakech once more receded. Although it still maintained an important role in the control of the south, the story of the city from the seventeenth through to the nineteenth century was one of decline and much of the trade which had generated its wealth dwindled away. Only in the last decades before the arrival of the French, when **Moulay al-Hassan** (1873-94) and **Moulay Abd el Aziz** (1894-1908) reversed this trend with their preference for Marrakech over the northern cities, did Marrakech begin to rise once again.

During the period of the **French Protectorate** (1912-56), the administration of the city was placed in the hands of **T'hami el Glaoui**. An extraordinary tribal leader who had rapidly emerged from the obscurity of Telouet in the Central High Atlas Mountains, he was created Pasha of Marrakech by the French. By allying himself neatly with the colonial rulers, he was able to rival the power of the sultan himself and, under his influence, the city once more blossomed, attracting wealthy traders who built extravagant homes and palaces amid the city's olive groves and palms.

In collaboration with the Glaoua family, the French then built the new areas of Guéliz and Hivernage to form a Ville Nouvelle to the west of the old Medina. Yet Marrakech was still not able to keep pace with the twentieth-century development of Rabat and Casablanca which, with their easier access to Europe, became the leading industrial and power centres of the country.

In recent times, particularly since the 1960s, Marrakech has increasingly relied upon tourism for its prosperity. Although other Moroccan cities have also tried to capitalise on the growth in the world travel market, none has managed to harness it as successfully as Marrakech, certainly not without sacrificing its original cultural identity. Up until 2008, therefore, with the growth in the number of airline companies offering cheap flights into Marrakech, along with a widening awareness of the potential of the High Atlas and Anti-Atlas Mountains for trekking, it seemed that Marrakech's continued prosperity was assured. However, with the recent worldwide economic downturn, once again many Moroccans feel that their city may be at the crossroads.

ARRIVAL AND DEPARTURE

By air

The recently redeveloped and expanded Aéroport Marrakech-Menara (☎ 0544-44 78 65; 🖳 www.onda.org.ma) lies 7km south-west of the city centre. Both petits taxis and grands taxis complete the 15-minute run to and from Djemaa al-Fna. The official charge is 50dh, although it is difficult to get one at this price. Taxi drivers will typically ask for above 100dh and you will do well to get them to agree to accept much below this figure. Other official taxi prices from the airport include: avenue de la France, 50dh; Guéliz, 60dh; and the Palmeraie, 80dh. Alternatively, bus No 19 runs reliably every 30 minutes in both directions between Djemaa al-Fna and the airport (20dh single, 30dh return, tickets valid for two weeks, between 6.15am and 12.15am, daily). From the airport, the bus reaches Djemaa al-Fna in 15 minutes and Bab Doukkala in 20 minutes, before heading for the Ville Nouvelle.

At the airport, both Banque Populaire and BMCE offer the convenience of exchange facilities and newly installed cash machines, obviating any previous difficulties caused by landing in Morocco outside regular banking hours without local currency.

By train

The train station (*gare ferroviaire*; ☎ 0524-44 77 68), on avenue Hassan II in Guéliz, is a 10dh petit taxi ride from the Medina, although expect to be asked to pay 20dh. It may well also cost 10dh to go to/from the Ville Nouvelle, despite its closer proximity. There are also regular buses (see opposite) which run between the Medina and the train station.

By bus

Most long-distance bus companies use the main bus station, or *gare routière*, just inside the city walls close to Bab Doukkala, although Supratours (☎ 0524-43 55 25) is based at the train station (see above). Also there is a service, additional to those listed in the next column, to Asni departing from near Bab er Robb (see Getting to Imlil, pp134-5). There are several buses which run between Bab Doukkala and Djemaa al-Fna (see opposite). Alternatively, expect to pay 10dh for a petit taxi or walk, 20 minutes at best, and possibly a lot longer if you lose your way trying to find the direct route through the streets of the north-western souk. If you decide to walk it is perhaps better to stick to the main streets, turning left out of the bus station and following the Medina walls round until turning left once more opposite the Koutoubia straight into the square.

Long-distance bus tickets can be purchased within the main building of the gare routière where each bus company has its own booth for its own route. Daily services of particular interest to trekkers include: **Asni** Line 3; 10am; 1½hrs; 20dh; **Azilal** Line 18; 8.30am, 12.30pm, 3.30pm; 3hrs; 45dh; **Boumalne du Dades** Line 6; 10am, 11am, 2pm, 3.30pm, 9pm; 6½hrs; 110-130dh; **Qalaa't Mgouna/El Kelaa M'gouna** Line 6; 10am, 11am, 2pm, 3.30pm, 9pm; 6hrs; 110-130dh; **Ouarzazate** Line 29; 6am, 8.30am, 9.30am, 10am, 11am, noon, 2pm, 3.30pm, 5pm, 6pm, 8pm, 10pm; 4hrs; 70-80dh; **Taliwine** Line 17; 9pm; 7hrs; 65dh.

A host of other destinations are also served by a plethora of bus companies. CTM (☎ 0524-43 39 33) has its own window offering the following (daily) services of interest to trekkers: **Boumalne du Dades** 7am; 5½hrs; 110dh; **Qalaa't Mgouna/El Kelaa M'gouna** 7am; 5hrs; 100dh; **Ouarzazate** 7am, 11.15am, 4.30pm, 12.30am; 4½hrs; 90dh. CTM also lists **Agadir** (6/day), **Fes** (3/day) and **Zagora** (2/day) in its schedule and has a second office (☎ 0524-44 83 28) in the Ville Nouvelle on boulevard Mohammed Zerktouni.

Supratours runs a daily bus service to **Ouarzazate**, departing at 4pm and arriving by 9pm (70dh); this bus continues to **Zagora**, arriving at midnight. Other destinations served by Supratours include **Essaouira** (4/day, 3hrs, 65dh) and **Agadir** (5/day, 4½hrs, 90dh).

The gare routière has a *consigne* (left-luggage office) which is always open to receive baggage, except for 7-8pm when it is closed for cleaning. It charges 10dh for a large bag, 7dh for a small one and 5dh for a *tout petit* for each 24-hour period. There is also a small **police station**.

By taxi

All long-distance grands taxis, except for taxis operating to and from Asni, arrive and depart from the taxi stand just outside the city wall opposite Bab Doukkala. Taxis for Asni depart from the taxi stand just outside the city walls opposite Bab er Robb (see relevant pages of intended destination towns for further details). Your driver may need to stop off to pick up permit papers before leaving the boundaries of town.

LOCAL TRANSPORT

Taxi

Marrakech is a fairly compact city so it's easy to get around on foot or by taxi. Yellow **petits taxis** operate in town while beige **grands taxis** cover journeys beyond Marrakech and between towns (see Arrival and Departure opposite).

Petits taxis are easy to find almost anywhere in the city and can be hailed down. They have meters which officially should be turned on but you are unlikely to have any success in achieving this. Consequently, it is important to negotiate the price of your ride before you get into the taxi. A ride from Djemaa al-Fna to Guéliz, for example, should cost 10dh but expect to be asked for 20dh: over to you. The best place to pick up a grand taxi for a trip across town is Djemaa al-Fna.

Calèches

Calèches, or open horse-drawn carriages, which frequent the Medina, can be quite an efficient, and certainly the most romantic, way to get around Marrakech. Once again there are official prices for set journeys. A trip from Djemaa al-Fna to Bab Doukkala should cost 17.50dh, to Palais El Bahia 30dh and to the Majorelle Gardens 40dh; a sight-seeing tour should cost 90dh per hour. Even though prices rise by 25% after 7pm, these prices are for the whole carriage and, given that there are seats for five people, this can make the price per head very reasonable.

However, even though these official prices are clearly displayed both on large fixed signs erected at calèche stands and on stickers on the inside of calèche wind-screens, in practice, most calèche drivers try to charge what they feel they can get away with. Even the advice given on the fixed signs encouraging dissatisfied customers to contact the Wilaya de Marrakech (☎ 0524-33 27 39) does little to deter the outright aggression that some drivers freely exhibit towards anyone questioning their unofficial pricing practice. Whatever else you do, agree the price in advance.

There are several places from which calèches can be picked up, including Djemaa al-Fna, Palais el-Badi, place de la Liberté and from outside some of the classier hotels: expect to have a tougher time negotiating prices from outside some of the latter.

> **❑ Pssst!**
> Moroccans have a habit of hissing loudly when they want to get your attention. So if you hear someone hissing at you, look around; it might mean you are about to get run over. Another sort of hissing, more appreciative and less imperative in tone, equates to the wolf whistle.

Bus

Since Marrakech is very easy to negotiate there is little need to grapple with the local bus service. If you do feel inclined to wedge yourself onto a bus, however, fares are very cheap; most range from just 2dh to 5dh.

Place de Foucauld, just off Djemaa al-Fna, is a good place to pick up a local bus to almost anywhere. Amongst them:

- **No 1** heads along avenue Mohammed V to Guéliz.
- **Nos 3, 8, 10, 13 and 14** all go to Bab Doukkala and then to the train station.
- **No 4** will also take you to Bab Doukkala and then on to the Majorelle Gardens.
- **Nos 6 and 20** go to the Agdal Gardens.
- **No 19** is the airport bus, first looping around the Ville Nouvelle.

Car hire

Driving your own vehicle through Marrakech's frenzied streets is an even more alarming experience than travelling on a Moroccan bus. Although cars aren't particularly useful in the city itself, they do provide great potential to explore further afield (see By car, pp66-7).

Most international car-hire companies are found both at the airport and in Guéliz. Some you may wish to consider include:

• **Avis** (☎ 0524-43 25 25), 137 avenue Mohammed V; (☎ 0524-43 31 69), Menara Airport
• **Budget** (☎ 0524-43 11 80), 68 boulevard Mohammed Zerktouni; (☎ 0524-43 88 75), Menara Airport
• **Europcar** (☎ 0524-43 12 28), 63 boulevard Mohammed Zerktouni; (☎ 0524-43 77 18), Menara Airport
• **Hertz** (☎ 0524-44 99 84), 154 avenue Mohammed V; (☎ 0524-44 72 30), Menara Airport.

Two well-known local car-hire companies are: **First-Car International** (☎ 0524-43 87 64), 234 avenue Mohammed V; **Lune Car** (☎ 0543-43 43 69), 111 rue de Yugoslavie. If you really want to research the local market further, the following are all located in the same building above the Hertz office at 154 avenue Mohammed V: **Concorde Car**, **Asfaria Car**, **Missil Car** and **Hatim Car**. Concorde charges from 400dh per day, tax and unlimited mileage included, for a Ford Fiesta or Peugeot 206 with air conditioning. Fully comprehensive insurance is available for a further 100dh per day.

Mopeds

Mopeds are a popular, if invasive, way of getting around Marrakech and can even be driven through the souks if you really want to make a nuisance of yourself. Try **3R** (☎/🖷 0524-44 10 11; GSM ☎ 0663-06 18 92; 💻 www.Marrakech-Roues.com), at 3 rue Bani Marine, where you can rent for half a day (250dh), a full day (300dh) or for a whole week (1500dh). As with rental cars, take time to check the terms of the rental agreement first (see Car hire, above).

Bicycles

It is fairly easy to rent a bicycle in Marrakech: try the outlets at the bottom of rue Bani Marine, at the far end from Djemaa al-Fna. Cycles can be hired by the hour (20dh), by the half-day (80dh), or by the day (120dh). Alternatively, in Guéliz, try **Marrakech Motors** (☎ 0524-44 83 59) at 31 avenue Mohammed Abdelkrim el Khattabi.

Take time to check the brakes and tyres before hiring and bear in mind that the level of consideration cyclists receive from car drivers might be lower than you are used to at home. One popular cycle route is from the Medina out to the Palmeraie, although, given the ruggedness of the unpaved roads, you might find that you would need at least a mountain bike for this.

ORIENTATION

We passed through narrow lanes where camels jammed us almost to the wall; along the foot-paths beggars sat and showed their sores; dogs, yellow, ulcerous and wild as jackals, skulked between our horses' legs, until at last we came out on an open space under the tower of the Kutubieh.

R B Cunninghame Graham, *Mogreb-el-Acksa*, 1898

Marrakech sits at an altitude of 470m above sea level in the heart of the fertile Haouz plain, within reach of the High Atlas Mountains and the sub-Saharan south. The city, like many in Morocco, is divided between the old town, or Medina, to the east, and the new town, or Ville Nouvelle, to the west, which is itself split between the areas of Guéliz, to the north-west, and Hivernage, to the west.

Hivernage is of little appeal to most travellers, although well-heeled visitors will find some of the superior, if rather bland, hotels here and a casino. **Guéliz** is the modern, commercial hub of the city where most banks, offices, shops and a number of mid-priced modern hotels are situated.

The medieval **Medina**, enclosed by its earthen walls, holds much more interest: its souks, cafés and cheap, but often charming, hotels evoke the Marrakech that most travellers seek. Its main square, Djemaa al-Fna, is the city's cultural heart and it is here that you are also most likely to find its soul. Heading out from Djemaa al-Fna, and leaving the labyrinthine alleys of the old town behind, the western edge of the Medina is marked by the beautiful, imposing Koutoubia mosque: from here the 4km road north-west to Guéliz is clear and straight.

SERVICES

Banks and currency exchange

Banks, currency-exchange facilities and ATMs are all widely available in Marrakech. Most banks have branches in both the Medina and in Guéliz, many with exchange facilities alongside them which often stay open longer than the banks themselves. When in the Medina, the streets leading away from the south side of Djemaa al-Fna offer numerous possibilities, particularly along rue piétonne Prince Moulay Rashid (previously known as rue Bab Agnaou) and rue Moulay Ismail. In Guéliz, the main area is along avenue Mohammed V north of place du 16 Novembre. For **BMCE** go to 144 avenue Mohammed V or rue Moulay Ismail on place de Foucauld, for **Banque Populaire** go to rue piétonne Prince Moulay Rashid where there are two branches, for **Crédit du Maroc** go to 215-7 avenue Mohammed V or rue piétonne Prince Moulay Rashid, for **Crédit Agricole** and for **Attijariwafa** go to rue Moulay Ismail.

Book shops and newspaper stands

Book shops are not common in Marrakech. The best seems to be **Librairie Chatr** at 19 avenue Mohammed V; it has a good range of French titles though few in English. Also in Guéliz, at 55 boulevard Mohammed Zerktouni, is a **Librairie d'Art** which sells a beautiful range of art and coffee-table books. **Librairie Ghazli**, a small bookshop on rue piétonne Prince Moulay Rashid, near the junction with Djemaa al-Fna, offers a smaller range along with some stationery.

Such is the lack of competition in the city that, within the souk, a small covered stall, **Fanaqoe Berbère**, can claim to be *La première Librairie à Marrakech*. Despite its size, it does indeed stock an impressive selection of books on Marrakech and Morocco. To find it, head north from Djemaa al-Fna down rue Laksour onto rue Mouassine, then start asking.

A number of **newspaper stands** are dotted around the city. One of the more longstanding is the one on the south side of Djemaa al-Fna at the top of rue des Banques, by the side of Café Glacier.

Cinema

If in the Medina, the most conveniently located cinemas are **Cinéma Mabrouka** on rue piétonne Prince Moulay Rashid (Stalls 25dh, Circle 20dh, Orchèstre 15dh) and the more downmarket **Cinéma Eden** on derb Debbachi. There is more choice in Guéliz where the pick is probably the **Colisée** on boulevard Mohammed Zerktouni.

Hammams

For an authentic experience in the Medina, try the hammam on **rue Riad Zitoun el Jedid** (8dh plus 50dh for an optional massage from Mohammed), but choose your time carefully: men's hours are 5am-1pm and 8pm to midnight, whilst 2-7pm is the preserve of women. It might be safer to go along to **rue Riad Zitoun el Kedim** where there are separate entrances for men and women. The price for the hammam is similarly priced at 8dh, although, I am cheerfully told, 15dh for foreigners. The massage costs 50dh for all-comers.

For a step up, try either ***Hotel Ali*** (see p104) or ***Hotel Jnane Mogador*** (see p106). At Hotel Ali a massage with soap costs 100dh or 120dh with both soap and oils. At Hotel Jnane Mogador a hammam is available for 125dh; a ¾hr back massage costs 180dh, a 'relaxing' massage 200dh and an 'energetic' massage 250dh.

Alternatively, you may wish to visit one of the growing number of hammams being set up with the tourist market clearly in mind. **Hammam Ziani** (GSM ☎ 0662-71 55 71; 💻 www.hammamziani.ma) at 14 rue Riad Zitoun el Jedid offers a wide range of services ranging from a simple steam bath (35dh) to complete packages including seaweed therapy (up to 300dh). If in Guéliz try **Wellness Plus** at 221 avenue Mohammed V.

Communications

• **Telephone** Apart from street telephones, which, for example, can be found both on the south side of Djemaa al-Fna and outside the two main post offices in Marrakech, téléboutiques abound within the city.

• **Internet access** Until recently quite slow to embrace the internet, cyber cafés are now appearing everywhere. **Cyber Café Tayni** on rue des Banques, and **Hanan Internet** and **Hassan Internet**, both on rue piétonne Prince Moulay Rashid, are amongst the most central. Probably the best access, however, is provided by **Moulay Abdeslam Cyber-Park** opposite the Ensemble Artisanal at the Medina end of avenue Mohammed V.

• **Post** The main post office is in the Medina, on the south side of Djemaa al-Fna. That in Guéliz, to which all *poste restante* mail is delivered, is on place du 16 Novembre.

Tourist Information office (ONMT)

The ONMT (☎ 0524-43 62 39) is at the junction of avenue Mohammed V and rue de Yugoslavie in Guéliz. You might try to elicit some information from its reluctant staff but be prepared to meet a wall of indifference.

Embassies and consulates

See Embassies and consulates, p70.

Laundry

If you are staying in a higher quality hotel, you may be able to use its laundry service. Otherwise, if in the Medina, the **small laundry** on rue Riad Zitoun el Kedim will turn around your washing in two hours, charging 6dh for each large piece and 3dh for each small piece of clothing. If in Guéliz, try **Pressing Oasis** at 44 rue Tarik ben Zaid.

Medical emergencies

• **Emergency medical aid** SOS Médecins (☎ 0524-40 40 40) charges 400dh per call-out.

• **Emergency accident** ☎ 0524-40 14 01.

Clinics

Polyclinique du Sud (☎ 0524-44 79 99), at the corner of rue de Yugoslavie and rue Ibn Aicha in Guéliz, has a long-standing high reputation for dealing efficiently with travellers' medical issues. Make sure you take your medical insurance details with you.

Doctors and dentists

Dr Abdelmajid Ben Tbib (☎ 0524-43 10 30), at 171 avenue Mohammed V in Guéliz, is a recommended doctor. He speaks English. **Dr Bennani** (☎ 0524-44 91 36), on the first floor of 112 avenue Mohammed V in Guéliz, a dentist, also comes recommended. He speaks some English.

Pharmacies

There is an abundance of good pharmacies in Marrakech, including a number both around Djemaa el-Fna and along avenue Mohammed V. **Pharmacie de la Place**, looking directly onto the square at rue piétonne Prince Moulay Rashid and **Pharamacie du Progrès**, at the far end of the same street, are both recommended. In Guéliz, try **Pharmacie de la Liberté**, just off place de la Liberté. There's an all-night pharmacy (*pharmacie de nuit*) by the Commissariat de Police on Djemaa al-Fna and another in Guéliz on rue Khalid ben Oualid. Otherwise, check the notice in any pharmacy window giving details of all other all-night chemists.

Police

Tourist Police ☎ 0524-38 46 01.

Supermarkets and shopping

The most convenient food shopping in Guéliz is at the municipal market on avenue Mohammed V. When in the Medina, head for the covered market between avenue Houmane el Fetouaki and arset el Maach. There is an **Ensemble Artisanal** at the Medina end of avenue Mohammed V.

Swimming pools

There is no longer a municipal pool in Marrakech. Try visiting one of the hotel pools or **Oasiria Water Park** (☎ 0524-38 04 38; 💻 www.oasiria.com; 10am-6pm daily; 180dh, 140dh after 2pm) which has waterslides, wave machines and a pirate ship. Located 4km from the centre of Marrakech, a free shuttle service (every 45 mins 9.30am-3pm) runs to and from Djemaa el-Fna between June and August. If in the Medina, ***Le Grand Hotel Tazi*** (see p106) allows the public to use its pool for 100dh; if in Guéliz, head for ***Hotel Al Bustan*** (see p106) which charges 50dh.

Trekking agencies

Agencies are not always good value for money, especially since it is relatively easy to organise a mountain guide and muleteer independently (see pp9-12). If you do decide to go with a trekking agency, consider the following:

- **Adrar Aventure** (☎ 0524-43 56 63, 🖳 www.morocco-travel-adventure.com), 111 Cité Saada, Menara
- **Atlas-Sahara Trek** (☎ 0524-31 39 01/03; 🖳 www.atlas-sahara-trek.com), 6 bis rue Houdoud, Quartier Marrakech
- **Trekking Tour Maroc** (☎/🖷 0524-30 98 62), 107 rue Saad ben Errabia, Issil.
- **Sahara Expeditions** (☎ 0524-42 79 77/42 97 47; 🖳 www.saharaexpe.ma), at the junction of rue Mouahidine and rue Bani Marine.

WHERE TO STAY

Hotel areas

Many of Marrakech's more interesting hotels are located within the **Medina**. The cheapest of these are often found squeezed into the narrow, bustling streets to the south of Djemaa al-Fna, although there's also a growing number of more expensive hotels, including some truly beautiful riads, within this area. More modern hotels, including some of the more expensive, can be found in the calmer, cleaner Ville Nouvelle areas of **Guéliz** and **Hivernage**. There's also the option of staying in the green and peaceful haven of the **Palmeraie**, just a few kilometres to the north of Marrakech: often the refuge of the rich and famous, fabulous accommodation here need not necessarily cost the earth.

Prices

Most of the cheapest hotels start at around 60dh for a single room without bathroom and with an extra charge for breakfast. At the other end of the scale it is quite possible to spend several hundred euros per night and more. The top hotels do, however, often offer seasonal discounts, particularly during the hot summer months of July and August. On the other hand, some close their doors altogether at this time of the year.

Budget hotels

Medina The following are but a selection of the hotels in the southern Medina. Often formerly the houses of affluent merchants, two or three storeys high, built around an open courtyard, there are simply too many, even in this small part of the city, to list all. Take comfort, however, from the fact that there is a remarkable consistency in room pricing amongst these budget hotels: quite simply, the more you are prepared to pay, the better the quality of the accommodation. Inclusion in this book does not therefore necessarily imply recommendation. All that are listed have been visited and checked, but since there so many hotels it's not possible to know them well and one author's passing anecdote should not be allowed to make or break the reputation of any one of them. It is better that you explore and have fun. Venture down any of the narrow, high-walled labyrinthine streets mentioned below, as I did, to find them, then take a left turn, take a right and see which door you end up at.

Another remarkable consistency: in all probability the high walls lining the streets will fail to inspire you, but then they were never meant to inspire. On the contrary, the beauty of the Moroccan home, above all that of the *riad*, is consciously turned inwards for the pleasure of those who reside behind its walls, without a thought to try and impress any passers-by through an outward flash of arrogance.

So, one tip: once across the threshold, look beyond any apparent material deficiencies, as judged by customary modern hotel standards; once you have stepped into the sanctuary of an inner courtyard, listen to your heart. If you do not at once warm to the soul of the riad, retreat, always courteously, and seek another, perhaps just around the very next corner, or even closer. Sooner or later you will cross a threshold and your heart will tell you that you are in the right place. Only this way will you find your temporary home. Welcome to Marrakech.

Many of the cheaper rooms in the Medina will be simple rooms without bathrooms; instead you will be offered communal toilets and showers. Sometimes there is an extra charge for showers, sometimes not, but this will be indicated in

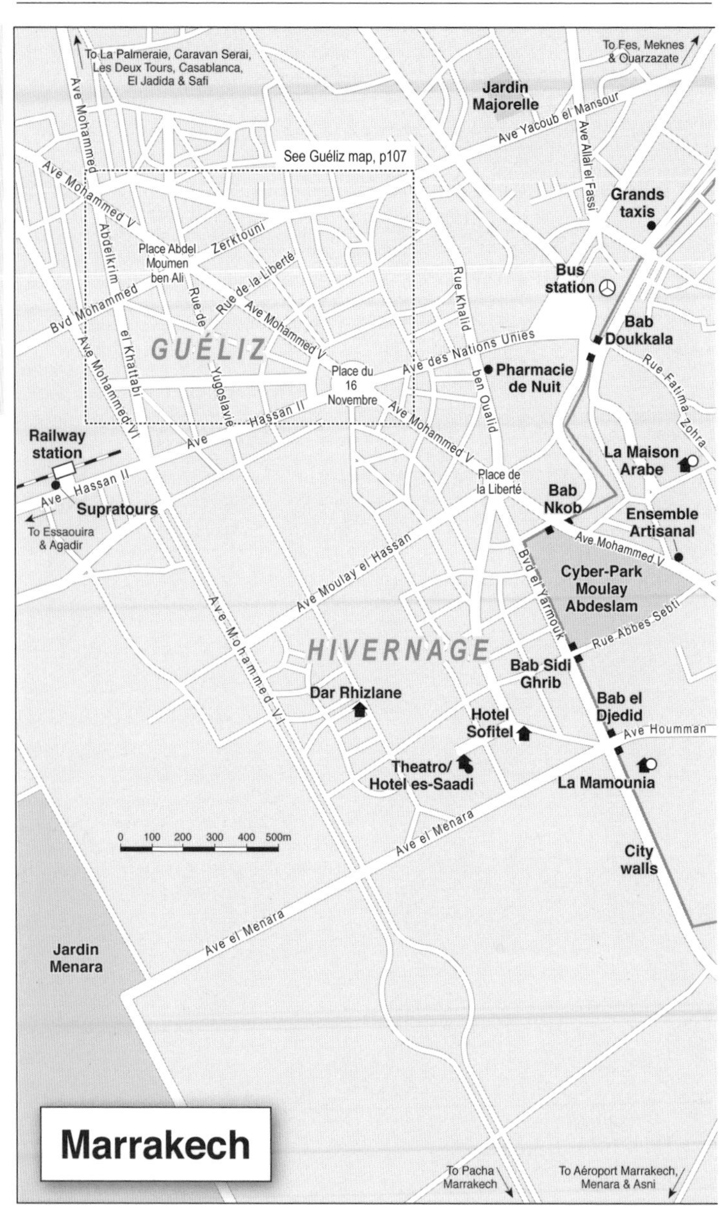

Marrakech
To La Palmeraie, Caravan Serai, Les Deux Tours, Casablanca, El Jadida & Safi
To Fes, Meknes & Ouarzazate
Jardin Majorelle
Ave Yacoub el Mansour
Ave Allal el Fassi
See Guéliz map, p107
Grands taxis
Bus station
Ave Mohammed V
Zerktouni
Place Abdel Moumen ben Ali
Rue de la Liberté
Abdelkrim
Bvd Mohammed
Rue de Yugoslavie
el Khattabi
Ave Mohammed VI
GUÉLIZ
Rue Khalid ben Oualid
Ave des Nations Unies
Pharmacie de Nuit
Bab Doukkala
Rue Fatima Zohra
Place du 16 Novembre
Ave Hassan II
Railway station
Supratours
To Essaouira & Agadir
Place de la Liberté
Bab Nkob
La Maison Arabe
Ensemble Artisanal
Ave Moulay el Hassan
Bvd el Yarmouk
Cyber-Park Moulay Abdeslam
Rue Abbes Sebti
HIVERNAGE
Bab Sidi Ghrib
Bab el Djedid
Ave Houmman
Dar Rhizlane
Hotel Sofitel
Theatro/ Hotel es-Saadi
La Mamounia
Ave el Menara
City walls
0 100 200 300 400 500m
Jardin Menara
To Pacha Marrakech
To Aéroport Marrakech, Menara & Asni

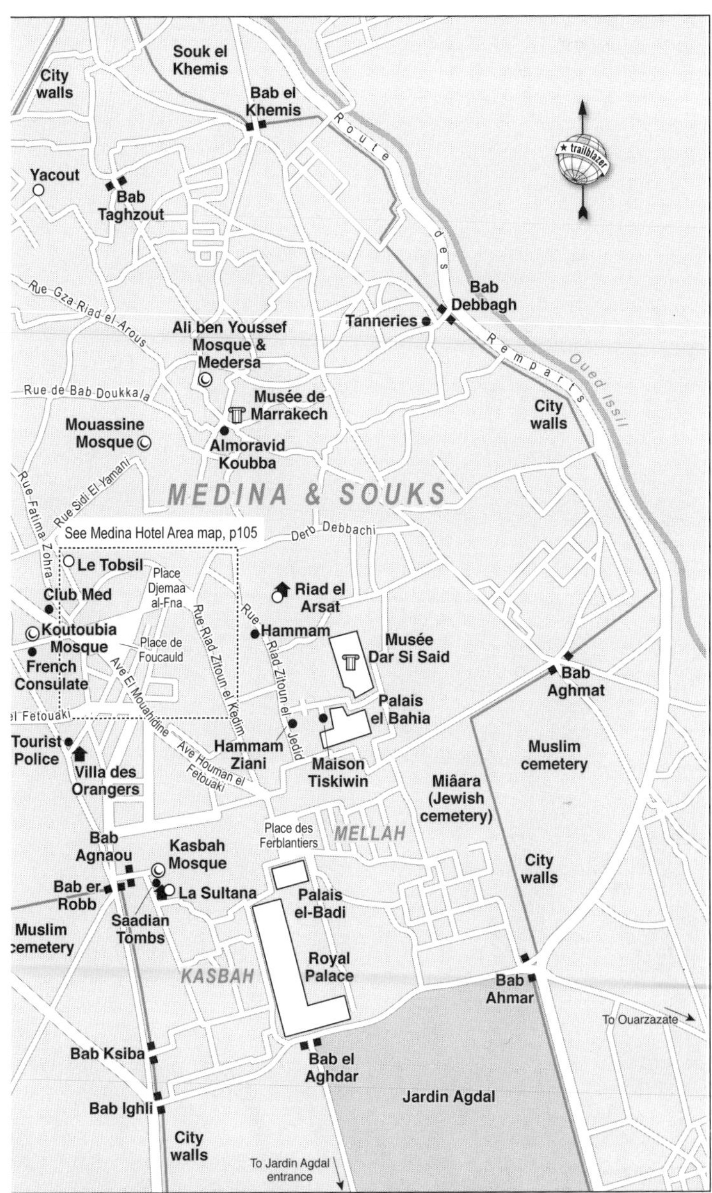
Souk el Khemis
City walls
Bab el Khemis
Route des Remparts
trailblazer
Yacout
Bab Taghzout
Rue Gza Riad el Arous
Bab Debbagh
Tanneries
Ali ben Youssef Mosque & Medersa
Oued Issil
Rue de Bab Doukkala
Musée de Marrakech
City walls
Mouassine Mosque
Almoravid Koubba
Rue Sidi El Yamani
Rue Fatima Zohra
MEDINA & SOUKS
See Medina Hotel Area map, p105
Derb Debbachi
Le Tobsil
Place Djemaa al-Fna
Riad el Arsat
Club Med
Rue Riad Zitoun el Kedim
Rue Riad Zitoun el Jedid
Hammam
Koutoubia Mosque
Place de Foucauld
Musée Dar Si Said
French Consulate
Ave El Mouahidine
Bab Aghmat
Palais el Bahia
el Fetouaki
Tourist Police
Hammam Ziani
Muslim cemetery
Villa des Orangers
Ave Houman el Fetouaki
Maison Tiskiwin
Miâara (Jewish cemetery)
Place des Ferblantiers
MELLAH
Bab Agnaou
Kasbah Mosque
City walls
Bab er Robb
La Sultana
Palais el-Badi
Muslim cemetery
Saadian Tombs
Royal Palace
KASBAH
Bab Ahmar
To Ouarzazate
Bab Ksiba
Bab el Aghdar
Jardin Agdal
Bab Ighli
City walls
To Jardin Agdal entrance

the details for each hotel. Normally the rates given indicate the charge for one/two people but sometimes additional tariffs are given to show the rate for three/four people.

Hotel Hilal (☎ 0524-38 38 82), at 14-15 rue de la Recette, is one of the hotels which offers rooms with multiple occupancy at 60/120/160/200dh (plus 10dh for a hot shower), as does the very simple ***Hotel el Farah*** (☎/🖹: 0524-44 15 46) just next door at 13 rue de la Recette, which charges 60/120/180/240dh. Rooms at ***Hotel Sahara*** (☎ 0524-72 01 71), a hotel of similar quality at 87 rue Sidi Bouloukate, are available for 60/120/180/240dh (with cold/hot showers for 5/10dh).

For a slight step up-market, head for ***Hotel el Atlal*** (☎ 0524-42 78 89), at 48 rue de la Recette. Here, the choice is of simple rooms for 80/150/300dh (triple rooms with air conditioning), or double and triple rooms with both air conditioning and en suite shower for 250/300dh. Back on rue Sidi Bouloukate, at No 3, ***Hotel Essaouira*** (☎/🖹 0524-44 38 05) offers rooms at 70dh and 100dh for two or more guests sharing, with the option of breakfast for 20dh. A luggage storage service is also available for 5dh. On the same street, at No 43, ***Hotel Eddakhla*** (☎/🖹 0524-44 23 59; 💻 hotel_eddakhla@menara.ma) provides rooms for 60/120dh regardless of whether showers are communal or en suite. Happily, plenty of communal showers and toilets are available, even if they are rather rundown. The hotel also boasts a pleasant courtyard with a central fountain, which unfortunately, like many in Morocco, is switched off in summer. Nevertheless, there are the benefits of a popular roof-top terrace and owners who are keen to emphasise their passion for their hotel.

Hotel Provence (GSM ☎ 0662-81 73 52), on rue Riad Zitoun Lakdime, has no single rooms but offers doubles and triples for 120/210dh with no additional charge for use of the communal hot showers. ***Hotel de France*** (☎ 0524-44 30 67) at 197 rue Riad Zitoun el Kedim has not raised its prices in at least seven years: rooms remain available for 40/80/120dh. Back at 45 rue Sidi Bouloukate, ***Hotel Afriquia*** (☎ 0524-44 24 03) charges 70/130/180dh with free communal hot showers; en suite double rooms are also available for 200dh. Just along the street, ***Hotel Imouzzer*** (☎ 0524-44 53 36; 💻 www.hotel-imouzzer.com) at 74 rue Sidi Bouloukate, has a particularly lovely central courtyard and charges 70/140/210dh. ***Hotel de la Paix*** (☎ 0524-44 54 31/37.62.21; 💻 paix@yahoo.fr), at No 46, offers rooms for 70/130/170/230dh of which only the rooms for four people have en suite toilets and showers.

Hotel Central Palace (☎ 0524-44 02 35/44 39 71/44 35 10; 💻 www.lecentralpalace.com), at 59 rue Sidi Bouloukate, offers double rooms (from 155dh with communal shower and bathroom to 405dh for air-conditioned suites) around a very pleasant central courtyard. Breakfast is provided for 25dh per person, half-board for 100dh and full board for 150dh. In addition the hotel offers both a currency exchange and a laundry facility. The roof terrace, where meals are served, offers impressive views.

Hotel la Gazelle (☎ 0524-44 11 12; 💻 hotel_lagazelle@hotmail.com), at 12 rue Bani Marine, offers rooms with communal toilets and showers for 100/150/200dh, while those with en suite and air-conditioning cost 150/200/250dh. Close by, ***Hotel Ichbilia*** (☎ 0524-38 15 30), at 1 rue Bani Marine, has no single rooms but offers doubles for 180-300dh, triples for 270-380dh, quadruples for 400-430dh and even rooms for five for 450dh. Some rooms have TV and air conditioning while others have en suite showers.

At the higher end of the Medina budget hotels is ***Hotel Ali*** (☎ 0524-44 49 79; 💻 www.hotel-ali.com), on rue Moulay Ismail, just 100m from Djemaa al-Fna; it charges 200/300/400/500dh. Breakfast is included in this price (which is also available to non-residents for 70dh). Half-board is also available for 200dh per person. If you wish to be right on the square itself, the long-established ***Hotel CTM*** (☎ 0524-44 23 25) can offer its older rooms for 120/190dh (without shower) or 160/230/350dh (with shower) or its new rooms for 320/430/650dh (with shower and air-conditioning), all prices including breakfast.

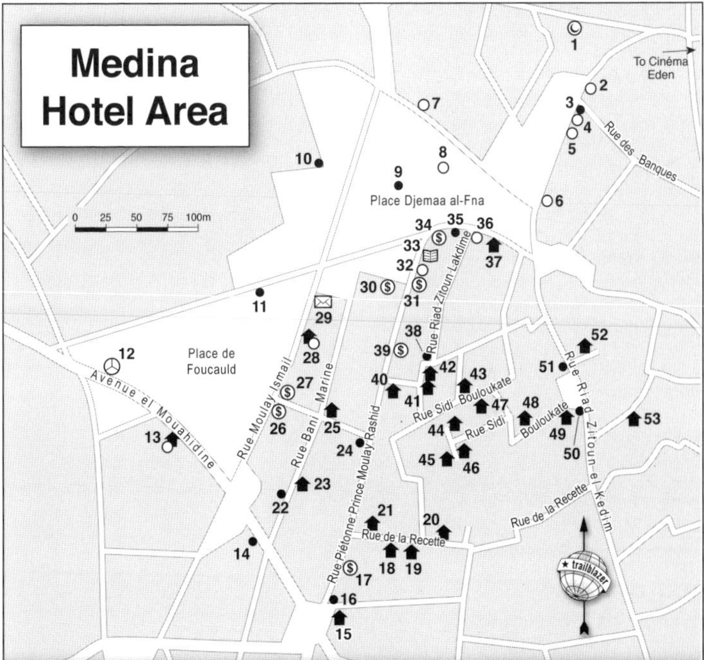

Where to stay
13 Hotel de Foucauld
15 Le Grand Hotel Tazi
18 Hotel el Farah
19 Hotel Hilal
20 Hotel Gallia
21 Hotel el Atlal
23 Hotel la Gazelle
25 Hotel Ichbilia
28 Hotel Ali
37 Hotel CTM
40 Hotel Central Palace
41 Hotel de la Paix
42 Hotel Provence
43 Hotel Eddakhla
44 Hotel Afriquia
45 Hotel Sahara
46 Hotel du Tresor
47 Hotel Imouzzer
48 Hotel Essaouira
49 Hotel Jnane Mogador
52 Hotel de France
53 Hotel Sherazade

Where to eat and drink
2 Chez Chegrouni
4 Café Glacier
5 Café de France
6 Covered food market
7 Café-Restaurant Argana
8 Food stalls
32 Café Restaurant l'Etoile
36 Café du Grand Balcon

Other
1 Qessabin Mosque
3 News stand
9 Taxis
10 Commissariat de Police
11 Calèche stand
12 City buses
14 Sahara Expeditions
16 Pharmacy
17 Banque Populaire
22 3R Moped Hire
24 Cinéma Mabrouka
26 BMCE
27 Attijariwafa
29 Post Office
30 Bank al Maghrib
31 Crédit du Maroc
33 Librairie Ghazli
34 Banque Populaire
35 Pharmacy
38 Hammam
39 Crédit du Maroc
50 Launderette
51 Hammam

Guéliz Good, cheap hotels have always been difficult to find in the Ville Nouvelle. Thankfully, plans to demolish the historic one-storeyed ***Hotel Franco-Belge*** (☎ 0524-44 84 72), on boulevard Mohammed Zerktouni, to make way for flats were not carried through. Rooms, built around a pleasant, green courtyard, are charged at 160/200dh, including private toilet and shower.

Close by, on the same street at No 40, the charm of ***Hotel des Voyageurs*** (☎ 0524-44 72 18) fortunately also survives into the twenty-first century. Built in 1935 and claimed by the owners to be the oldest hotel in the Ville Nouvelle, you will forgive the *Jingle Bells* tune of its door-ring. The hotel is essentially a series of rooms off a long corridor that faces onto a tiled courtyard with a central fountain and shade provided by a canopy of vines.

Around the corner, at 50 boulevard Mohammed V, is ***Hotel Oasis*** (☎ 0524-44 71 79) which charges 130/200dh for a room with its own shower or 150/250dh for a room with both shower and toilet.

Mid-priced hotels

Although the Ville Nouvelle, particularly Guéliz, has traditionally been the best area for moderately priced hotels, the recent trend towards opening some exquisite traditional riads within the Medina leaves travellers with a genuine choice as to which part of the city in which to stay.

While hotels in the Ville Nouvelle tend to be more modern with more facilities, those in the Medina can offer traditional Moroccan charm, usually in a smaller, often more intimate, setting.

Medina ***Hotel Sherazade*** (☎ 0524-42 93 05; 💻 www.hotelsherazade.com), at 3 derb Djemaa, off rue Riad Zitoun el Kedim, is housed in a traditional riad, formerly the home of wealthy merchants. The rooms, centred round a very pleasant tiled courtyard, cost from 180/230dh to 640/690dh.

Hotel de Foucauld (☎ 0524-44 08 06/44 54 99; 📠 0524-44 13 44), on avenue El Mouahidine, is a popular hotel with trekking groups. It offers rooms for 250/350dh including breakfast or 360dh/285dh per person half-board. Breakfast (6-10am) is also served to non-residents for 30dh; an evening buffet is served 7.30-10.30pm for 150dh.

Hotel Gallia (☎ 0524-44 59 13/39 08 57; 💻 hotel.gallia@menara.ma), at 30 rue de la Recette, offers a range of rooms costing 195-275/230-410dh, with a suite for 630dh. Breakfast is an additional 40dh. Established in 1929 and owned by the Galland family, the hotel is beautifully decorated in traditional Moroccan style and offers a wonderful terrace.

Le Grand Hotel Tazi (☎ 0524-44 27 87; 📠 0524-44 21 52) which has its own restaurant and licensed bar, is at the junction of rue piétonne Prince Moulay Rashid and avenue El Mouahidine. Rooms cost 275/410dh with an extra 40dh for breakfast and 150dh for evening meal. The hotel also has a swimming pool: the 100dh entrance charge includes a complimentary sandwich. In its hey-day, this was clearly quite a grand hotel and nowhere is this more apparent than in the finesse of the stucco ceilings in its main foyer which doubles as a public bar.

One exquisite yet moderately priced riad in this category is ***Hotel Jnane Mogador*** (☎ 0524-42 63 24/24; 💻 contact@jnanemogador.com), at 116 rue Riad Zitoun el Kedim at the junction with rue Sidi Bouloukate. High-season room prices are 360/480/580/660dh and 850dh for a suite. Breakfast is served for 40dh and meals at other times for 90-150dh.

At 77 rue Sidi Bouloukate, the newly opened ***Hotel du Tresor*** (☎ 0524-37 51 13, 💻 http://p52975.typo3server.info/eng/history.php) is already attracting good reviews. Of the 14 rooms, four are singles and three are suites; rates, including breakfast and wifi access, are €38/47 (low season), €47/52 (high season). Every room has a television, a bath, air-conditioning, a fireplace and a terrace with a view.

Guéliz One hotel in this category which can be recommended is ***Hotel Al Bustan*** (☎ 0524-44 68 10/11/12; 💻 hotel_albustan@wanadoo.net.ma) at 66 boulevard Mohammed Zerktouni. The hotel can offer rooms with balconies and two large restaurants, one of which, the traditional Moroccan

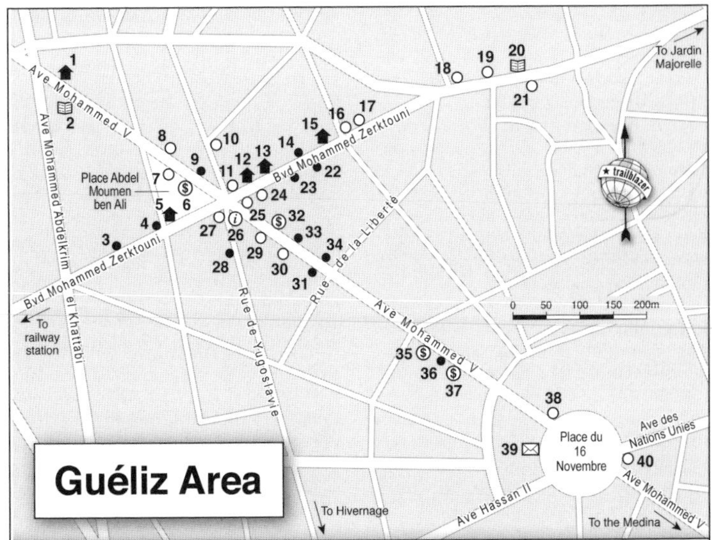

Where to stay
1 Hotel Oasis
5 Hotel Tachfine
12 Hotel des Voyageurs
13 Hotel Franco-Belge
15 Hotel Al Bustan

Where to eat and drink
7 Chez Jack'Line
8 Café Agdal
10 Pâtisserie Hilton
11 Le Jacaranda
16 Café Le Grand Dades
17 Le Dragon d'Or
18 Jazzo
19 Dreamland Food
21 Chez Casanova
24 Al Fassia
25 Café des Négociants
27 Grand Café et Restaurant de l'Atlas
29 Chesterfield Pub
30 Brasserie Nassim
38 McDonald's
40 Pizza Hut

Other
2 Librairie Chatr
3 CTM Office
4 Colisée Cinema
6 Banque Populaire
9 News stand
14 Budget
20 Librairie d'Art
22 Europcar and petrol
23 British Consulate
26 Tourist Information Office
28 Lune Car
31 Avis
32 BMCE
33 Pharmacy
34 Hertz
35 Attijariwafa
36 Royal Air Maroc
37 Crédit du Maroc
39 Post Office

restaurant, has 500 seats, and two bars. There is also an outdoor pool (open to non-residents; 50dh) which has a shallow area for children and has some shade. Rooms cost 160/240dh, including breakfast.

On the same street is ***Hotel Tachfine*** (☎ 0524-44 71 88; 💻 www.amalay-tachfine.ma) which charges 341/412/512dh for rooms with TVs. Breakfast (39dh) is charged separately and is available in the hotel's two restaurants; they also offer a *menu touristique* for 138dh along with traditional Moroccan cuisine.

Expensive hotels

The choice of first-class hotels in and around Marrakech is great and the first dilemma to be faced is whether to aim for the bustling crowds of Marrakech itself or whether to head away for the peace and tranquility of the Palmeraie which, though on the city's northern flanks, still remains within striking distance of the Medina. The second dilemma is to choose between the polish of an opulent purpose-built modern hotel or a beautifully restored historical building which might capture more of the Morocco you came to see. Whichever way you turn, there remains a big choice of accommodation and, although it is easily possible to pay a rate which would match that of the most expensive hotels anywhere in the world, it is equally possible to find wonderful hotels in Marrakech at a much more modest price which will still make your heart skip a beat with delight.

Medina Within the Medina itself you might consider one of a number of breathtaking small, luxury riad hotels. ***La Villa des Orangers*** (map p103; ☎ 0524-38 46 38; 💻 www.villadesorangers.com), at 6 rue Sidi Mimoun, offers the best of Moroccan architectural traditions exquisitely blended with French sophistication, reflecting its current French ownership. While its roof terrace looks outwards to Koutoubia, its heated pool offers inner sanctity within its own enclosed garden. Prices range from 3700dh for a de luxe room to 7700dh per night for a master suite with balcony, private pool and garden view for two people sharing, including breakfast and light lunch. Price reductions (30%) are available in the low season between mid-June and mid-August.

La Sultana (map p103; ☎ 0524-38 80 08; 💻 www.lasultanamarrakech.com), 403 rue de la Kasbah, consists of four historic riads, one even sharing a wall with the Saadian Tombs, all displaying stunning craftsmanship, beautifully adorned with marble, *tadlekt* (a traditional lime-based wall plaster) and chiselled stucco. A heated pool and a spa could provide the relaxation you might be craving. Prices range from 2800dh for a prestige room to 10,500dh for an apartment, including breakfast and use of the spa.

La Maison Arabe (map p102; ☎ 0524-38 70 10; 💻 www.maisonarabe.com), at 1 derb Assehbe near Bab Doukkala, built around two flower-filled patios, began life as a restaurant yet, through the use of traditional crafts, materials and furnishings, including cedarwood ceilings and floors made of *bejmat* (small sand-coloured bricks), has developed into the most atmospheric of small hotels. More than this, the hotel's own shuttle service will whisk you to its private garden beyond the city, fifteen minutes away, where you can enjoy a wonderful swimming pool reserved for guests of the hotel. Rates, which include breakfast and tea, start at 1900dh for a standard room and go up to 6400dh for the royal suite.

At the edge of the Medina, on Avenue Bab el Djedid, is ***La Mamounia*** (map p102; ☎ 0524-38 86 00; 💻 www.mamounia.com), the most famous hotel in Marrakech, if not in the whole of Africa (see box opposite). It has 136 rooms and 71 suites. Rates in the low season start at 4000dh for a classic room, located on the lower floors, whilst suites on the middle floors begin at 6400dh, with the most luxurious, the Al Mamoun suite, priced at 35,000dh. Children up to two years of age can stay free of charge when using existing beds in their parents' room, although children aged three years and over are fully charged. Should you really want to indulge, there are also three riads (from 56,000dh), each containing three bedrooms, in the hotel's gardens. Note: a dress code applies in all public areas of the hotel. See also ***Riad el Arsat*** (p123).

La Mamounia

La Mamounia was designed in 1923 by the architects Prost and Marchisio, who paid due respect to the twin influences of Moroccan tradition and the orders of the Compagnie des Chemins de Fer du Maroc (the Moroccan Railway Company), their financial patron. Built between 1925 and 1929, Art Deco touches were first provided by Jacques Majorelle, with additional significant work carried out in 1986 by French designer, André Paccard.

The hotel closed in July 2006 for extensive renovation and only reopened its doors at the end of November 2009. The inspiration for this latest evolution of La Mamounia was provided by Paris-based interior designer, Jacques Garcia, who chose to develop the hotel's traditional Arabo-Andalusian craftsmanship.

The auctioning of over 6000 items associated with the 'old' hotel, ranging from sofas to crockery to sheets, in May and June 2009 raised three million euros.

Once the favourite retreat of Sir Winston Churchill, who visited Morocco frequently during the 1930s and 1950s, often to paint, the hotel is a Marrakech landmark in its own right and has since been visited by scores of politicians and celebrities from around the world. Amongst these are US presidents Theodore Roosevelt and Ronald Reagan, South African giants Nelson Mandela and Desmond Tutu, film idols Charlton Heston, Tom Cruise, Nicole Kidman and Sharon Stone, fashion moguls Yves Saint Laurent and Jean-Paul Gaultier, along with a plethora of music stars including The Rolling Stones and Elton John.

Indeed today many less famous visitors to the city choose to come simply to enjoy an orange juice or pot of mint tea on its rear terrace. From here you, too, can wander through its historic gardens (see What to see, p123) or simply admire them from across its outdoor, heated swimming pool, closed to non-residents. The hotel also has the benefit of four restaurants, five bars, a spa, a fitness pavilion and an attached casino. In all, the hotel has 136 rooms and 71 suites.

As Jacques Garcia himself has said of the hotel, 'Combining the best the modern world has to offer with traditional values, La Mamounia provides an experience so unique, it becomes an integral part of the myth that defines it.'

Hivernage Most of the expensive hotels in the Ville Nouvelle are found within Hivernage. They can be large, modern buildings with excellent facilities, including swimming pools, but, in keeping with much of this area of Marrakech, tend to be somewhat soulless.

Perhaps the best of the big chain hotels in Hivernage is the five-star ***Hotel Sofitel*** (map p102; ☎ 0524-42 56 00/42 05 05; 🖳 www.sofitel.com), rue Harroun Errachid, Quartier de l'hivernage, 4000 Marrakech, close to the Medina and within easy walking distance of Djemaa al-Fna. Managing to combine modernity with some traditional features, all 260 of its air-conditioned rooms have either a balcony or a terrace. Surrounded by a beautiful garden with fountains and heated outdoor pools, the hotel also has a well-equipped health and fitness centre which includes a Jacuzzi, a hammam and a gym. Three restaurants offer a choice of Moroccan and international cuisine, and its three bars provide a range of meeting points. Prices start at 1500dh for a standard double room rising to 6000dh for a superior suite with two king-size beds, room only; breakfast costs around 20dh.

For a more intimate setting in Hivernage, try the 19-roomed ***Dar Rhizlane*** (map p102; ☎ 0524-42 13 03; 🖳 www.dar-rhizlane.com), avenue Jnane El Harti,

Quartier de l'hivernage, 4000 Marrakech. Again within walking distance of the Medina, the heart of this hotel is a 1940s house, more recently extended and renovated. Reflecting the elegance of a bourgeois Marrakech villa, designed in the style of a small palace, it is set in a wonderfully lush and varied garden with its own pool, enclosed by high walls. The quality of the cuisine from its restaurant is renowned throughout Marrakech.

Prices start at 2625dh for a double room in the low season, rising to 3150dh in the high season, whilst suites rise from 5000dh to 5800dh. Rates include breakfast and afternoon tea. Transfer to and from the airport can be arranged for a further 120dh.

Outside Marrakech Eight kilometres north of the pink walls of Marrakech ***Caravan Serai*** (☎ 0524-30 03 02; 💻 www.hotel-caravanserai.com), 264 Ouled Ben Rahmoune, 4000 Marrakech, provides an oasis of calm and relaxation to all travellers who seek its refuge. Suitably, its very name means an 'inn for desert caravans'. Ingeniously created through the restoration and renovation of three tumble-down pisé houses, in the traditional village of Ouled Ben Rahmoune, into a single structure, today it offers a haven of 17 bedrooms and suites. All are different in size and form, built around a central, communal, lantern-lit heated pool, and linked by a series of small inter-connected courtyards.

Designed with the intention of conveying the charm of rural simplicity at its best, its ceilings, made with the thick trunks of eucalyptus and palm trees, its traditional Berber furnishings, its indulgent tadlekt bath tubs and its large, open fireplaces succeed in achieving just this.

Swathes of billowing white fabric framing the monumental gateway to its central courtyard, and the shade of jacaranda trees in its garden, add to the prevailing atmosphere of peace. What is more, Caravan Serai has its own hammam and spa, while its restaurant, ***La Route des Épices***, serves a choice of Moroccan and French cuisine. Should you need any more pampering, no fewer than 40 staff stand on hand. Double rooms start at €110 in the low season (July and August) rising to €165 in the high season, whilst the cost of the master suite, with its own private, heated pool, increases from €225 to €330. All tariffs include breakfast and access to a non-alcoholic mini-bar, airport transfer, plus a shuttle service to and from Marrakech three times daily. Advance booking is essential, at which time you would be wise to pre-arrange a time and place to be collected and taken to the hotel. Otherwise, take the Casablanca Road (N9, the old P7) northwards out of Marrakech for 8km, cross the bridge and turn right for Ouled Ben Rahmoune.

The Palmeraie ***Les Deux Tours*** (☎ 0524-32 95 25; 💻 www.les-deuxtours.com), Circuit de la Palmeraie, BP513, Marrakech, is located in the heart of the Palmeraie within the village of Douar Abiad, close to Oued Tensift, eight kilometres north of Marrakech and just 20 minutes' drive from Djemaa al-Fna. It is accessible from both the Fes Road (N8, the old P24) and the Casablanca Road (N9, the old P7). Simply pick up the signs for the 'Circuit de la Palmeraie' and follow the road around, looking out for further signs indicating turnings off for your hotel.

The entrance to its walled grounds is marked by the eponymous two towers (*les deux tours*), large and unmistakable. Designed by brilliant architect, Charles Boccara, the series of rooms and suites within, each with its own distinctive character, reflect the Frenchman's creative inspiration from sources as diverse as Morocco, Turkey and Egypt. All are finely crafted and beautifully adorned with *zellij* (mosaic) floors, tadlekt walls and traditional wooden ceilings, for which the highly poisonous, evergreen Oleander wood is often employed.

In total, there are 30 rooms and junior suites, some of which have fireplaces whilst others have impressive, domed bathrooms. There are also five luxury suites, each with their own small, heated pool as well as a private garden. The hotel has a communal, heated outdoor pool, too, and a spa, plus two restaurants, one of which serves pool-side meals, while the other, ***Salaambô***, recently received the prestigious one-star award from Michelin. There is much to enjoy within this green haven; above all, the sweet fragrance of the jacaranda as the sun sets.

WHERE TO EAT

At its finest, Moroccan cuisine is amongst the best in the world and in Marrakech there is a wealth of opportunity to enjoy this. The city boasts a number of fabulous restaurants, often located within wonderful settings, which, while sometimes quite expensive in relation to the local economy, furnish the visitor with experiences which might only be dreamed of at home. Either as a send off into the mountains or as a return celebration, the trekker would be unwise to visit Morocco and fail to indulge at least once. On the other hand, it is very easy to eat inexpensively in Marrakech, even cheaply, and well.

The key consideration is to avoid picking up a stomach bug before setting off on your trek. Contaminated water is the likeliest source of upset. Although this will not often cause a problem to locals, Westerners should adhere to drinking bottled water while in Marrakech, always checking that the seal of the bottle is unbroken. Do not become complacent: even if you feel you have been in the country for a long time, your system will not have become strong enough to cope with local tap water. To further minimise your chances of becoming ill eat hot, freshly cooked food and avoid salads which have not been freshly prepared and ice cream which will almost certainly have been prepared using contaminated water. Peel fruit. Water absorbed into your food, such as rice or couscous, that has been well boiled in the cooking process should be rendered safe, but if in any doubt that the water has been properly boiled, simply avoid. This equally applies to water in hot drinks, including tea and coffee.

Medina

Even before the evening storytellers and drummers have arrived in force, a growing number of rows of **food stalls** are set out across **Djemaa al-Fna** under the setting sun. White-coated chefs man the stalls, offering fish, salads, couscous, kebabs, chicken or simple egg sandwiches, brought to your table by friendly and efficient waiters. Noisy conversation hangs over the square, along with smoke from the barbecues which, when lent an orange glow by the evening lights of the stalls, give an almost supernatural atmosphere to the proceedings.

Tourists and locals alike, seated shoulder to shoulder on benches at crowded tables, come together to enjoy one of the cheapest meals to be had in Marrakech. A small feast of lamb kebabs, olives, bread and tea will cost around 40dh; the feeling that you have truly arrived in Marrakech comes free of charge.

Should you prefer to eat inside, however, Djemaa al-Fna is surrounded by inexpensive, pleasant restaurants. One of these, ***Chez Chegrouni***, on the east side of the square near rue des Banques, offers tagines (60dh), couscous (60dh) and omelette (30dh); typical prices for restaurants in this category. With balconies on the first and second floor, good views can be gained of the theatre of life being played out in the square below. In truth, almost any of the restaurants around the Djemaa could provide you with similar experiences. Try ***Café-Restaurant Argana***, for example, which towers over the square on its north side. Its best views, rivalled only by those from the large balcony of ***Café Glacier*** on the south side of the square, are from its top terrace where, unfortunately, only drinks are served; meals are served on the terrace below.

Another good place to look for inexpensive restaurants is **rue Bani Marine** which leads directly from the southern side of Djemaa al-Fna. In the next street, rue Moulay Ismail, ***Hotel Ali*** (see Where to stay) has a simple public restaurant (harira 10dh, pizza from 30dh, brochettes from 45dh) which is popular with guides and can therefore be a good place to make enquiries about organising a trek. Of a higher quality is the hotel's recommended evening buffet (80dh), served upstairs. Another hotel-restaurant offering an evening buffet (150dh; 7.30-10.30pm), considered to be of a slightly higher standard but at a slightly higher price, is ***Hotel de Foucauld*** (see p106).

Further from Djemaa al-Fna, yet arranged in a fashion which is reminiscent of it, a series of stalls have recently begun to set up for business in **place des Ferblantiers** (map p103), near the walls of Palais el-

MARRAKECH

Badi. Here, diners eating simple, traditional fare, sit *al fresco* at tables lining the square.

At completely the other end of the range of eating possibilities and considered one of the great experiences of Marrakech, is a visit to ***Yacout*** (see map p103; ☎ 0524-38 29 29/00; 🖳 yacout@menara.ma; Tue-Sun). Hidden deep within the Medina at 79, Sidi Ahmed Soussi, you are unlikely to find it without a lot of guidance; most people order a taxi to help them find their way out again afterwards. Set in the opulent surroundings of a former palace, this restaurant is truly an institution in Marrakech. Fine, traditional Moroccan four-course set meals (700dh per person) are served in very generous portions by immaculately and traditionally dressed waiters. Even better than the meal, however, is the aperitif which you will first be offered on the roof terrace, providing special views over the Medina, to the accompaniment of hypnotic *Gnaoua* musicians.

Another way to eat very well in beautiful surroundings is to dine at one of Marrakech's finest hotels. At the sumptuous ***La Sultana*** (see p108), for example, French-influenced Moroccan cuisine can be enjoyed on the hotel's roof terrace. A three-course meal would cost around 400dh. At ***La Maison Arabe*** (see p108) there is even a choice of restaurants; while one, the smaller and more intimate, evokes the colonial Africa of the 1930s, the other offers a more traditional Moroccan experience. A three-course meal is set at 400dh. ***La Mamounia*** (see p108) incredibly has four restaurants, including the celebrated ***Le Marocain***. The other three – ***Le Français***, ***L'Italien*** and ***Le Pavillon de la Piscine*** – offer further fine dining opportunities, made all the more special by the opportunity to visit one of the most famous hotels in Africa.

Currently deemed by many to be the finest restaurant experience in Marrakech, however, is ***Le Tobsil*** (map p103; ☎ 0524-44 40 52) at 22 derb Abdellah Ben Hessaien. Exquisite traditional Moroccan cuisine is served in an intimate riad on two levels around a central courtyard. Additional atmosphere is supplied courtesy of Gnaoua musicians. A set meal here, including aperitifs and wine, costs around 600dh.

In Guéliz

Many of the places to eat in Guéliz are clustered along the length of **avenue Mohammed V** north of place du 16 Novembre and around the streets immediately off it. Although restaurants are not all expensive in this part of Marrakech, there is not, however, the number of cheap restaurants which can be readily found in the Medina. But if you have just returned from the mountains and are weary of tagine and couscous, there are good opportunities here to indulge in some quality international cuisine.

One of the more popular moderately priced restaurants is the licensed ***Chez Jack'Line*** (☎ 0524-44 75 47), at 63 avenue Mohammed V. Renowned as much for the resident parrot as for the good-value food, both French and Italian dishes are available here, although the set menu based upon a selection of Moroccan dishes is the less expensive option (80dh).

For a complete change of scenery, ***Le Dragon d'Or*** (☎ 0524-43 06 17/44 62 48), at 82 boulevard Mohammed Zerktouni, serves Chinese and Vietnamese cuisine amidst oriental décor including golden dragons, Chinese lanterns and lacquered tables. A typical main course of beef chop suey would cost 65dh.

If, however, you are still seeking Moroccan cuisine, the pleasant ***Brasserie Nassim*** within the four-star Nassim Hotel, just a little north of the tourist information office at 115 avenue Mohammed V, offers fish brochettes for 75dh and chicken tagine for 80dh. For traditional Moroccan cuisine with a twist, go to ***Al Fassia***, on boulevard Mohammed Zerktouni, where you can enjoy lamb tagine with aubergine (130dh) or, for a change of menu, head further along the same street to ***Chez Casanova*** where a good Italian menu includes lasagne al ragu (80dh) and tagliatelle al salmone (100dh).

Alternatively, for a sophisticated taste of France, head back along boulevard Mohammed Zerktouni to the junction with avenue Mohammed V to find the well-established ***Le Jacaranda*** (☎ 0524-44 72 15). During the day you can opt for the two-course *menu rapide* (85dh), the three-course *menu touristique* (105dh), or even the *menu du marché* (190dh). In the evening, as the lights soften and a more romantic mood envelops the restaurant, the à la carte menu offers such delicacies as fillet of beef with oysters (145dh). Don't come here, however, if you are in a hurry. As a sign at the door reads, *'La cuisine est oeuvre d'art, elle demande du temps, soyez comprehensive.'*

Pâtisseries
If it is the sweet things in life you have been missing while on the trail, Marrakech provides plenty of opportunities to redress that balance. There are several fine pâtisseries, notably in the Ville Nouvelle. The easiest to find is the centrally located ***Café des Négociants*** on place Abdel Moumen ben Ali. Here, at the intersection of avenue Mohammed V and boulevard Mohammed Zerktouni, is a wonderful opportunity to watch the world go by, while sitting on the café's large pavement terrace.

NIGHTLIFE
The rapid increase in popularity of Marrakech as a tourist destination has resulted in a city which is changing quickly. Nowhere has this rapid development been more apparent than in the increase in nightlife which now extends well beyond the traditional entertainers of Djemaa al-Fna and the cafés which overlook it. Indeed Marrakech has a fast-growing reputation for its nightlife which even attracts international weekend visitors.

Bars
Quite apart from those to be found inside Marrakech's higher class and international hotels, several bars and smaller hotels serve alcohol, notably those in the Ville Nouvelle. A good selection line avenue Mohammed V, particularly clustered around place Abdel Moumen ben Ali. One such is the ***Chesterfield Pub*** at 119 avenue Mohammed V, next to Nassim Hotel (see Brasserie Nassim opposite). In the Medina, where the options are more limited, try the popular bar on the ground floor of ***Le Grand Hotel Tazi*** (see p106) which offers a selection of local and imported beers.

Clubs
Pacha Marrakech (☎ 0524-38 84 00; 💻 www.pachamarrkech.com), which claims to be the biggest club not just in Morocco but in all Africa, is to be found in the Hivernage district of Marrakech on boulevard Mohammed VI (formerly avenue de France). The inconvenience of the location is compensated for by the free shuttle service provided to and from town which can be arranged by calling. The pull of Pacha is such that DJs come from as far as Europe and New York to be seen here. There is a price to pay: Sunday to Thursday, 100-150dh; Friday and Saturday, 200-250dh or more for a big event (first drink included).

Also in Hivernage, in the grounds of Hotel es-Saadi on avenue Qadissia, ***Theatro*** (☎ 0524.44.88.11; 💻 www.theatromarrakech.com) is the club with currently the fastest-rising reputation.

WHAT TO SEE
Djemaa al-Fna
The largest crowds are drawn by the storytellers. It is around them that people throng most densely and stay longest. Their performances are lengthy; an inner ring of listeners squat on the ground and it is some time before they get up again. Others, standing, form an outer ring; they, too, hardly move, spellbound by the storyteller's words and gestures. Sometimes two of them recite in turn. Their words come from farther off and hang longer in the air than those of ordinary people. **Elias Canetti**, *Storytellers and scribes*, from *The Voices of Marrakech*, 1967

The original meaning of Djemaa al-Fna is ambiguous. Rooted in Arabic, it might either be a reference to the 'assembly of the dead', and a time when the heads of executed criminals were displayed on poles around the square, or else a reference to the 'place of the vanished mosque', the destruction of an Almoravid mosque here long ago.

Its function, however, is clear: since time immemorial, it has provided a meeting place for merchants drawn to this magical city from both near and far. Most significantly for its development these included those who came here from the deep south.

After days or even weeks on the trail, having traversed the heat of the desert and clambered over the lofty passes of the High Atlas, they finally reached Marrakech. It was here that their caravans finally stopped and their entertainment at last began.

Although those days of the caravans have sadly passed, the entertainers have continued to gather here; today their performances are enjoyed equally by Moroccans and tourists alike. Such is the vitality of the square that all attempts by the French administration, in the final throes of their colonial grip on Morocco, to have it closed down and turned into a car park, were surely bound to end in failure. So it proved.

This vast open square at the heart of the Medina continues to be one of the most extraordinary sights, not only in Morocco but throughout Africa, because of the people who work here: story-tellers, snake charmers, healers, clairvoyants, musicians, cooks, dentists and water carriers; together they form a constantly shifting scene of vivid colour. During the day the square is relatively quiet. A few snake-charmers might sit under parasols while traders set out their wares on faded carpets; water carriers in their outlandish costumes stroll about attracting attention by shaking bells; a score of identical orange-juice stalls are set up around the perimeter. However, as night falls, the square hits a more urgent note, intoxicating, intimidating, insistent, timeless; crowds gather as drummers and Berber musicians compete, the players shrouded in smoke from the many food stalls.

If, however, you tire of jostling your way around this bustling square, or would simply prefer to watch in relative peace, head for one of the many cafés and restaurants overlooking all this activity. For the price of a drink, you can have a front row seat at one of the best theatres in the world.

Koutoubia mosque

What is inside I believe no Christian knows. Had I that moment, dressed as I was, sunburned and dirty, got off and entered it, I might have seen, but the thought did not cross

Safety in Djemaa al-Fna

With the increase in their numbers in recent years, tourists are no longer so conspicuous in Djemaa al-Fna. However, you are still likely to attract some attention, at least when you stop to enjoy one of the many performances in the square. Most hustlers are simply salesmen trying to make some money, or perhaps Djemaa al-Fna regulars offering to pose for photographs in return for some coins. Remember that if you listen, watch or take photographs, you will be expected to pay and it is useful to be ready with a pocketful of small change. Naturally you need to be confident that the subject of any photograph you take does not object to being photographed in the first place (see Cultural impact pp90-1).

Of course, in any place where large gatherings congregate, there is always a risk posed by would-be thieves and pickpockets, particularly at night. Djemaa al-Fna is no exception. Happily, in recent years there has been a major crackdown by the police on tourist-related crime through the engagement of designated plain-clothes tourist police (see Security, crime and the police, p87) who themselves mingle with the crowds; you might even find yourself rubbing shoulders with one as you join the circle of spectators gathered around the snake charmers. Similarly, the chances of being hassled by *faux guides* (unofficial guides) and 'students', claiming to want to practise their English, have certainly receded of late. Nevertheless, be on your guard and keep your valuables close to you; better still, travel lightly through the square.

my mind, and afterwards, when known for a European, it might have cost my life.

RB Cunninghame Graham, *Mogreb-el-Acksa*, 1898

Koutoubia, at 220ft the tallest mosque in Marrakech, towers over the Medina. It is the most visible landmark in the city; at night, when its minaret is lit, it can be seen quite clearly from the distant Palmeraie and for miles beyond. The mosque was built on the site of a kasbah in the twelfth century by the Almohads. Its design adhered to traditional Almohad patterns which formed the basis for much classical Moroccan architecture which followed. Unfortunately, though it is possible to walk around its landscaped surroundings, the building itself is closed to non-Muslims.

The souks

Marrakech has long thrived as an economic and cultural hub, its spokes extending to every part of southern Morocco and beyond, and the splendour of its souks reflects that importance. From merchants trading daily necessities to craftsmen demonstrating the skills of their guild, all of Morocco can be found here.

An increasing number of shops, particularly along main thoroughfares such as rue Souk Smarine, are beginning to diversify in what they sell, believing that this will give them more chance of catching the eye of passing tourists. It is, however, still true that for the most part each souk has its own specialism. Thus you will find many silver dealers clustered in one area and most textile merchants grouped in another. Shops within the souks have been organised in this way throughout the Islamic world for centuries, and the markets of medieval Christian Western Europe would not have appeared so very differently.

Souk Smarine forms the main route through the souks from the northern side of Djemaa al-Fna and it is traditionally the textiles souk. Since it sees the bulk of tourist traffic, however, it has become something of an all-purpose crafts market with larger shops selling everything from carpets to jewel-encrusted travelling chests. However, many textile merchants remain here.

After passing the clothes *kissaria* on the left, you will come to **Rahba Kedima**. This square, once the corn souk, is fascinating for its wool market on the south side and animal skin souk on the east. You must get to the wool market early in the morning to see any trading taking place. The ancient skins market is open for business all day. There are also several stalls selling traditional remedies and potions here. Many of the goods on offer seem extraordinary to Western visitors – and the merchants' claims are often even more staggering; you will find here 'cures' for all manner of illnesses, aphrodisiacs and bizarre ingredients for working black magic.

After Souk Smarine the street divides. The right-hand fork, Souk el-Kebir, leads next to **La Criée Berbère**. This was a slave market until the French occupation in 1912 and kidnapped black Africans were sold like mules at auctions here. These days the small square is dominated by carpet-sellers.

Anyone with any experience of Morocco will know that carpet-sellers are nothing if not persistent, so it takes steely determination to keep a cool head and find a genuine bargain here where there are more carpet-sellers per square foot than anywhere else in the country! There are bargains to be had, though, and you will no doubt be shown beautiful carpets from various regions in Morocco. Different patterns show regional variations and most of the designs have some meaning. It can be an education to have your carpet dealer teach you about the symbolism within them. There will often be a carpet auction during mid-afternoon. Only participate if you're confident you know what you're doing (see Carpets pp85-6).

The next souk after La Criée Berbère is **Souk aux Bijoutiers** – for jewellers – after which you will find yourself in the tight streets of Souk Cherratin. Before reaching Souk Cherratin, however, you will pass the kissarias to the left; these rather tacky stalls sell mainly Western goods, or copies of Western goods, at inflated prices. **Souk Cherratin** is the place to come for leather goods. Haggle here for handmade shoes, bags and jackets.

To loop back to Djemaa al-Fna, head left after the leather workers' souk before reaching **Ali ben Youssef Mosque** (see opposite). This will take you to **Souk Haddadine** where blacksmiths ply their trade with noisy enthusiasm. From here walk south along **Souk el-Attarin**, the souk for perfumes and spices, to **Souk aux Chourai** (for carpenters) and, just a little further on, to **Souk des Huivres** where oils are bought and sold. Beyond here the colourful **Souk des Teinturiers**, or dyers' souk, is for many visitors the most attractive feature in this labyrinthine market. Dyed

SURVIVING THE SOUKS

Orientation

On first impression the souks may seem to have developed to no particular plan at all. In fact they have been shaped by both religion and economics: only goods deemed 'clean' in the Islamic sense can be sold close to mosques. Thus, in the Marrakech souks, the coppersmiths' trade, for example, is 'clean'; valuable products like silver are generally made and sold close to the main streets while less impressive or cheaper products, dyed wool perhaps, will normally be found deeper in the side streets.

Guides or touts?

Do not go into the souks with a faux guide. They act as agents for merchants, simply guiding tourists to particular carpet dealers where they then take a commission. There are qualified guides in Marrakech but there is, in fact, little need to take a guide into the souks at all. Just pay close attention to where you are and take care not to get lost.

The simple art to surviving the souks is to appear confident and where possible to give the impression that you know where you are going. There was a time when to fail in either of these respects would have invited unwanted, sustained and even aggressive attention. In truth, the greatly increased number of Westerners now appearing in Marrakech has proportionately diluted this problem.

If you do get lost, choose your moment and simply ask for directions from a friendly stall holder back to Djemaa al-Fna, or wherever else you might want to be.

What to pay

Haggling will go more smoothly if you are polite. Haggling will go better still if you manage to convey the impression that you are not really interested in the item at all. One way of doing this is to decline any request to name your price while respectfully acknowledging the beauty of the item. Do not enthuse too much, always let the merchant suggest his price first and even then do not be rushed into stating yours.

By the time you agree a price it is often said that you might typically expect to be offered a price of about a third of that initially suggested by the merchant. Clearly this is not a scientific rule: despite the common folklore about the trials of shopping in the souks, some vendors will actually offer you a pretty fair price in the first place.

Whatever your approach, do not haggle for any item you are not genuinely interested in as this would be unfair on the merchant and would set a bad precedent for those who follow you. You would also be well advised not to touch items, for this too will create the impression that you want to buy and may even push up the price. Only start to touch items when your haggling has advanced reasonably, to be sure that the item is of the quality you believe.

wool is hung out above the sun-dappled streets to form a beautiful, bright and colourful canopy. Continue south on Souk el-Attarin to return to Souk Smarine and Djemaa al-Fna. Alternatively you could go right before reaching the dyers' souk. This street takes you to **Mouassine Mosque** and its sadly delapidated sixteenth-century Saadian fountain. Turn left at the mosque onto rue Mouassine to head back to Djemaa al-Fna. There is another interesting souk, **Souk des Forgerons** (coppersmiths) along a narrow street behind the mosque.

The first time you visit the souks they may seem like an impossible maze but you will soon begin to feel more confident and realise that you cannot get so very lost even if you try. Therefore, do not restrict yourself to this brief tour. There is often just as much of interest, arguably even more, along any number of the many side streets you will pass. Less frequented by tourists and, therefore, perhaps with more original curiosities; even the merchants might respond more freshly to your inquisitiveness. Take a risk.

Ali ben Youssef mosque and medersa

The Ali ben Youssef **mosque** is found at the northern end of the souks in place Ben Youssef. It is the largest in the Medina, recognisable by its green-tiled roof and minaret. It was first built by the Almoravid sultan, whose name the mosque still bears, in the twelfth century but, after numerous alterations, it was completely rebuilt in the Merenid style in the nineteenth century. Sadly, non-Muslims are not admitted.

The **medersa**, one of the most impressive in Morocco, stands alongside the mosque. Originally founded in the fourteenth century by the Merenid Sultan Abu Hassan, it was transformed in under a year into the largest religious establishment in the whole of the Maghreb on the order of the Saadian Sultan Abdullah el Ghalib in 1564. His motivation was for the ben Youssef Mosque to overtake Fes as the prime intellectual centre for the whole of North Africa. His name is commemorated in dedications in Kufic lettering on the lintel of the main entrance and also around the prayer hall within.

In line with tradition, the medersa was built around a central courtyard at the centre of which is a rectangular pool. The walls of the courtyard are decorated at ground level with beautiful zellij, above which is exquisite stucco decoration, and finally, high above, intricately carved cedar.

This is no traditional medersa, however; even its entrance, along a right-angled passageway, is highly irregular. What is more, the students, up to 900 at a time, were accommodated in just 132 small, plain cells located on the second storey. Here they stayed for up to six years while they learned to recite the Qu'ran from memory. While some of the cells look inwards over the central courtyard, others, contrary to custom, look outwards over the street. Another unusual feature is the series of small internal courtyards with skylights above, providing additional natural light for the students.

Open daily 9am-7pm (Apr to Sep), 9am-6pm (Oct to Mar), including to non-Muslims; entry 40dh, 20dh for children, or 60dh for a combined ticket that includes the medersa, the koubba (see below), and Musée de Marrakech, see pp121-2.

Almoravid Koubba

On place de la Kissaria, next to Musée de Marrakech and about 40 metres south of the Ali ben Youssef Mosque, stands an early twelfth-century Almoravid koubba. Though badly damaged, this domed pavilion is hugely important as it is one of the few Almoravid buildings in Marrakech to have survived the Almohad rampage which destroyed much of the city in the mid-twelfth century. It originally formed an annexe to the original Almoravid Ali ben Youssef mosque, which no longer stands, providing washing facilities to the faithful before prayer; remains of fountains and one of the original ablution basins can still be seen.

A two-storeyed rectangular building, measuring 7.3m x 5.5m at its base, is crowned by a brick dome decorated with blind arcades and chevrons centred upon a seven-pointed star. Beautiful decoration, which includes geometric patterns and flowers, is particularly notable for the inscription to Ali ben Youssef, the founder, which is the oldest surviving example of cursive writing throughout North Africa.

Long buried under one of the outbuildings of the succeeding ben Youssef mosque, the koubba was only rediscovered in 1948, below several metres of earth and ash, and finally excavated during 1952-3. Considered to be an exceptional piece of architecture by scholars of Muslim art, it is open to both Muslims and non-Muslims (9am-12.30pm and 2.30-6pm, Oct to Mar; until 7pm, Apr to Sep; entry 10dh. Tickets available from Musée de Marrakech, see p121).

The Jewish quarter (The Mellah)

On the third morning, as soon as I was alone, I found my way to the Mellah. I came to a crossroads where there were a great many Jews standing about. The traffic streamed past them and round a corner. I saw people going through an arch that looked as if it had been let into a wall, and I followed them. Inside the wall, enclosed by it on all four sides, lay the Mellah, the Jewish quarter. **Elias Canetti**, *A visit to the Mellah*, from *The Voices of Marrakech*, 1967

Elias Canetti was entering the Mellah from close by place des Ferblantiers. This remains the main entrance today although regrettably few Jews are now to be found within. The Mellah was created at the command of the Saadian Sultan Abdullah al-Ghalib in 1558 with the specific purpose of housing the Jewish population of Marrakech. It was built as a walled enclosure on the former site of the royal stables under the shadow of the royal palace. On the one hand the Sultan thereby provided protection for the Jewish community, who now lived securely in a city within a city; the Mellah could only be entered by two gates. On the other hand, the Jewish bankers, traders, linguists and craftsmen could easily be controlled and exploited by him.

With its narrow, parallel streets, the Mellah looks and feels different to the rest of the Medina. Although the souk, with its traditional rush roofing intact, still thrives, today it is largely run by Muslims. Only around 300 Jews and a solitary synagogue remain within its walls: the Mellah is in decline. The old synagogue can be visited and although it is hard to find, small boys will offer to lead the way for you through the surrounding dilapidated streets.

At the eastern end of the Mellah lies the run-down Jewish cemetery (the *miâara*) overseen by a self-appointed *guardien*. He will emerge from nowhere and provide you with a guided tour if you wish, or even if you don't.

Tanneries

Close by Bab Debbagh (Tannin Gate), confusingly also sometimes known as Bab El Sebbagh (meaning 'gate in the east of the Medina'), at the north-east corner of the Medina, are the tanners of Marrakech. They continue to produce and dye leather using traditional techniques passed down from father to son, techniques which have hardly changed since the Middle Ages.

The whole production process, from untreated fleece to finished article ready for sale, can be seen here, acted out in the open air without even shade to protect the backs of the workers from the ferocity of the beating sun. First the animal skins, those of sheep, goat, cow and camel, are soaked in a lime solution to clean away the remnants of flesh, fat and hair. In order to make them supple, the skins are then washed, soaked and trodden underfoot for several weeks in large stone vats containing a concoction of animal urine and pigeon droppings. Many stages follow before finally, and necessarily, they are washed in a fragrant mixture of bark and flowers to chase away any remaining foul odour. Even today the dyes are all natural: bright lemon yellow, the *ziouvani*, for example, so popular with purveyors of babouches, is achieved from pomegranate bark.

It is no coincidence that the tanneries are on the eastern edge of the Medina: the Oued Issil, at least until the recent droughts, provided a reliable source of water, so vital in the production process. Even more critically, the westerly breeze takes the foul smells created away from the city.

The tanneries are not easy to find; you will probably need a friendly local to help you. If he is worth his tip, he will provide you with a sprig of mint along the way to help combat the truly awful stench. You will probably feel a moral obligation to reward him, and even to make a purchase from the adjacent tannery shop, too: there is, after all, no admission charge to witness this special performance.

Saadian tombs

Considered by many to be the most prized attraction in Marrakech, the Saadian tombs lay buried for 350 years and were only rediscovered by French archaeologists in 1917 after they spotted them through studying aerial photographs. Situated between Bab er Robb and Palais el-Badi, they have since been restored to their former glory.

The mausoleum was built in the late sixteenth century for the Saadian sultans and their families, but when their dynasty was toppled by the rampaging Alaouites in the late seventeenth century, Moulay Ismail, the new, dynamic Alaouite sultan, had the tombs of his enemies sealed. The world is fortunate that the tombs survived at all, however. Whereas Ismail methodically dismantled much of Palais el-Badi (see Palais el-Badi) and much else of the Saadian legacy in Marrakech, the Saadian tombs avoided a similar fate probably only because of his fear of supernatural retribution.

The entrance to the tombs today is inauspicious but, once inside their high-walled enclosure, there are attractive gardens sheltering two separate beautiful mausoleums. Between them they contain 66 tombs with a further 100 or more located around the gardens – tombs of princes, soldiers and servants, including those of a few Jews, who had connections with the royal family.

The first mausoleum, on the left as you enter, is the more impressive of the two. Perhaps this is because it houses the tomb of Sultan Ahmed al-Mansour Eddahbi (the 'Golden One'), and those of his male heirs, during whose reign the mausoleum was built. The delicate yet spectacular designs inside the mausoleum's three inner chambers are breathtaking. The central room has twelve columns, exquisitely decorated with *zellij* and finely sculptured stucco plaster. It is said to mark the zenith of Hispano-Moorish art in Morocco, recalling the magnificence of the Alhambra in Grenada.

The second mausoleum, the older, also has three chambers. It contains the tomb of Ahmed al-Mansour's mother as well as the body, if not the head, of Mohammed esh Sheikh, the founder of the Saadian dynasty. He was killed in the Atlas Mountains by Turkish mercenaries who then took his head back to Istanbul. There it was placed on public display as proof of his demise.

As the Saadian tombs are probably the most popular tourist attraction in Marrakech, you would be well advised to arrive early in order to avoid lengthy queues.

Open daily 8.30am-noon and 2.30-6.30pm. Entry 10dh.

Palais el-Badi

If you ask a Moorish boy why he is so kind to the stork alone among the birds, he will tell you at once that the stork was once a Sultan, no less. **John Finnemore**, *Peeps at Many Lands Morocco*, 1908

Just like the Saadian Tombs, Palais el-Badi was built in the heyday of Sultan Ahmed al-Mansour in the sixteenth century and it too would come to suffer its demise at the hands of the Alaouite Moulay Ismail in the seventeenth century.

The construction of 'The Incomparable Palace' was the result of al-Mansour's ambition to build a new showpiece for his capital to rival any palace in the world. With more than 300 rooms, organised around a central courtyard measuring 135 metres by 110 metres, with a 90-metre by 20-metre pool at its centre, this ambition was made clear. Nor did he stint on either materials or workmanship: the building, which he had adorned with gold, white marble and multi-coloured onyx, imported from all over the Maghreb and southern Europe, took over ten years to complete.

Still standing at the western end of the courtyard is the Koubba el Khamsiniya, once the great hall for state occasions, famed for its 50 giant marble columns, shipped to Morocco from Italy, in exchange, it is said, for their equivalent weight in sugar. Regrettably, the koubba's columns and the pyramid-shaped roof they once supported are no more. Indeed, little more than the shell of the palace remains and it can take some imagination for the visitor to get a sense of its past glory. Only the height of its exterior walls, on the tops of which storks have built untidy, straggling nests, give a hint at the vast scale of the rooms and courts that once were; only the central pool and orange groves within its sunken gardens remain to remind us of its former finesse.

Sadly, much of the beautiful building material was removed to aid the construction of Meknes, Moulay Ismail's personal choice as the new capital for his dynasty. Beyond the courtyard, in the south-west corner of the site, amidst scant remains of some lesser buildings, are the former stables and some pitch black, cavernous underground dungeons; take a torch so you can explore them. Housed in a small room in the south-east corner of the site is a finely decorated and proudly restored seventeenth-century minbar rescued from the historic Koutoubia.

Found just off place des Ferblantiers through Bab Berrima. Open daily, 8.30am-noon and 2.30-6.30pm. Entry 10dh (with an additional 10dh charge to see the minbar).

Palais el Bahia

The el Bahia, meaning 'the Brilliant', was built towards the end of the nineteenth century by two grand *viziers*: Si Mousa, a former palace slave, and his son, Bou Ahmed, who reputedly became the most influential man in Morocco until his death in 1900.

The palace also became home to Bou Ahmed's four wives, 24 concubines and huge numbers of offspring. He was a tough and cruel man. Immediately after his death, his slaves and harem ransacked the palace, stealing everything of value. His family was driven out and the state took possession of the palace itself, which remains intact. Its craftsmanship, however, while undeniably impressive and certainly extravagant, would not have compared to the splendour of the Palais el-Badi in its prime.

Although built for the most part to traditional patterns reflecting Muslim preferences for privacy within the home, the palace is by no means a classical model of Moroccan architecture having been gradually pieced together over two generations. It consists of a series of intricately linked, richly decorated rooms, secluded Andalusian gardens and inner courtyards, all built around a huge garden planted with orange and lemon trees, jasmine and cedars.

Each member of Bou Ahmed's court, each of his wives, and his collective harem, had their own private area and courtyard within the complex which others were not to enter. Today there are restrictions upon the modern visitor, too, as part of the palace is occupied by members of the current royal family.

Open daily, 8.30am-noon and 2.30-6.30pm, entry 10dh. Guided tours available.

Musée Dar Si Said (Museum of Moroccan Arts)

Not far from el Bahia, close to the bottom of rue Riad Zitoun el Jedid, the sign-posted Palace Dar Si Said today houses an excellent Museum of Moroccan Arts. Built at the end of the nineteenth century by Bou Ahmed's brother (see Palais el Bahia), though less grand than its near neighbour, the palace provides a truly opulent setting.

The collection is beautifully displayed in a series of rooms over several floors in a building set around leafy, pooled courtyards. It includes Atlas jewellery, Haouz carpets, Safi pottery, Taroudannt oil lamps, mountain village doors, Marrakech leather, traditional costumes and weapons, and more besides. You will also hopefully come across one of the museum's most prized exhibits, a 1000-year-old marble basin brought to Marrakech from Spain by Ali ben Youssef to be placed in his mosque. It was transferred to the museum some years ago but, unfortunately, it is not always on display. Remember to look onto the central courtyard and up at the finely carved ceilings which adorn many of the rooms and which are among the most impressive in Marrakech.

The museum (☎ 0524-38 95 64, rue Riad Zitoun el Jedid) is open 9-11.45am and 2.30-5.45pm Sat-Mon and Wed-Thu; 9-11.30am and 3-5.45pm Fridays; closed Tuesdays. Entry 20dh.

Maison Tiskiwin

Just around the corner from the Musée Dar Si Said is Maison Tiskiwin at 8 rue de la Bahia. This very attractive riad, built in Andalusian-Moroccan style at the turn of the century, was transformed into a museum of Berber culture by Dutchman Bert Flint. A succession of rooms takes you through an exhibition of carpets, clothes, jewellery and artefacts on an anthropological tour of southern Morocco and the desert beyond.

Try to go on a Tuesday when the near-by Musée Dar Si Said is closed as tour groups, which normally try to cover both in the same half day, will be absent.

See the box below on Bert Flint for a fuller appreciation of this museum.

Open daily, 9am-12.30pm and 3-6pm. Entry 20dh, 10dh for children (☎/📠: 0524-38 91 92; 💻 tiskiwin@yahoo.fr).

Musée de Marrakech

Opened as recently as 1997 on place Ben Youssef, Musée de Marrakech is the result of the restoration of a derelict late nineteenth-century palace, Dar Mnebbi, brought about through the drive of patron of the arts, Omar Benjoullan.

At one point in its distinguished history, the building was owned by T'hami el Glaoui (see pp50-1) when he was Pacha of Marrakech. With the advent of Moroccan independence in 1956, the palace fell into the hands of the state, yet was neglected and gradually fell into a state of ruin. Today, however, it houses a wonderful collection of both contemporary and historic arts and crafts, artefacts and documents.

The museum also offers the benefits of a small bookshop and an open-air café in its courtyard.

Bert Flint

Having first visited Marrakech in 1954, Bert Flint settled in the city three years later, before buying the beautiful building which now houses his private anthropological collection as a home in 1976. The first part of the house was opened to the public in 1989. Now in his 80s, he has since donated the whole of it to the Cadi Ayyad University of Marrakech on the understanding that he may continue to live within. Not surprisingly, it is often still referred to as Bert Flint's House.

Bert Flint was first attracted to Marrakech by his interest in the Andalusian tradition which he saw living on in the architecture and interior designs of private houses in the city. In time he found himself steadily drawn to the visual arts and the music of the surrounding countryside. So much so that he is now best known for his celebration of the art and culture of the Moroccan peasant and nomad.

More recently still, he has grown increasingly interested in Marrakech's long-standing, once deep, cultural links with peoples across the Sahara and with the countries of the Sahel. These, he recognises, have been so critically important in the shaping of the south of Morocco in general and Marrakech in particular. He believes strongly that unless these cultural links, now precarious and withering, are nurtured and restored, they will soon be lost forever.

The museum is the manifestation of Bert Flint's determination to play his part. The permanent exhibition is entitled 'The Art of Dress and Ornament in the Sahara, Maghreb and Sahel' and the museum is indeed a tour of Berber history, of Toureg, Hausa, Djerma, Maure and others. It is a demonstration, too, of the importance of the ancient trans-Saharan trade cities, of the likes of Gao and Timbouctou, to the formation of the Marrakech that we know today. If, like Bert Flint, you believe that we can only understand ourselves through knowing our cultural heritage, small though it is, this is probably the most important museum to visit in Marrakech.

Open daily 9am-6.30pm. Entry 30dh (including entry to Almoravid Koubba) or 60dh with entry also to ben Youssef Medersa (☎ 0524-44 18 93; 💻 www.museedemarrakech.ma).

Old walls and gates

Arguably the most impressive feature of today's Marrakech is the twelfth-century Almoravid defensive wall which completely encircles the Medina. Eight to ten metres high, built with local red earth, it is punctuated by no fewer than 209 towers and 20 gates. Whilst some of these gates are plain and simple, others are impressive military structures exhibiting ingenious defensive design, amongst them **Bab Aghmat**, **Bab Taghzout** and, flanked by its twin bastions, **Bab Doukkala**. Moreover, no fewer than nine of these gates are decorated with beautiful Almoravid art of which **Bab Agnaou** stands out as the finest example.

The orange-pink walls make a splendid sight, particularly under a setting sun. It is worth walking out to the olive groves south-west of the Medina during sunset when the glow of the walls and the backdrop of the High Atlas Mountains is quite wonderful.

The gates can also be very useful to help with orientation. Bab er Robb, to the south-west, is the place to pick up a grand taxi to Asni whilst just beside Bab Doukkala, to the north-west, is the main bus station. Close to Bab Debbagh, on the east side, are the tanneries.

Gardens

Nearly half the area of the city, which is nearly nine miles in circumference, is occupied by gardens. The Moor believes not only that a garden was the original birthplace of mankind but also that the souls of virtuous Moslims will realise supreme beatitude in the radiant bowers of the Mohammedan paradise. **George D Cowan and RLN Johnston**, *Moorish Lotos Leaves,* 1883

Marrakech is rightly famous for its gardens which serve both a practical and a spiritual need. However, as Muslim architecture places great emphasis on privacy, many of the most beautiful of the city's gardens, just like many of the city's most beautiful homes, are kept hidden, a secret from prying eyes. Few, for example, even know of the largest garden in the Medina (see Riad el Arsat opposite).

However, Marrakech is also famous for its public gardens which were first created by the Almoravids in the twelfth century. They were greatly aided by their creation of a revolutionary irrigation system which enabled water to be brought all the way to the city from the distant Atlas Mountains. Should you ever feel the need to escape the heat and hubbub of Marrakech, you could seek relaxation in any of the following.

Jardin Agdal First established by the Almoravids, who laid out an orchard garden in the twelfth century, it was irrigated by water brought from the Ourika Valley, more than 30km to the south, by a network of underground channels and ditches. Today, the gardens have expanded to cover more than 400 hectares.

The name '*Agdal*' derives from the Berber, meaning 'meadow on the banks of a wadi enclosed with a stone wall'. Its surrounding walls, with gates in each corner, in fact date to the nineteenth century when the gardens were enlarged and then enclosed with *pisé* walls. The largest of the pools, *Sahraj el Hana* or 'Tank of Health', is probably as old as the orchards themselves but was re-shaped at this time with *menzehs* (summer pavilions) constructed to overlook the water. The last of the pre-colonial sultans would have retreated here from the heat of the city to enjoy their summer picnics. You can do likewise along the shaded pathways which surround the pool's edge. The gardens are located just outside the southern walls of the Medina.

Usually open 9am-6pm, Fri and Sun, although closed when the king returns to Marrakech due to the garden's proximity to the royal palace. Entry free.

Jardin Menara Formerly the property of sultans, created in the twelfth or thirteenth century, these gardens are best recognised by the menzeh, a two-storey, nineteenth-century summer pavilion, presiding over them from their centre. The pavilion's pyramidal green roof, reflected in a huge artificial rectangular lake stretching before it, is filled with water flowing all the way from the distant Atlas Mountains on the southern horizon.

The views from the pavilion are marvellous, first beyond the immediate lake to the surrounding gardens of olive, palm and Cyprus trees, then across the walled red city, some three kilometres away to the east, and finally around to the peaks of the Atlas themselves. This is a perfect place to escape the hustle of the city and to enjoy a picnic. It is also a popular meeting place for lovers.

The gardens (☎ 0524-43 95 78; open daily 8am-6pm, entry free) are located south-west of Hivernage. The menzeh is open daily, 8am-12.30pm and 3-6pm, entry 15dh.

Jardin Majorelle Designed by artist Jacques Majorelle in 1924, deep within the French colonial period, and first opened by him to the public in 1947, the garden was purchased by business partners and lovers Pierre Berget and Yves Saint Laurent in 1980. Plants from all five continents can still be enjoyed here, including cacti, palms, bamboos, potted plants and aquatic plants.

At the heart of the garden lies the bold, blue Art Deco **Islamic Art Museum**, once the pavilion home of Berget and Saint Laurent, which now houses in just five small rooms their personal art collection of jewellery, weapons, carpets and more, gathered from as near and far as the Maghreb, the Orient, Africa and Asia.

In truth the garden, covering 12 acres, is just a little too small and a little too frequented to offer the peace and tranquillity which it once brought its owners, and its images published in glossy style magazines frankly appear more beautiful than the reality. Nevertheless, it was here that Saint Laurent chose to have his ashes scattered in June 2008.

The garden (☎ 0524-30 18 52; 🖳 www.jardinmajorelle.com) is just north-east of Guéliz, off avenue Yacoub el Mansour. It is open daily 8am-5pm, Oct to May; 8am-6pm, Jun to Sep. Entry 30dh, 15dh more for museum.

Hotel La Mamounia Spread over 20 acres in traditional Moroccan design, 'Arset el Mamoun', the gardens of the most famous hotel in Africa, are fit for royalty. Being a wedding gift from the Alaouite Sultan Mohammed ben Abdellah, who ruled Morocco in the eighteenth century, to his fourth son, Prince Moulay Mamoun, they predate the hotel and even lend their name to it. Today, a team of 34 gardeners is required to maintain their beauty and no fewer than 140,000 new plants are added each year. Officially reserved for the enjoyment of hotel guests, you will need to at least buy a drink on the hotel rear terrace in order to be allowed to enter the gardens. To enjoy them at their very best, as with so much in Morocco, come either at sunrise or at sunset.

The gardens, for so long closed during the renovation of the hotel (see Where to stay p108 and box p109), are now open once again.

Riad el Arsat The largest private garden, and the only true riad garden, in the Medina is behind the high walls of Riad el Arsat .

Within are 1600 square metres of rich, jungle-like greenery, plentiful singing birds, a splashing fountain, a fish pond and a small pool. The property itself was built by the Kabbaj family at the end of the nineteenth century but fell into multi-occupancy and decline in the 1960s. The current owner, Nicole Arbousset, has renovated it using a blend of European and Andalusian styles and furnished it with Moroccan rugs and artefacts. You are welcome to knock on the large wooden door and ask to view its garden.

Alternatively, you could stay for a meal, freshly prepared by Fatimah, the resident chef, or even book to stay in one of its four rooms (double rooms and suites are charged at €70-330 per room). This small hotel (☎ 0524-38 75 67; GSM ☎ 0661-21 21 40; 🖳 www.riad-elarsat-marra kech.com) offers a wonderful haven at the end of a strenuous trek.

MARRAKECH

5 OUARZAZATE

Although Ouarzazate has a long history, the town on view today dates almost exclusively from the modern colonial and post-colonial periods. From relatively humble origins, it was strategically developed and rapidly expanded during the period of French occupation at the end of the 1920s to fulfil the functional requirements of empire. It was thus transformed into an administrative centre, customs post and garrison town for the French Foreign Legion. The very name 'Ouarzazate' derives from Berber words, meaning 'without noise' or 'without confusion'; although a name given long ago, it is one that remains appropriate still and the air of functionalism which it breathed in the era of the French Protectorate continues.

The town's chief distinction, providing the main crossroads to the south, is admirably maintained and, if you are heading for Jbel Sirwa or Jbel Sahro, or even to the Sahara beyond, you will almost inevitably pass through here. Ouarzazate, however, is unlikely to offer you much more than a stopping-off point on your way to or from your trailhead. Given its good communication links, you may not need to be here longer than the time it takes for you to change a bus or taxi. However, should you decide to stay, you will find a modern, agreeable, easy-going town which can provide all the services you are likely to require, plus one or two pleasant distractions.

HISTORY

The origins of Ouarzazate are largely lost in the mists of the past but it is known to have grown in importance in ancient times as a crossing point for African traders who travelled from the deserts of the south to the cities of northern Morocco, and even to Europe, with their cargos of gold, salt and slaves. The ancient strategic importance of Ouarzazate is apparent from its position close to the confluence of the Draa, Dades and Ouarzazate valleys.

The rapid rise of the town to national and even international prominence is irrevocably linked to the rise in fortunes of the previously obscure Berber House of Glaoua at the turn of the nineteenth century. From their base at Telouet, high in the Atlas Mountains, their expansion of control over rival clans included their absorption of Ouarzazate. With time, this family came to rival even the authority of the crown and during the 1950s would play a key role first in deposing and then restoring the sultan to the throne of Morocco (see p51).

Ouarzazate was raised to dizzy heights once more during the 1980s by the twin forces of the film industry and tourism. First encouraged by the establishment of the Atlas Corporation Studios here (see pp131-2) and then internationally promoted to tourists as the gateway to the oases and the deserts of the south, a revival in hotel construction followed. The resulting period of optimism and fresh belief in the potential of the town, however, proved to be rather brief.

ARRIVAL AND DEPARTURE

By air

Royal Air Maroc (☎ 0524-88 23 48/88 32 36/88 51 02; 🖳 www.royalairmaroc.com) operates daily flights out of Taourirt Airport (☎ 0524-88 23 83), about 2km to the north-east of the town centre, to Casablanca from where connecting domestic and international flights can be caught. Flights to and from Casablanca, which take about one hour and cost from around 230dh, can also be booked at RAM's town office at 1 avenue Mohammed V (☎ 0524-89 91 50; 🖷 0524-89 91 59).

By bus

There are two bus stations in Ouarzazate: Mahta bus station (gare routière) 2km north-west of the town centre, and the older CTM bus station on avenue Mohammed V, at the eastern end of the town centre. Services from the CTM bus station (☎ 0524-88 24 27) are: **Agadir** 12.30pm; 130dh; 7hrs; **Agdz** 5.15am, 4pm; 30dh; 1hr; **Aoulouz** 12.30pm; 70dh; 3½hrs; **Boujdour** 12.30pm; 400dh; **Boumalne du Dades** noon; 45dh; 2hrs; **Casablanca** 10.30am, 10pm; 190dh; 10hrs; **Dakhla** 12.30pm; 480dh; **Errachidia** noon; 90dh; 6hrs; **Fes** 10.30am, 10pm; 290dh; **Goulimine** 12.30pm; 210dh; **Goulmima** noon; 80dh; 6hrs; **Laayoune** 12.30pm; 340dh; **Marrakech** 8.30am, 10.30am, 11.45am, 10pm; 100dh; 4hrs; **Meknes** 10.30am, 10pm; 275dh; **M'hamid** 4pm; 80dh; 6hrs; **Ouled Teima** 12.30pm; 100dh; 6½hrs; **Ouled Barhel** 12.30pm; 100dh; 4½hrs; **Qalaa't Mgouna/El Kelaa M'gouna** noon; 35dh; 1½hrs; **Rabat** 10.30am, 10pm; 225dh; 10½hrs; **Taliwine** 12.30pm; 60dh; 3hrs; **Tan Tan** 12.30pm; 260dh; **Tangier** 10.30am, 10pm; 330dh; **Taroudannt** 12.30pm; 90dh; 5½hrs; **Tazenacht** 12.30pm; 30dh; 1½hrs; **Tinejdad** noon; 70dh; 4hrs; **Tinerhir** noon; 60dh; 3hrs; **Zagora** 5.15am, 4pm; 50dh; 3hrs.

CTM (☎ 0524-77 20 15 33) also have a ticket office at the gare routière where all other bus companies, including SATAS (☎ 0524-88 30 53), Trans Ghazala, Chia Tours (☎ 0524-30 11 25/53 79), Marhaban Tours, Diana Viajes, Marhaban Tour and Trans Bougafer, are based, offering a huge number of alternative departure times, fares and journey durations. SATAS, for example, runs buses to **Marrakech** at 9am, to **Agadir** at 10am and to **Taroudannt** at 10am, as well as international buses, departing at 9am on Mondays, Thursdays and Saturdays to **Paris** (850dh), to **Strasbourg** (900dh) and to **Italy** (1000dh).

The gare routière offers the service of a left-luggage office *(consigne)* charging 5dh per item for each 24hr period. There is also a range of small café-restaurants as well as a *Poste de Police*.

LOCAL TRANSPORT

Taxis

A seat in a grand taxi costs 90dh to or from Marrakech and 30dh to or from Qalaa't Mgouna. The main grand taxi rank is just in front of Mahta bus station.

Should you arrive in Ouarzazate either by grand taxi or on a bus run by any company other than CTM, you may wish to take a petit taxi ride from Mahta bus station into the centre of town for around 10-15dh. If you arrive by plane, a taxi ride from Taourirt Airport will cost around 20-30dh.

Car hire

There is a wide range of car-hire dealers from which to select in Ouarzazate, mostly located either along avenue Mohammed V or around place du 3 Mars; while some are international companies, others are local to Morocco. They include:

- **Toudra Cars** (☎ 0524-88 85 48) avenue Mohammed V
- **Draa Car** (☎ 0524-88 81 06; GSM ☎ 0661-64 64 46; 🖳 draacar05@yahoo.fr) avenue Mohammed V

- **Hertz** (☎ 0524-88 20 84; GSM ☎ 0663-61 42 10; 🖳 ouarzazate@hertz.ma) 33 avenue Mohammed V
- **Budget** (☎ 0524-88 42 02; 🖳 www.budget.ma) 4 avenue Mohammed V
- **Tiflit Car** (☎/🖹 0524-88 48 17) avenue Mohammed V
- **Europcar** (☎ 0524-88 20 35; GSM ☎ 0661-17 13 16) place du 3 Mars
- **Avis** (☎ 0524-88 80 00) avenue Mohammed V
- **National/Alamo** (☎ 0524-88 20 84; 🖳 avisozz@menara.com) place du 3 Mars.

ORIENTATION

The main focus for trekkers passing through Ouarzazate is almost bound to be avenue Mohammed V, the principal road through the centre of the town. Nearly all services and points of interest lie along or immediately off this thoroughfare, particularly between Mahta gare routière to the west and Kasbah Taourirt to the east. Allow up to an hour to walk between these two points.

SERVICES

Banks and currency exchange

Numerous banks line avenue Mohammed V, including Crédit du Maroc, Banque Populaire, Crédit Agricole and Société Générale; nearly all with an ATM. There are also several currency-exchange facilities provided by Western Union and Attijariwafa (see town plan p128).

Churches

Église Sainte Thérèse, just south of avenue Mohammed V close to the central mosque, celebrates mass at 7pm on Sundays and Thursdays.

Communications

There are several **téléboutiques** in central Ouarzazate, a number of which also provide a **fax service**. If in need of making a reverse charge call, head for the main post office (see column opposite).

There are a number of centrally located **internet cafés**. The most convenient is likely to be Cyber Café on avenue Mohammed V close to the Hertz rental office (see town plan p128).

The main **post office**, which offers a *poste restante* service, is at the junction of avenue Mohammed V and rue de la Poste at the eastern end of the town centre.

Medical emergencies

The **public hospital**, Hôpital Bougafer (☎ 0524-88 24 44) is at the far eastern end of avenue Mohammed V between the town centre and Kasbah Taourirt.

There are a few **pharmacies** along avenue Mohammed V from Pharmacie de la Renaissance, close to place du 3 Mars in the west, to Pharmacie Annour, near the main post office in the east. They are open Monday to Friday 8am-10.30pm, as well as on Saturday 8.30am-12.30pm. Try also Pharmacie Centrale (☎ 0524-88 26 01) at 31 avenue Mohammed V, next to Hertz, or Pharmacie du Nuit (sic; ☎ 0524-88.24.90), the all-night chemist, also on avenue Mohammed V, opposite the post office.

Supermarkets and shopping

Super Marché (open daily 8am-10pm) about halfway along avenue Mohammed V, close to the BMCE bank and opposite Restaurant Chez Dimitri, quite apart from holding a reasonable selection of groceries, also sells alcohol. Supermarché Dades (open daily 8am-1pm and 4-10pm) on avenue Moulay Rachid has a better selection of groceries.

For arts and crafts, you might want to head out to the **ensemble artisanal** (open daily 9am-12.30pm and 3-6pm) opposite Kasbah Taourirt, about 30 minutes' walk to the east of the town centre along avenue Mohammed V.

Swimming pools

The municipal swimming pool, reached by following avenue Mohammed V, is situated 2km east of the town centre close by the municipal campsite and a new tourist complex. In addition La Perle du Sud (see Where to Stay p130) allows public use of its outdoor pool (50dh) at the rear of the hotel.

Tourist information office

The tourist information office (☎ 0524-88 24 85; 🖹 0524-88 52 90), open Monday to Friday 8.30am-4.30pm, is reached by following avenue Mohammed V to the east to the point just past the post office at the Zagora road junction.

Trekking agencies

The experienced **Désert et Montagne** (☎ 0524-85 49 46/49; 🖳 www.desert-montagne.ma), Douar Talmasla, Tarmigt, BP93, 45000 Ouarzazate, offers a wide range of specialised treks in the Atlas, Anti-Atlas and along the Atlantic coast, including camel treks and excursions by 4x4.

Try also **La Baraka du Sud** (☎ 0524-88 57 52; GSM ☎ 0661-86 39 97/071-84 10 03; 🖳 www.labarakadusud.com) on avenue Mohammed V, a little east of Hotel Royal; they offer a wide range of excursions, specialising in desert treks, including a 15-day epic from Ouarzazate to M'hamid.

There are a number of smaller organisations along avenue Mohammed V which offer tours and excursions, including **Iriqui Excursions** (☎ 0524-88 57 99; 🖳 www.iriqui.com) place du 3 Mars and **Cheguagua Tours** (☎ 0524-88 43 66; 🖷: 0524-88 43 68) opposite the Royal Air Maroc offices.

WHERE TO STAY

A good number of hotels, including most of the budget hotels, many of which are satisfactory or better, are located in central Ouarzazate. However, many of the mid-priced hotels are in the suburb of Tabounte, 2km to the south across the Oued Ouarzazate, but are not included in this guide as they are a little out of the way to be of interest to those passing through on their way to or from a trek. Nonetheless, should you decide to aim for Tabounte, the two star ***Hotel Saghro*** (☎ 0524-85 43 05) comes strongly recommended, largely because of the friendliness of the staff.

Budget accommodation

The municipal campsite, ***Camping-Restaurant Ouarzazate*** (☎ 0524-88 40 26/46 36), 2km east of the centre, next to a new tourist complex, offers the cheapest accommodation of all, although reportedly the washrooms are often not so clean. The campsite is shaded and usually quiet, with hot showers available for 5dh and a simple menu for 40dh. One benefit of opting for the campsite is the easy access that it offers to the municipal swimming pool which is just next door.

At 13 rue du Marché the newly decorated, 42-roomed ***Hotel Atlas*** (☎ 0524-88 77 45; 🖷 0524-88 64 85), fresh with bright paint, provides very good value for money. Any inconvenience of noise emanating from the busy street immediately outside its front door is likely to be offset by the friendliness of the very hospitable manager and his son, who speaks English well. Simple rooms (40/80/100dh) as well as en suite rooms (60/120/150dh) are available.

The slightly grander 33-roomed ***Hotel Royal*** (☎ 0524-88 22 58), on avenue Mohammed V, offers a choice of simple rooms (45/80/100dh), rooms with shower only (70/100/140dh) and en suite rooms (90/120/160dh), all of which are generally both light and spacious. The hotel has the added benefit of a very pleasant restaurant with a terrace which spills onto the main street.

If these two are full, try the basic ***Hotel Hicham*** (☎ 0524-88 54 59), a little more difficult to find off avenue Mohammed VI, formerly avenue Prince Héritier Sidi Mohammed, on the edge of the market. Not quite of the same standard as the previous two hotels, simple rooms are available for 45/80/110/140dh and rooms with showers for 70/120/170dh. A television can be provided (10dh), as can a ventilator (10dh) and a heater (30dh).

It is more difficult to recommend ***Hotel Es-Salaam*** (☎ 0524-88 25 12), back on avenue Mohammed V, when the management proved so obstructive to my visit. Of all the hotels I visited in the writing of this book, this was the only occasion where I was not permitted so much as a viewing of a room nor even a *carte visite*. Nevertheless, if you want to push your luck, simple rooms are available for 45/90/120dh and rooms with shower for 70/130/160dh.

Mid-priced hotels

The slightly old-fashioned, one-storeyed ***Hotel La Gazelle*** (☎ 0524-88 21 51; 🖷 0524-88 47 27) is conveniently situated

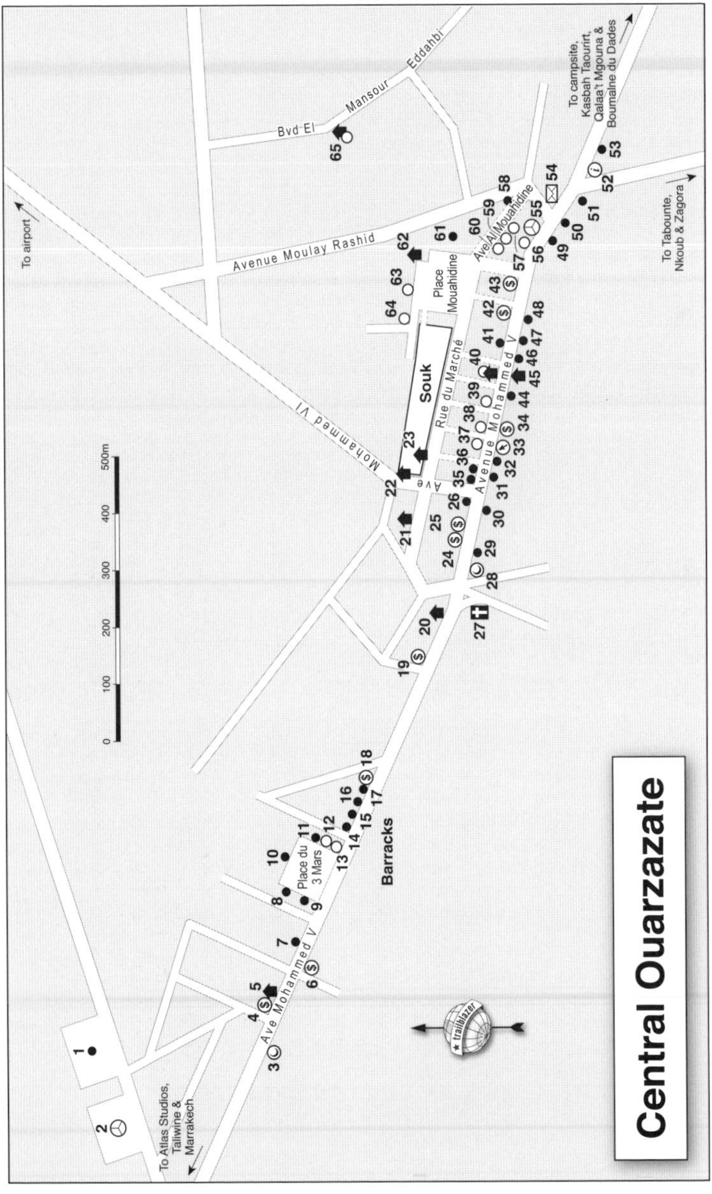

Central Ouarzazate

OUARZAZATE MAP KEY

Where to stay

5 Hotel La Gazelle
20 La Perle du Sud
21 Hotel Amlal
22 Hotel Hicham
23 Hotel Atlas
40 Hotel Royal
45 Hotel Es-Salam
62 Hotel Bab Essahara
65 Le Berbère Palace

Where to eat and drink

5 Hotel La Gazelle
12 Glacier 3 Mars
13 Café Glacier Snack Delphine
20 7ème Art/Safari Club
37 Café Restaurant La Renaissance
38 La Fibule
39 Chez Dimitri
40 Café Picasso & Restaurant Royal
56 Café Restaurant des Voyageurs
57 Restaurant Erraha
59 Café Restaurant Sable d'Or
60 Restaurant Pizzeria La Halte
63 Café Restaurant Aux Bon Amis
64 Boulangerie Patisserie Glacier
65 Le Berbère Palace

Other

1 Taxi rank
2 Mahta bus station
3 Mosque
4 Banque Crédit du Maroc
6 Banque Populaire
7 Shell petrol station
8 National & Alamo car rental
9 Ksour Voyages
10 Palais des Congrès
11 Europcar
14 Pharmacie de la Renaissance
15 Avis
16 Toudra Car
17 Iriqui Excursions
18 Société Générale (ATM & Western Union)
19 Crédit Agricole (no ATM)
24 Crédit Agricole (ATM)
25 Wafa
26 Royal Air Maroc (RAM)
27 Église Saint Thérèse
28 Central mosque
29 Draa Car
30 Cheguagua Tours
31 Pharmacie Centrale
32 Hertz
33 Cyber Café/Téléboutique
34 BMCI Bank (ATM)
35 Budget
36 Launderette
41 La Baraka du Sud
42 Attijariwafa (ATM)
43 Banque Populaire (ATM & Moneygram)
44 Supermarket
46 Tiflit Car
47 Pharmacie Ouarzazate
48 Shell petrol station
49 Pharmacie Annour
50 Pharmacie du Nuit
51 Fountain
52 Tourist Information Office
53 Co-operative Artisanale de Tapis
54 Post Office
55 CTM bus station
58 Atlas Cinema (closed)
61 Water tower

close to Mahta gare routière should you arrive by bus or grand taxi late at night. The downside is that you are likely to be awoken by other travellers either arriving or departing well into the small hours. This is somewhat offset by the hotel's old-fashioned charm, set well back from the road and built around a small central garden. Rooms, all en suite, are charged at 127.50/159/212.50dh. Extra beds can be provided for 53dh and breakfast for 21dh, served in the attached licensed bar-restaurant.

Also in this price range is ***Hotel Bab Essahara*** (☎ 0524-88 47 22; 📠 0524-88 44 65) in the corner of place Mouahidine. Front rooms overlook the square and its two restaurants, on the first and ground floors, are open to the public. En suite rooms are charged at 120/180dh, including breakfast.

The most expensive hotel in this category is ***Hotel Restaurant Amlal*** (☎ 0524-88 40 30; GSM ☎ 0661-36 88 03; 📠 0524-88 46 00) off rue du Marché, which provides good, clean rooms at 200/250/300/350dh or at 285/440/585/740dh for half-board. The hotel has a restaurant which is open to the public and offers a car rental service, although its low-level lighting creates a bit of a dingy atmosphere.

Finally, should you decide to venture out to visit the Atlas Film Corporation Studios, you may opt to stay at their Oscar Hotel (see p132).

Upmarket hotels

The most conveniently situated hotel in this category is the modern, 68-roomed ***La Perle du Sud*** (☎ 0524-88 86 40/41; 💻 www.hotelperledusud.com) at 40 avenue Mohammed V, which has been designed with half an eye for Berber traditions, evident from its fine reed ceilings. Rooms start from 360/500dh (with shower) to 950/1100dh for the senior suites. Breakfast is charged at an additional 60dh and lunch or dinner at 150dh. The restaurant, open to the public, puts on a buffet of Moroccan and international cuisine whenever 50 or more guests are expected, at a charge of 100-120dh per head. The spacious salon has wifi; at the rear of the hotel is an open-air swimming pool, admission 50dh for non-residents, with a separate, shallow area for children. The hotel also has a piano bar and night club (see opposite).

The outstanding hotel in Ouarzazate is the beautifully and traditionally furnished five-star ***Le Berbère Palace*** (☎ 0524-88 31 05; 💻 www.ouarzazate.com/leberberepalace) in the nearby Quartier el Mansour Eddahbi, just north-east of the previously listed hotels. Rooms start at 2300dh rising to 12,000dh for the Grand Visir suite. Buffet breakfast is available for 150dh, buffet lunch and buffet dinner each for 300dh. Three restaurants specialise in Moroccan, French and Italian delicacies respectively.

In addition to three tennis courts, the hotel also has a fitness centre providing a hammam, a Jacuzzi, a gymnasium and a sauna, as well as a hairdressing and massage service.

WHERE TO EAT

There are many simple and inexpensive places to eat in central Ouarzazate. Several line the south-facing side of avenue Mohammed V providing sunny terraces in the mornings on which to enjoy French-style breakfasts. There are others on place du 3 Mars and on rue du Marché, with some around the market itself, and yet more around place Mouahidine.

One of the more popular café-restaurants on avenue Mohammed V is ***La Fibule*** which, typical of most in Ouarzazate, clears away breakfast to offer grills, tagines and salads both in the afternoon and evening. Try also one of the three pleasant restaurants, all with terrace seating, on the section of avenue Al Mouahidine which leads east from the square itself towards the post office: ***Restaurant Pizzeria La Halte***, ***Café Restaurant Sable d'Or*** and ***Restaurant Erraha***, virtually next door to each other, provide the usual slightly cosmopolitan menu of pastas, pizzas, salads, couscous and tagines at good prices.

More expensive, perhaps even overpriced, is the historic and slightly chic ***Chez Dimitri*** (☎ 0524-88 73 46; 💻 oalimentaire@menara.ma) at 22 avenue Mohammed V. Founded in 1928 in one of the oldest buildings in Ouarzazate, previously a post office, a petrol station and also the first public house in town, this fully licensed restaurant offers a range of Moroccan and continental dishes. Apparently frequented by both political personalities and film stars, signed photographs of the likes of Omar Sharif, Orson Welles and Hilary Clinton adorn its walls. It is just a pity that the vegetable tagine served to me was not a patch on those produced by my cuisinier on a single gas burner while on the trail in the Jbel Sahro.

In addition, a number of hotels have restaurants open to the public, the much celebrated ***Le Berbère Palace*** (see opposite) providing the best restaurant in central Ouarzazate.

NIGHTLIFE

By 10pm the streets of Ouarzazate empty and there is little to be enjoyed in terms of entertainment. It is a sad irony that the town which boasts the Atlas Film Corporation Studios (see column opposite) cannot support a cinema: even the centrally located Atlas Cinéma, just off place Mouahidine, has been closed for many a year and shows no signs of reopening. This is an irony not lost on the local youth kicking about in the street.

If in search of a late-night drink, amongst the better possibilities are those provided by some of the hotels. ***Hotel la Gazelle*** has a quiet licensed bar. La Perle du Sud has ***7ème Art***, a tapas bar, referred to by the staff as a piano bar, adjacent to the main building. La Perle also has a nightly discotheque, ***Safari Club***, inside the hotel, to which there is a separate, external access door from the street for those who are not clients of the hotel.

WHAT TO SEE

Kasbah Taourirt

The only genuine tourist attraction in Ouarzazate, the impressive structure of Kasbah Taourirt (daily 8am-6.30pm; entry 10dh) is a 30-minute walk along avenue Mohammed V to the east of the town centre. Built in the nineteenth century by Berber chiefs belonging to the House of Glaoua, it was then probably the largest Kasbah in Morocco. Its importance grew with the fortunes of the family, reaching its zenith when, in the 1950s, the Glaoua family, already the most powerful in the country outside the royal family, successfully challenged the power of the Sultan (see History p51). Although Glaoua chiefs themselves never lived in the kasbah, its control, and with it a firm grip of the important trade routes to the south, was maintained by their close relatives.

Following independence in 1956, the kasbah was taken over by the government. Unfortunately, like many Glaoua monuments during this period, it was then allowed to fall into decline. Many would argue, given the unlikely power previously held by the House of Glaoua, that the government was making a political point. Although recently some restoration work has at last been funded, many parts have already fallen into complete ruin or even collapsed entirely, whilst others, towards the rear, continue to be occupied by those who, for decades, have made the kasbah their home.

Amongst those rooms to which access is still possible are some fine decorations, including painted stuccos and cedar-wood ceilings. Perhaps most intriguing of all is the 77mm Krupps gun, which is on view outside the kasbah. Given in gratitude by Sultan Moulay al-Hassan to the House of Glaoua in 1893, its ownership was the single most important factor responsible for the rise to prominence of this family. For a gripping account of this remarkable episode in Moroccan history, see Gavin Maxwell's *Lords of the Atlas, the Rise and Fall of the House of Glaoua*.

Atlas Film Corporation Studios

Following the shooting of the widely acclaimed *Lawrence of Arabia* at the Aït Benhaddou Kasbah in 1962 in the nearby Atlas Mountains, others were awakened to the enormous potential for film production offered by southern Morocco. The resulting Atlas Film Corporation Studios (☎ 0524-88 22 12; daily 9am-6pm; entry 50dh for a 30-min tour) begun in 1983 by Mohamed Belghmi, owner of the Salam hotel chain, were the first film studios to be built in the country, 5km west of Ouarzazate on the Marrakech road.

Many internationally renowned films have been shot here in recent years, including *Jewel of the Nile, Kundun, Gladiator*, and *Asterix and Obelisk*. Spread over 150 hectares, here is an opportunity, restrictions imposed by film-shooting permitted, to wander around some of the original film sets.

Regrettably the studios have of late received poor reviews from those taking the tour, complaining in particular that the scenery is not well maintained. However, should you wish to extend your stay the well-equipped ***Oscar Hotel*** (☎ 0524-88 22 12; 💻 www.oscarhotel.ma) is within the grounds. There are 65 first-floor air-conditioned rooms (€30/41/58 including breakfast), all with satellite television. The hotel has its own outdoor swimming pool as well as an appropriately named Cleopatra Restaurant and Gladiator Bar.

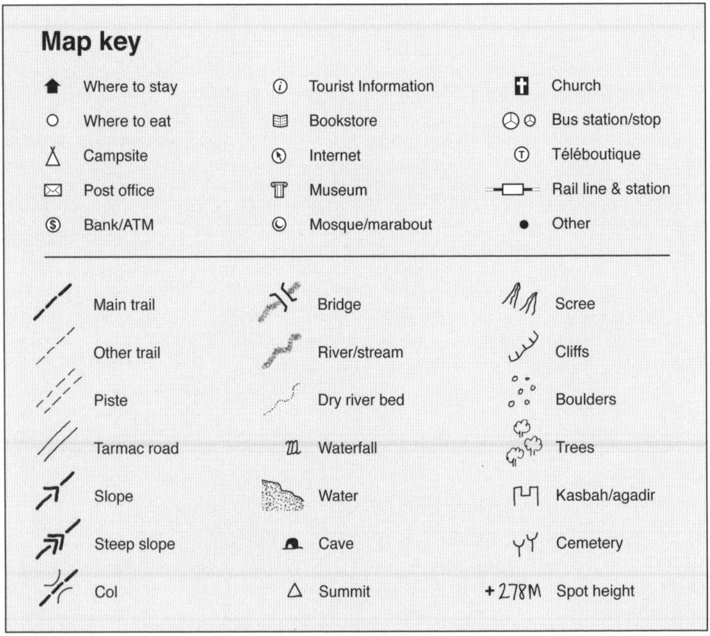

Map key

Where to stay	Tourist Information	Church
Where to eat	Bookstore	Bus station/stop
Campsite	Internet	Téléboutique
Post office	Museum	Rail line & station
Bank/ATM	Mosque/marabout	Other
Main trail	Bridge	Scree
Other trail	River/stream	Cliffs
Piste	Dry river bed	Boulders
Tarmac road	Waterfall	Trees
Slope	Water	Kasbah/agadir
Steep slope	Cave	Cemetery
Col	Summit	+278M Spot height

TRAIL GUIDE & MAPS 6

Using this guide

ROUTE MAPS

Scale and walking times

Timings in any mountains, no less in the Moroccan Atlas, can be one of life's great imponderables. Nevertheless, I have attempted to organise the treks in this book into convenient stages equating to the amount of ground you might reasonably expect to cover with enough time to rest at the end of each day and still enjoy your destination. Since everyone walks at a different speed, all timings given should be treated as approximate. Don't feel compelled to divide your trek into these exact same stages and do walk at your own pace (see p11). Until you do work out how your speed relates to those suggested, allow extra time.

Timings are given along the side of each trail map with arrows showing the direction to which the time refers. Black triangles depict the points between which the timings were taken. Since these timings are for actual walking you will need to add on time for rests or stops along the way. If you are planning a longer trek than those described in this book, allow a rest day every five days or so. Finally, try not to cover too much ground too quickly; the appeal of trekking is, after all, the slow pace that gives you the chance to really see the country.

Up or down?

The trail is shown on the maps as a dotted line. An arrow across the trail depicts a slope; two arrows show the slope is steep. The arrows point to the higher part of the trail. If, for example, you were walking from A (at 900m) to B (at 1100m) and the trail between the two were short and steep, it would be shown thus: A– – –>> – – –B. The spot heights on the trail maps have, for the most part, been taken from the Division de la Carte 1:100,000 map series.

Place names

Any word printed on a Moroccan map in Roman letters has been transcribed from either a Berber dialect, itself rarely written, or from Arabic (see p70). This can lead to a lot of problems. Place names in particular can often be spelled differently from one map to another. Different spellings of place names are shown in this route guide but

only on the first mention of that place name eg'Imlil/Imelil' (below). Where places referred to in the text are not shown on any of the recommended maps, an attempt has been made to spell these names phonetically (see also Glossary, pp254-6).

Water sources

Natural water sources, or springs, usually provide the safest water to drink on the trail and trekkers should replenish their bottles whenever such opportunities arise. An attempt has been made to mark all water sources on the route maps. Nonetheless, it is recommended that even source water should be treated with some caution (see Water Purification Systems, p29); always treat before drinking.

The Toubkal region

Most High Atlas trekkers make Jbel Toubkal (4167m/13,670ft), the highest peak in North Africa, their first goal. Indeed, in season about 90% of trekkers in the Atlas Mountains are likely to be in the Toubkal Region at any one time. Toubkal is easy to reach from Marrakech and, although it is not advised here, the summit can be tackled in just a couple of days (see pp138-44).This is a stark but exceptionally striking region. The views from the summit of Toubkal provide a wonderful opportunity to see the way in which the Atlas Mountains form a spine across the length of Morocco, dividing a gleaming Atlantic coast to the north and west from the scorching vastness of Saharan Africa to the south and east.

GETTING TO IMLIL/IMELIL

By far the simplest and most efficient way to get from Marrakech to Imlil is to take a *grand taxi*. If you have just landed at Aéroport Marrakech-Menara, you may choose to negotiate a direct ride without entering Marrakech at all. Otherwise you will need to get to the taxi rank just outside Bab er Robb, the gate on the south-west edge of the Medina. The journey from Marrakech to Imlil takes 75 minutes; a place should cost 30dh or you could book a private taxi for 200dh. Alternatively, buses from Marrakech (20dh) run as far as Asni (47km) in 90 minutes. A morning bus (Line 3) runs from the *gare routière* at Bab Doukkala leaving at 10.30am, but is unreliable at the best of times and grinds to a halt altogether during Ramadan. A much more trustworthy afternoon bus departs from Bab er Robb, by the taxi rank, at 1pm. Additionally, minibuses (20dh) also leave from Bab er Robb for Asni every two hours.

From Asni you would then need to organise transport for the final 17km to Imlil. The asphalting of the road means this journey is now easy. Although trucks (10dh) still frequent the route, particularly on Saturdays, the day of the Asni souk, one of the most important in the region, it is frowned upon to take a lorry when taxis are available. A place in a shared taxi from Asni to Imlil costs 15dh and a private taxi 50dh. There are also five or six minibuses daily (15dh).

At the time of writing there were no regular taxis to take trekkers back to Imlil from Tacheddirt at the end of the trek. It would be best therefore to organise your return taxi before first setting out on your trek. There is, of course, no set price for this trip though a taxi from Tacheddirt back to Marrakech, via Imlil if you need to drop off your guide, could cost around 500dh (£40/$60), or even 600dh should you opt for a 4x4.

Asni

There is little reason to spend time in Asni itself, being but a lively roadside village offering little more for most of the week than a handful of cheap cafés. Granted, the Saturday **souk** would provide a good opportunity to stock up on supplies. If, however, you seek luxurious accommodation there's Richard Branson's ***Kasbah Tamadot*** (☎ 024.36.82.00, 💻 www.kasbahtamadot.virgin.com; 24 rooms) just outside Asni along the road to Imlil. Rates start at €360 per night in the low season rising to €1700 in the high season for the master suite which consists of three bedrooms and a private pool. This truly beautiful hotel, built around a series of courtyards and gardens, also has an indoor and outdoor pool, a hammam, a gym, tennis facilities, a restaurant and a bar.

IMLIL

This busy, colourful trailhead (1740m/5707ft) in the Aït Mizane Valley serves trekkers well. There are several cafés, places to stay and a Bureau des Guides through which you can very easily organise your trek using official guides. Do, however, make sure that you have sufficient dirhams with you before you arrive in Imlil as there is neither a bank nor a currency-exchange facility here.

Services

The simple **alimentation générale** (grocery) and the **pharmacie**, on the left-hand side of the street as you climb a little further beyond Hotel Étoile du Toubkal, could furnish you with basic needs.

Trekking agencies and guides

- The **Bureau des Guides** (☎/📠 0524-48 56 26), situated in the rear corner of the car park opposite Café Resta, is the best place to find an official guide or for general advice about trekking in the Toubkal region. There are 32 official guides based in Imlil of whom five to ten are likely to be available at any one time. Their named photographs are on display inside the bureau. They operate a rota system amongst themselves so you will be offered whichever guide is next in line for work. Mules, muleteers, food and equipment can all be organised very swiftly. The bureau is keen to emphasise their expertise in all areas of both the High and the Anti-Atlas Mountains and indeed their ability to lead treks throughout Morocco.
- **Jamal Imerhane** (GSM ☎ 0671-15 76 36; 💻 www.toubkalguide.com) is an extremely positive and helpful official guide based at the Bureau des Guides who speaks excellent English.

Where to stay

There are a quickly growing number of places to stay both in and around Imlil.

One of the less expensive, near to the northern entrance of the village, is ***Dar El Aine Auberge Café Restaurant*** (GSM ☎ 0670-40 56 70) which charges 50dh, including hot shower, and serves breakfast (15dh) and meals (30-60dh).

The ***CAF refuge and campsite*** (☎/📠 0524-48 51 22; GSM ☎ 0677-30 74 15), conveniently located next to the Bureau des Guides, charges members 35dh for dormitory accommodation, non-members

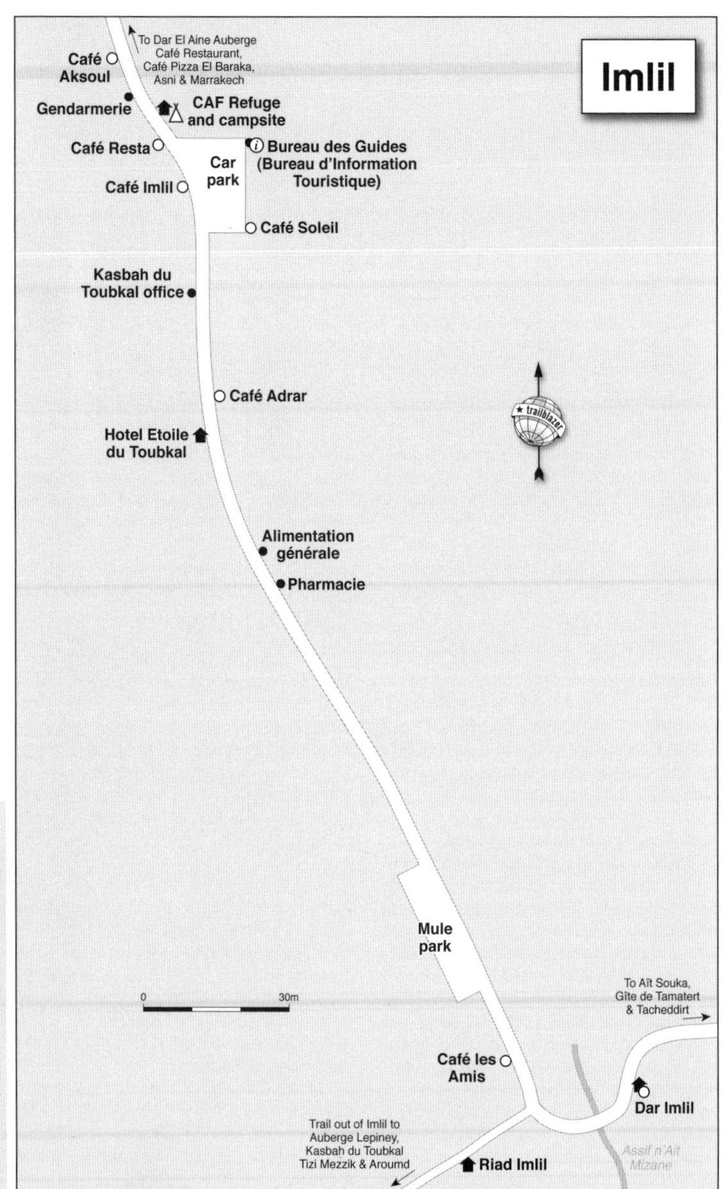
Imlil
To Dar El Aine Auberge
Café Restaurant,
Café Pizza El Baraka,
Asni & Marrakech
Café Aksoul
Gendarmerie
CAF Refuge and campsite
Café Resta
Bureau des Guides (Bureau d'Information Touristique)
Car park
Café Imlil
Café Soleil
Kasbah du Toubkal office
Café Adrar
Hotel Etoile du Toubkal
trailblazer
Alimentation générale
Pharmacie
Mule park
0
30m
To Aït Souka,
Gîte de Tamatert
& Tacheddirt
Café les Amis
Dar Imlil
Trail out of Imlil to
Auberge Lepiney,
Kasbah du Toubkal
Tizi Mezzik & Aroumd
Riad Imlil
Assif n'Aït Mizane

carrying the *Guide Routard* 60dh, and all others 85dh per night. A hot shower is 10dh, breakfast 30dh and meals 80dh. It costs 15dh plus 20dh per person to pitch a small tent in its grounds. Campers must pay 12dh for a hot shower. The kitchen is available to all residents for a 15dh charge. Another good, inexpensive option is ***Auberge Lepiney*** (☎ 0524-48 56 88; GSM ☎ 0668-67 35 84; 💻 www.imlil.org/auberge_lepiney.htm) about 500m along the piste leading west from the centre of Imlil towards Tizi Mezzik. This small, bright, clean and friendly gîte has its own café, restaurant and small camping ground. Single beds in dormitories are available for 130dh and twin rooms for 300dh (including breakfast).

At the southern end of Imlil are three newer, more comfortable establishments, all of which have been built in keeping with Berber traditions. The rather dark and austere ***Riad Imlil*** (☎/📠 0524-48 54 85; GSM ☎ 0661-24 05 99; 💻 www.imlil.org/riad_imlil.htm) has 20 rooms (€45/70 half-board).

Just above Imlil, on the trail to Aroumd, is the much-celebrated ***Kasbah du Toubkal***. Owned by British-based Discover Ltd (UK ☎ 01883-744392; 💻 www.kasbahdutoubkal.com), rates including breakfast range from €130 for a small Berber salon for three people to €160 for a standard double room, and up to €430 for the apartment suite. In addition there is a 5% surcharge which goes towards the Imlil Village Association (*Association des Bassins d'Imlil*) to fund community projects such as an ambulance service and rubbish clearance. Lunch (15dh) and dinner (20dh) can be ordered. Most unusually in the Atlas Mountains, the hotel accepts Visa and MasterCard. A hammam is available for guests free of charge. Both accommodation and treks, including guided ascents of Jbel Toubkal, can be booked through the **Kasbah du Toubkal** office in Imlil.

Back in Imlil, on the far eastern bank of the river, just away from the main thrust of the village, is the exquisite ***Dar Imlil***, also owned by Discover Ltd. Created through the renovation of an old riad, this *maison d'hôte* provides a true haven amidst leafy plants, old pots and traditional lanterns spread over three storeys. Opened in 2005, prices range from 1300dh for a standard double to 2000dh for a suite, including breakfast. Even the standard rooms are so big that they would be called suites in most other hotels. The additional 5% levy charged at Kasbah du Toubkal is also raised here.

Across the road, and just a little higher up from the Bureau des Guides, the completely rebuilt ***Hotel Étoile du Toubkal*** (☎ 0524-48 56 18, GSM: 0661-34 31 40, 💻 www.hotel-etoile-toubkal.com) reopened in 2009. It has 18 en suite rooms with balconies; rates are €20-25/30-35/40-45 including breakfast, and €30-35/50-55/80-85 for half-board. The hotel has a two restaurants and a fine garden.

There are several gîtes in the villages surrounding Imlil, notably in Aït Souka, and no shortage of owners on the main street of Imlil willing to tell you about theirs too. However, try the impressive ***Gîte de Tamatert*** (GSM ☎ 0667-16 89 06/ 0671-15 76 36; 💻 www.atlasguest.com), owned by three brothers, Mohamed, Jamal and Rachid Imerhane, all official mountain guides, about 1km along the road to Tacheddirt. It offers good, clean rooms (half-board 160dh/320dh) and lovely views over Imlil.

Where to eat

There are a number of inexpensive places to eat lining the main road through Imlil. First as you enter from Marrakech is ***Café Pizza El Baraka***. You pass ***Dar El Aine Auberge Café Restaurant***, ***Café Aksoul***, and ***Café Resta*** before you have even reached the Bureau des Guides. All serve satisfactory traditional, if limited, fare for as little as 30dh, as do the more central ***Café Imlil***, ***Café Soleil*** and ***Café Adrar***. Towards the top of the village, just after the mule park on the right-hand side of the road, is the very popular terrace of ***Café les Amis***.

If you're looking for something a little more sophisticated, ***Dar Imlil*** serves both lunch and dinner (€20) to non-residents. If you are prepared to undertake the short climb to ***Kasbah du Toubkal***, non-residents can take lunch for €30 and dinner for just €5 more.

TOUBKAL CIRCULAR TREK

> **TOUBKAL CIRCULAR TREK**
> - **Level of difficulty** Strenuous
> - **Duration** 6-7 days
> - **Maps** Either *Okaïmeden-Toubkal* 1:100,000 (Division de la Carte, Morocco Survey) or *Jbel Toubkal* 1:50,000 (Division de la Carte, Morocco Survey)

This route involves a climb to the summit of Jbel Toubkal (4167m/13,670ft). All trekkers should be aware of the symptoms and dangers of altitude sickness and the necessary response to them (see box pp258-9). Because of the proximity of Toubkal to Marrakech and the potential for a rapid ascent to the summit, many trekkers ascend too quickly and suffer the consequences. The route described here is the classic trek in the region and the one likely to be suggested by your guide, although it is perhaps not the ideal route to the summit. There are alternatives which would offer a more gradual, gentle approach and more time for acclimatisation. See the routes indicated by red dots on the 1:50,000 map for suggestions.

If you do choose to follow the route described here, do not rush straight from Imlil (1740m/5707ft), despite the lure of the peaks ahead of you, but spend a night there and even possibly a second at Aroumd/Around (1960m/6428ft), albeit that Aroumd is just a short morning's walk beyond Imlil. The trail, even from Aroumd to Neltner Refuge (3207m/10,520ft), involves a steady but demanding climb of well over 1000m. The route description for this trek is arranged as a six-day trek. Allow seven days if you stay overnight at Aroumd.

Imlil–Aroumd/Around–Neltner Refuge [Map 1, p140]

From the Bureau des Guides, walk south through Imlil, passing first Hotel Étoile du Toubkal and then the mule park on your right. After five minutes, just beyond Café les Amis, turn right onto the road to Tizi Mezzik/Mzik. After just two more minutes the path climbs to the left from the road and winds through trees towards **Kasbah du Toubkal**.

Leaving the Kasbah behind, the path crosses an irrigation channel after 20 minutes then climbs more steeply still in a series of zigzags along a mule trail to the right. Follow the trail south for 25 minutes along the right-hand (west) bank of the valley until you are opposite the village of **Aroumd**. At this point turn steeply down to the river and cross by the bridge towards the village on the far side.

You may choose to enter the village itself. Behind the initial façade of a few newly built concrete houses, wind your way through its lanes to find a maze of traditional dwellings which form the heart of the old village. Aroumd has grown quickly in recent years and today 60% of its 1600 inhabitants are involved in tourism in some capacity. Accommodation is available: try ***Gîte Tourtatine*** (☎ 0524-36 16 80; GTM ☎ 0666-94 56 61; half-board 150dh, hot shower 10dh) at the eastern end of the village; it's owned by Aït Tadrart Ahmed.

From Aroumd, pass a small walled orchard on your right and pick up the trail along the left (eastern) edge of the river bed which quickly opens out into a wide floodplain. Thirty minutes from the village, the trail leaves the valley floor, briefly climbing in zigzags to the left.

The Marabout of Sidi Chamharouch

According to Berber tradition, on a night of nights one of these house-size boulders came crashing down from Adrar Tichki to entomb the famous saint, Chamharouch, as he lay fast asleep in his little hut. On the actual site, a shrine has been built to one side of the boulder... **Michael Peyron**, *Great Atlas Traverse*, Vol 1, 1989

If you watch the comings and goings carefully you will notice a steady stream of pilgrims from as far as Marrakech arriving, often on muleback, with animals in side baskets to sacrifice on the flat terrace immediately behind the *marabout*. Their faith brings them in the belief that Sidi Chamharouch may cure them or their loved ones of any mental health problem or emotional burden.

Once the animal has been sacrificed, the meat is shared with the poor, some of whom wait in hope close by. The tomb of the saint is enshrined by a huge white-painted boulder with colourful flags flying from the top. The building extending from the marabout is in fact a mosque. Close by, two water sources, concealed by a single small stone building, divided internally with separate entrances, provide the opportunity for men and women to bathe privately before undertaking their prayers. Non-Muslim visitors should note that the whole site, which is clearly visible across a small bridge, is reserved for those of the Muslim faith.

Sadly the annual *moussem*, which used to be held here in September, has been abandoned due to difficulties following celebrations in 2000. People from outside the region took it upon themselves to indulge in the wanton destruction of trees in and around Imlil, scenes which the local authorities felt they could not risk re-occurring.

Follow the path past one small isolated **shop** selling soft drinks to a second, neither usually open before 10am. Do not, however, assume that the nearby irrigation channel provides clean water as it merely siphons from the river water flowing higher up in the main valley.

Continue to follow the path, climbing steeply in places, for a further 80 minutes, enjoying beautiful views both up and down river. Then, shortly after passing a series of small waterfalls, descend once more to the valley floor to cross the river close to the *marabout* of **Sidi Chamharouch** (2310m/7579ft).It's possible to camp within the vicinity and very simple rooms are also available, although there are unlikely to be vacancies in summer particularly at weekends. There is no fixed price. A number of shops selling meals and drinks, as well as carpets and other Berber artefacts, face the religious complex from the right (western) bank. For a better view of proceedings return to the trail and climb up the right bank behind the shops, away from both the river and the throng surrounding the marabout, to a solitary **café** set upon a magnificent natural terrace offering a bird's eye view.

From the café, the path continues to climb, yet more gently, to the south and south-west, before reaching another small café at **Doudmet** (not marked on either the 1:100,000 or the 1:50,000 maps) after about 60 minutes. Here drinks

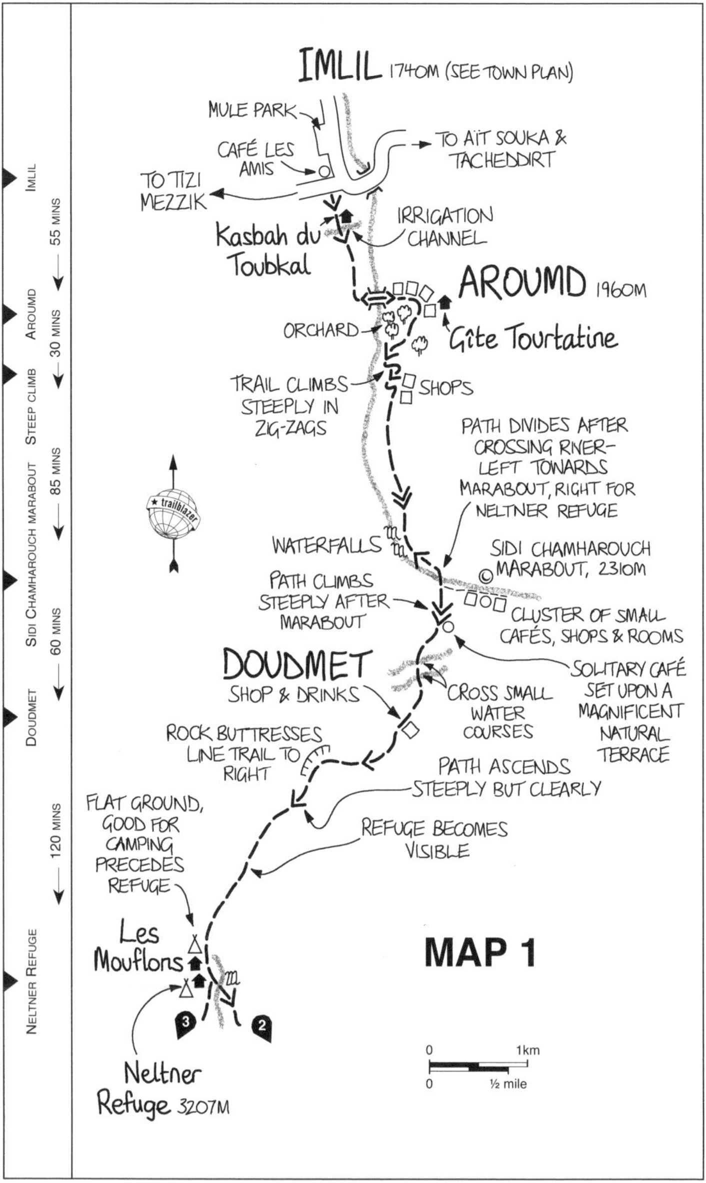

Imlil
55 mins
Aroumd
30 mins
Steep climb
85 mins
Sidi Chamharouch Marabout
60 mins
Doudmet
120 mins
Neltner Refuge

IMLIL 1740M (SEE TOWN PLAN)
MULE PARK
CAFÉ LES AMIS
TO AÏT SOUKA & TACHEDDIRT
TO TIZI MEZZIK
Kasbah du Toubkal
IRRIGATION CHANNEL
AROUMD 1960M
ORCHARD
Gîte Tourtatine
TRAIL CLIMBS STEEPLY IN ZIG-ZAGS
SHOPS
PATH DIVIDES AFTER CROSSING RIVER– LEFT TOWARDS MARABOUT, RIGHT FOR NELTNER REFUGE
WATERFALLS
SIDI CHAMHAROUCH MARABOUT, 2310M
PATH CLIMBS STEEPLY AFTER MARABOUT
CLUSTER OF SMALL CAFÉS, SHOPS & ROOMS
DOUDMET
SHOP & DRINKS
CROSS SMALL WATER COURSES
SOLITARY CAFÉ SET UPON A MAGNIFICENT NATURAL TERRACE
ROCK BUTTRESSES LINE TRAIL TO RIGHT
PATH ASCENDS STEEPLY BUT CLEARLY
FLAT GROUND, GOOD FOR CAMPING PRECEDES REFUGE
REFUGE BECOMES VISIBLE
Les Mouflons
Neltner Refuge 3207M
3
2
MAP 1
0 1km
0 ½ mile

can be found cooling naturally in water falling from a rock buttress; the drinks and Berber artefacts can be bought from an adjacent shop.

The path remains clear until the CAF Neltner Refuge comes into view 90 minutes after Doudmet from which point you will still need a further 30 minutes to reach your goal for the day. During your approach you will cross several flat spaces which would be suitable for **camping** but if you decide to pitch tent, choose a sheltered spot if you can: the wind here can be very strong.

The long-established 90-bed, dormitory-style ***Neltner Refuge*** (also known as ***Refuge du Toubkal***) never closes but is unfortunately often overcrowded, especially at weekends. Its price structure is somewhat complicated. CAF and British Mountaineering Council members pay as little as 46dh in summer (May to end Oct) and 92dh in winter (end Oct to end Apr); YHA members pay 69dh in summer and 115dh in winter; non-members pay 92dh in summer and 150dh in winter. There is ample sheltered **camping** space in the grounds of the refuge for 10dh per person per night. Breakfast is 25dh, lunch 40dh and evening meals 50dh. Alternatively the kitchen can be hired for a charge of 10dh per person. Showers can be taken for 10dh and a small shop sells cold drinks, including freshly squeezed orange juice (10dh), and other basic provisions, notably chocolate.

Registration is compulsory on arrival, both in the *Register d'hotel* and in the *Fiche de nuitée refuge*, for all staying in the refuge, although not for campers.

For 70 years the Neltner Refuge stood alone in the valley below Toubkal. Recently, however, new accommodation, Moroccan-owned ***Les Mouflons***

The Neltner Refuge

The concept of the Refuge du Toubkal dates back to an ill-fated expedition to the summit of Toubkal in September 1933. Although the expedition successfully reached the summit, illness affected the party during its descent and it was decided that a return to Aroumd that day was not possible. Instead, a bivouac was made in a cave at the foot of the mountain. Amongst the group, who were left with a long and cold evening during which to reflect upon the lack of adequate provision for mountaineers in this area, was one Louis Neltner, French geologist and Atlas specialist. The product of his reflection was the Neltner Refuge which still stands today.

With him that night was a certain Omar Aït Elkadi, since 1925 the first and only guide in the valley. It was appropriate, therefore, that, when the Neltner Refuge opened in 1938, he was appointed its first *guardien*. This was a position he would hold until he was succeeded in 1968 by none other than his son, Lahcen Aït Elkadi, who himself would hold the position until his own retirement in 1985.

Even now the responsibility of guardien remains within his family. Reflecting the constantly increasing pressure on the refuge from growing numbers of trekkers, the responsibility of guardien has been shared equally between Lahcen's three sons for the last two decades and more. Already there are plans that one day their position should be passed on to a fourth generation of the family. In many ways the family history of the Aït Elkadis is the history of the Neltner Refuge: quite fittingly, a photograph of Lahcen Aït Elkadi is still proudly displayed in one of its dining rooms.

(☎ 0524-44 97 67, GSM: 0663-76 37 13, 0661-21 33 45/46, 💻 www.refugetoubkal.com) has been constructed alongside. Built with Berber-architectural traditions firmly in mind, grilled windows and coloured lanterns add atmosphere to very clean and spacious accommodation. Dormitory beds are available year-round for 80dh in summer and 100dh in winter. Breakfast is offered for 30dh (summer) and 40dh (winter) while a typical tagine costs 60dh (summer) and 70dh (winter). The kitchen can be rented for 25dh to cook a meal and showers are available for 10dh (summer) and 15dh (winter). A well-stocked shop provides essentials.

All trekkers who have not yet read the section on the symptoms and dangers of altitude sickness and the necessary response to them on pp258-9 are strongly advised to do so before setting out on Day 2.

Neltner Refuge–Jbel Toubkal summit [Map 2]

Three people crowded into a two-man tent in a jet stream wind on top of the highest mountain in North Africa sounds as attractive as an undeserved parking ticket but truth to tell, I would not have been anywhere else. I was hugely happy to be there and was as warm, cosy and well fed as long experience and good gear allowed. Outside the tent was a different world. **Hamish Brown**, *The Mountains Look on Marrakech*, 2007

The route described here, the South Cwm ascent, is by far the most popular for the ascent of Toubkal even though the loose scree makes the ascent difficult and the descent worse. Jbel Toubkal is a graveyard for walking boots and none too kind to ankles. Make sure that your boots are fit for purpose (see p31). In particular, ensure they have plenty of tread to cope with the scree. It is often very cold at the summit: on my first ascent in 1986, although in August, it actually snowed, albeit briefly. There is no opportunity to refill water bottles en route. You should allow a day to get from the refuge to the summit and back, although it is perfectly feasible for walkers in a hurry to reach the summit and return all the way to Imlil in the same day.

Many trekkers depart for the summit as early as 4 or 5am. Usually there is not, however, the problem of afternoon storms in the Toubkal region which beset the ascent of Mgoun (see pp164-7) and the motive of these trekkers is simply to reach the summit as early in the day as possible. If you do not wish to become part of their procession wait until around 7am, by which time the tranquillity of the mountain is usually restored.

From Neltner Refuge, look up into the large side valley entering the main valley from the east as this is the route that you will follow towards the summit. At first, head south from behind the refuge, following the small **gully** for five minutes until you reach a small **waterfall**. Cross the stream in front of the waterfall to climb the scree path to the left (east). The path, which at times is unclear, scrambles over an expanse of large boulders. Small cairns mark the route, although at this stage you simply need to keep heading eastwards and upwards.

After 40 minutes, cross in front of a large and very obvious **rock overhang** which is visible from the refuge and walk back over the top of it to resume the climb. By now the path is clearer although it has degenerated into rather frustrating scree. Once in the dominant cwm of the mountainside it splits into three.

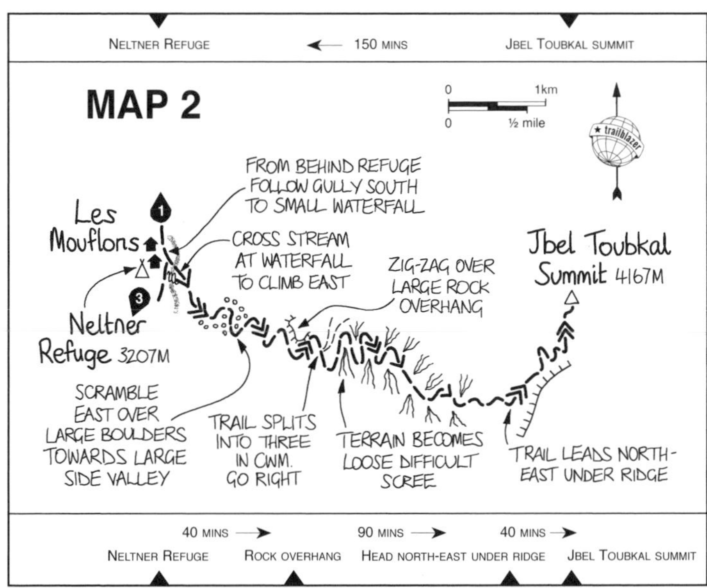

Take the right-hand route as the others have the worst scree and are more demanding. After a further 90 minutes the path swings and climbs to the left (north) just below a ridge which will have been visible for some time.

The summit, which is marked by a metal tripod, is visible after a further 15 minutes and you should reach it some 25 minutes after this. The views from the **summit** (4167m/13,670ft) are magnificent although often hazy. Look for Jbel Sirwa, with its unmistakable volcanic plug, to the south and the less clearly

The first ascent of Jbel Toubkal

The first European ever to visit Aroumd was British botanist and director of Kew Gardens, Sir Joseph D Hooker, in 1871, accompanied by fellow-traveller J Ball. Their gripping account of their adventures can be read in *Journal of a Tour in Marocco* (sic) *and the Great Atlas* published in London in 1878.

Although they became the first Europeans to climb a 3000m peak in the Atlas, Jbel Gourza near the Tin Mal mosque on the Tizi-n-Test road, the ascent of Jbel Toubkal would be left to others. Indeed the highest mountain in North Africa would remain unclimbed by Europeans until the Marquis de Segonzac, Vincent Berger and Hubert Dolbeau finally scaled its heights on 12th June 1923. If ever their efforts were predated by those of local people, there is no surviving historical record to verify this.

defined expanse of the Jbel Sahro range to the south-east. For many, the ascent of Toubkal is a deeply spiritual experience and you should not be surprised should you witness a grateful trekker offering thanks to Allah.

Allow 120 to 150 minutes for the descent which follows in reverse the same route as the ascent. First, however, as you leave the summit, wander briefly from the path a little to the north. If you did not notice the village behind you during the final moments of your ascent, views of Aroumd are now to be gained ahead, to the north and far below.

Neltner Refuge–Tizi-n-Ouanoums–Lac d'Ifni [Map 3]

This breathtaking walk offers great views from Tizi-n-Ouanoums, a 3664m/12,071ft-high col, followed by a rewarding descent to the serene Lac d'Ifni (2312m/7583ft). Though the descent is rather lengthy and even arduous, you can take some comfort from the fact that any trekkers you meet travelling in the opposite direction are enduring one of the longest and most punishing ascents anywhere in the Atlas.

Head due south from the refuge along a clear trail which climbs fairly steeply for 15 minutes before levelling off into a beautiful stretch of the Aït Mizane Valley. The path then climbs again, weaving around a series of large **rock outcrops**, until it reaches a flat, grassy area which would make an outstanding campsite.

Continue for a further 20-25 minutes, across the stream and zig-zag steeply up the side of the valley to the left (east). After passing under a large overhang, the path continues up to the **Tizi-n-Ouanoums**, some 45 minutes later, offering a fine view of the beautiful Lac d'Ifni on its far (eastern) side. Immediately after the col, there are wonderful views once more of both Jbel Sahro, straight ahead, and Jbel Sirwa, to the right. The lake, however, quickly disappears from sight and will not be seen again until after you have completed your descent.

The path descends sharply after the col and continues its downward thrust for a full 1352m, its steep hairpins demanding concentration, particularly during intermittent scree-covered sections. Two hours later the source, which feeds Lac d'Ifni, emerges as a trickle from under a large boulder. Shortly afterwards, permanent snow lies in a deep ravine on the far right. From the source the path follows the small stream, crossing it several times.

Some 90 minutes later the path drops down onto a large, flat **rocky plain**, which once formed part of a larger lake bed, and which leads to the lake itself, finally now visible again. Head left towards the **north shore of the lake** across a rather awkward boulder field to reach, after a further 25 minutes, a row of **cafés** selling drinks and basic provisions along with a number of purpose-built stone **bothies** providing shelter to trekkers for a nominal charge. Mohammed, the owner of the first, original shop here, bears a striking resemblance to American actor, screenwriter and film producer, Tom Selleck.

Although it's possible to pitch a tent here, the recognised **campsite**, which can be seen from this point, is 20 minutes further on. Climb the high path around the northern edge of the lake before descending again to the right onto a broad, flat alluvial fan which runs right up to the very water's edge.

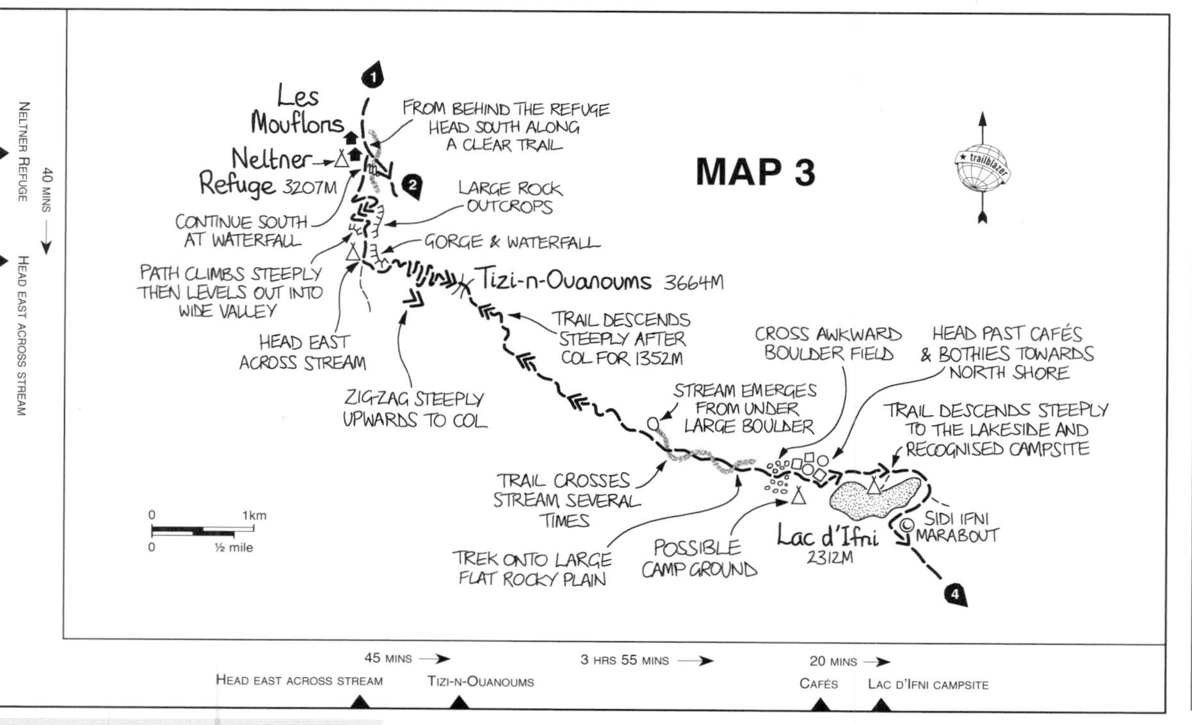

MAP 3
trailblazer
1
2
4
Les Mouflons
Neltner Refuge 3207M
FROM BEHIND THE REFUGE HEAD SOUTH ALONG A CLEAR TRAIL
CONTINUE SOUTH AT WATERFALL
LARGE ROCK OUTCROPS
PATH CLIMBS STEEPLY THEN LEVELS OUT INTO WIDE VALLEY
GORGE & WATERFALL
HEAD EAST ACROSS STREAM
ZIG-ZAG STEEPLY UPWARDS TO COL
Tizi-n-Ouanoums 3664M
TRAIL DESCENDS STEEPLY AFTER COL FOR 1352M
STREAM EMERGES FROM UNDER LARGE BOULDER
TRAIL CROSSES STREAM SEVERAL TIMES
TREK ONTO LARGE FLAT ROCKY PLAIN
POSSIBLE CAMP GROUND
CROSS AWKWARD BOULDER FIELD
HEAD PAST CAFÉS & BOTHIES TOWARDS NORTH SHORE
TRAIL DESCENDS STEEPLY TO THE LAKESIDE AND RECOGNISED CAMPSITE
SIDI IFNI MARABOUT
Lac d'Ifni 2312M
0
1km
0
½ mile
40 MINS →
NELTNER REFUGE
HEAD EAST ACROSS STREAM
45 MINS →
HEAD EAST ACROSS STREAM
TIZI-N-OUANOUMS
3 HRS 55 MINS →
20 MINS →
CAFÉS
LAC D'IFNI CAMPSITE

Lac d'Ifni–Amsouzart/Amsouzerte [Map 4]

This relatively short and easy walk provides a chance to see cultivated valleys, small villages and traditional Berber life. This is the more colourful face of the Toubkal region and as such contrasts with the sharply spectacular but rather bleak scenes of the trek so far.

Rejoin the path above the **campsite** and follow it around the eastern edge of the lake to its southern side and the **marabout of Sidi Ifni**, claimed by its guardien to be 300 years old. Its religious importance is particularly apparent not only during the annual moussem, which is held here in mid-August, but also at weekends when large numbers of finely dressed Muslim women make the pilgrimage to the tomb of the saint to pray for blessings on their fertility. This they follow with ceremonial ablutions in the lake below. Sidi Ifni was the brother of Sidi Chamharouch, whose marabout you encountered on the trail from Imlil to the Neltner Refuge.

Now follow the historic pilgrimage trail around the back of the marabout towards the south-east, climbing a little at first, for a largely gentle descent all the way to the village of Aït Igrane (named only on the 1:50,000 map). As a reflection of the modern demand for access to the lake, the trail quickly grows into a piste, which comes as something of a relief after the previous two days' rather arduous walk across scree.

After about 30 minutes the appropriately named village of **Aït Igrane**, (igrane meaning 'land of agriculture') comes into view, along with a string of pretty villages beyond to the east through which you will soon walk, all sitting in a very green and fertile valley. A further 30 minutes on, the road leads past walnut and silver birch trees to the entrance of Aït Igrane itself. At this point the dramatic village of Andous (not named on either the 1:100,000 or the 1:50,000 maps), perched precariously on a cliffside, set amongst its terraced fields, bordered by an impressive waterfall cascading from high above, attracts your attention just across the valley to your left (north).

Aït Igrane has four cafés, reached in quick succession. The most notable are ***Café Andous*** and ***Café Toubkal***. The latter, owned by the Belaid family, offers cold drinks and snacks under the pleasant shade of a walnut tree. The Belaids also sell a limited range of everyday products such as toilet paper and soap. Beds in very clean **dormitory rooms** are available for 50dh per night, including breakfast and hot shower. There is also a shady **campsite** for 30dh per night including shower but without breakfast. Attractive views across the family's cornfields should have made this a pleasant place to relax but sadly our sojourn was tainted by the proprietor's attempts to heavily overcharge us for our lunch, one of the very few experiences of this sort we encountered on our trek. No amount of apologetic kissing of our cheeks on his part could subsequently compensate for this.

Continue down valley to the village of **Imhilene** on the left and its mosque which has decorative stucco, painted white, on its minaret. A clock face forms part of this decoration, eternally declaring the time to be three o'clock. The trail turns left here at right angles, passing by the mosque, and crosses a small ford before again heading down valley (east) on the opposite bank.

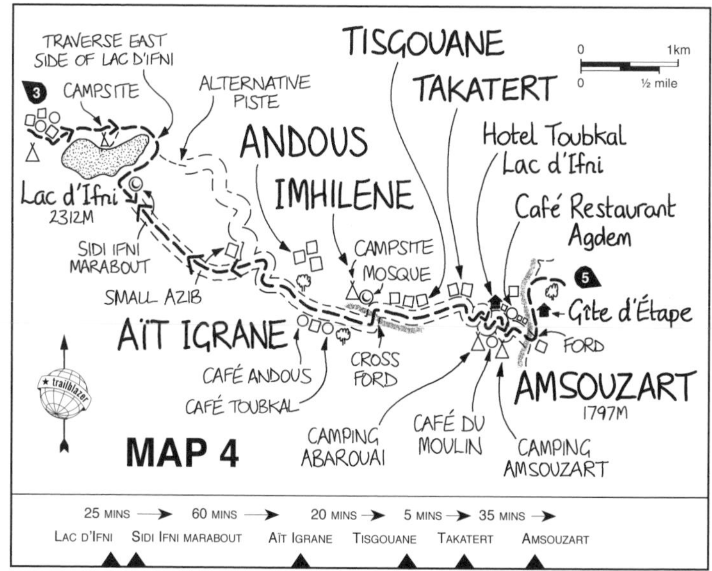

After another 20 minutes' gentle walk you will reach the village of **Tisgouane** and then, five minutes later, **Takatert**. After Takatert the road hairpins downwards into **Amsouzart** (1797m/5894ft).

You will pass several small cafés as you enter the village, including ***Café du Moulin***, although the pick would appear to be ***Café Restaurant Agdem***, especially if you are looking to eat. There is a choice of two campsites, both on the right-hand side of the road offering good, flat, grassy land under the shade of trees close to the river. The first, ***Camping Abarouai***, you will encounter at the very entrance to the village although it might be harder to find anyone in charge. The second, ***Camping Amsouzart***, is just a few yards further on in the main part of the village.

If you are feeling the need for a little more comfort at this stage of your trek, you might want to try ***Hotel Toubkal Lac d'Ifni*** (☎ 0619-47 94 05; 💻 m_him mi@menara.ma) sited just below the road on your left shortly before entering the village. A restaurant and a swimming pool are included in the development plan. The manager, Himmi Mohamed, tells us that he is more interested in people staying at the hotel than setting fixed rates.

There is also a good, clean ***gîte d'étape***. For this, walk down through the village and cross the ford at the bottom. Continue to follow the road on the other side for just a few yards before climbing the stone steps running alongside a small tributary stream almost immediately on your left. Look out for the gîte signpost on your right which you will meet within seconds. Owned by Omar ben Abdullah, it seems a very popular place with trekkers to judge by the happy faces on its panoramic terrace and the glowing comments in the visitors' book. A bed with breakfast costs 50dh, lunch 30dh and evening meal 50dh. Hot showers are available for 10dh. The guardien, Bergden Mohamed, is pleasant, attentive and conscientious.

If for any reason you need to abandon your trek at this stage, it is quite possible to get back to Marrakech or even Agadir from here; ask when the next lorry or 4x4 is expected to leave. Alternatively, a place in a full grand taxi costs around 100dh to Marrakech and around 200dh to Agadir.

Amsouzart–Azib Likemt [Map 5]

This stage is characterised by a long, steep climb to the Tizi-n-Ouraï/n'Ououraïne (3109m/10,200ft), with further stunning views, followed by an almost continuous gentle descent along the pretty Assif Tinzart/n'Tinzer to the pastoral Tifni Valley (2600m/8528ft).

Follow the trail past Omar ben Abdullah's gîte (see above) and follow the stream uphill (north-east) for five minutes before turning right again off the main trail and leaving the stream behind. After a further five minutes the path crosses a piste and zigzags slowly upwards, at first to the east and then to the north-east, bringing in to view the valley through which you descended yesterday to the west and a new perspective on Amsouzart below, which can now clearly be seen to be divided into three parts. Each of these three parts is associated with one family; the Amsouzart population of one part of the village traditionally chooses its marriage partner from either of the other two parts, but not from any other village.

You are in fact climbing up to the ridge of the right-hand (eastern) bank of the valley which descends from the Tizi-n-Ouraï. Although there are several alternative trails up to this col, including one along the ridge of the left-hand (western) bank of the valley and another via the floor of the valley itself, the route described here is the preferred option of official guides on account of the amazing views that it offers during the ascent. Jbel Toubkal can be seen standing proud over all the other peaks to the west, the green Assif-n-Tifnout Valley which leads south all the way to Taliwine (the trailhead for treks in the Jbel Sirwa region), and Jbel Sirwa itself, once again recognisable by its volcanic summit on the southern horizon.

The winding path to the col is clear although the ascent will ultimately require about four hours. After about three hours of steep climbing the trail straightens and swings around first to the north and then quickly to the north-west to cut across the head of the valley that you left behind outside the gîte at the beginning of the day. Here it joins the two alternative trails mentioned in the previous paragraph. The col itself now suddenly appears to be within easy striking distance, but prepare yourself for disappointment as 30 minutes later you reach only a **false summit**. Take heart, however, as Tizi-n-Ouraï is just a further 30 minutes beyond.

The descent to the **valley floor** on the far (northern) side of the col requires only a rapid 20 minutes. In summer, the flat, grassy area which greets you is

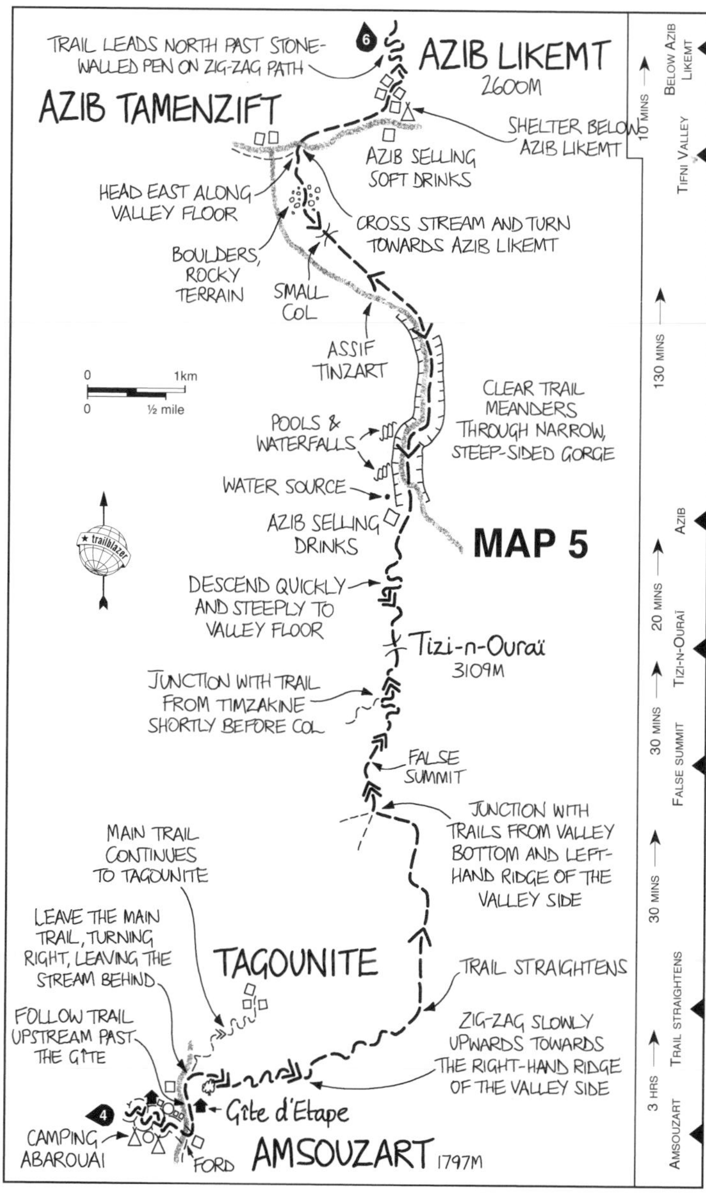

TRAIL GUIDE AND MAPS

good for camping, taking a break or making lunch. There is even an **azib** selling water and soft drinks. In winter, however, the area might be too wet.

Follow the trail through the **gorge** straight ahead (north) just past the azib. After five minutes you will find a **water source** emerging at knee height from a group of rocks on the left (west) side of the path. For the next 90 minutes you will enjoy gentle walking along the banks of the **Assif Tinzart**. As it meanders its way northwards, you may be tempted by its numerous deep pools and small waterfalls that make this a beautiful, gradual descent.

Finally the path climbs up to the right, cutting across the spurs of the Tinzart Valley, leaving the river behind, to a small col 30 minutes later, the last landmark before you reach the Tifni Valley, your destination for the day. Once at the col, you will look down into the valley and see a series of azibs on its far (northern) slopes, an idyllic pastoral scene and the perfect overnight resting place at the end of a long day's walk.

There are several good **camping** places to choose from close down by the river. The pick, however, is the area below Azib Likemt (2600m/8528ft), close to the junction of the Tifni and Likemt valleys. Quite apart from putting you in prime position for your ascent to **Tizi-n-Likemt** tomorrow, this spot has the benefit of

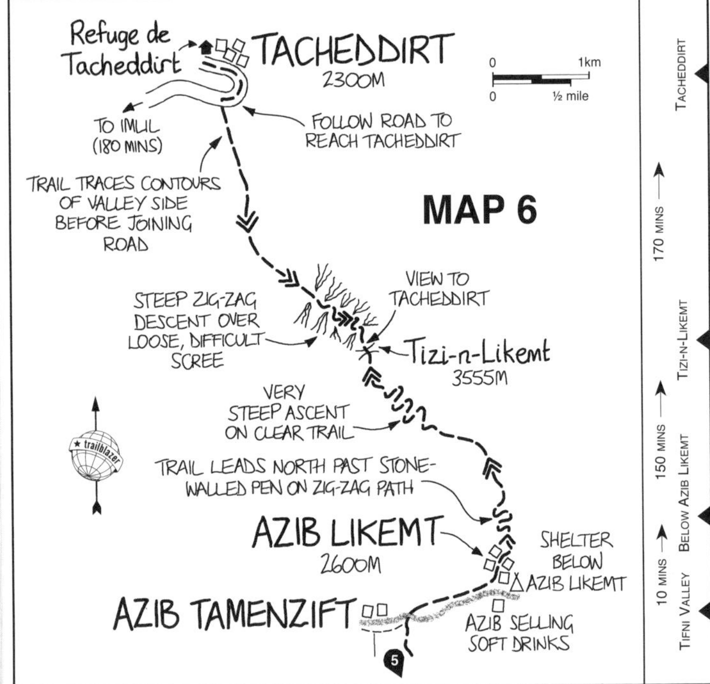

a wooden-roofed stone structure providing shelter, should it be required, plus another small azib selling water and soft drinks. Make sure you are carrying enough water for tomorrow as this will be an arduous stage. Indeed the Likemt Valley becomes notoriously hot and an early start before sunrise is advised.

Azib Likemt–Tacheddirt [Map 6]

Follow the trail steadily upwards (northwards) behind the **stone shelter** to quickly reach Azib Likemt and continue climbing, leaving the Assif-n-Tifni behind, as you zigzag towards the left (western) bank of the Likemt Valley. The well-trodden path turns gradually towards the north-west and continues to meander upwards for a rather punishing 150 minutes to **Tizi-n-Likemt** (3555m/ 11,660ft). The col can be very cold and extremely windy, even in the height of summer. Just before you reach the col, make sure you glance over your left shoulder to witness Jbel Toubkal fleetingly come back into view, before this glorious mountain disappears for a final time on this trek. Cross the col and start a steep but clear zigzag descent of a vast scree slope on the far side: 'the grandfather of all Atlas scree slopes' according to Michael Peyron (*Great Atlas Traverse,* Vol 1, 1989). You are met by a wonderful view of the **Imenane Valley** floor with traditional Berber villages strung alongside its south-facing slopes.

After about 150 minutes the trail meets a road just before reaching the valley floor. You are now faced with a choice. Either follow the road to your right into the next village, **Tacheddirt** (2300m/7544ft), a further 20 minutes' walk away, or have your transport pre-arranged to pick you up at this point and to take you back to Imlil along the road to your left.

Tacheddirt is a pleasant village, surrounded by a quilt of fields, with a small, basic CAF refuge (***Refuge de Tacheddirt***) which, despite the absence of hot water, is popular with trekkers. Dormitory accommodation costs 52dh per person per night.

Should you choose to walk back to Imlil, the old trail below the road can be followed easily. Allow at least three hours for the final push. However, the very presence of the road, recently asphalted, is likely to offset your enthusiasm to trek beyond this point.

The Mgoun region

(Mgoun) … the most extensive area of terrain above the 3000m contour in Morocco…
Michael Peyron, *Great Atlas Traverse*, Vol 2, 1990

Mgoun is the second most popular trekking destination in the Atlas Mountains. While the climate here can be just as challenging and the peaks only marginally lower than those in the loftiest areas of the Toubkal region, Mgoun has a softness and a rich fertility not usually shared by other Atlas regions described in this guide. Though still tough, life in the region is certainly less harsh than in the bleaker, more dramatic southern terrains of Sirwa and Sahro. Without doubt, however, Mgoun offers some of the most inspiring views in the Atlas and to reach the summit itself, at 4068m/13,343ft, is a truly rewarding experience. In order to reach the trailhead at Tabant, it is necessary to journey via Azilal.

GETTING TO AZILAL

Three buses a day undertake the 170km journey of three hours and upwards from Marrakech to Azilal. They depart from the main gare routière near Bab Doukkala at 8.30am, 12.30pm and 3.30pm. In order to ensure your seat, tickets, which cost 45dh, should be bought from the Line 18 office inside the station as far in advance of your journey as possible. For a more immediate departure, take a grand taxi to Azilal for 70dh from the taxi rank just five minutes' walk around the corner from the gare routière, immediately outside the medina walls, and shave a little off your journey time, too.

AZILAL

There is no good reason to delay in Azilal. Though a perfectly pleasant modern town, its attractions are limited. Supplies could be picked up here, but their transportation to Tabant, where everything you are likely to need is available, would be extremely cumbersome, especially if travelling by public transport. Do, however, make sure that you have sufficient dirhams with you before you leave Azilal as there are no banks and no currency-exchange facilities in Tabant.

Services

Azilal is a rapidly growing and increasingly well-resourced administrative town. Largely built up on either side of the main street, avenue Hassan II, which runs from south-west to north-east, orientation is straightforward.

The area of interest to the passing trekker is likely to be restricted to the central 800 yards of its length (see map opposite). All essential services are within this strip including a **post office**, a **police station**, numerous **pharmacies** and hairdressers (*coiffeurs*), and several **doctors**, one of whom is located on the pedestrianised street between Café des Voyageurs and Hotel Souss (GSM ☎ 0662-05 89 18). The **hospital** is off the main road towards the north-east end of town.

The **tourist information office** (☎ 0523-45 87 22; open Mon to Fri 9am–noon and 3-6pm) can provide basic information on local matters. A selection of **téléboutiques**, an **internet café** and several **banks** are at your disposal, although the **ATMs** in Azilal are well known for being a little temperamental.

If you are short on reading material, you might try your luck at the single, centrally located **bookshop**, although the chances of finding something in a European language that you would really want to read are precarious.

Should you decide to stock up on food supplies before moving on, there is a choice of several small **supermarkets** as well as a small, but cheerful and colourful, **souk**. You might even find simple souvenirs here. On the other hand, if you want to be sure of buying good-quality products, you may wish to try the **Ensemble Artisanal,** found about 15 minutes' drive to the north-east of the centre of Azilal, where a range of traditional handicrafts are available under one roof at fixed and regulated, if slightly inflated, prices.

Finally, there are also a few basic places to eat and a handful of well-priced hotels in Azilal, if you were to get stuck here.

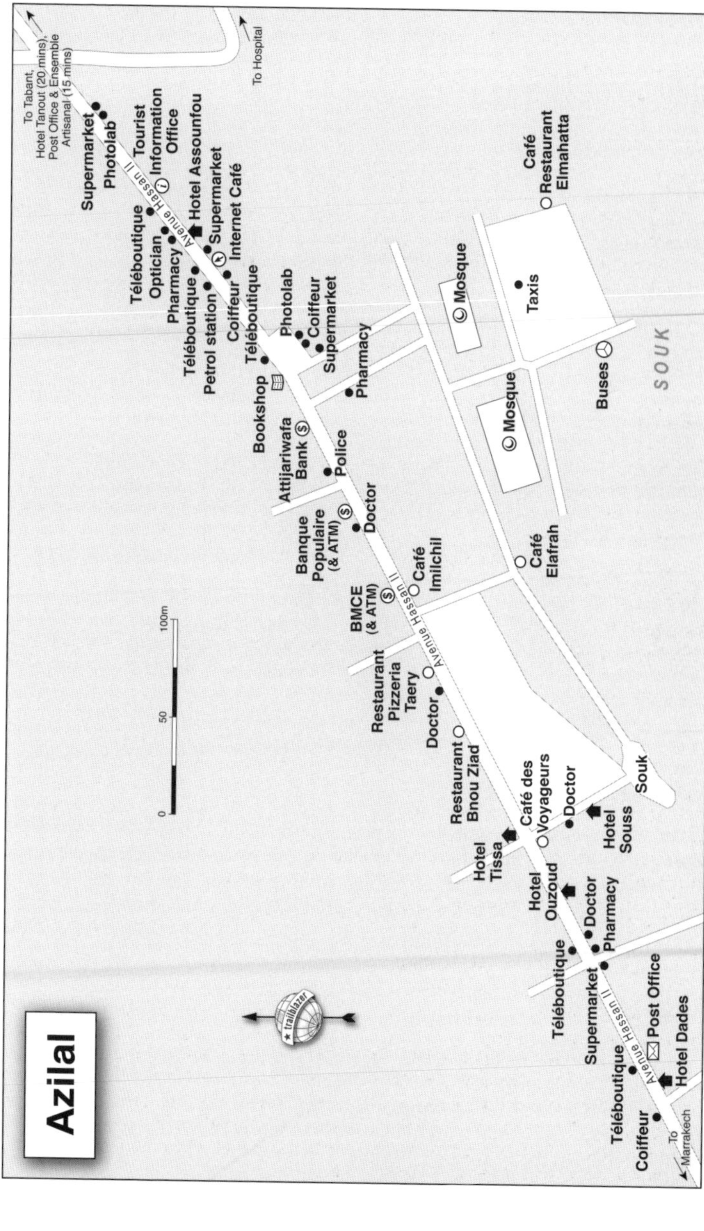

Azilal

To Tabant, Hotel Tanout (20 mins), Post Office & Ensemble Artisanal (15 mins)
To Hospital
Supermarket
Photolab
Tourist Information Office
Téléboutique
Optician
Hotel Assounfou
Pharmacy
Supermarket
Internet Café
Téléboutique
Petrol station
Coiffeur
Téléboutique
Photolab
Coiffeur
Supermarket
Bookshop
Pharmacy
Attijariwafa Bank
Police
Mosque
Mosque
Café Restaurant Elmahatta
Taxis
Buses
SOUK
Banque Populaire (& ATM)
Doctor
BMCE (& ATM)
Café Imilchil
Café Elafrah
Restaurant Pizzeria Taery
Doctor
Restaurant Bnou Ziad
Avenue Hassan II
0
50
100m
Souk
Café des Voyageurs
Doctor
Hotel Tissa
Hotel Souss
Hotel Ouzoud
Doctor
Pharmacy
Téléboutique
Supermarket
Post Office
Téléboutique
Hotel Dades
Coiffeur
To Marrakech
trailblazer

Where to stay

There are several inexpensive, basic hotels along the central stretch of the main thoroughfare, avenue Hassan II. Hotel tariffs in the town have hardly moved in the last decade which suggests that business has been slow. Indeed there is little sign of any recent improvements to any of the following established hotels.

Hotel Tissa (GSM ☎ 0666-48 26 31) charges only 30/60/90dh. This includes access to a hot shower although there is only one in the whole hotel.

Hotel Ouzoud (☎ 0662-33 46 46; 💻 ministrek@yahoo.fr) similarly charges 30/60/90dh, with an additional 4dh payable for hot showers. The slightly superior ***Hotel Dades*** (☎ 0523-45 82 45; 💻 hoteldades@yahoo.fr) charges 40/80dh (hot showers 5dh). The hotel has the benefit of a restaurant on site which serves meals, including breakfast for 10-15dh. Finally in this bracket, ***Hotel Souss*** (GSM ☎ 0672-32 84 95) charges 35/70dh.

If these do not meet your requirements, the recent appearance of the more sophisticated ***Hotel Assounfou*** (GSM ☎ 0672-17 48 55; 100/150/200dh) also on avenue Hassan II, obviates the need to travel out to ***Hotel Tanout*** (☎ 0523-45 93 23; 💻 www.hoteltanout.com) which provides basic traveller rooms for 75/120dh, as well as en suites for 140/230dh (room only) and air-conditioned suites for 190/280dh (including breakfast). Breakfast is 20dh and three-course meals 90dh.

Where to eat

Seemingly the most popular place to eat for locals travelling into Azilal from Tabant is the centrally positioned ***Restaurant Bnou Ziad***. This might be a good place to begin making useful Tabant contacts in advance of your trek. Simple cafeteria meals, including tagines and omelettes, can be ordered here for about 25dh. Only a few doors away to the north-east is ***Restaurant Pizzeria Taery*** which provides pizza and roast chicken with salad for very similar prices.

Continuing along avenue Hassan II to the north-east, ***Café Imilchil*** is on the opposite side of the road, immediately behind which is the busy ***Café Elafrah***. The well-positioned ***Café des Voyageurs*** can be recommended if you are seeking a drink; it does not serve food. If you are anxious about missing your onward transport out of Azilal you might avail yourself of ***Café Restaurant Elmahatta*** conveniently located within the walls of the taxi rank itself, and close to the minibus stand; the staff will provide you with a bottle of coke and even prepare you a chip butty.

GETTING TO TABANT

Several mini-buses, the number varying with demand, leave Azilal for Tabant during the course of each day from beside the main mosque. They depart when full and the journey takes between three and four hours. The fare has recently fallen from 40dh to 30dh. This is on account of growing competition from the *grands taxis* which set out from the compound adjacent; for 35dh a seat, they cover the same ground to Tabant in as little as two hours.

TABANT

[see map p156]

Tabant (1850m/6068ft) is one of the most appealing trailheads in the Atlas. As a small, friendly, laid-back market town, which sits in the Aït Bou Guemez Valley, it offers a beautiful setting, the best of Berber hospitality and all essential services which trekkers might need to prepare for a long trek, except, importantly, currency-exchange facilities.

Services

Tabant provides both the economic and administrative focal point for the region, serving the relatively prosperous Aït Bou Guemez Valley well. Although having no banks or currency-exchange facilities, there is a **post office**, a number of **téléboutiques**, a **gendarmerie** and the **local government office**. There are also quite a few shops, including grocers and butchers.

A glimpse of the weekly Sunday **souk** (Souk el Had) at Tabant's eastern exit is possible on Saturday evening when meat goes on sale early.

A small **women's co-operative** at the western end of Tabant is indicative of a slow shift in the balance of economic power in rural Morocco. By purchasing from the array of rugs, textiles, artefacts and post-cards on sale here, you would be supporting local women in securing greater control over their own financial affairs. You would also be helping them to free themselves from their historic dependence upon a middleman to sell their goods; the middleman has traditionally taken a cut from the sale far greater than the payment that the women themselves have received as reward for their labour.

The **Moroccan mountain guide training centre** (CFAMM; Centre de Formation aux Métiers de la Montagne) is situated just outside Tabant near the village of Aït Imi. It should be no surprise, therefore, that many guides and muleteers are found both in Tabant and in the surrounding villages; they can be most easily contacted through your chosen accommodation. Be warned, however, that the ever-increasing number of larger, organised trekking groups passing through Tabant, typically on their way to the Vallée des Roses (see box p224), is beginning to put pressure on the local supply of mules. Even so, this should not present an insurmountable problem and at worst even in summer should only require a little patience to resolve.

Trekking agencies and guides

- **Mohamad Imharkan** (GSM ☎ 0654-57 49 12; 💻 mimharkan@yahoo.fr), official mountain guide, also contactable via Gîte d'étape Tawada in Imelghas, see below.
- **Dar Itrane** (☎ 0544.31.39.01/03; 💻 www.atlas-sahara-trek.com), the hotel in Imelghas, see below, is experienced in organising treks not only in the Mgoun area in summer but also into the desert in winter.

Where to stay

Both the **hotels** (Dar Si Hamou and Dar Itrane) in the area are quite new and were designed with Berber traditions in mind.

Tabant

- ***Dar Si Hamou*** (GSM ☎ 0661-07 34 82) is at the western entrance to town. Rates are 250-400/320-450dh including breakfast, or an extra 80dh per person for half-board.

Imelghas

- The beautiful French-owned ***Dar Itrane*** (☎ 0523-45 93 12; 💻 www.atlas-sahara-trek.com) charges from €25 per person per night, half-board.

Gîtes in the area include:

- *No name*; Ali el Ouakhoumi (☎ 0671-95 09 37). Has a small library on the Atlas Mountains and Berbers.
- *No name*; Mohamad Azorki ben Ichou (☎ 0678-36 00 59). Terrace with beautiful views of the valley; small shop on ground floor.
- Sign outside reads ***Départ des Randos***, owner insists it is called ***Tawada***; Mohamad Imharkan (☎ 0523 45 87 39/0670-01 96 66; 💻 mimharkan@yahoo.fr). M Imharkan is both President of Aït Bou Guemez Gîte Association and an official mountain guide. He is consequently extremely well informed. His terrace provides beautiful views of the valley.
- *No name*; Tigami n'Ouayour. Almost the last building in Imelghas heading north-east towards Iskattafene.

Iskattafene

- *No name*; Mohammed el Ouassea.
- *No name*; Brahim Maskour (☎ 0523-45 89 59/0668-24 75 72). Very hospitable.

Ikhf-n-Ighir

- ***Dar Alfarda***; Youssef Mustafa Ortglaout (☎ 0666-16 95 44). An impressive gîte, first on main road arriving from Iskattafene, right-hand side.

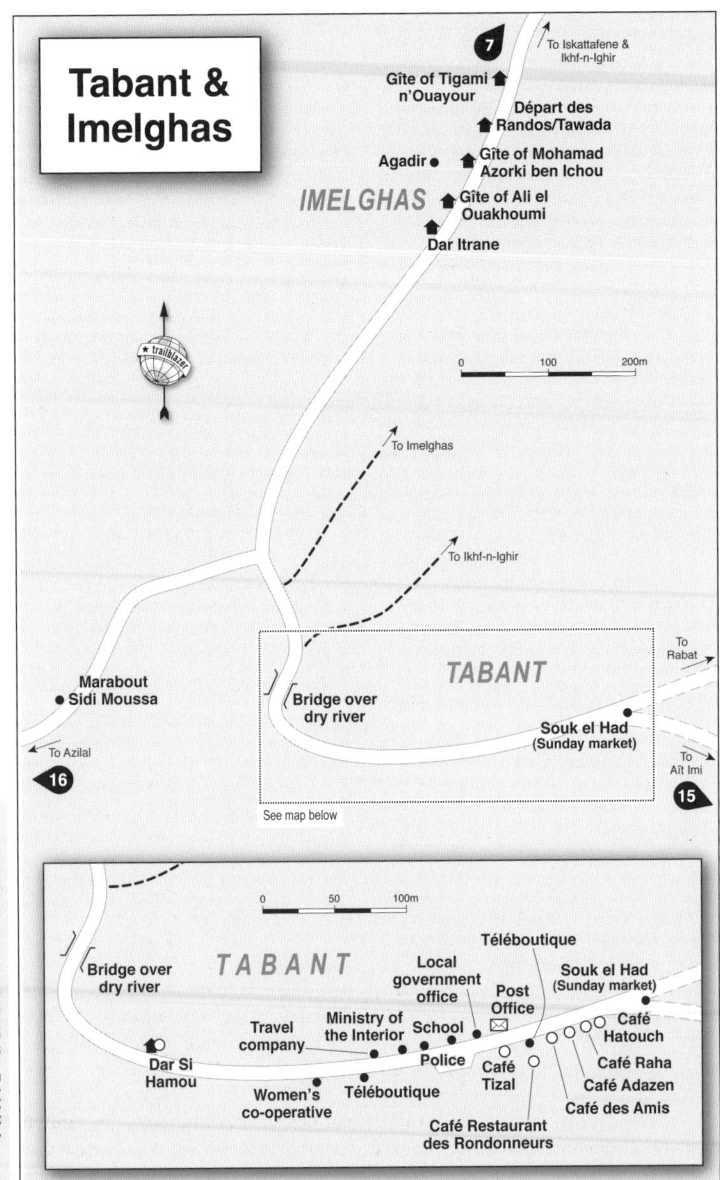
Tabant & Imelghas
To Iskattafene & Ikhf-n-Ighir
7
Gîte of Tigami n'Ouayour
Départ des Randos/Tawada
Agadir
Gîte of Mohamad Azorki ben Ichou
IMELGHAS
Gîte of Ali el Ouakhoumi
Dar Itrane
trailblazer
0
100
200m
To Imelghas
To Ikhf-n-Ighir
To Rabat
TABANT
Marabout Sidi Moussa
Bridge over dry river
Souk el Had (Sunday market)
To Azilal
To Aït Imi
16
15
See map below
0
50
100m
Téléboutique
TABANT
Bridge over dry river
Local government office
Souk el Had (Sunday market)
Post Office
Travel company
Ministry of the Interior
School
Café Hatouch
Dar Si Hamou
Police
Café Tizal
Café Raha
Café Adazen
Women's co-operative
Téléboutique
Café des Amis
Café Restaurant des Rondonneurs

• ***Bonnaceur***; Mohammed Bonnaceur Iqfnirir (☎ 0524-45 91 75). Just off main road, signposted left side on approach from Iskattafene.
• ***Marhaba***; On main road, left side on approach from Iskattafene.
• ***Tamounte***; Ali Imeddahen (☎ 0670-65 21 86). Close to the valley floor, follow sign from main road, beautifully maintained.
• ***No name***; Mohammed Imharkan (☎ 0616-45 00 15). Large gîte on valley floor; need to ask directions; very warm reception; hammam available.

In all these gîtes expect to pay 50dh for a bed, 20dh for breakfast and 50dh for other meals.

Where to eat

There are a number of basic cafés serving simple, traditional dishes along the main road, all on the right-hand side when entering Tabant from the west. They include ***Café Tizal***, which has a pleasant garden with tables and parasols, ***Café des Amis***, ***Café Adazen*** and ***Café Hatouch***. The more limited and unattractive ***Café Raha*** appears to serve only tea and bread. There is also ***Café Restaurant des Rondonneurs*** [sic] behind Café Tizal which, likewise, has a small garden. For a better class of meal, however, you will need to make a reservation at the restaurant of ***Dar Si Hamou*** (GSM ☎ 0661-07 34 82).

UPPER AïT BOU GUEMEZ CIRCULAR TREK [Map 7, p159]

The Bou Guemez is often, justifiably, called La Vallée Heureuse and this verdant swathe among stony mountains, lit by spring blossom and shining waters, poplar rows, orchid meadows and darting black damselflies, can astonish.

Hamish Brown, *The Mountains Look on Marrakech*, 2007

UPPER AïT BOU GUEMEZ CIRCULAR TREK
• **Level of difficulty** Easy
• **Duration** 3 hours
• **Maps** Either *Zawyat Ahancal* (1:100,000), Division de la Carte, Morocco Survey, or *Mgoun Massif* (1:100,000), West Col.

Aït Bou Guemez actually translates as 'the people of the man who scratches'. The name of the valley is derived from the legend of its first inhabitant. Suffering from an unfortunate condition which he did not want to inflict on others, he came here to live alone. Whatever the basis of this legend, there is no sign of such misfortune in the valley today. Indeed it is with some justification that French trekkers have nicknamed Aït Bou Guemez 'la vallée heureuse', the happy valley.

This trek, a simple circular tour of the villages to the north and north-north-east of Tabant, provides a gentle introduction to the pleasures of the Aït Bou Guemez Valley. It offers opportunities to wind through a series of picturesque settlements and gain panoramic views towards the south-west along the length of this fertile valley. While the route might require as little as three hours to complete, you should certainly allow double this time if you at all wish to avail yourself of the generous hospitality which you will almost certainly encounter along the way. Besides, invitations to drink mint tea and nibble sweet biscuits in people's homes can only be declined so often before offence is caused.

Head west and then north out of Tabant (1850m/6068ft) along the **Azilal road** for 15 minutes, crossing the river course, until you meet a small **road junction**. From here the road is tarmacked. Ignore the left (west) turn for Sidi

Sidi Moussa

The dual-purpose agadir and marabout circular stone structure of Sidi Moussa, partially restored between 1993 and 1996, sits at 2008m/6583ft atop a natural conical hill about two kilometres north-west of Tabant. It can be seen for miles around and makes a straightforward trek from anywhere in the vicinity. The views from its rooftop alone make the trip worthwhile.

An agadir is a traditional fortified Berber granary used to hide food, animals and even people in times of tribal war (see Berber architecture, pp58-9). Within Sidi Moussa are store rooms for grain, space for animals and sleeping quarters for individual families, as well as a millstone, a kitchen area and prayer mats. There are more rooms on the second storey while, on the flat roof above, four towers, one at each corner, aid its defence.

A marabout is the tomb or shrine of a holy man (see Holidays and festivals, p75 and Religion, pp57-8). This is the tomb of Sidi Moussa at which local girls are encouraged to pray for a husband, marriage and children. There is a traditional ritual, apparently still occasionally practised, by which a young girl sleeps outside the marabout on a Thursday night after which she first kills and then eats a cockerel. Other beliefs include one claiming that mad people can be brought here in chains and left for three nights in order for them to regain their sanity.

Tradition has it that visitors should make a pot of mint tea to leave for subsequent callers. These days an old guardian will slowly open a creaking door, welcome you and prepare the tea while you, torch in hand, visit an inner chamber which contains the tomb of Sidi Moussa himself. Curiously, upon your return to the guardian, he will present three glasses on a silver tray, one for you, one for him, while the third he leaves empty.

Moussa (see box p158) and Azilal. Instead aim for Imelghas, either by continuing ahead along the road (north-east) and then immediately bearing right as it turns towards Imelghas, or, just 10 yards before the junction, leave the road and cut through a copse of poplar trees on your right (east). Follow this trail through cultivated fields for about 20 minutes before turning back to your left to rejoin the road which you just left, leading to the **village centre**.

Continue to follow the road towards the north and east through Imelghas. It was in this village that Karin Huet and Titouan Lamzou spent 'Un Hiver Berbère' (see Other books, p37). Pass the ancient agadir on your left and head towards the village of Iskattafene.

Twenty minutes after leaving the centre of Imelghas the road veers slightly to the left into a valley towards the area of **Ansous** just at the point where a piste leads away to the right. Iskattafene, directly ahead, its houses prettily clustered on south-facing slopes, looks down at you from across cultivated fields just five minutes away. Follow a meandering path through these fields, bisecting the road and the piste, while now keeping Iskattafene straight ahead.

Climb through the village and then bear right (east), before dropping into a north–south running tributary valley flanking its eastern edge. Cross the flat

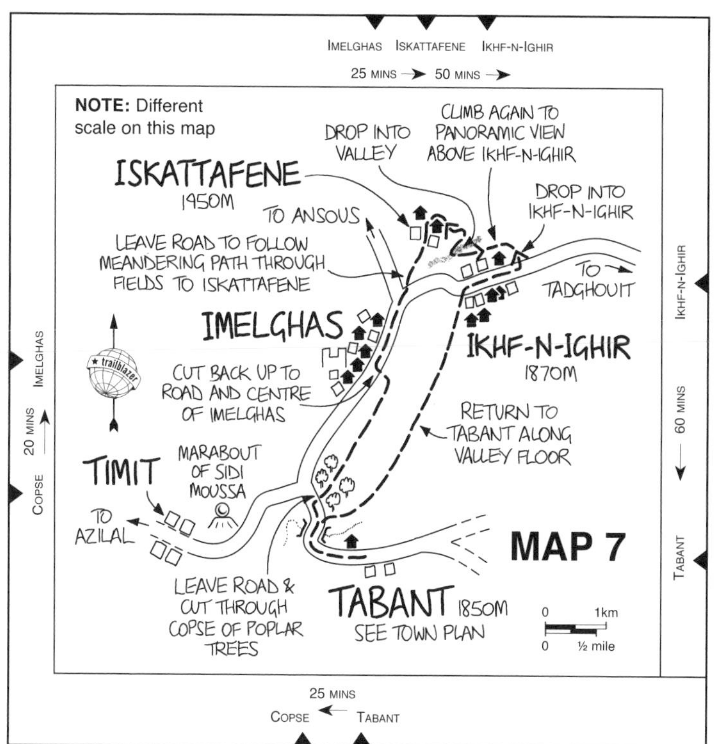

valley floor and climb to the top of the ridge which forms its far (eastern) bank. From here, there are spectacular views in all directions, particularly of the main, green Aït Bou Guemez Valley to the south-west with Sidi Moussa dominating the mid-ground. Both the Mgoun circular trek and the Mgoun traverse lie in this direction.

Below you, over the eastern edge of the ridge, lies the linear village of Ikhf-n-Ighir, hemmed in on one side by the ridge itself and on the other by the upper reaches of the Aït Bou Guemez Valley. It is tantalisingly close but, in order to descend to it, you will first need to head further north-east along the ridge in the direction of the village of Tadghouit until the gradient of the ridge allows for a comfortable descent.

Once at Ikhf-n-Ighir, you could simply follow the road south-west all the way back to Tabant. For a more picturesque return, wind your way along the flat valley floor, more or less in parallel with the road, until you rejoin the section along which you walked out of Tabant at the beginning of your day's ramble.

MGOUN CIRCULAR TREK

This route involves a climb to the summit of Ighil Mgoun (4068m/13,343ft) and all trekkers who undertake it have a responsibility to make themselves aware of the symptoms and dangers of altitude sickness and the necessary response to them (see pp258-9). The route description is organised as for a five-day trek with an optional one-day circular side trek which would require a sixth day.

MGOUN CIRCULAR TREK
- **Level of difficulty** Strenuous
- **Duration** 5-6 days
- **Maps** Either *Zawyat Ahancal, Azilal, and Qalaa't Mgouna* (1:100,000), Division de la Carte, Morocco Survey (most of route is on the Zawyat Ahancal map but the ascent of Ighil Mgoun is on the edge of the Azilal and Qalaa't Mgouna maps) or *Mgoun Massif* (1:100,000), West Col.

Tabant–Aït Sa'id/Ayt Said–Azib n'Ikkis [Map 8]

This is quite a gentle day's trek. It provides opportunities to enjoy the natural beauty of the fertile Aït Bou Guemez Valley and to wander through some of its traditional Berber villages.

From Tabant (1850m/6068ft), head west along the **Azilal road** but turn off left (south-west) after just five minutes, immediately before **Dar Si Hamou Hotel**, to snake through the neatly cultivated fields of the wide valley floor on a narrow but clear path. You may become aware that sadly some of the outlying houses have been built in unusual forms with new, obtrusive materials: these are the constructions of Europeans who presumably appreciate the beauty of the valley enough to want to live in it without properly respecting its culture and traditions.

After 20 minutes the trail leads through the quiet village of **Aguerd-n-Ouzrou**. Ask to be shown the fossilised **dinosaur footprints** preserved on a rock slab in the centre of the village. As the path climbs over a rocky outcrop towards its western exit there's a panoramic view of the village and its fields before you descend back into the valley yourself.

After a further 15 minutes you will reach the village of **Tamalout n'Aït Ziri**. From here your muleteer will need to follow the main track in the valley, a piste which is flat and uninspiring but easy to see. It heads in a south-westerly direction along the left (south) side of the valley, cutting across the **Tamzrit Plain** and moving gradually further away from the Aït Bou Guemez River veering towards the hills to the south. Meanwhile, your indirect but more interesting route meanders through more fields – those you were previously admiring from the rocky outcrop at Aguerd-n-Ouzrou. You will not be reunited with your muleteer until the entrance to the Assif-n-Arous Valley, about 80 minutes after parting.

From Tamalout n'Aït Ziri you should cross over the river to its right-hand (northern) side. You will be presented with a multitude of small paths from which to choose but, so long as you keep the **marabout of Sidi Shita**, in the village of Idoukaln, in view and aim to pass it to the left, you cannot go wrong. The marabout of Sidi Shita, like that of Sidi Moussa, is sited on a near-perfect natural conical hill. Unlike Sidi Moussa, however, it is in a poor state of repair internally. You will reach it about 25 minutes after leaving Tamalout n'Aït Ziri.

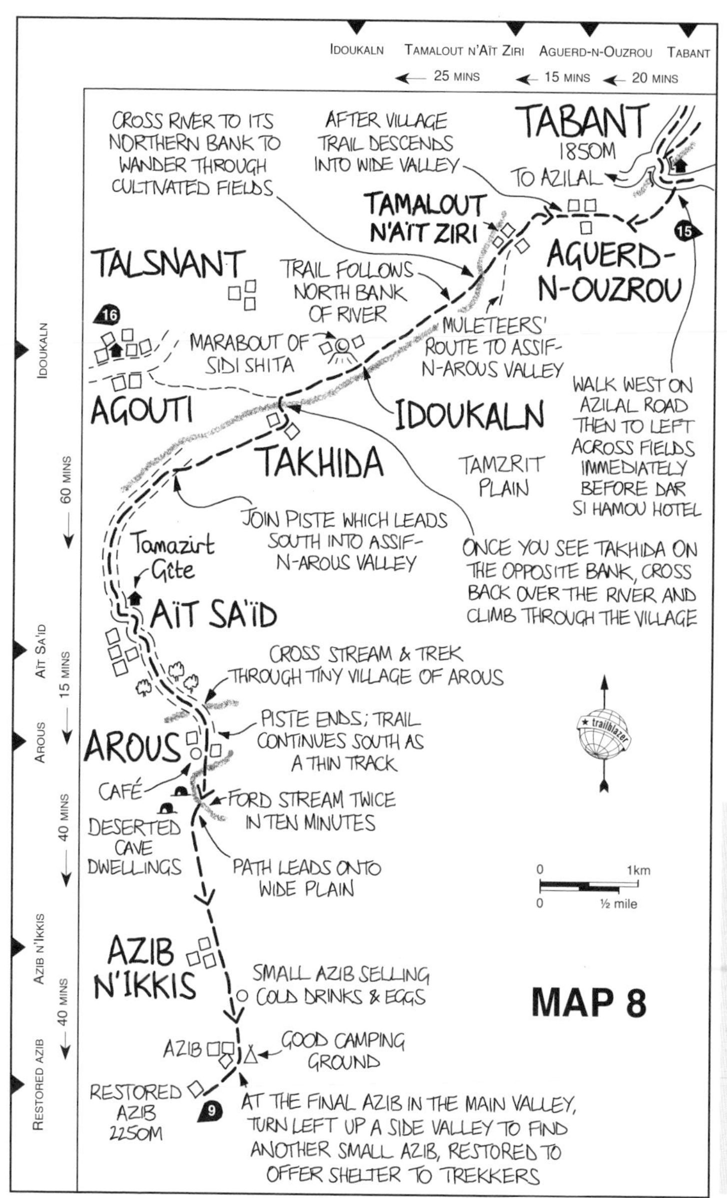
IDOUKALN
TAMALOUT N'AÏT ZIRI
AGUERD-N-OUZROU
TABANT
25 MINS
15 MINS
20 MINS
CROSS RIVER TO ITS NORTHERN BANK TO WANDER THROUGH CULTIVATED FIELDS
AFTER VILLAGE TRAIL DESCENDS INTO WIDE VALLEY
TABANT
1850M
TO AZILAL
TAMALOUT N'AÏT ZIRI
AGUERD-N-OUZROU
15
TALSNANT
TRAIL FOLLOWS NORTH BANK OF RIVER
16
MARABOUT OF SIDI SHITA
MULETEERS' ROUTE TO ASSIF-N-AROUS VALLEY
WALK WEST ON AZILAL ROAD THEN TO LEFT ACROSS FIELDS IMMEDIATELY BEFORE DAR SI HAMOU HOTEL
AGOUTI
IDOUKALN
TAKHIDA
TAMZRIT PLAIN
JOIN PISTE WHICH LEADS SOUTH INTO ASSIF-N-AROUS VALLEY
ONCE YOU SEE TAKHIDA ON THE OPPOSITE BANK, CROSS BACK OVER THE RIVER AND CLIMB THROUGH THE VILLAGE
Tamazirt Gîte
AÏT SAÏD
CROSS STREAM & TREK THROUGH TINY VILLAGE OF AROUS
PISTE ENDS; TRAIL CONTINUES SOUTH AS A THIN TRACK
AROUS
CAFÉ
FORD STREAM TWICE IN TEN MINUTES
DESERTED CAVE DWELLINGS
PATH LEADS ONTO WIDE PLAIN
trailblazer
0
1km
0
½ mile
AZIB N'IKKIS
SMALL AZIB SELLING COLD DRINKS & EGGS
MAP 8
AZIB
GOOD CAMPING GROUND
RESTORED AZIB 2250M
9
AT THE FINAL AZIB IN THE MAIN VALLEY, TURN LEFT UP A SIDE VALLEY TO FIND ANOTHER SMALL AZIB, RESTORED TO OFFER SHELTER TO TREKKERS
IDOUKALN
60 MINS
AÏT SA'ID
15 MINS
AROUS
40 MINS
AZIB N'IKKIS
40 MINS
RESTORED AZIB

Continue to follow the river on its northern bank until, about 15 minutes later, you see the village of Takhida on the opposite (south) bank, not to be confused with the village of the same name along the road on the north bank. Climb gently up through **Takhida** and then south-west back to the Tamzrit plain, finally turning away from the Aït Bou Guemez River. Continue south-west and, after a further 20 minutes, rejoin the main trail, the piste, along which your muleteer should have already passed since your parting. At this point the large village of Agouti will be behind you on the northern side of the Aït Bou Guemez Valley.

Twenty minutes after rejoining it, the piste will turn south and then quickly south-east, entering the narrow **Assif-n-Arous Valley**. You should have arranged either to rejoin your muleteer here or else in the small village of Aït Sa'id/Sayd, just 10 minutes ahead.

Once in the Arous Valley, the mighty Mgoun summit suddenly appears straight ahead to the south, staring forbiddingly down upon you. The piste now runs alongside the Arous River, here just a slow-moving stream. At the entrance to **Aït Sa'id** there is a small gîte, ***Tamazirt***, where drinks are served at tables in a garden shaded by trees. The old man who owns it used to sell soft drinks cooled in buckets of stream water, evidence that years of labour can bring its just reward. Continue through Aït Sa'id for a further 15 minutes to reach **Arous**, a larger village which lends its name to the valley. You will find another welcome ***café*** at its exit, although simply by sitting in the garden by the stream you may incur a 20dh charge additional to the 10dh for your Coke. The village marks the end of the piste; from here the route continues as a trail.

Immediately after the café, ford the stream and continue south into the narrowing Arous Valley but 10 minutes later cross back again to the right-hand (eastern) bank. Look out here for deserted **cave dwellings** high up in the cliff face to your right, once the homes of goatherds. Shortly afterwards the trail climbs up to a wide, rolling plain, across which several azibs are scattered. You reach the first, **Azib n'Ikkis**, about 40 minutes after leaving Arous. Gradually the river falls away below to the left and the emerging views of the summit of Ighil Mgoun, directly ahead, are quite wonderful.

Continue climbing gently to the south for a further 35 minutes, passing other azibs and a **small stall** selling soft drinks and eggs, to the point where a side valley enters from the south-west. This is where the best **camping** area is to be found, close to a further azib. The ground is soft and flat and good water flows in the stream: the source itself is only about 20 minutes further up the side valley. Alternatively, you might choose to head up the side valley itself for less than five minutes towards the source to find one more **azib** (2250m/7380ft). This, the last this side of the Aghouri Est pass, has been kindly restored, cleaned and maintained by a local goatherd to provide shelter for anyone in need of it.

Azib–Tarkeddid Refuge [Map 9]

Today's walk is demanding, requiring the crossing of two cols, Tizi n'Oumskiyq/Oumskiyk (2909m/9541ft) and Aghouri Est (3400m/11,152ft). The views from both are magnificent and, for the first time on this trek, the trekker can properly appreciate the grandeur of the High Atlas Mountains. There follows a

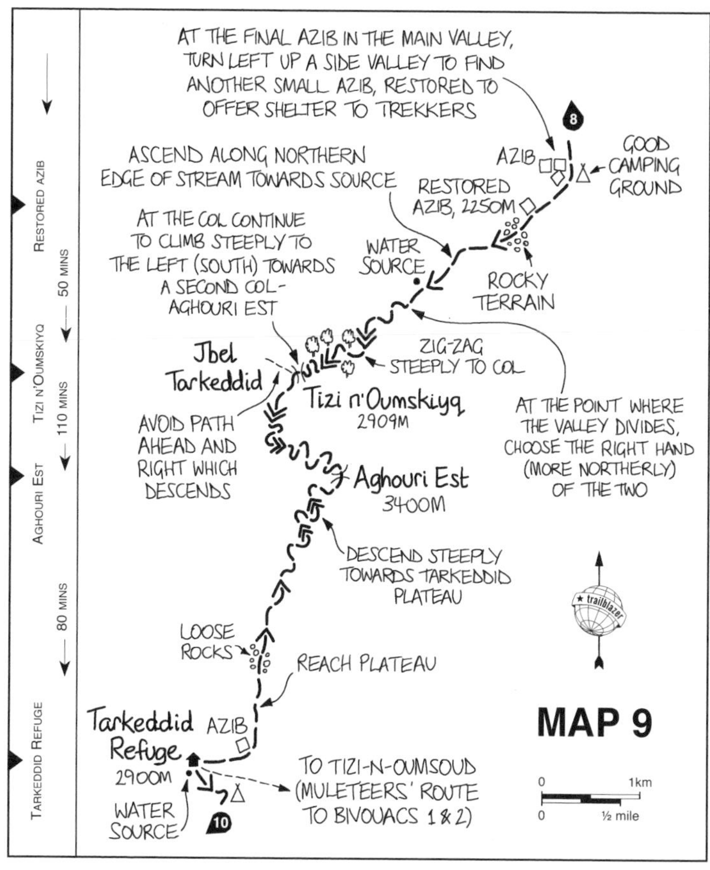

steep descent to the beautiful pastures of the Tarkeddid/Tarkeddit Plateau. The trail ascends steadily from the camping ground in a south-westerly direction up the side valley, closely following the northern edge of the stream towards its source. The route is obvious and the terrain, though becoming rocky, is pleasant. Once past the source, as the trail continually steepens, the **valley divides**. Head into the right-hand (more northerly) of the two valleys and zig-zag to the col, **Tizi n'Oumskiyq**, reached 45 minutes into the day's trek. Once at the col, there is a choice of directions; be sure not to be tempted to descend into the next valley, ahead and right, but select the trail which climbs steeply to the left (south) towards a second, higher col, **Aghouri Est**. Although at first out of sight, it will soon come into view once you have climbed a little higher.

The trail in fact steepens still further as it approaches Aghouri Est which you should reach 110 minutes after passing over Tizi n'Oumskiyq. Once you have crossed this second col you will have traversed Jbel Tarkeddid which faces Mgoun. The col offers magnificent views in all directions including clear views not only of Ighil Mgoun summit, standing high in the south-east, but also of the Tarkeddid Refuge, marking the end of the day's trek, lying low on a fertile plateau to the south-west.

The path descends in **tight zig-zags** from the col in a generally south-westerly direction over occasional loose rocks for 60 minutes before levelling out onto the plateau itself. Skirt around the **azib** and its aggressive dogs before heading west across the plateau for another 20 minutes to reach the refuge.

The **Tarkeddid Plateau** is one of the most beautiful settings anywhere in the Atlas Mountains, but do not be lulled into a false sense of security. Despite your rapid descent and the gentle pastoral scene which greets you, the plateau still stands at 2900m above sea level. I am told that in October 2006, before the restoration of the refuge, three French women died here in their tents during an overnight snowstorm.

Happily, ***Tarkeddid Refuge*** (☎ 0524-43 99 68; GSM ☎ 0672-38 68 79; 📠 0524-43 99 69; 💻 sporttravel.resa@menara.com) has recently been renovated and now provides a range of excellent facilities and services, including hot and cold drinks (starting at 10dh and 20dh respectively), breakfasts (20dh), meals (100dh), kitchen facilities, comfortable dormitory accommodation (80dh, reductions for children below 15 years, free to guides) and warm showers (20dh). Reservations are obligatory for groups in winter when charges are also slightly higher and showers are not available. There is a source about 150m directly in front of the refuge.

Given the nature of the next stage, it is important that trekkers familiarise themselves with the following route description before light fails.

Tarkeddid Refuge–Ighil Mgoun summit–Oulilimt bivouacs 1 and 2 [Map 10; Map 11, p168; Map 12, p170]

This route focuses on the ascent to the summit of Ighil Mgoun (4068m/13,343ft) and the descent to the Oulilimt bivouacs. All trekkers who have not yet read the section on the symptoms and dangers of altitude sickness and the necessary response to them on pp258-9 are strongly advised to do so before setting out.

The ascent of Mgoun is clearly inappropriate for your mule. An alternative, direct route to reach the Oulilimt bivouacs, at the end of this stage, is therefore detailed for your muleteer to follow, a route which of course you might also undertake if health, weather or any other considerations prevent you from reaching the Mgoun summit. Be aware that poor weather regularly prevents trekkers from reaching it even in summer. Days which start with fine weather regularly change for the worst; afternoon storms are a common occurrence.

The best advice is to set out for the summit very early in the morning, perhaps at 5am, and to begin your descent well before midday: a descent in bad weather can be just as dangerous as an ascent. As it will be dark when you set

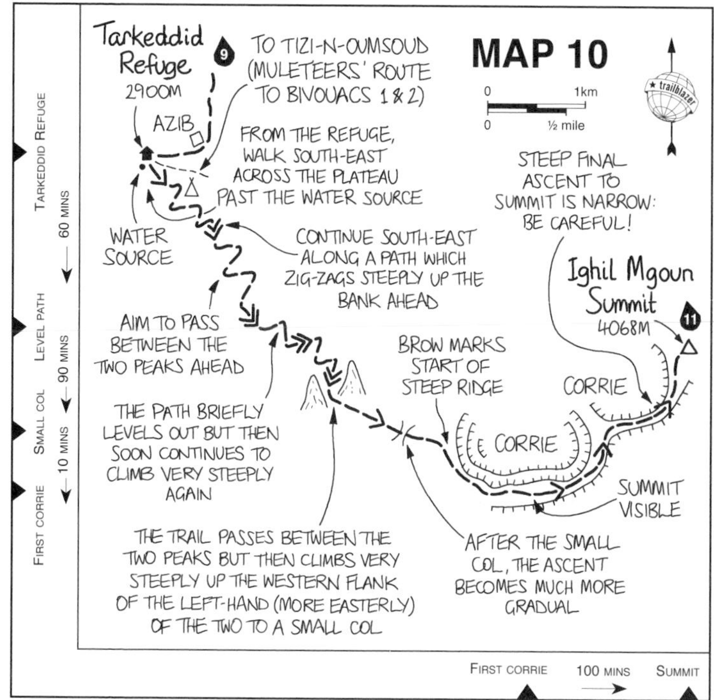

off, you will need a torch and you will need to have spent time the day before on the plateau visualising your ascent.

From the refuge walk south-east across the plateau past the water source and five minutes later, taking care not to be misled by numerous erroneous animal tracks, take a path which clearly continues south-east up the bank ahead of you. This path **zig-zags** steeply upwards and eventually heads between **two peaks** which stand out very noticeably when viewed from the refuge. Keep these peaks in your sight against the backdrop of the lightening sky and keep aiming to pass between them.

After 60 minutes the track levels out briefly and then quickly climbs again, still to the south-east, gently at first, between the two peaks, before working very steeply up the western flank of the left-hand (more easterly) of the two. You will arrive at a col on its shoulder 90 minutes later. Even after the col, the path still continues to climb, although much more gently, heading east-south-east around the back of this same peak. It reaches a huge and spectacular **corrie** 10 minutes later bounded on its southern edge by a steep-sided ridge with massive drops on both sides, both to the north, into the corrie itself, and to the south.

Safety tips

- Do not carry mobile phones or watches with metal straps during a storm, especially on summits.
- In very high winds, either stop as a group or, to continue, hold hands and form a human chain.
- Take even steps and breathe evenly. These steps should be short when you are ascending or descending and your breathing ought to be deep, through an open mouth if necessary.
- Enjoy the scenery around you but never turn around while walking; always stop to look around.

This ridge is likely to induce many trekkers familiar with the English Lake District to think of a giant Striding Edge. By now Ighil Mgoun summit, though still some way away, is clearly visible on the far side of the corrie to the north-east. Follow the trail around the ridge of the corrie's southern edge, at first heading south-east, then east, then north-east, for 30 minutes while always taking great care: the ridge is narrow and in high winds can be especially dangerous.

Having rounded the southern flank of this first corrie, the trail quickly leads onto the southern edge of a second, the equally steep-sided and dramatic **Assif Ikraween Valley** (not named on the 1:100,000 maps) immediately east of and adjacent to the first. This forms the head of the larger Oulilimt Valley. Massive drops continue both to your left (north) into the second corrie and right (south). Follow the trail around the southern head of the second corrie first to the east and then north-east, for a further 20 minutes before you come to a final steep section of ascent which will require 30 minutes more to complete. The climb then becomes much more gentle and the Mgoun summit ridge, now due north and marked by a stone cairn, is just 20 minutes away.

The first ascent of Mgoun

There is some mystery surrounding the first successful European ascent of Mgoun. Perhaps the honour belongs to Frenchman Jacques Felze who is known to have battled his way in adverse weather conditions to the summit from Qalaa't Mgouna via the south face, probably in 1932. On the other hand, he may have been pipped by compatriot René Euloge, a French civil servant based in Azilal, also renowned as a writer, painter and poet, whose personal records suggest that he may have reached the summit as early as 1928. Disguised in Berber clothing and speaking the local tongue, he travelled through hostile territory at great personal risk on a number of occasions during the 1920s. Sadly, his ascent of the second highest mountain in North Africa remains unconfirmed.

The views are tremendous for much of the latter stages of your ascent; from the **summit** they are truly spectacular. From the Oulilimt Valley, which you have just rounded immediately to the west, to the Arous Valley and Aghouri Est away to the north, to the Anti-Atlas deep in the south, the 360-degree panorama is one truly to savour. Rarely have I so strongly felt the presence of a Creator.

The descent to the Oulilimt bivouacs is rapid and quite straightforward. Continue past the summit cairn for just a few metres northwards along the summit ridge and, just before the ridge ends, pick up the very clear path which leads down its left (western) side and into the eastern side of the steep-sided **Assif Ikraween Valley**. It zig-zags through huge amounts of scree, very clearly leading you towards the valley bottom and ultimately northwards. As the path eventually becomes less steep, the valley narrows and soon you will be looking back up at its steep sides, admiring the beauty of the rock face, particularly to your left on the opposite (western) bank. The path remains on the right-hand (eastern) side of the valley.

After about 90 minutes from the summit you will arrive at a **meadow**. The flat bottom of the Oulilimt Valley is clearly in view ahead though still below you, just 50 minutes more away. Most of the descent and significant risk is now behind you and you may therefore decide to rest at this point. The meadow has some rocks offering limited shade. To seek greater shelter and the small **Oulilimt stream**, scramble down the nearby narrow crags to your left.

Continue across the meadow, keeping to the right-hand (eastern) side of the valley as it veers steadily round towards the north-east. Only when the trail and the valley finally begin to flatten out, 40 minutes after the meadow, close to where the valley swings round fully to the east, will you find yourself switching backwards and forwards across the stream. Five minutes later you will pass a **natural rock tower** standing on the left of the trail and five minutes more will bring you to a potential bivouac, here called **Bivouac 1**, on the right-hand side of the main valley floor. The valley is again dry at this point in summer, as it has been since the rock tower; indeed the stream does not reappear until Bivouac 2.

Bivouac 1 offers a choice between a raised area of stony ground providing reasonable camping ground and, 100m further, a small cave on the right side of the valley. There are in fact two inter-joining caves, one in use as a shop selling water, soft drinks and a few Berber textiles, the other seemingly owned by the shopkeeper. On my stay here, the shopkeeper helped us eat the meal that we had prepared, slept with us in the cave that night, and charged us 20dh the next morning for his hospitality. If this does not appeal, carry on to the next potential bivouac, here called Bivouac 2. To reach it, continue eastwards from Bivouac 1 along the wide Oulilimt Valley floor. Almost immediately pass a side valley on your left which leads down from Tizi-n-Oumsoud (2969m/9378ft), the route which your muleteer will have taken to get this far. A **large azib** stands opposite on the right (south) bank of the main valley. Immediately afterwards the trail leaves the valley floor and follows its left (north) bank.

About 35 minutes later, pass a **second azib**, to the left of the trail, which has been built under a flat layer of overhanging rock; a third, very picturesque, large azib soon appears on the far (southern) side of the valley. After a further 35 min-

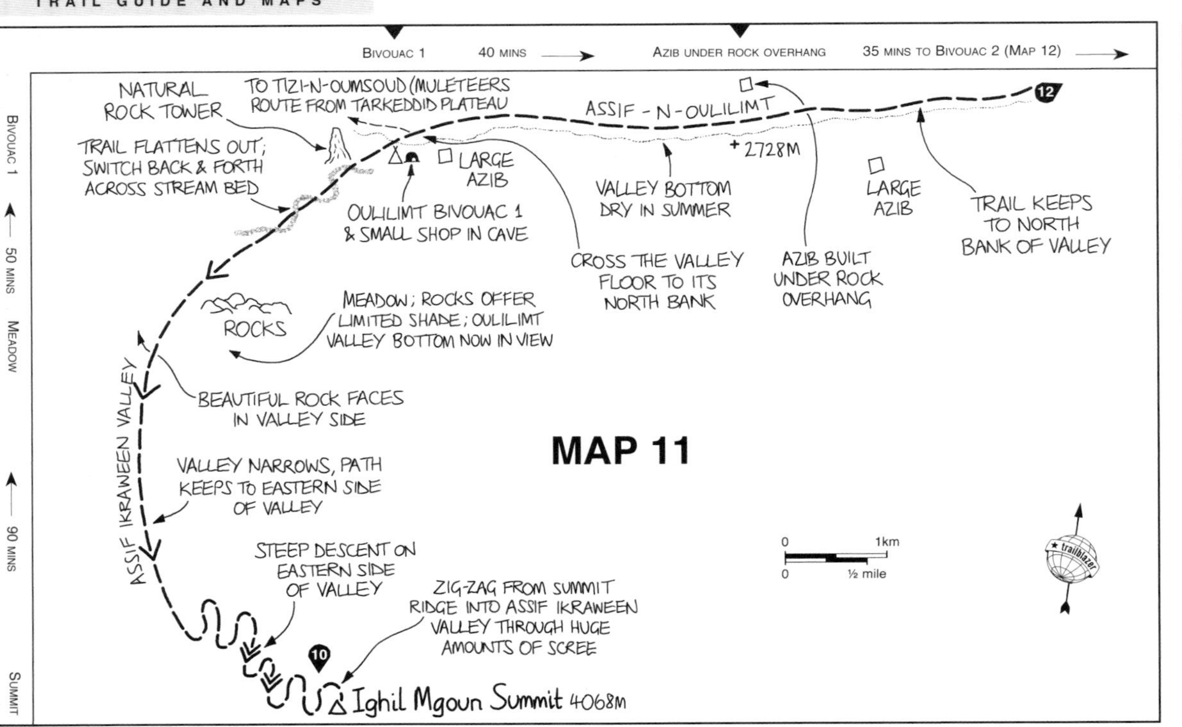
BIVOUAC 1
40 MINS
AZIB UNDER ROCK OVERHANG
35 MINS TO BIVOUAC 2 (MAP 12)
NATURAL ROCK TOWER
TO TIZI-N-OUMSOUD (MULETEERS ROUTE FROM TARKEDDID PLATEAU
ASSIF - N - OULILIMT
12
TRAIL FLATTENS OUT; SWITCH BACK & FORTH ACROSS STREAM BED
LARGE AZIB
+2728M
LARGE AZIB
OULILIMT BIVOUAC 1 & SMALL SHOP IN CAVE
VALLEY BOTTOM DRY IN SUMMER
TRAIL KEEPS TO NORTH BANK OF VALLEY
CROSS THE VALLEY FLOOR TO ITS NORTH BANK
AZIB BUILT UNDER ROCK OVERHANG
ROCKS
MEADOW; ROCKS OFFER LIMITED SHADE; OULILIMT VALLEY BOTTOM NOW IN VIEW
BEAUTIFUL ROCK FACES IN VALLEY SIDE
MAP 11
ASSIF IKRAWEEN VALLEY
VALLEY NARROWS, PATH KEEPS TO EASTERN SIDE OF VALLEY
0 1km
0 ½ mile
trailblazer
STEEP DESCENT ON EASTERN SIDE OF VALLEY
ZIG-ZAG FROM SUMMIT RIDGE INTO ASSIF IKRAWEEN VALLEY THROUGH HUGE AMOUNTS OF SCREE
10
Ighil Mgoun Summit 4068M
BIVOUAC 1 ← 50 MINS MEADOW ← 90 MINS SUMMIT

utes the valley suddenly grows very narrow, almost closing. Just before this lies a small, soft area of meadow, **Bivouac 2**, at the centre of which a natural water source may spring. If it is dry, the Oulilimt River re-emerges in the main valley here in summer, but, of course, this is not source water and should not be considered safe to drink without purification (see box p29). This is a good place to camp, but it lacks shade.

Alternative route Meanwhile, your muleteer, will have followed an alternative route from Tarkeddid Refuge to the Oulilimt Valley, first heading eastwards across the Tarkeddid Plateau. After about one hour, still heading eastwards, the trail begins a 30-minute descent via a steep zig-zagged path, to the floor of the Arous Valley. Having crossed the Arous stream at the bottom, the route climbs again to a col, **Tizi-n-Oumsoud**, reached in about 2¼ hours from the refuge, crossing a second stream bed en route.

On the far, eastern side of the col, the trail descends steeply at first to the north, but quickly levels out and then, after about 15 minutes, runs eastwards through a narrow corridor of rocks before emerging shortly afterwards onto the floor of the Oulilimt Valley. If you have agreed to meet your muleteer at Bivouac 1, he will need to turn right (west) here and trek back up the Oulilimt Valley for just two minutes to reach the raised area of stony ground and the caves. If, however, you have headed for Bivouac 2, he will need to continue down valley (east), as described above.

Oulilimt Bivouac 2–Refuge Aïn Aflafal [Map 12, p170]

This short, attractive stage is easy to follow since it simply traces the Oulilimt Valley, often along its floor, and periodically climbs the left-hand (northern) valley side to offer beautiful views to both east and west.

From Oulilimt Bivouac 2, immediately pass two **natural rock towers** and a small **stone cottage** and briefly climb to the left (north) up the valley side before turning to follow the valley eastwards at a higher level. After 20 minutes the path descends to cross a **tributary stream** and returns briefly to the floor of the Oulilimt before immediately ascending gently for 10 minutes and continuing down valley. After passing numerous natural rock towers, it again descends steeply back to the valley floor 15 minutes later.

For the next 40 minutes the trail follows the valley bottom, passing another azib under a **rock overhang** after 20 minutes on the left, before turning away sharply at 90 degrees, again climbing the valley side very steeply. Then, once more turning to follow the valley at a higher level, the first of three successive **small cols** is reached 40 minutes later. After the third col, reached 20 minutes after the first, the trail descends for the final time today, for 15 minutes, in zig-zags back to the Oulilimt floor.

This time cross over to the southern side of the valley. **Refuge Aïn Aflafal** (2320m/7609ft) will come into view, now just 20 minutes away, seemingly in the valley bottom. In fact it sits at the confluence of the Oulilimt and a tributary river flowing from the south-east. Sadly, though structurally very sound, the refuge offers no more than rudimentary shelter between November and April. Worse still, between May and October, it is completely taken over for use as a *bergerie*

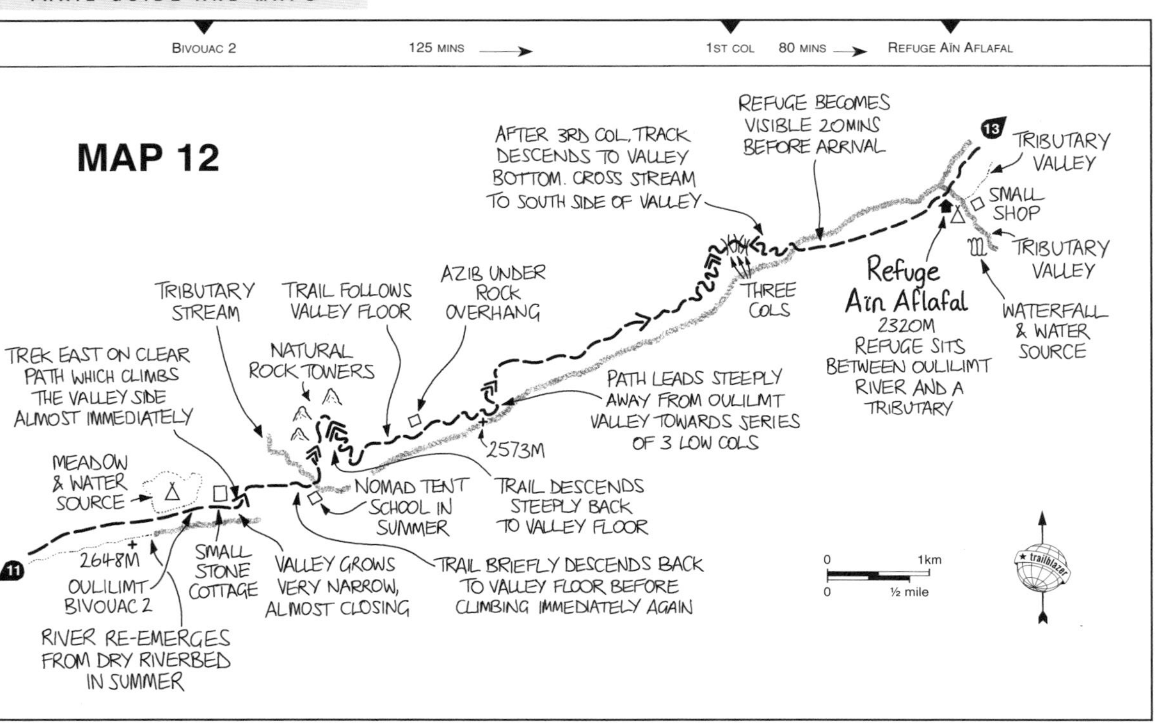
BIVOUAC 2
125 MINS
1ST COL
80 MINS
REFUGE AÏN AFLAFAL
MAP 12
TREK EAST ON CLEAR PATH WHICH CLIMBS THE VALLEY SIDE ALMOST IMMEDIATELY
MEADOW & WATER SOURCE
2648M
OULILIMT BIVOUAC 2
RIVER RE-EMERGES FROM DRY RIVERBED IN SUMMER
SMALL STONE COTTAGE
VALLEY GROWS VERY NARROW, ALMOST CLOSING
TRIBUTARY STREAM
NATURAL ROCK TOWERS
TRAIL FOLLOWS VALLEY FLOOR
NOMAD TENT SCHOOL IN SUMMER
AZIB UNDER ROCK OVERHANG
TRAIL BRIEFLY DESCENDS BACK TO VALLEY FLOOR BEFORE CLIMBING IMMEDIATELY AGAIN
TRAIL DESCENDS STEEPLY BACK TO VALLEY FLOOR
2573M
PATH LEADS STEEPLY AWAY FROM OULILMT VALLEY TOWARDS SERIES OF 3 LOW COLS
AFTER 3RD COL, TRACK DESCENDS TO VALLEY BOTTOM. CROSS STREAM TO SOUTH SIDE OF VALLEY
THREE COLS
REFUGE BECOMES VISIBLE 20MINS BEFORE ARRIVAL
Refuge Aïn Aflafal
2320M
REFUGE SITS BETWEEN OULILIMT RIVER AND A TRIBUTARY
TRIBUTARY VALLEY
SMALL SHOP
TRIBUTARY VALLEY
WATERFALL & WATER SOURCE
0
1km
0
½ mile
trailblazer

(goat pen). The building becomes completely uninhabitable and degenerates into a stinking cesspit, the floor entirely caked in animal excrement and urine.

Nevertheless, in the tributary valley just behind there is plenty of soft, level grass to provide excellent **camping** ground and just five minutes further upstream, on the southern side of the tributary valley, is a wonderful source in the form of a small **waterfall** which cascades from high out of the rock. Also, a small azib, found in the first side valley on the north bank of the tributary valley, serves as a small **shop** selling the usual soft drinks; it will also provide live chickens and goats should your meat supply be running low. The shop-keeper can even accommodate you in an equally small and basic outbuilding for 20dh.

Refuge Aïn Aflafal–Taghreft–Tighremt n'Aït Ahmed [Map 13, p172]

It would be possible to complete the circuit back to Tabant and the Aït Bou Guemez Valley, just a five-hour trek from the refuge to the north-west, in one day. However, you might consider making an excursion to the east along the pretty Mgoun Valley as far as the village of Taghreft and back to Tighremt n'Aït Ahmed. This is a pleasant and fairly easy trek which allows time to explore a series of Berber villages. Despite the increasing numbers of organised trekking groups which pass this way on their way to the Vallée des Roses and Qalaa't Mgouna directly from Tabant, they retain a sense of being beautifully remote.

Allow about five hours to walk from the refuge to Taghreft and to return as far as Tighremt n'Aït Ahmed, although you should make sure that you build in additional time for inevitable tea breaks in the villages through which you pass. Bear in mind also that there is no need to replicate your route exactly on the return to Tighremt n'Aït Ahmed: a number of variants are possible, ranging from a trail along the riverbed to tracks that climb high above the villages, although you will be obliged to stay within the valley itself. Also, for a different experience, consider giving your muleteer a rest day. He might guard your bags and prepare the evening camp while you try your hand at riding his mule. On one trek here I reached this point on my birthday; it emerged, rather uncannily, that it was also the birthday of my muleteer. By changing our roles for the day, we felt that we had both been given a birthday treat by the other.

Rejoin the route by returning from your overnight camp to the refuge in the main valley and follow the River Oulilimt to the right (north-north-east). You might need sandals to follow this stretch of the river, even in summer. After 30 minutes you will encounter **Tighremt n'Aït Ahmed** (2235m/7330ft), the shell of a small and dilapidated abandoned agadir. This is the spot to which you will return to camp this evening and where you might now choose to leave your muleteer for the day. Conveniently, there is also a small **shop** here, owned by Moha Outfrit, which sells water and soft drinks. Should the shop be closed, the key might be available from one of the small azibs to the north-west on the far side of the river, although my guide returned very frustrated without it. Adjacent to the shop is a small rock overhang and a constructed **stone shelter** which would provide adequate accommodation for a small group; you might be asked to pay a nominal charge.

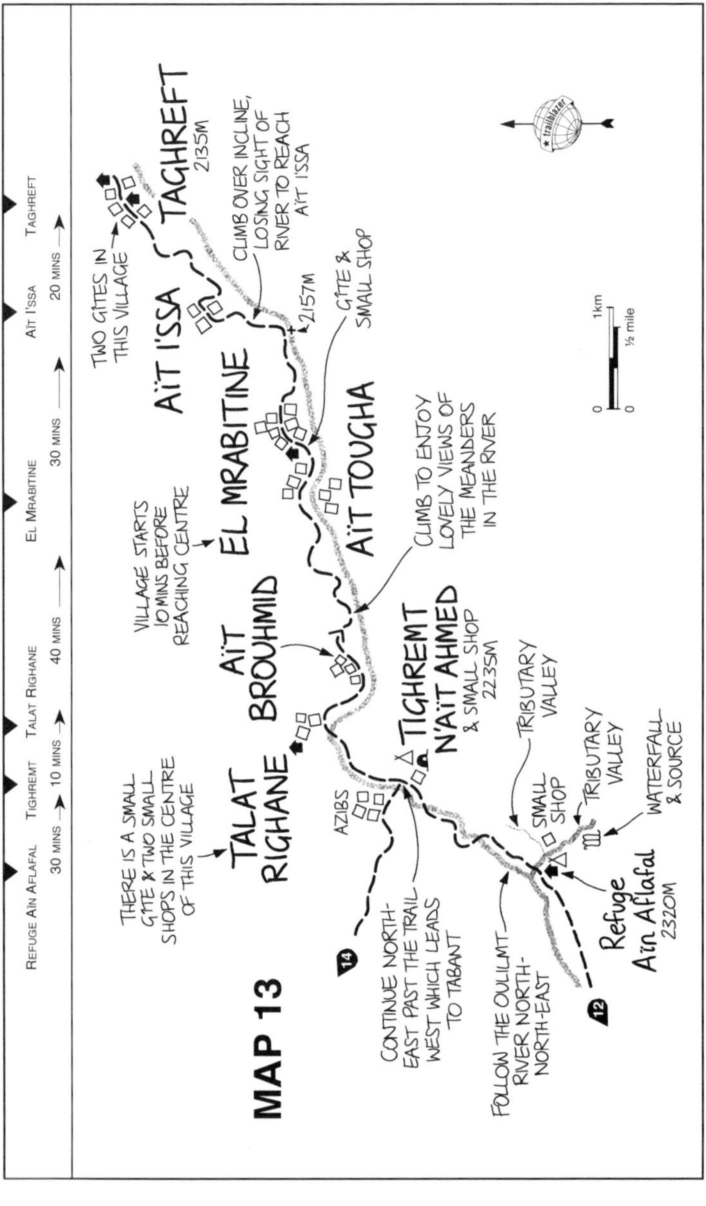

REFUGE AÏN AFLAFAL
30 MINS
TIGHREMT
10 MINS
TALAT RIGHANE
40 MINS
EL MRABITINE
30 MINS
AÏT I'SSA
20 MINS
TAGHREFT
MAP 13
THERE IS A SMALL GÎTE & TWO SMALL SHOPS IN THE CENTRE OF THIS VILLAGE
TALAT RIGHANE
AÏT BROUHMID
VILLAGE STARTS 10 MINS BEFORE REACHING CENTRE
EL MRABITINE
AÏT I'SSA
TWO GÎTES IN THIS VILLAGE
TAGHREFT
2135M
CLIMB OVER INCLINE, LOSING SIGHT OF RIVER TO REACH AÏT I'SSA
2157M
GÎTE & SMALL SHOP
AÏT TOUGHA
AZIBS
CONTINUE NORTH-EAST PAST THE TRAIL WEST WHICH LEADS TO TABANT
TIGHREMT N'AÏT AHMED
& SMALL SHOP
2235M
CLIMB TO ENJOY LOVELY VIEWS OF THE MEANDERS IN THE RIVER
FOLLOW THE OULILMT RIVER NORTH-NORTH-EAST
TRIBUTARY VALLEY
SMALL SHOP
TRIBUTARY VALLEY
WATERFALL & SOURCE
Refuge Aïn Aflafal
2320M
12
14
0
1km
0
½ mile
trailblazer

Continue to follow the valley to the north-east. Look back to the azibs on the left on the far side of the river where you might have searched for the key to the shop. Take note of the side valley behind them through which a trail leads to the west, as this is the route back to Tabant that you will take tomorrow.

Ten minutes later, having crossed over to the north bank of the Mgoun River, you will reach the pretty village of **Talat Righane**. A small ***gîte d'étape***, owned by Aït Lehcen Brahimat, at the back of the village, with just two rooms but with an attractive courtyard, charges 30dh per person: his price has not shifted in years. The village also boasts two small shops, one either side of the gîte. The village looks out over neat and carefully farmed fields which border the river as it wends its way out of sight to the south-east.

Continue to follow the north bank of the river for about 20 minutes to reach the next village of **Aït Brouhmid** before climbing a little to gain lovely views of occasional hamlets and further meanders in the river. Ten minutes after Aït Brouhmid you will see the small village of Aït Tougha on the opposite (south) bank, before descending once again to reach the first houses of the much larger village of **El Mrabitine/Mrabtin** (also known locally as Egrarmen) at the river's edge. A further 10 minutes will bring you towards the village centre where Youss Lehcen Atifi would allow you to stay in his house for 30dh per night including a hot shower. Should you wish not to linger so long you might at least take the opportunity to enjoy a pause for tea in his first-floor salon. Conveniently, there is also a small, friendly **shop** next door.

Continue along the river for a further 30 minutes to the village of **Aït I'ssa/ Ayt Issa** where a small sign fastened to a tree invites you to take more tea, ***Chez Ahmed***. Once you have passed a grand old house at the exit of the village, 20 minutes more will bring you to the attractive village of **Taghreft** (2135m/ 7002ft).

Taghreft is a relatively large village with a population of about 1000 made up of 90 families. There are two ***gîtes d'étape***. The first you are likely to encounter is run by the very personable former mayor, Oujahuoch Addi, which can offer only cold showers, although it does have the benefit of electric lights. Follow the signs from the path to find it in the middle of the village. The second, a new and larger **gîte**, ***Chez Jamal***, with a picturesque setting close to the river, was only completed in 2008. Located at the eastern exit to the village, beds are offered for 30dh and hot showers are available.

To return to Taghreft, head back (west) in the direction from which you have just come, but consider varying your path either by climbing higher over the cliffs or else by wading through the river, season permitting.

Tighremt n'Aït/Ayt Ahmed–Tizi-n-Aït/Ayt Imi–Tabant
[Map 14, p174; Map 15, p175]

Cross the Oulilimt River to its western bank. Head to the left of the *azibs*, now clearly visible to the north, and into the side valley of **Assif Amougr Sain**, which enters the Oulilimt Valley from the west. At this point, the col towards which you are trekking, Tizi-n-Aït Imi (2905m), can be seen some way ahead towards the far end of the side-valley on its right-hand (northern) side.

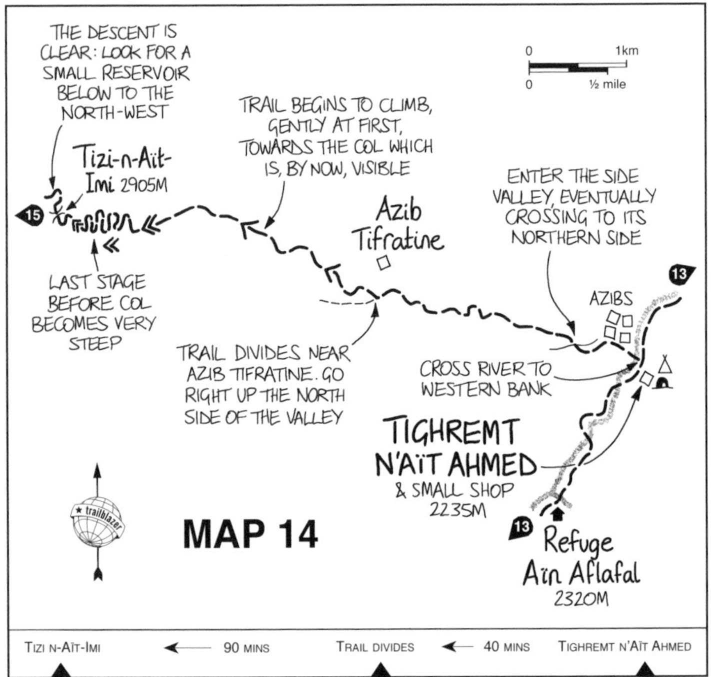

Some 40 minutes later, below **Azib Tifratine**, the trail divides; from here it will take another 90 minutes to reach the col. Veer to the right (north-north-west) up the fork which climbs the north side of the side-valley. The incline is initially fairly gentle, although after about 15 minutes it begins to zig-zag more steeply, becoming very steep just before the col. Assuming that you have recently ascended Ighil Mgoun, however, you certainly have nothing to fear.

On the final approach to **Tizi-n-Aït Imi**, pause to enjoy views back to the Mgoun Valley and across to Tizi-n-Oumsoud: this is the col which your muleteer crossed on his way to meet you at the Oulilimt bivouacs on Day 3. At the col you can also enjoy marvellous views of the Aït Bou Guemez Valley which open up to the north.

The path descends steeply on the far side of the col to the north-west across some loose scree. Take care: this is the only place in the Atlas where I have encountered the body of a fallen mule. Should the weather be poor and Tabant not be visible, the path is nevertheless very clear. Aim first for a small **reservoir**, reached in about 85 minutes and then for the village of **Aït/Ayt Imi** (1900m/6232ft) reached 35 minutes later. The village gîte d'étape, which once offered respite here to weary trekkers on their descent, is now closed. Nonetheless, **Tabant** (1850m/6068ft) is now just 25 tantalising minutes away across a few cultivated fields.

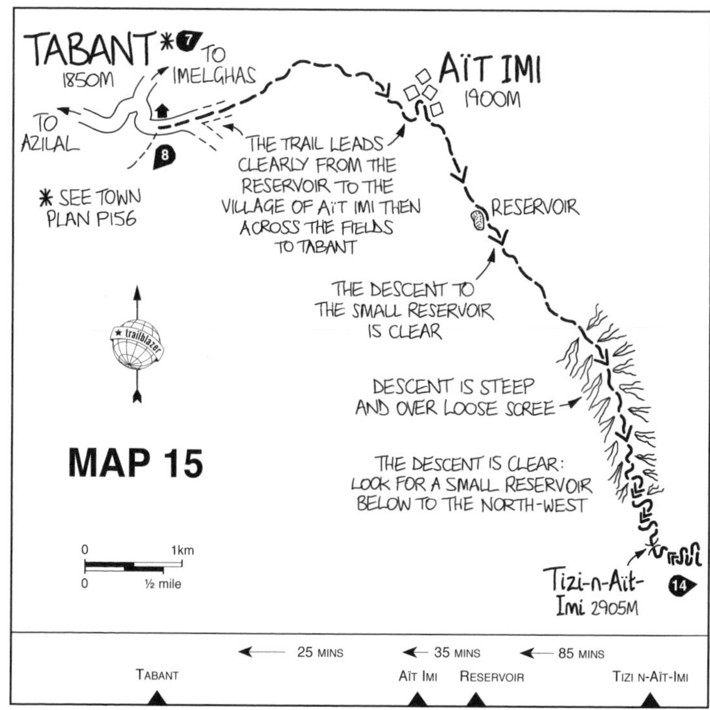

MGOUN TRAVERSE

This trek, mostly low level and winding through beautiful valleys, includes just one climb of note, to cross Tizi-n-Rouguelt/Rougoult (2860m/9380ft). The route description is in six stages, though some may wish to organise transport after the fifth to avoid a final day walking on a track suitable for vehicles. Allow an extra day, however, if you decide to take a side trip to Megdaz.

> **MGOUN TRAVERSE**
> - **Level of difficulty** moderate
> - **Duration** 5, 6 or 7 days
> - **Maps** Either *Zawyat Ahancal, Azilal and Skoura* (1:100,000), Division de la Carte, Morocco Survey, or *Mgoun Massif* (1:100,000), West Col, which covers the whole route except for the last nine kilometres to Aït Tamlil.

Tabant–Agouti–Taghia–Abachkou [Map 16, p176; Map 17, p177]

The first stage is long but the valley scenery is quite beautiful and the trekking easy. Indeed it is possible to walk along road and piste the whole way to Abachkou, the end of the first stage.

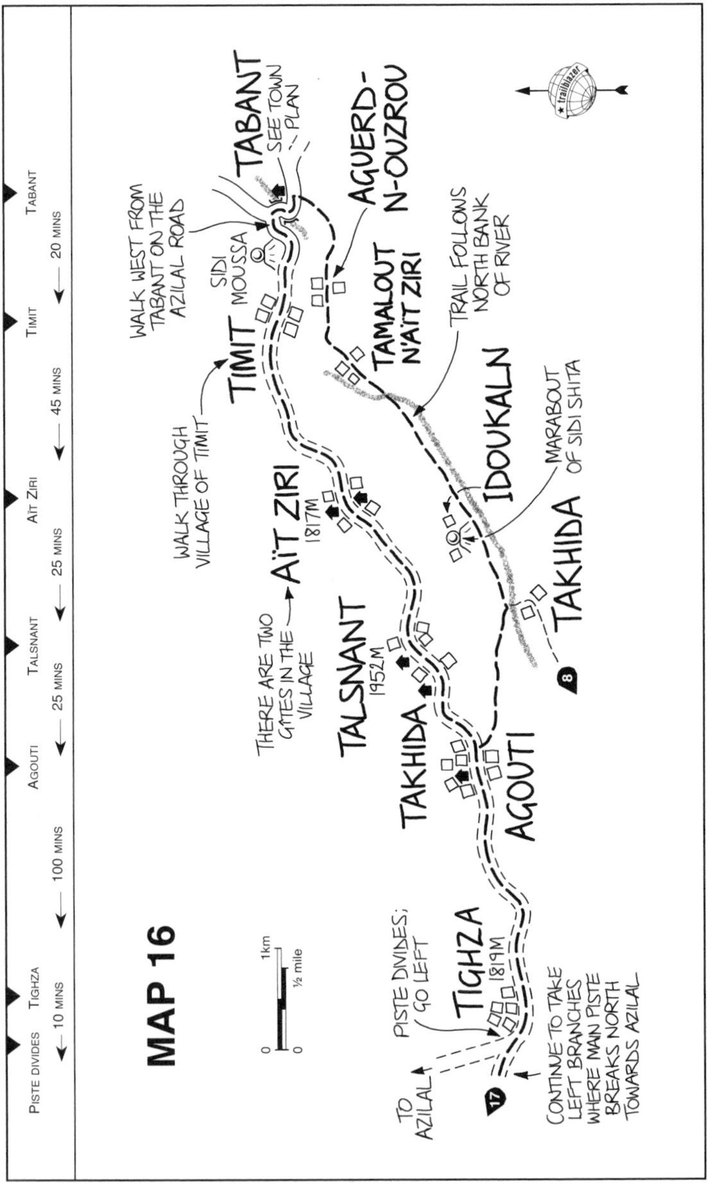

PISTE DIVIDES ← 10 MINS TIGHZA ← 100 MINS AGOUTI ← 25 MINS TALSNANT ← 25 MINS AÏT ZIRI ← 45 MINS TIMIT ← 20 MINS TABANT

MAP 16

0 1km
0 ½ mile

WALK WEST FROM TABANT ON THE AZILAL ROAD
WALK THROUGH VILLAGE OF TIMIT
TIMIT
SIDI MOUSSA
TABANT
SEE TOWN PLAN
THERE ARE TWO GÎTES IN THE VILLAGE
AÏT ZIRI
1817M
TALSNANT
1952M
AGUERD-N-OUZROU
TAMALOUT N'AÏT ZIRI
TO AZILAL
PISTE DIVIDES; GO LEFT
TAKHIDA
TIGHZA
1819M
17
AGOUTI
TRAIL FOLLOWS NORTH BANK OF RIVER
IDOUKALN
CONTINUE TO TAKE LEFT BRANCHES WHERE MAIN PISTE BREAKS NORTH TOWARDS AZILAL
8
TAKHIDA
MARABOUT OF SIDI SHITA
trailblazer

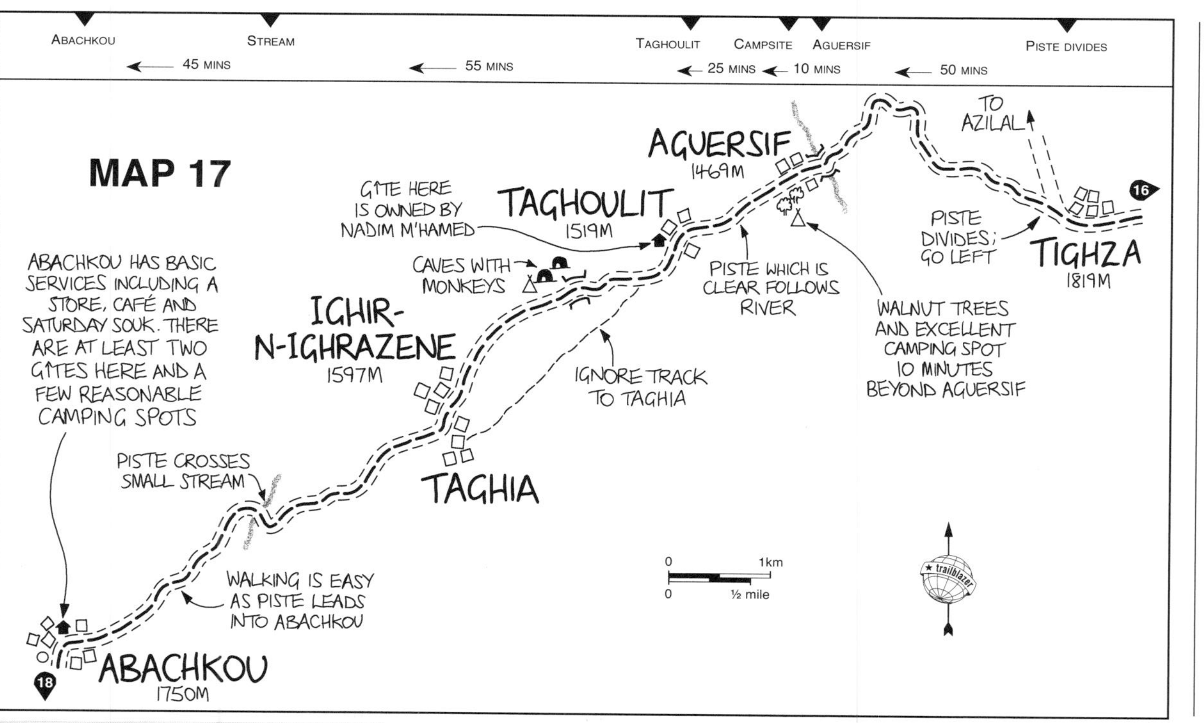
ABACHKOU
STREAM
TAGHOULIT
CAMPSITE
AGUERSIF
PISTE DIVIDES
45 MINS
55 MINS
25 MINS
10 MINS
50 MINS
MAP 17
GÎTE HERE IS OWNED BY NADIM M'HAMED
TAGHOULIT 1519M
AGUERSIF 1469M
TO AZILAL
16
PISTE DIVIDES; GO LEFT
TIGHZA 1819M
ABACHKOU HAS BASIC SERVICES INCLUDING A STORE, CAFÉ AND SATURDAY SOUK. THERE ARE AT LEAST TWO GÎTES HERE AND A FEW REASONABLE CAMPING SPOTS
CAVES WITH MONKEYS
IGHIR-N-IGHRAZENE 1597M
PISTE WHICH IS CLEAR FOLLOWS RIVER
WALNUT TREES AND EXCELLENT CAMPING SPOT 10 MINUTES BEYOND AGUERSIF
IGNORE TRACK TO TAGHIA
PISTE CROSSES SMALL STREAM
TAGHIA
0
1km
0
½ mile
trailblazer
WALKING IS EASY AS PISTE LEADS INTO ABACHKOU
ABACHKOU 1750M
18

First head west and then north out of Tabant (1850m/6068ft; see pp154-7) along the Azilal road for 15 minutes, crossing the river course, until you meet a small **road junction**. Here, a left turn (west) heads immediately to Sidi Moussa (see box p158) after which the road passes the villages of **Timit** (20 minutes, not shown on the West Col map) and **Aït/Ayt Ziri** (65 minutes), where there are two **gîtes**, before reaching **Talsnant** (1952m/6402ft; 90 minutes). The ***gîte*** in the centre of the village here is owned by Boukhayou Mohammed. Mohammed himself is something of a legend in the valley. He was once caught in extreme weather on Mgoun with clients who refused to follow his advice to descend. The helicopter had to be called but it was too late for one trekker. Such tragedies are rare in the Atlas but serve to highlight the importance of trusting local guides who know the area and are weatherwise. There is another ***gîte*** just five minutes further on in the adjacent village of **Takhida**, owned by Jellou Brahim and his French wife. It is a friendly place with much-better facilities than most gîtes, including hot showers.

Agouti (115 minutes from Tabant) also has a ***gîte***, not quite so impressive, which is run by Aït Ben Ali Mohammed. Prices are very similar in all these gîtes. Expect to pay 50dh for a bed, 20dh for breakfast and 50dh for other meals. To avoid tarmac from Tabant to Agouti, it is much more pleasant to follow the route as described at the beginning of the Mgoun Circular trek (see p160). Once the village of Agouti is almost on your right, turn right (north) along a track which at first doubles back a little before heading across the fields to reach it. From Agouti, continue west on the road until you see the village of **Tighza** (1819m/5966ft; 3 hours 35 minutes from Tabant), 10 minutes after which an obvious piste (signposted) to the left leaves the tarmac road, descends into the valley to the west and continues all the way to Abachkou (185 minutes from the tarmac road). At the time of research this piste was being improved to enable better vehicle access to Abachkou and so facilitate the excavation of minerals from the mountains.

Aguersif/Agerssif (1469m/4818ft) is reached 60 minutes after Tighza and 10 minutes beyond is an excellent area for ***camping***, under some walnut trees by the stream. From here, the piste follows the river to the south-west into the next village, **Taghoulit** (1519m/4982ft). The ***gîte*** here is owned by Nadim M'hamed.

Keep following the piste, ignoring the track which heads left to Taghia. Shortly afterwards some **caves** above a bridge provide home to some wild monkeys; a good ***campsite*** area lies below. Pass the village of **Ighir-n-Ighrazene** (1750m/5740ft) on the right and continue to Abachkou (almost 7 hours from Tabant). **Abachkou** has some services including a **general store**, a **café** and a Saturday **souk**. There are at least two ***gîtes*** here and a few reasonable pitches if you wish to **camp**, although there are much better areas to be found in the valley of Ghougoult/Rougoult just 75 minutes further on.

Abachkou–Ghougoult/Rougoult–Ifira [Map 18]

Walk through Abachkou (1750m/5740ft) past the **café** just below an aerial and look for a trail which leads south-east towards the stream on the valley floor. Cross the **stream**, for which there is no bridge, and follow it downstream on the right-hand side to an obvious mule track. Follow the track as it contours round into the **Ghougoult Valley**. The track climbs quite high before it levels out

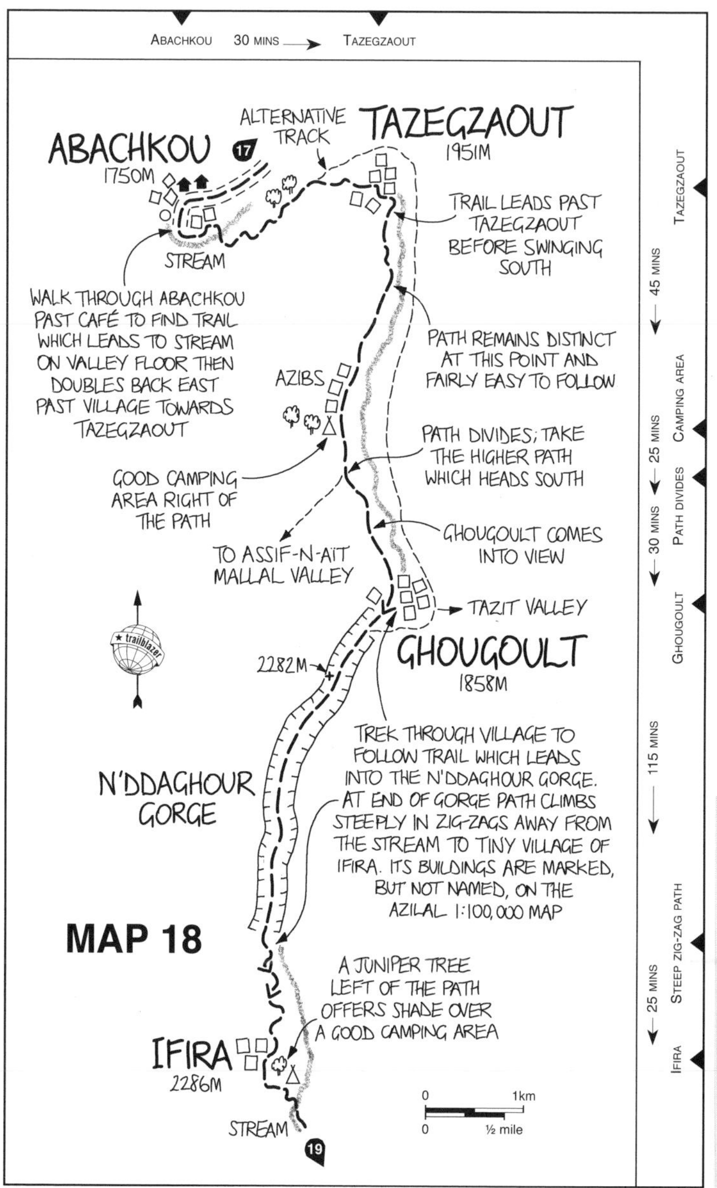

ABACHKOU 30 MINS → TAZEGZAOUT
ALTERNATIVE TRACK
TAZEGZAOUT
1951M
ABACHKOU
17
1750M
STREAM
TRAIL LEADS PAST TAZEGZAOUT BEFORE SWINGING SOUTH
WALK THROUGH ABACHKOU PAST CAFÉ TO FIND TRAIL WHICH LEADS TO STREAM ON VALLEY FLOOR THEN DOUBLES BACK EAST PAST VILLAGE TOWARDS TAZEGZAOUT
PATH REMAINS DISTINCT AT THIS POINT AND FAIRLY EASY TO FOLLOW
AZIBS
PATH DIVIDES; TAKE THE HIGHER PATH WHICH HEADS SOUTH
GOOD CAMPING AREA RIGHT OF THE PATH
GHOUGOULT COMES INTO VIEW
TO ASSIF-N-AÏT MALLAL VALLEY
TAZIT VALLEY
trailblazer
2282M
GHOUGOULT
1858M
TREK THROUGH VILLAGE TO FOLLOW TRAIL WHICH LEADS INTO THE N'DDAGHOUR GORGE. AT END OF GORGE PATH CLIMBS STEEPLY IN ZIG-ZAGS AWAY FROM THE STREAM TO TINY VILLAGE OF IFIRA. ITS BUILDINGS ARE MARKED, BUT NOT NAMED, ON THE AZILAL 1:100,000 MAP
N'DDAGHOUR GORGE
MAP 18
A JUNIPER TREE LEFT OF THE PATH OFFERS SHADE OVER A GOOD CAMPING AREA
IFIRA
2286M
STREAM
19
0 1km
0 ½ mile
TAZEGZAOUT
45 MINS
CAMPING AREA
25 MINS
PATH DIVIDES
30 MINS
GHOUGOULT
115 MINS
STEEP ZIG-ZAG PATH
25 MINS
IFIRA

along the right side of the valley and passes the village of **Tazegzaout** before it reaches **Ghougoult** (2 hours 10 minutes from Abachkou). It is possible to stay '*chez l'habitant*' (in a local's home) in Ghougoult; ask at the school.

The path climbs to the south-south-west as it crosses to the far (south) side of Ghougoult and into the **n'Ddaghour Gorge**. The gorge is quite obvious; just take care not to be drawn eastwards from Ghougoult along the larger Tazit Valley.

After almost two hours in the gorge, the trail starts to zig-zag steeply to the right (south-west) away from the stream to the tiny village of **Ifira** (2286m/7498ft), reached in a further 25 minutes. Not named on either of the 1:100,000 maps, its location is, however, indicated by buildings marked on the Azilal map. Keep your eyes open: Ifira is little more than a bergerie that is only inhabited in summer and would be missed easily in winter. Alternatively, you might consider continuing to the camping area mentioned below.

Ifira–Amezri [Map 19]

Continue south-east from Ifira. The path begins to climb steeply but continues to trace the stream and its ravine. About one hour beyond the bergerie the valley divides. Take the steeper, narrower valley to the left (east) which heads towards **rock towers** and cliffs.

Later the ravine quite suddenly widens out to reveal a gentle, sweeping valley, just below the approaching Tizi-n-Rouguelt/Rougoult. There is a tempting, grassy area, which would be ideal for **camping** and might be considered as an alternative end to the first stage instead of Ifira.

Keep ascending with the trail as it gradually steepens and zig-zags more sharply and emerges onto the wide col of **Tizi-n-Rouguelt** (2860m/9380ft), 145 minutes from Ifira, just as another, higher path meets yours from the left (east). Once over the col, the track divides within minutes. Ignore the left (east) branch which leads to the village of Tassawt-n-Oufella and the Tarkeddid Plateau: take the right (south-west) branch which descends along the west side of the Tessaout Valley to the village of **Tasgaïwalt/Tasgaywalt** about 75 minutes south of the col.

At this point the valley is a spectacular mixture of colours created by the combination of grasslands, cultivated areas, red rock foothills and snow-capped mountains. You will now follow the beautiful **Tessaout Valley** for the remainder of the trek until the final approach to Aït/Ayt Tamlil.

Shortly after Tasgaïwalt, as you continue down the valley, pick up an obvious piste that will lead you southwards to **Amezri** (2250m/7380ft) within about 20 minutes. Here there are three small **shops**. To find the only ***gîte d'étape*** in the village, either follow the signpost or ask for Aguemed Mohammed. Alternatively, there are **camping** opportunities a little further along the valley.

Amezri–Aït/Ayt Hamza–Aït 'Ali-n-Ito/Ayt Ali n'Ittou [Map 20, p182; Map 21, p183]

This stage of the traverse is over five hours long, but relatively easy both in terms of terrain and navigation. There are no demanding climbs or descents and the path is clear. The scenery is fantastic almost all the way. However, you will

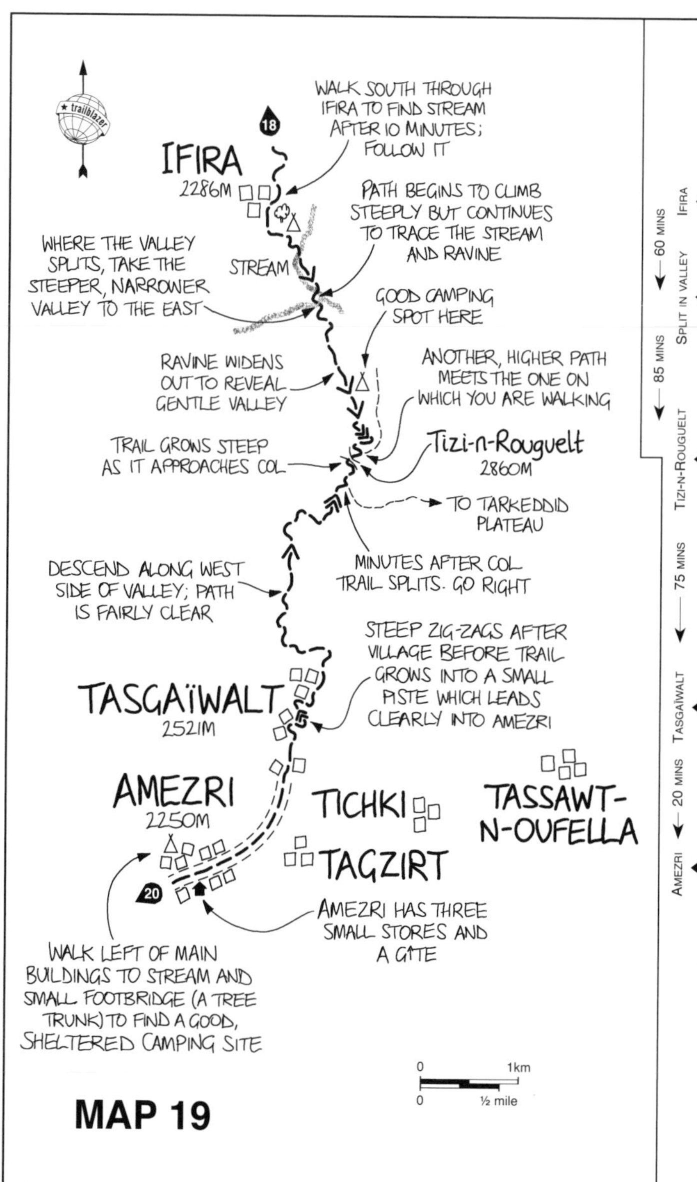
WALK SOUTH THROUGH IFIRA TO FIND STREAM AFTER 10 MINUTES; FOLLOW IT
IFIRA
2286M
PATH BEGINS TO CLIMB STEEPLY BUT CONTINUES TO TRACE THE STREAM AND RAVINE
WHERE THE VALLEY SPLITS, TAKE THE STEEPER, NARROWER VALLEY TO THE EAST
STREAM
GOOD CAMPING SPOT HERE
RAVINE WIDENS OUT TO REVEAL GENTLE VALLEY
ANOTHER, HIGHER PATH MEETS THE ONE ON WHICH YOU ARE WALKING
TRAIL GROWS STEEP AS IT APPROACHES COL
Tizi-n-Rouguelt
2860M
TO TARKEDDID PLATEAU
DESCEND ALONG WEST SIDE OF VALLEY; PATH IS FAIRLY CLEAR
MINUTES AFTER COL TRAIL SPLITS. GO RIGHT
STEEP ZIG-ZAGS AFTER VILLAGE BEFORE TRAIL GROWS INTO A SMALL PISTE WHICH LEADS CLEARLY INTO AMEZRI
TASGAÏWALT
2521M
AMEZRI
2250M
TICHKI
TASSAWT-N-OUFELLA
TAGZIRT
AMEZRI HAS THREE SMALL STORES AND A GîTE
WALK LEFT OF MAIN BUILDINGS TO STREAM AND SMALL FOOTBRIDGE (A TREE TRUNK) TO FIND A GOOD, SHELTERED CAMPING SITE
trailblazer
18
20
0
1km
0
½ mile
MAP 19
IFIRA
60 MINS
SPLIT IN VALLEY
85 MINS
TIZI-N-ROUGUELT
75 MINS
TASGAÏWALT
20 MINS
AMEZRI

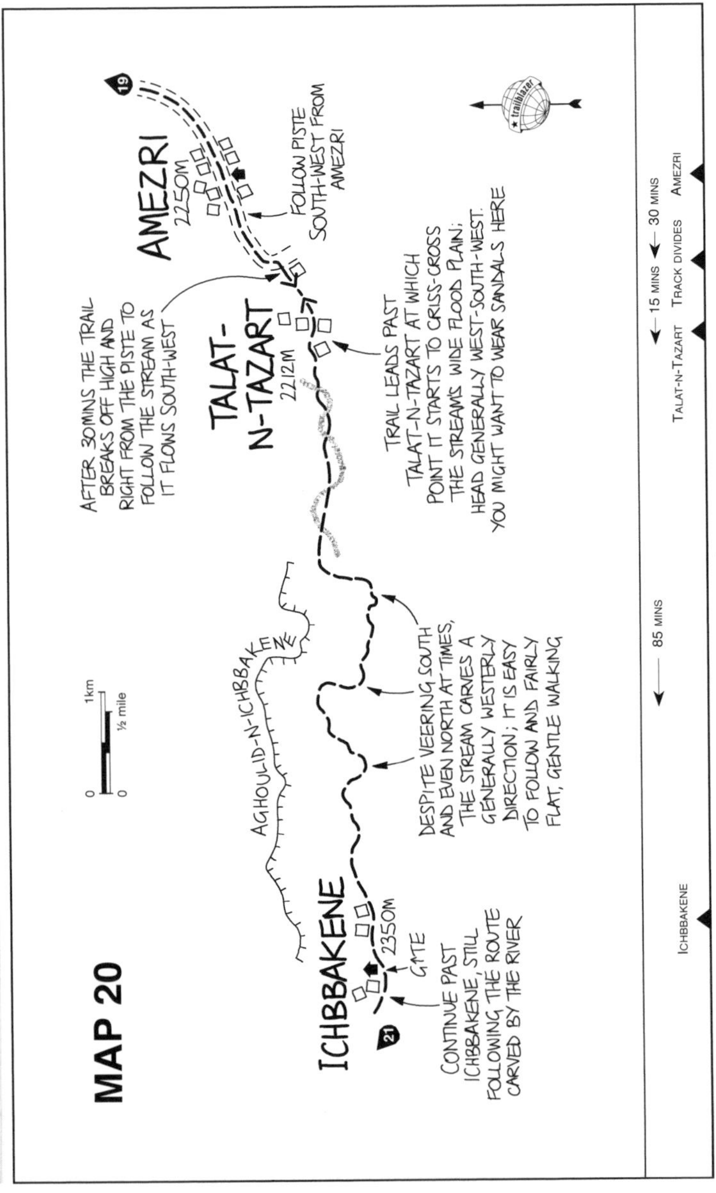

MAP 20

0 1km
0 ½ mile
AMEZRI
2250M
AFTER 30MINS THE TRAIL BREAKS OFF HIGH AND RIGHT FROM THE PISTE TO FOLLOW THE STREAM AS IT FLOWS SOUTH-WEST
FOLLOW PISTE SOUTH-WEST FROM AMEZRI
TALAT-N-TAZART
2212M
TRAIL LEADS PAST TALAT-N-TAZART AT WHICH POINT IT STARTS TO CRISS-CROSS THE STREAM'S WIDE FLOOD PLAIN; HEAD GENERALLY WEST-SOUTH-WEST. YOU MIGHT WANT TO WEAR SANDALS HERE
AGHOULID-N-ICHBBAKENE
DESPITE VEERING SOUTH AND EVEN NORTH AT TIMES, THE STREAM CARVES A GENERALLY WESTERLY DIRECTION; IT IS EASY TO FOLLOW AND FAIRLY FLAT, GENTLE WALKING
ICHBBAKENE
2350M
GATE
CONTINUE PAST ICHBBAKENE, STILL FOLLOWING THE ROUTE CARVED BY THE RIVER
21
19
trailblazer
85 MINS
15 MINS
30 MINS
ICHBBAKENE
TALAT-N-TAZART
TRACK DIVIDES
AMEZRI

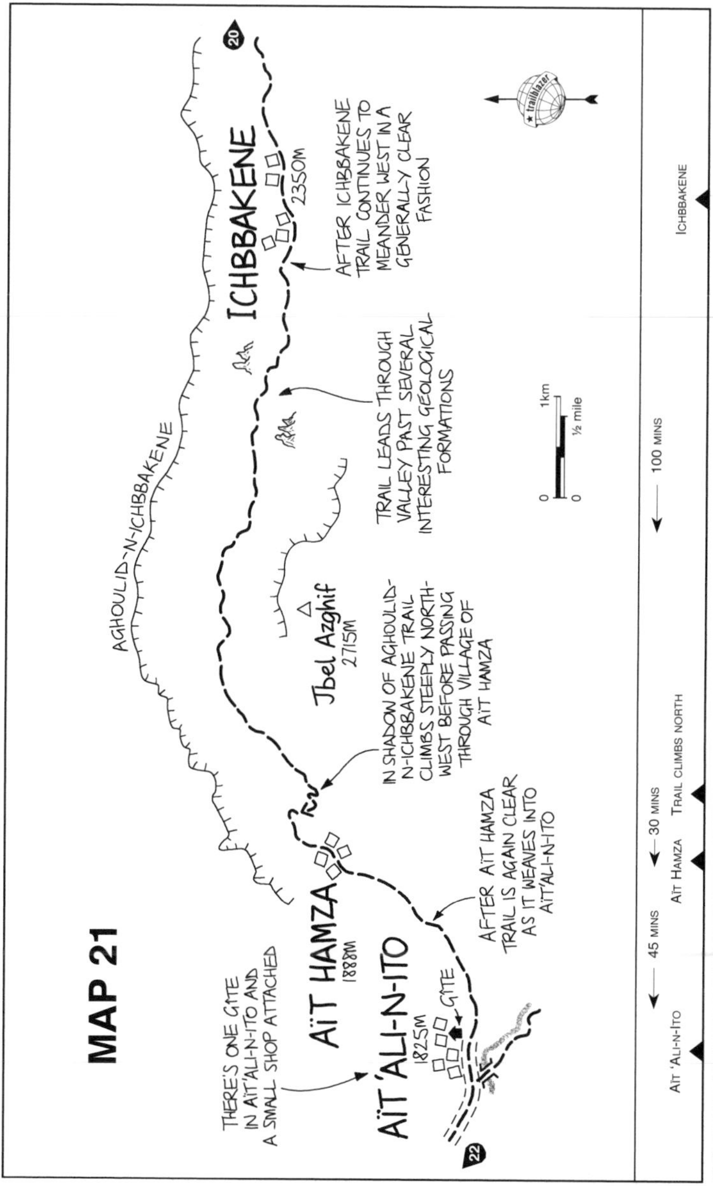

MAP 21

AGHOULID-N-ICHBBAKENE

THERE'S ONE GÎTE IN AÏT'ALI-N-ITO AND A SMALL SHOP ATTACHED

AÏT HAMZA
1888M

AÏT 'ALI-N-ITO
1825M

GÎTE

22

AFTER AÏT HAMZA TRAIL IS AGAIN CLEAR AS IT WEAVES INTO AÏT'ALI-N-ITO

IN SHADOW OF AGHOULID-N-ICHBBAKENE TRAIL CLIMBS STEEPLY NORTH-WEST BEFORE PASSING THROUGH VILLAGE OF AÏT HAMZA

Jbel Azghif
2715M

TRAIL LEADS THROUGH VALLEY PAST SEVERAL INTERESTING GEOLOGICAL FORMATIONS

ICHBBAKENE
2350M

20

AFTER ICHBBAKENE TRAIL CONTINUES TO MEANDER WEST IN A GENERALLY CLEAR FASHION

0 1km
0 ½ mile

trailblazer

← 45 mins ← 30 mins ← 100 mins

Aït 'Ali-n-Ito | Aït Hamza | Trail climbs north | Ichbbakene need to cross water several times so might want to keep a pair of sandals handy to avoid getting your boots wet. The trail follows the Tessaout riverbed but frequently changes its route after heavy rain or snow melt. Moreover, if heavy rains fall, the river is likely to be deep and fast-flowing and can be impossible to get through at all.

Follow the wide path heading south-west straight out of Amezri. After 30 minutes a trail leads off high to the right and then quickly down to join a wide, stony floodplain which continues to meander generally south-west. Keep following the valley floor, past the village of **Talat-n-Tazart** (wrongly named Ichbbakene on the Skoura map; 2212m/7255ft). In summer cross and re-cross from one side of the floodplain to the other to negotiate the many streams and rivulets which trace complicated paths across the valley floor. At times the valley veers briefly south and even north but maintains a generally westerly course.

Pass through the fields of **Ichbbakene/Ichebakan** (2350m/ 7710ft; wrongly named Talat-n-Tazart on the Skoura map) some 130 minutes after setting out from Amezri. Within this brooding village, which towers above its green fields in the valley below, is a ***gîte*** belonging to Mohamed Massreura. Just west of the village, natural rock formations punctuate the sensational surroundings.

Continue westwards to the exceptionally pretty village of **Aït/Ayt Hamza** (1888m/6192ft), stacked neatly against the valley side, reached in 130 minutes from Ichbbakene, then continue south-west for a further 45 minutes to reach the hamlet of **Aït 'Ali-n-Ito/Ayt Ali n'Ittou** (1825m/6074ft). The ***gîte d'étape*** here, run by Bourchouq Abdellah, has clean, adequate shared rooms. There is also a small **shop** attached and a **telephone**.

A road of sorts leads from Aït 'Ali-n-Ito west to Aït/Ayt Tamlil. Irregular transport, usually lorries, can therefore sometimes be available. As Aït 'Ali-n-Ito has a Saturday souk, Saturday afternoons or Sunday mornings are the best days to look for transport out. From Aït Tamlil there are connections to Azilal.

Aït 'Ali-n-Ito–Megdaz and return/onwards to Ifoulou [Map 22]

It would be a great shame to miss this short diversion from Aït 'Ali-n-Ito to Megdaz/Magdaz, one of the most attractive Berber villages in the entire Atlas range. The trek to Megdaz takes a little under two hours, so allow four hours for the return back to Aït 'Ali-n-Ito.

Alternatively, it is possible to make a longer, circular route by traversing west from Megdaz to Tagoukht/Tagourt in the Assif–n-Tasselnt/Teslant Valley, then north to Tasselnt and finally back down to Ifoulou in the Tessaout Valley where one can resume the westward trail to Aït/Ayt Tamlil. Allow a full day for this.

To get from Aït 'Ali-n-Ito to Megdaz, trek south from the gîte d'étape into the valley of the **Assif-n-Tifticht/Tittacht**. Simply cross the **concrete bridge** opposite the gîte and follow the valley south-east, heading upstream. Where the main valley turns eastwards towards Tifticht/Tittacht after 40 minutes, head south up the tributary valley towards Megdaz, passing through the village of **Imziln**. This is a relatively busy route so you will no doubt pass a number of Berbers on donkeys journeying between Megdaz and Aït 'Ali-n-Ito. Megdaz will come into view 60 minutes later and, after trekking for just

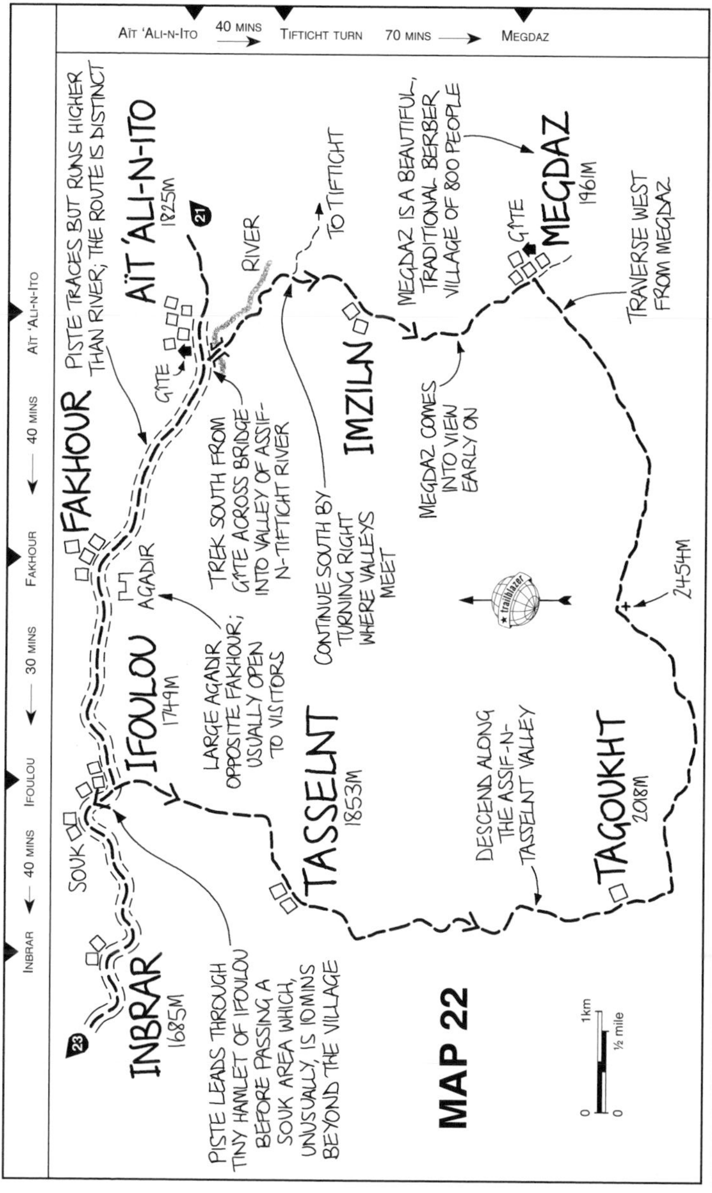

Aït 'Ali-n-Ito 40 mins → Tifticht turn 70 mins → Megdaz

Inbrar ← 40 mins Ifoulou ← 30 mins Fakhour ← 40 mins Aït 'Ali-n-Ito

MAP 22

INBRAR
1685M

PISTE LEADS THROUGH TINY HAMLET OF IFOULOU BEFORE PASSING A SOUK AREA WHICH, UNUSUALLY, IS 10MINS BEYOND THE VILLAGE

SOUK

IFOULOU
1749M

LARGE AGADIR OPPOSITE FAKHOUR; USUALLY OPEN TO VISITORS

AGADIR

FAKHOUR

PISTE TRACES BUT RUNS HIGHER THAN RIVER; THE ROUTE IS DISTINCT

GATE

AÏT 'ALI-N-ITO
1825M

TREK SOUTH FROM GATE ACROSS BRIDGE INTO VALLEY OF ASSIF-N-TIFTICHT RIVER

RIVER

TO TIFTICHT

CONTINUE SOUTH BY TURNING RIGHT WHERE VALLEYS MEET

IMZILN

MEGDAZ COMES INTO VIEW EARLY ON

MEGDAZ IS A BEAUTIFUL, TRADITIONAL BERBER VILLAGE OF 800 PEOPLE

GATE

MEGDAZ
1961M

TRAVERSE WEST FROM MEGDAZ

2454M

TASSELNT
1853M

DESCEND ALONG THE ASSIF-N-TASSELNT VALLEY

TAGOUKHT
2018M

0 1km
0 ½ mile

Mririda n'Aït Attik
Its beauty apart, Megdaz is also renowned as being the place of birth of the highly regarded Berber poetess, Mririda n'Aït Attik. Her works about her life in the Tassaout Valley, first translated into French by René Euloge, have been published under the title *Les Chants de la Tassaout* and in English as *The Songs of Mririda*.

10 more minutes, you will reach the first of its buildings. This is a large village of about 800 people with stout, square buildings, some up to 450 years old, stacked up against one another. Residents often have to climb over each other's homes in order to reach their own front doors. The houses, constructed with pale brown earth, blend into the mountainside and the whole village provides a perfect example or traditional, organic Berber architecture.

There is one enormous house in the centre of the village which stands out from the rest. It is almost a self-contained village for one extended family. Guests can stay here. Alternatively, there's a small unclassified ***gîte*** next door. The owner of this place, Hasou Nasser, is also the mayor. The people of Megdaz are particularly friendly and welcoming. They are used to visitors but haven't changed the village to accommodate tourism. Five small **shops** dispense the usual essentials such as toothpaste and water. Unless you plan to make the long loop round to Ifoulou, there is little alternative but to re-trace your steps back to Aït 'Ali-n-Ito.

Aït 'Ali-n-Ito–Aït/Ayt Tamlil [Map 22, p185; Map 23]

This last stage is entirely along a track that is suitable for vehicles so you may wish to end your trek at Aït 'Ali-n-Ito. If so, you will ideally have pre-arranged transport to collect you from this point. Nevertheless, should you wish to continue on foot, this long stage is again clear and easily navigated as it follows the Tessaout Valley almost all the way from Aït 'Ali-n-Ito to Aït/Ayt Tamlil.

Set out from Aït 'Ali-n-Ito on the piste which heads west and then turns north-west parallel with the river. The trail leads higher than the river but keep tracing the valley for 40 minutes to the hamlet of **Fakhour**, huddled on its right-hand (north) side. On the opposite (south) side of the valley stands an **agadir**, usually open to visitors.

At this point, the track swings sharply left (west) as it continues to pursue the valley and, in another 30 minutes, takes you to the small village of **Ifoulou** (1749m/5736ft). Those who choose to complete the small circuit via Megdaz and Tasselnt (see p184) will rejoin the main trail here. The track starts to ascend, passing an area purpose-built for the Ifoulou **souk**, which is held every Monday, 10 minutes beyond the village.

The next village, **Inbrar**, will take another 30 minutes to reach and 10 minutes beyond you will pass to the north of **Toufghine/Toufghin** (1685m/5527ft). From here the road, which again swings away to the right (north-west), is metalled. It leads first to the souk of **Aït/Ayt Alla**, which takes place every

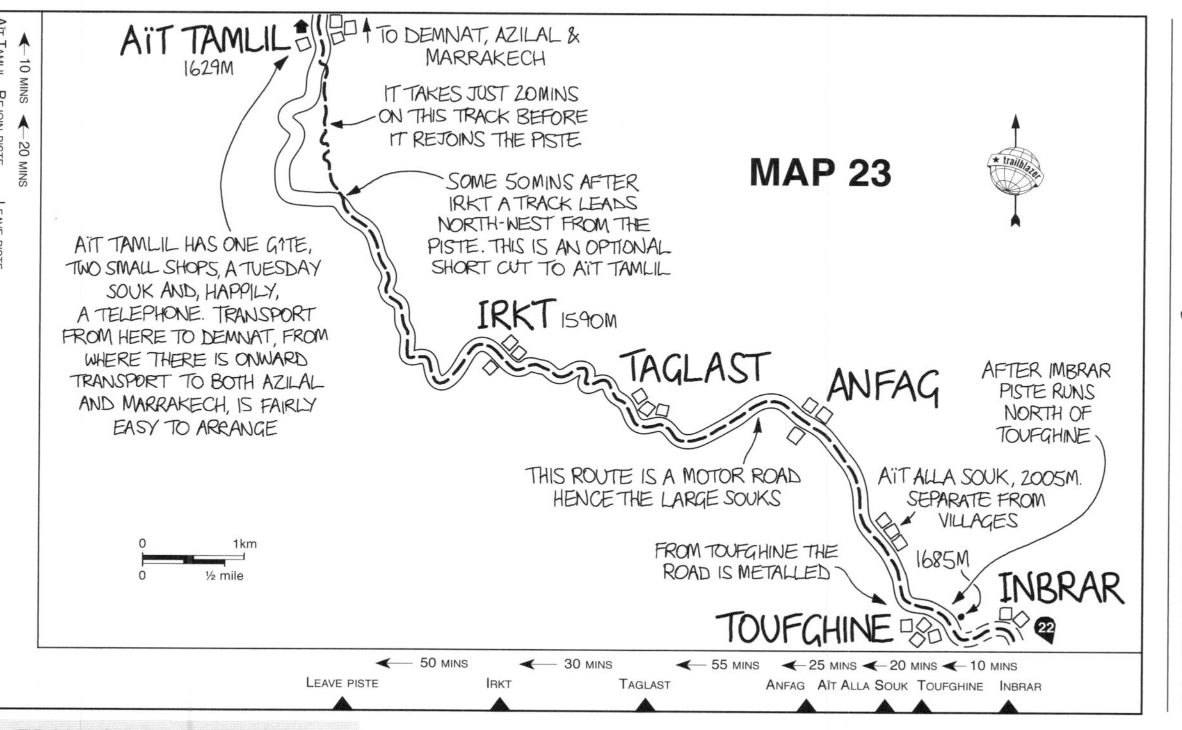
AÏT TAMLIL
1629M
TO DEMNAT, AZILAL & MARRAKECH
IT TAKES JUST 20MINS ON THIS TRACK BEFORE IT REJOINS THE PISTE
SOME 50MINS AFTER IRKT A TRACK LEADS NORTH-WEST FROM THE PISTE. THIS IS AN OPTIONAL SHORT CUT TO AÏT TAMLIL
MAP 23
AÏT TAMLIL HAS ONE GÎTE, TWO SMALL SHOPS, A TUESDAY SOUK AND, HAPPILY, A TELEPHONE. TRANSPORT FROM HERE TO DEMNAT, FROM WHERE THERE IS ONWARD TRANSPORT TO BOTH AZILAL AND MARRAKECH, IS FAIRLY EASY TO ARRANGE
IRKT 1590M
TAGLAST
ANFAG
AFTER IMBRAR PISTE RUNS NORTH OF TOUFGHINE
THIS ROUTE IS A MOTOR ROAD HENCE THE LARGE SOUKS
AÏT ALLA SOUK, 2005M. SEPARATE FROM VILLAGES
FROM TOUFGHINE THE ROAD IS METALLED
1685M
INBRAR
TOUFGHINE
22
0 1km
0 ½ mile
← 10 MINS ← 20 MINS
AÏT TAMLIL REJOIN PISTE LEAVE PISTE
← 50 MINS ← 30 MINS ← 55 MINS ← 25 MINS ← 20 MINS ← 10 MINS
LEAVE PISTE IRKT TAGLAST ANFAG AÏT ALLA SOUK TOUFGHINE INBRAR

Monday, 20 minutes beyond Toufghine, and then on to the village of **Anfag** in a further 25 minutes.

Turning back to the west, the road leads through **Taglast/Tagfast** 55 minutes later and then, 30 minutes afterwards, through **Irkt** (1590m/5215ft). Beyond Irkt the road again swings round to the right to head north-west. Look out for a steeper but smaller path which cuts away further right (north-north-west) from the road some 50 minutes after the village. Follow it for 20 minutes after which the narrow track rejoins the main road for the final 10-minute walk into **Aït/Ayt Tamlil** (1629m/5343ft). Aït Tamlil has one ***gîte d'étape***, that of Ben Kezza ben Mohammed, two small **shops** and a **telephone**. There is a **souk** on Tuesdays. Transport is available from here to Demnat (often Demnate) via Imi-n-Ifri, where a bizarre natural bridge carries the road over a stream. You might need to rely on a *camion* (lorry) to get from Aït Tamlil to Imi-n-Ifri but from there there is a mini-bus service to Demnat.

From Demnat transport, including grands taxis, is available both east to Azilal and west to Marrakech. **Demnat** also has a number of cheap **hotels**, **télé-boutiques**, **cafés**, **shops** and an interesting **kasbah** should you wish to linger.

The Sirwa region

Isolated and magnificent, Jbel Sirwa (3305m/10,840ft) offers some of the most exciting trekking in the Atlas Mountains. Its distinctive, volcanic summit, largely hidden from view to the south, can be seen from miles to the north, from as far as the distant High Atlas, and a trek to its summit is both varied and challenging. Lying between the High Atlas and Anti-Atlas ranges, the Berbers around Sirwa see fewer trekkers than those of either the Toubkal or the Mgoun regions further north. This remoteness can make trekking here difficult. Happily, the maps for the most part are quite accurate but, as in Sahro, paths can be hard to find and fewer locals speak English or even French than in the High Atlas.

This six-day circular route not only takes in the summit of Jbel Sirwa but also some of the most fascinating and unusual villages and valleys found anywhere in the Atlas Mountains. A visit to its agadirs alone would almost make this trek worthwhile.

GETTING TO TALIWINE

Reaching Taliwine by public transport can sometimes be a little problematic. A daily Taliwine bus leaves Marrakech at 9pm from the gare routière at Bab Doukkala. Tickets for this gruelling 200km, 7-hour journey are available from kiosk No 17 at a cost of 65dh per person. It is advisable to check whether the bus will take you all the way to Taliwine since it sometimes stops at Aoulouz some 30km west. If you do end up in Aoulouz, you will probably need to complete your journey by taking a seat in a grand taxi. The bus journey from

Marrakech might be long but it is also spectacular, crossing the spine of the High Atlas Mountains by winding up to the Tizi-n-Test (2100m/6888ft) before descending on its southern side to the Sous Plain and the Anti-Atlas beyond.

You can enjoy the same route by grand taxi, although again it can be difficult to find transport direct from Marrakech and may involve a change at Aoulouz. For 800dh you can book a private taxi all the way from Bab Doukkala to Taliwine. On the return journey, the local recommendation is first to take a place in a grand taxi from Taliwine to Taroudannt (35dh) and then from Taroudannt to Marrakech (100dh). The leg from Taroudannt involves travelling along the P40 to Chichaoua and then east along the P10, thereby skirting the western flanks of the Western Atlas and avoiding any serious mountains.

TALIWINE/TALIOUINE (984m/3227ft)

Taliwine is the main trailhead for reaching Sirwa. However, since relatively few trekkers explore this harsh and spectacular region, trekking has a low profile within the town. Even so, you should have very little trouble finding guides and muleteers here. Also, though quite small, Taliwine is a market town which serves a large region, so you will also find ample supplies of fresh fruit and vegetables and a reasonable range of other everyday goods. When a friend arrived here with scarcely more than the boots on his feet, his bag having gone astray in Marrakech, he was able to equip himself with a new wardrobe and refill his wash bag in not much more than an hour. What's more, although largely a functional town, its main architectural attraction being an inspiring, if decaying, Glaoua kasbah about two kilometres to the east of the town centre, Taliwine is a pleasant place in which to spend some time both at the beginning and end of your trek.

Services

You will find all the services you might expect of a small Moroccan town here, including **téléboutiques**, **pharmacies**, a **post office** and a Shell **garage**. All centrally located, there is also a convenient permanent **vegetable market** and a municipal **souk**. Perhaps more surprisingly, the town even has a **bar** in Grand Hotel Ibn Toumert which is open to non residents (see p190).

Taliwine, however, has only one **bank**, a branch of Crédit Agricole (Mon-Thu 8.30-11.30am & 2.30-5pm, Fri 8.30-11am & 3-5pm). It does not have an ATM. Although money can also be changed at the post office, it too is closed at weekends. Note that on Mondays, the day of the weekly Taliwine souk, there can be lengthy queues for money in both these places.

The location of the **souk** is a little inconvenient, east of the town centre and about half a mile along a track to the south of the main street.

Trekking agencies and guides

- **Ahmed Jadid** (contact via Auberge Souktana, see p190). A six-day trek, taking in the summit of Jbel Sirwa, starting and finishing at the auberge, including half-board the day before starting and an evening meal on your return, costs 3510dh per person for two people, the price decreasing per head as the number in the party increases.
- **Mahjoub Bajja and Annie Lauvaux, Maroc Inedit** (☎ 0528-85 36 48 or, for information in English, GSM ☎ 0676-31 67 43; 💻 www.maroc-inedit.com).

Where to stay

There are a number of agreeable places in which to stay, mostly found just out of town to the east. Long-established as the place to go to for trekking information and for help with the organisation of any trek in the region, ***Auberge Souktana*** (☎/🖷 0528-53 40 75; 🖳 souktana@menara.ma/aubsouktana@yahoo.fr) is directly opposite the kasbah, across the bridge and 2km to the east of town. This very pleasant hotel is run by *Homme Bleu*, Ahmed Jadid, originally hailing from Goulimine and the first mountain guide in Taliwine, and Michelle, his French wife. It provides four en suite rooms (180/220/300/360dh) in the main building plus five rooms which have communal toilets and bathrooms (from 90/140dh) in self-contained buildings, and four tent rooms (50/80dh) lit by candle. A half-board tariff is available. Heating or air conditioning can be provided in the interior rooms for a 40dh supplement. These interior rooms are built around a central lounge-dining area which is heated by a wood-burning stove. Due to the popularity of the hotel, it is advisable to book ahead.

Should Souktana be full, try ***Auberge Askaoun*** (☎ 0528-53 40 17; 🖳 aubergeaskaoun@yahoo.fr). Just a little nearer the town centre, this is another friendly place in which to stay. Rooms are available for 110/150/200dh (family rooms, 250dh); plus half-board for 170dh per person.

The same owner runs ***Auberge Campin*** (sic) ***Car Toubkal*** (☎ 0528-53 43 43; 🖳 www.maghrebtourism.com/aubergetoubkal), 3km east of the town centre. Here there are both en suite rooms (from €18/36) and suites (from €50). Traditional Moroccan meals can be taken either in the restaurant or on the terrace and the hotel also offers the further benefit of a swimming pool.

If you wish to stay in the centre of town, there are two simple hotels you might consider. The least expensive, ***Hotel Renaissance***, is conveniently situated by the bus stop, but otherwise has little to recommend it, being somewhat short on both comfort and facilities. It seems even to lack a telephone, precluding the possibility of making contact prior to arriving in Taliwine. Close by is ***Hotel Atlass*** (sic; ☎ 0528-53 45 13); given that it offers hot water, it does at least represent a small step up in quality. The most comfortable hotel in town by far is ***Grand Hotel Ibn Toumert*** (☎ 0528- 85 12 31). Set back from the main road, close to the Kasbah, it offers the additional facilities of a swimming pool and a licensed bar, as well as a tourist shop selling traditional Moroccan goods, predictably somewhat expensively.

Where to eat

There are a number of inexpensive **café-restaurants** spread along the main street of Taliwine. Additionally, enjoyable, traditional Moroccan meals might be taken either in ***Auberge Souktana*** or ***Auberge Askaoun***. The latter serves breakfast from 25dh and meals at other times of the day for between 50 and 70dh. If you wish to pay a little bit more, ***Hotel Ibn Toumert*** can also provide both breakfast and meals.

What to see

• **The kasbah** While the upper floors are in ruins, the lower floors are still largely occupied by local families, most of whom are descended from those who originally worked in the kasbah as servants of the House of Glaoua (see p51). Visits within the kasbah are sometimes welcomed by these families for a small fee. Otherwise, a tour of the outside of this still very impressive structure is rewarded with glimpses of some beautiful original moulding around its windows and wall patterning. Close by, across barren fields to the west, are the picturesque colonnaded remains of the ancient judiciary.

• **The Saffron Museum** Given that the countryside around Taliwine is the only region of Morocco that grows saffron and that its quality is amongst the very best in the world, it is not surprising to find a small dedicated museum (open daily, 8am–8pm, admission free) on the main road towards the eastern end of town. The museum is the project of the Co-operative Souktana de Safran (☎ 0528-39 52 15; GSM ☎ 0666-97 90 02; 🖳 www.safran-souktana.mezgarne.com). Should you wish to buy a sample of saffron, one gram packets can be bought from the co-operative's office right next to the museum.

SIRWA CIRCULAR TREK

SIRWA CIRCULAR TREK
- **Level of difficulty** Strenuous
- **Duration** 6 days
- **Maps** *Taliwine* (1:100,000) Division de la Carte, Morocco Survey

Taliwine–Akhfamane [Map 24, p192]

This is a straightforward and pleasant four- to five-hour walk which takes in a number of picturesque villages. Their cultivated fields, yielding figs and carobs, olives and almonds, besides a host of other crops and beautiful wild flowers, offer a maze of lesser paths through which you might meander. Some trekkers choose to skip this stage, preferring instead to start from Akhfamane (1250m/ 4100ft) further into the mountains. Others would even advocate taking transport beyond Akhfamane as far as Mazwad (see p193) and to start the trek from there but this only serves to miss the delights of the approach to the mountains and the chance to appreciate a gentle contrast with what follows.

Follow the main road (P32) out of Taliwine to the east. After 15 minutes you will pass a sharp right-hand turning to the village of El Qaçba. Keep heading east but take the path which heads left (north-east) from the main road after a further five minutes or so. The path from here is very distinct and climbs at a gentle rate. Keep the **river bed** to your left as the path more or less follows it from here through the village of **Ighil-n-Imchguiln** to **Tirassat** (1062m/3483ft) which you should reach about 90 minutes after leaving Taliwine. Enjoy the views of the picturesque kasbah of Taourirt-n-Aït Lahsene which dominates the far (west) bank of the river once you have passed through Ighil-n-Imchguiln.

At this point you are presented with a choice. After Tirassat, one path turns to the right (east) away from the river bed, but then re-joins it 120 minutes later at the village of **Timicha**. From here, continue along the path and the river bed, still heading north-east, crossing the tributary stream which leads down from Amaliz to the south-east. You will reach **Tifourt** approximately 20 minutes after leaving Timicha. Just beyond Tifourt you will meet a wider road, large enough for vehicles, which forks left and right at the point at which you reach it. Take the right (south-east) fork and follow this road all the way into **Akhfamane** (1250m/4100ft) which you should reach some 40 minutes after leaving Tifourt.

Alternatively from Tirassat you could continue to follow the valley closely, even crossing to its far (west) bank to enjoy passing through the quiet villages of Taltenzoukht, Tabia-n-Ighil, Agadir-n-Aït Taleb, Tasrga and Ighzi and the orchards of their shaded gardens. This walk from Tirassat to Akhfamane takes around 3½hrs. Just take care not to wander into the side valley just after Ighzi as that leads north-east to Anammet; stay in the main valley. Whichever choice you make, some of the geological stratigraphy of the rocks, seen in the valley sides on the approach to Akhfamane, is quite stunning.

Akhfamane is a typical small, dusty Sirwa village wedged between two flat-topped ridges. You will find a small **kasbah**, a few **rooms for hire** and friendly locals, including muleteers. There is a very pleasant **camping** possibility in a copse immediately before the village, just at the point where the path following the valley bottom climbs the valley side to enter the village.

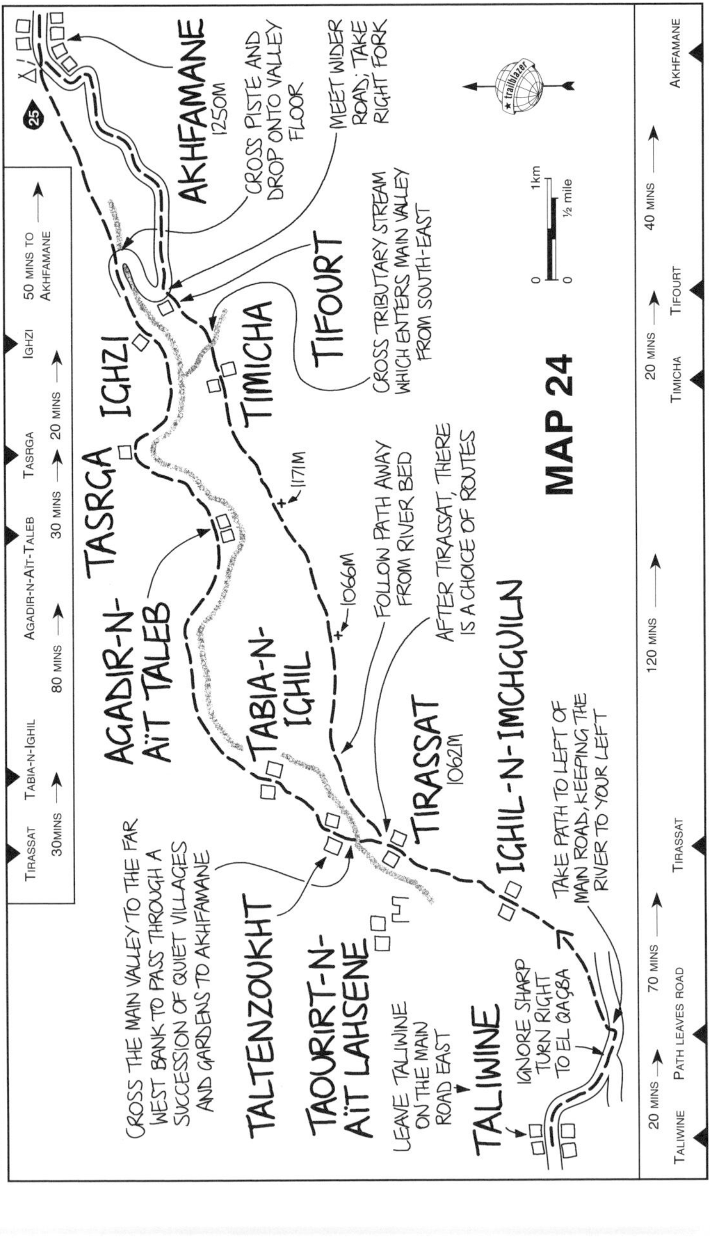

TIRASSAT 30MINS → TABIA-N-IGHIL 80 MINS → AGADIR-N-AÏT-TALEB 30 MINS → TASRGA 20 MINS → IGHZI 50 MINS TO AKHFAMANE →

25

AKHFAMANE
1250M

CROSS PISTE AND DROP ONTO VALLEY FLOOR

MEET WIDER ROAD; TAKE RIGHT FORK

IGHZI

TASRGA

AGADIR-N-AÏT TALEB

CROSS THE MAIN VALLEY TO THE FAR WEST BANK TO PASS THROUGH A SUCCESSION OF QUIET VILLAGES AND GARDENS TO AKHFAMANE

TIMICHA

TIFOURT

CROSS TRIBUTARY STREAM WHICH ENTERS MAIN VALLEY FROM SOUTH-EAST

1171M

TABIA-N-IGHIL

TALTENZOUKHT

TAOURIRT-N-AÏT LAHSENE

1066M

FOLLOW PATH AWAY FROM RIVER BED

TIRASSAT
1062M

AFTER TIRASSAT, THERE IS A CHOICE OF ROUTES

LEAVE TALIWINE ON THE MAIN ROAD EAST

TALIWINE

IGNORE SHARP TURN RIGHT TO EL QAÇBA

IGHIL-N-IMCHGUILN

TAKE PATH TO LEFT OF MAIN ROAD, KEEPING THE RIVER TO YOUR LEFT

MAP 24

0 1km
0 ½ mile

trailblazer

TALIWINE 20 MINS → PATH LEAVES ROAD 70 MINS → TIRASSAT 120 MINS → TIMICHA 20 MINS → TIFOURT 40 MINS → AKHFAMANE

Akhfamane–Mazwad–Ti-n-Iddr [Map 25, p194]

The route from Akhfamane to Mazwad simply follows a piste which is barren and volcanic and which offers very little shade for about 3½ hours. Though it is lined by occasional pistachio trees, there is an unfortunate prevalence of electricity pylons, too. What's more, there are fewer villages to enjoy than before: even the residents of Arg relocated their village away from this route into the Assif n'Warg side valley to the north some decades ago, apparently to escape an infestation of ants. If you decided to make private transport arrangements to get you as far as Akhfamane, therefore, you may wish to negotiate paying a little extra to take you on to Mazwad.

Otherwise, walk east through Akhfamane for about 500m until you reach a fork in the piste. Take the **right fork** which will take you up a gentle incline past the last few houses of the village and along the right (south) side of the gorge in an easterly direction. The river is usually dry in summer.

Thirty minutes after leaving Akhfamane, you reach a small **azib** on the right. Just afterwards the piste turns left (north). For a small shortcut, however, carry straight on and descend to the river bed where you will soon rejoin the piste. The route continues generally eastwards, weaving between the river bed and the sides of the gorge.

Some 30 minutes beyond the azib, as the trail turns to the south-east, you will reach a series of dry **ravines** that fall away to your right (south) every 200 metres or so. After a further 10 minutes, look to the left (north) where a collection of terraced, stone-walled fields indicate the village of **Aberniberka** (not marked on the 1:100,000 map). Just five minutes beyond this, the route splits. Take the right (east) fork leaving the village to your left.

About 35 minutes later the piste begins to climb into the hills, leaving the river bed behind, through a barren and volcanic landscape with very little shade. After a further 35 minutes you will come to a large **stone wall** to the right of the piste. Take advantage of the shade it offers as it's the last you'll see for quite a while. From the wall, a small footpath offers the chance to cut out a few hundred metres of piste. Either way, the route continues to ascend gently for another 75 minutes in a generally north-easterly direction before it starts to descend.

At this point you should see an area of more fertile land to the right (south-east) and some azibs across the valley. The route starts to snake and you soon round a corner to see the beautiful village of **Mazwad** (1441m/4728ft), built on both sides of a small ravine, up ahead. As you approach the village, the route forks again. The right fork heads south to Tagmoute, where you might choose to finish your trek, but for now take the left which heads north-east, down into Mazwad.

Mazwad makes a good place to stop either overnight or just for lunch. You may even receive the offer of accommodation *chez l'habitant* (in a local's home) as you pass through. There are a few good patches of ground on which to **pitch tents** and a pleasant copse with a water source just to the east of the village. For a little more privacy, continue through the village and then take the trail left (north-north-east), as if continuing to Ti-n-Iddr, to find shaded gardens on a terraced slope just a few minutes ahead.

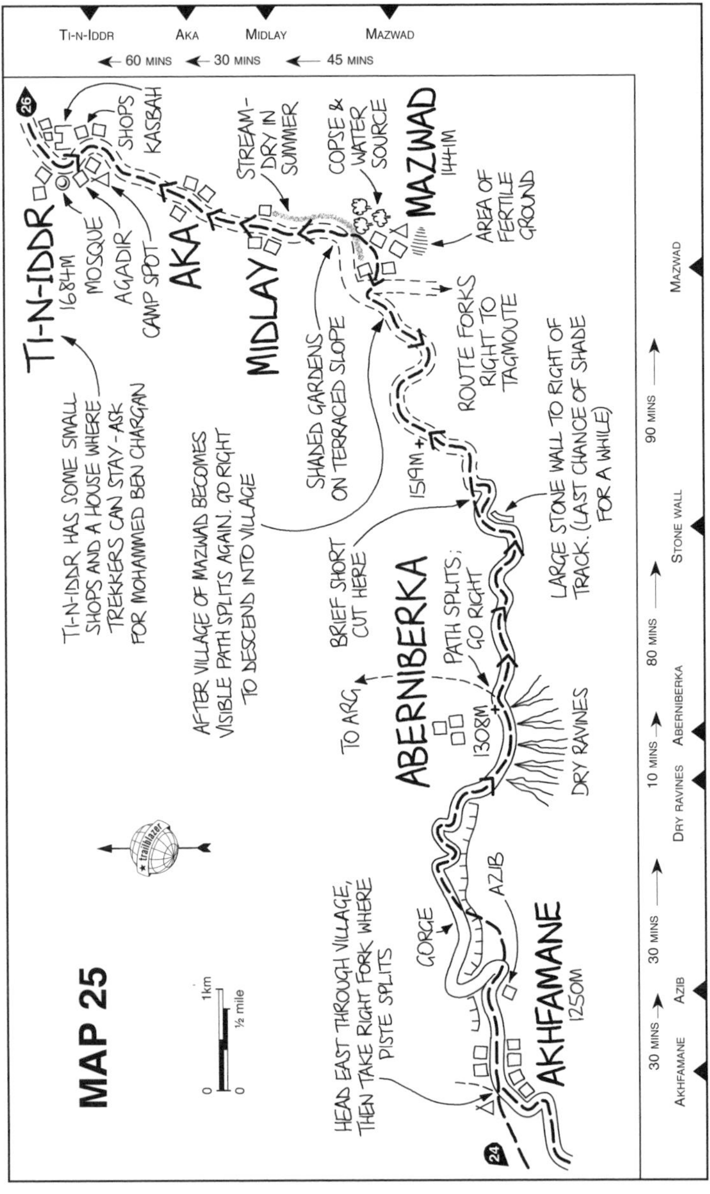

MAP 25

0 1km
0 ½ mile

AKHFAMANE
1250M
HEAD EAST THROUGH VILLAGE, THEN TAKE RIGHT FORK WHERE PISTE SPLITS
GORGE
AZIB
ABERNIBERKA
1308M
TO ARG
PATH SPLITS; GO RIGHT
DRY RAVINES
BRIEF SHORT CUT HERE
1519M
LARGE STONE WALL TO RIGHT OF TRACK. (LAST CHANCE OF SHADE FOR A WHILE)
AFTER VILLAGE OF MAZWAD BECOMES VISIBLE PATH SPLITS AGAIN. GO RIGHT TO DESCEND INTO VILLAGE
ROUTE FORKS RIGHT TO TAGMOUTE
SHADED GARDENS ON TERRACED SLOPE
MAZWAD
1441M
AREA OF FERTILE GROUND
COPSE & WATER SOURCE
MIDLAY
STREAM - DRY IN SUMMER
AKA
TI-N-IDDR
1684M
TI-N-IDDR HAS SOME SMALL SHOPS AND A HOUSE WHERE TREKKERS CAN STAY - ASK FOR MOHAMMED BEN CHARGAN
MOSQUE
AGADIR
CAMP SPOT
SHOPS
KASBAH

30 MINS → 30 MINS → 10 MINS → 80 MINS → 90 MINS →

AKHFAMANE | AZIB | DRY RAVINES | ABERNIBERKA | STONE WALL | MAZWAD

TI-N-IDDR ← 60 MINS ← AKA ← 30 MINS ← MIDLAY ← 45 MINS ← MAZWAD

The clear trail continues to climb steadily north-north-east following the valley of the Assif-n-Wamrane, usually dry in summer. A number of small tracks drop down to the river, below to your right (east), but the main trail climbs through two more villages, **Midlay** and **Aka** (neither marked on the 1:100,000 map) and finally onto Ti-n-Iddr. These three villages are reached approximately 45 minutes, 1¼ hours and 2¼ hours from Mazwad respectively. **Ti-n-Iddr** (1684m/5525ft), even more beautiful than Mazwad, is perched on a hillside, its houses built both between and upon huge boulders, set against the backdrop of growing mountains to the north. Take time to enjoy the narrow lanes of the village, its kasbah and its agadir (ask around for the key), along with the ancient doorways of its small houses.

You could **camp** on the threshing floors on the village approach. Alternatively, walk down through the village to the north where you will find some good shade and a stream providing fresh water. There is also a **house** in which trekkers can stay: ask for Mohammed Ben Chargan. The village has some small **shops**.

Ti-n-Iddr–Guiliz–Tegragra [Map 26, p196]

Walk through Ti-n-Iddr, passing small **shops** on the right, then turning left between the mosque and the Kasbah, to rejoin the piste on the far side. Up ahead you will see a series of beautiful ridges, both to the right (south-east) and left (north-west). The piste, climbing only slightly at first but later steepening, follows the Assif-n-Wamrane Valley to the north-east. It is obvious and easy to follow. Half-an-hour beyond Ti-n-Iddr, the village of Atougha (1705m/5594ft) will come into view. Its houses are stacked neatly against the valley side, and its terraced maize and wheat fields are spread out below, making it a very impressive sight. Look out, too, for the equally picturesque village of **Tihssant** to the right (north-east), a little higher up the Assif-n-Wamrane Valley, just beyond Atougha. Its terracing is even more impressive and continues along the valley high above the villages almost all the way to Tegragra.

The piste continues to steepen but then comes to an end as you reach **Atougha**, 50 minutes from Ti-n-Iddr. From here, a path continues, leading to the right of the mosque, towards the impressive **agadir** at the top of the village, reached in a further 60 minutes. Ask at the adjacent house about the key. Within, facing a central courtyard, are four walls of ancient chambers, built several storeys high, all protected by ancient, gnarled wooden doors. The image of the perfect village is only spoilt by the inevitable spread of satellite dishes along its roof tops. Passing to the left of the agadir, the path zig-zags steeply up to a ridge above the village.

Atougha is the last village you will pass through on your way to the summit of Jbel Sirwa. For now the path northwards remains clear, but it will become less obvious over the next two days as you continue your ascent, eventually disappearing altogether. It will, therefore, become important to maintain an awareness of the general direction of your trek, to the north and north-east.

As you climb out of Atougha to the north-east, you will again see the village of Tihssant, now down below, with its picturesque terraced fields to the right

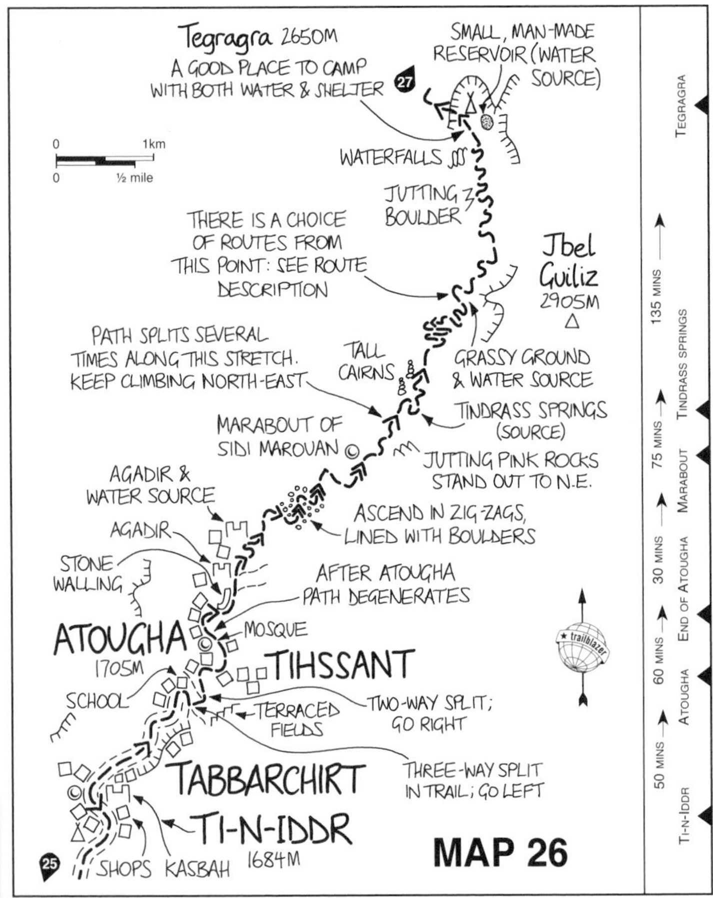

and a waterfall to the left (dry in summer). Continue to zig-zag upwards towards and then past a second agadir and a water source. At every split in the trail, keep heading upwards to avoid picking up any path which might lead you back down into the Assif-n-Wamrane Valley. Soon peaks appear ahead to the north and you pass the small **marabout of Sidi Marouan**, just below to the left, about 90 minutes from the centre of Atougha.

Continue to wind steadily up the mountain, passing some unusual, jutting, pink-coloured rocks to the right (north-east), after which the path zig-zags up over the next ridge. Terraced fields lie to the right of the track. The path is small but clear, contouring and climbing gently in a northerly direction to a flat terraced area, '**Tindrass Springs**' (2290m/7513ft), reached 105 minutes from the agadir at Atougha, directly south of spot height 2651m on the 1:100,000 map. A good **water source** makes this an ideal stop for lunch.

Soon **Jbel Guiliz** (2905m/9531ft) comes into view along with the valley to its left (west) that will lead you directly to Tegragra. Contour all the time round ravines, past some isolated bergeries and continue to ignore any paths that might fork right (east) and downwards until finally you have no choice but to descend into the main valley at the foot of Jbel Guiliz, approximately one hour from Tindrass Springs. Here is grassy ground, an **azib** which would provide some shelter and a further **water source**.

From here, it is possible to follow either side of the valley northwards to Tegragra. One path crosses to the right (east) side of the valley, climbing quite high to avoid waterfalls as it approaches Tegragra. Alternatively, another path follows the left (west) bank of the valley for about half an hour and then veers left towards some statue-like **rock formations**. There is no real path at this point but, once you gain a plateau above the river bed, contour round past a **waterfall** in a ravine and finally into **Tegragra**, 2¼ hours from Tindrass Springs.

This area of scattered bergeries and walled fields, set in a gorgeous valley and surrounded by steep, dramatic ridges, makes an excellent ***campsite***. A **reservoir** provides another good source of water. Tegragra is, however, notoriously cold at night. During my ascent we even picked up an additional mule at Ti-n-Iddr; this was for the sole purpose of carrying extra bedding for our two other mules which our muleteer feared would otherwise have felt too much of the cold.

Tegragra–Jbel Sirwa summit–Tizgui [Map 27, p198]

This relatively long and demanding stage requires an early start. This is to allow enough time for an ascent to the summit and a descent to a good camping area afterwards, even should the weather deteriorate after midday, as it has a tendency to do. Ideally the weather will be good and you won't need ropes but to be safe you should have them for the final ascent to the summit. Even with ropes, however, in bad weather this final ascent might not be possible. This is not a day for your mule or muleteer; they will need to take an alternative route to meet you afterwards at Tizgui.

There are no trails from Tegragra to the summit of Jbel Sirwa and the nature of the gorse-covered, rocky terrain through which you must now pass makes a precise description difficult to write and almost impossible to follow closely. The most important point to remember is that Jbel Sirwa lies due north from Tegragra: a compass is strongly advised for this section of the route.

Climb steeply north-north-west from Tegragra for about 60 minutes to the **col** on the ridge ahead of your camp. Once on this ridge, turn right (north-east) and ascend along it to a second, higher col above, reached in a further 30 minutes. At this **second col** turn left (north-west), scrambling for about 60 minutes more to reach the higher ground of a second, larger ridge.

The rocky summit of Sirwa (3305m/10840ft) suddenly comes in to view to the right (north-east). More than this, a fantastic panorama opens up to the north. The entire range of the High Atlas Mountains now lies bare before you, with both

THE SUMMIT OF SIRWA COMES INTO VIEW

WALK ALONG THE SECOND RIDGE TO THE BASE OF THE ROCKY SUMMIT

ROPES MAY BE NEEDED TO REACH THE PEAK ITSELF

CAIRN

Jbel Sirwa
3305M

AT THE SECOND COL, TURN LEFT AND SCRAMBLE TO REACH THE HIGHER GROUND OF A SECOND, LARGER RIDGE

BOULDERS

HEAD SOUTH-EAST OVER GORSE

MOSSY BOULDERS

BLACK ROCKS

ON THE RIDGE, TURN RIGHT AND ASCEND ALONG IT TO A SECOND, HIGHER COL

SMALL, MAN-MADE RESERVOIR

CAIRN

DRY GORGE

CLIMB STEEPLY NNW OUT OF TEGRAGRA TO THE COL ON THE RIDGE ABOVE YOUR CAMP

26

Tegragra
2650M

GORGE LEADS AWAY TOWARDS JBEL TISFELDAT WHICH IS VISIBLE ON THE DESCENT

MULE TRAIL FROM TEGRAGRA

FLAT BOULDER WITH CAIRN

Jbel Guiliz
2905M

Jbel Tisfeldat
2918M

FLAT AREA OF GORSE

0 1km
0 ½ mile

WATER SOURCE

TRAIL LEADS DOWN INTO THE GORGE FLOOR

AZIBS

PATH CLIMBS TO THE RIGHT AND REACHES A MORE OPEN AREA WITH CULTIVATED FIELDS

GORGE BECOMES IMPASSABLE WITHOUT ROPES; CLIMB OUT OF THE GORGE BOTTOM TO THE RIGHT

trailblazer

MULE TRACK LEADING TO TAGOUYAMT

TIZGUI
2200M

CAMP SPOT

28

MAP 27

Tegragra 165 mins → Base of summit 15 mins → Summit

Tizgui 60 mins ↓ Gorge becomes impassable 30 mins ↓ Gorge floor 30 mins ↓ Mule trail from Tegragra ↓ 90 mins Base of summit

Ighil Mgoun and Jbel Toubkal standing proud, while in the mid-distance, the smaller peaks of Tikniwine and Amzdour stand like stepping stones inviting you to leap across to meet them. Meanwhile, behind you to the south, the horizon is punctuated by the distant crests of the furthest Anti-Atlas Mountains.

Turn north-east for a final, gentle 15-minute amble along the ridge to the base of the rocky **summit of Sirwa**. Allow 2¾ hours to reach this base from Tegragra. To climb to the summit, allow another 15 minutes. Start by climbing the gully on the east face of the rock and continue up its south ridge. Take care: the rock is polished and becomes very slippery in wet or icy conditions, but once you have completed your ascent it will feel as though there is nothing between you and heaven.

The descent

Descend steeply south-east from the base of the summit rock through gorse and energy-sapping boulder fields into the head of the Assif n'Aït ou-Byal Valley, which runs between Jbel Guiliz to the south and Jbel Tisfeldat (2918m/9573ft) to the south-east. Just 15 minutes from the base of the rocky summit, a gorge leads away left (south-east) directly towards Jbel Tisfeldat. Your route, however, turns gradually to the right (south) and you will finally pick up a path as the Assif n' Aït ou-Byal Valley narrows to become a **gorge**. After about 1½ hours the path, still descending, turns back to the left (south-east) and a mule track appears on your right (west), climbing up to meet you from Tegragra.

The trail then cuts through a flat area of gorse before heading down to the gorge floor (120 minutes). The gorge is very pretty with patches of green grass, waterfalls and springs. The path begins to meander from left to right, repeatedly crossing the **stream bed** until it climbs to the right (south) and reaches a more open area with some cultivated fields. At this point, however, (150 minutes) the river drops away to the left (south-east) and the gorge beyond becomes impassable without ropes. To avoid this, take the path which climbs away from the gorge bottom, following a course high above the right-hand (south-west) side of the valley. Take care to avoid a mule track which heads off further still to the right (south-west) as it would lead you directly to Tagouyamt and by-pass the picturesque village of Tizgui.

Soon, **Tizgui** (2200m/7218ft) comes into view. You will reach the village about 3½ hours after leaving the base of the summit rock. Pass through the centre of the tiered village to find some soft, terraced areas and threshing floors which make excellent ***camping*** points. There is a **private residence** in Tizgui at which trekkers can stay: ask for Mohammed Mazouz Aznag.

Tizgui–Tagouyamt–Tislit [Map 28, p200]

Leave Tizgui, descending along the large piste which heads south, following the right (west) side of the gorge of the Assif n'Aït ou-Byal Valley. After only five minutes a fascinating **agadir** is seen to the right, built into the vertical rock face of the gorge side. The geology on show within the sides of the gorge here reveals a dramatic confusion of sedimentary and conglomerate rock; the huge, protruding boulders betray the chaotic violence of the earth's formation.

Five more minutes will bring you to the bottom of the gorge. As you descend, look out for the village of Tagouyamt ahead. It is overlooked by twin agadirs, further still down valley, facing each other from opposite hilltops, like two towers guarding the entrance to the village against anyone wishing to force entrance from the south. You reach the village about 60 minutes after leaving Tizgui.

Pass through **Tagouyamt** on the piste, but then take the small path on the left (east) just after the school and cross the river to head towards the minaret

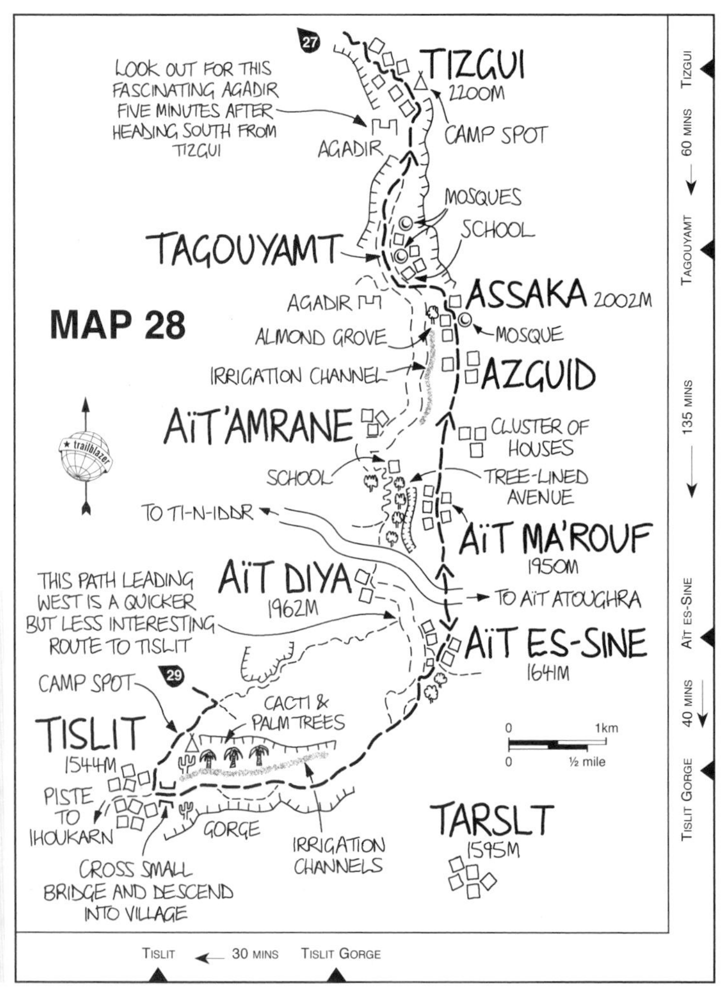

of **Assaka** (2002m/6568ft). If you are lucky enough to pass this way at a time which coincides with Mohammed's birthday, you could well chance upon the village's annual four-day moussem. From Assaka, a trail leads through Azguid to a cluster of houses and then on to **Aït Ma'rouf** after which the path becomes a little unclear but you can see the minaret of the next village, Aït es-Sine (1641m/5384ft), ahead (south). To reach it, cross a major piste, which runs east-west from Aït Atoughra to Ti-n-Iddr, and a small river bed before climbing up to the village, about 2¼ hours from Tagouyamt.

Upon leaving Aït es-Sine the path is again not clear but the going is easy. Continue straight (south) to head out of the village towards rocks on the right (east) of the valley which here narrows into a small gorge. At this point the path is defined with rocks although it soon becomes unclear again. Head right of the small gorge towards a small stone building. Here a sandy river bed appears which leads into the spectacular **Tislit Gorge**, 40 minutes from Aït es-Sine.

The gorge is adorned with fantastic rock tower formations, sandstone boulders and beautiful water pools. They are interspersed with lush green vegetation, including tall palm trees, quenched by man-made irrigation channels. Often 20ft above the ground, they provide wonderful walkways through this stunning, surreal landscape. The gorge would make an ideal campsite had not a local Tislit villager recently planted olives in the recognised camping spot, sadly one of the better pieces of ground in the gorge suitable for pitching a tent. You may now find you need to climb a little out of the gorge to find a flat, dry spot.

Alternatively, continue through the gorge for 30 minutes towards the wonderful, ancient village of **Tislit** (1544m/5066ft), its buildings carved into the rock itself. To enter the village, climb out of the gorge at the first house. Although there is no official gîte, there is a ***pink house*** in which trekkers can stay; ask for Ahmed el-Taleby.

Tislit–Ihoukarn or Tislit–Assaïs–Tagmoute [Map 29, p202]

There are two possibilities for the final day of the trek. Whichever you choose, you should prearrange transport for the journey back to Taliwine. For a short, gentle walk and a quick return to Taliwine, head south-west down the valley from Tislit to Ihoukarn; the walk should take two hours. There is little to be gained from trekking beyond Ihoukarn for the piste becomes quite large and busy with vehicles from this point all the way back to the main road (P32) and on to Taliwine. Alternatively, for a four-hour trek, consider the following route to Tagmoute (misprinted 'Tamgout' on the 1:100,000 map).

Head north out of Tislit on a clear piste which leads first past the school before turning to the north-east straight across open, cultivated land. On reaching a slightly larger piste, running north-west to south-east, after 20 minutes, follow it to the left (north-west) towards **Souk Larba** (Wednesday market) and **Assaïs** (1675m/5495ft) which come into view ahead in the Assif-n-Ousaïs Valley. Shortly afterwards another piste heads left (south-west) directly to Aït 'Icht but do not deviate; stay on the piste to reach Souk Larba. Once you arrive there, turn left (south-west) to head down valley through Assaïs and on to **Aït 'Icht**, reached in approximately 90 minutes from Tislit.

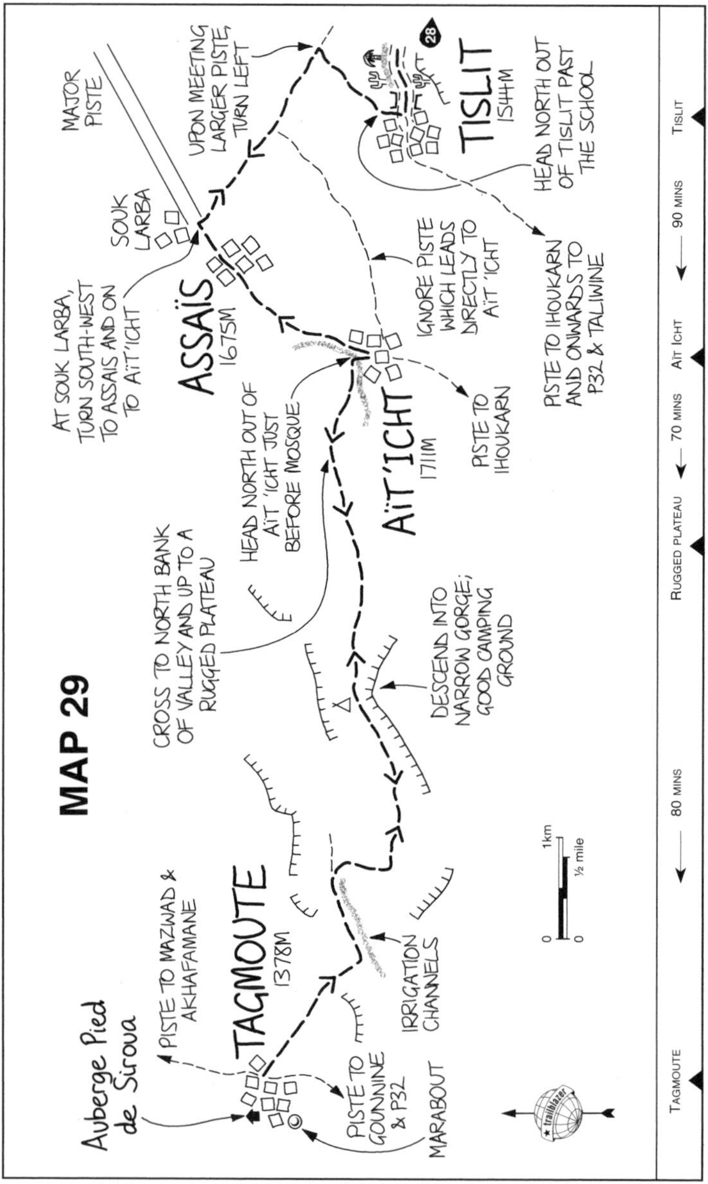

MAP 29

Auberge Pied de Siroua
PISTE TO MAZWAD & AKHAFAMANE
TAGMOUTE 1378M
PISTE TO GOUNNINE & P32
MARABOUT
IRRIGATION CHANNELS
CROSS TO NORTH BANK OF VALLEY AND UP TO A RUGGED PLATEAU
DESCEND INTO NARROW GORGE; GOOD CAMPING GROUND
HEAD NORTH OUT OF AÏT 'ICHT JUST BEFORE MOSQUE
AÏT 'ICHT 1711M
PISTE TO IHOUKARN
AT SOUK LARBA, TURN SOUTH-WEST TO ASSAIS AND ON TO AÏT 'ICHT
ASSAÏS 1675M
SOUK LARBA
MAJOR PISTE
UPON MEETING LARGER PISTE, TURN LEFT
IGNORE PISTE WHICH LEADS DIRECTLY TO AÏT 'ICHT
28
TISLIT 1544M
PISTE TO IHOUKARN AND ONWARDS TO P32 & TALIWINE
HEAD NORTH OUT OF TISLIT PAST THE SCHOOL

0 1km
0 ½ mile

trailblazer

TAGMOUTE ← 80 MINS RUGGED PLATEAU ← 70 MINS AÏT ICHT ← 90 MINS TISLIT

Turn north out of Aït 'Icht, just before the mosque, and make your way across **Assif-n-Ousaïs**, climbing up to its far (northern) bank to reach a clear path heading left (west) down the valley. Keep to high ground and follow the path up on to a **rugged plateau**, reached 70 minutes from Aït 'Icht, from where the path continues high on the right side of a steep valley. You should see the spectacular canyon of **Assif-n-Talmachacht** on your right approximately one hour later. The path heads left to go around a **small hill** before heading right (north-west) and then north to descend into the gorge, arriving at some bergeries, pretty waterfalls and palm trees. This would make a great place to **camp**.

Once in the **gorge**, head downstream past a small dam at the valley intersection, walking along either the river bed or the irrigation channels, reaching **Tagmoute** (1378m/4521ft), wrongly named Tamgout on the 1:100,000 map, about four hours from Tislit. There's a **shop**, places to **camp** and ***Auberge Pied de Siroua*** (☎ 0528-82 44 32; GSM ☎ 0670-28 20 37; 💻 www.auberge-siroua.com), which has four rooms (140dh per person or 280dh half-board); traditional Moroccan meals are willingly prepared for non-residents for very reasonable prices. From Tagmoute a major piste runs north-north-east back to Mazwad, Akhfamane and onwards to Taliwine whilst another runs south to the P32 via Gounnine.

Jbel Sahro

This staggeringly beautiful mountain range, with its unusual rock formations, formidable gorges and isolated communities, rises to the east of Ouarzazate. It extends eastwards, reaching towards the distant desert town of Rissani and the dunes of Erg Chebbi. It lies between the High Atlas Mountains to the north and the Sahara Desert to the south, at the eastern end of the Anti-Atlas Mountains which run south-west almost all the way to Tan Tan and the shores of the Atlantic. The forbidding, barren landscape is only occasionally punctuated by far-flung oases. Semi-nomadic Berbers, migrating north towards the High Atlas in summer and returning south again in winter, roam vast, barren valleys beneath strangely formed rocky outcrops and mountains. None but the hardy could live here: renowned for their spirit of independence, this is indeed the land of the infamous warriors of the Aït Atta tribe (see box p50), whose heroic resistance of French control right up until 1933 has guaranteed them a perpetual place in Berber folklore.

Tourism has only just begun to develop here and trekking is still relatively new. This makes Sahro a highly rewarding area in which to travel, although it also makes it a more difficult one. Accommodation is very scarce and you will need to carry all your supplies with you into the mountains. Summer days can be scorching, winter nights freezing, and in places water can be hard to find all year-round. Nevertheless, trekking in Sahro is an exhilarating adventure. You are more likely to feel like an explorer here than in any other part of the Atlas and your efforts will be rewarded through your encounters with fascinating individuals and communities and through sharing their epic landscape.

If you only take a **guide** with you once in Morocco, take one in Jbel Sahro. Maps of the area are often inaccurate, particularly on the plains towards the beginnings and ends of treks, at which times identification of landmarks for inclusion in the route descriptions which follow has been especially difficult. Whole villages and even valleys are sometimes unmarked; where they are marked they might not be named, and where they are named local people often know them by another. The trails are often unclear and you should therefore trek in this region prepared to lose your path. Even if you do not take a guide, at the very least take a **compass** and a willingness to converse at every opportunity with locals that you may meet along the way. At times you will have nothing more to guide you than a general sense of the direction in which you ought to be heading.

NKOUB/NEKOB/N'KOB

Too many tourists arrive in Nkoub in their 4x4s, enjoy a meal in their hotel and depart after breakfast the next morning on their tour of the Deep South without seeing much more of this remarkably unspoilt town than the main thoroughfare. Step off the main street, however, to the north of the town in particular, to see streets unchanged for centuries. Known as the town of the 40 kasbahs, the fabulous old structures here are testament to Nkoub's former prosperity; that some are now in a chronic state of disrepair only adds to the atmosphere. Take your time to enjoy the ancient door frames and door knockers of the old houses, as well as their traditional iron window grilles. It would also be a pity to leave Nkoub without venturing down into the palmery to wander along its shaded irrigation channels.

Arrival and departure

Getting to Nkoub can be more awkward than reaching many towns in Morocco. To reach it by bus or by **grand taxi**, from either Ouarzazate or Zagora, you will almost inevitably need to change at Tansikht, from where the best option is to join a grand taxi to Nkoub. Be warned, however, about arriving at Tansikht late in the afternoon (see below).

Buses between Ouarzazate and Zagora, which would allow you to alight at Tansikht, are not frequent and tend to depart either very early in the morning or in the afternoon. CTM, for example, runs two buses daily, departing Ouarzazate at 5.15am and 4pm (50dh).

You might even have difficulty finding a grand taxi to cover the two-hour journey direct from Ouarzazate to Nkoub (65dh per seat) if you leave it too late in the day, especially at weekends, despite the weekly Nkoub souk being held on a Sunday. Even the fallback option of taking a grand taxi bound for Zagora and changing at Tansikht falls flat if you do not make your connection before around 5pm; by then the Tansikht taxi drivers will have packed up for the day and gone home, leaving you nothing to look at but a desolate spot of dusty ground, for Tansikht itself is nothing much more than a road junction and a name on the map. If all else fails, you could book a private grand taxi from Ouarzazate to Nkoub for 400dh.

Orientation

Orientation in this small and simple town is easy. Its single road runs north-west to south-east with most services clustered around the western entrance, met on the approach from Ouarzazate.

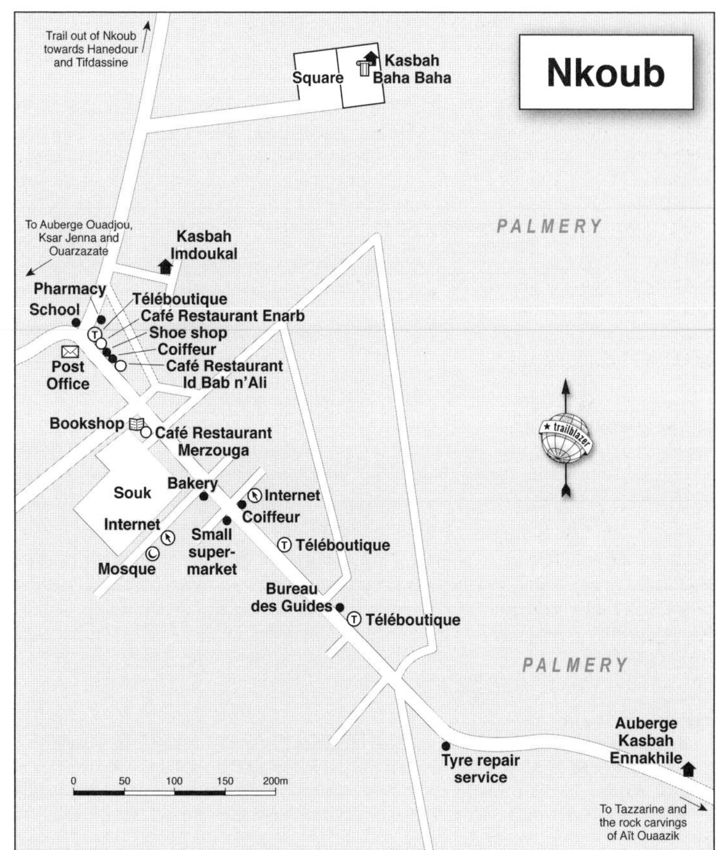

Services

In such a small town, services are limited, though the **post office**, the **pharmacy**, a **téléboutique** and even two **coiffeurs** (hairdressers) are all conveniently found at the western entrance to Nkoub along with a small **shoe shop** at which you can watch traditional shoes being made by hand; should your boots be in need of repair, this would be the right place to try. If it is repairs to your tyres you need, there is a **tyre repair service** (GSM ☎ 0670-72 33 56) at the far south-eastern end of town. Two **internet cafés** are found within the proximity of the town's centrally located main mosque. Don't get too excited about the **bookshop**, Librairie Aït Hmid; only an extremely limited supply of unheard-of cheap French fiction is kept under the counter.

The colourful weekly Sunday **souk** is well worth a visit, with villagers coming to town from far and wide to sell mostly vegetables and meat plus, all the way from Agadir, a variety of fresh (iced) fish. You could also pick up extra pans and utensils here. Any other day of the week, there is a small **super-**

market just east of the souk and numerous **bakers**, **butchers** and **grocers** spread along the length of the main street.

Trekking agencies

The Bureau des Guides on the main street is run by a solitary official guide:

• **Mohamed YaaQoub** (☎ 0524-88 47 95, GSM ☎ 0667-48 75 09; 💻 www.moroccotrek.net) BP 26, Bureau des Guides, Centre Nkoub, P. Zagora. He is also contactable via his UK co-ordinator, Jane Kiersch, tel: 07779 083 097, 💻 jane@moroccotrek.net. Should he be unavailable, all five hotels listed below could organise a trek for you given sufficient notice.

Where to stay

Nkoub has several very pleasant places in which to stay. The least expensive rooms are provided by ***Auberge Kasbah Ennakhile*** (☎ 0524-83 97 19; GSM ☎ 0672-64 15 11; 💻 www.auberge-ennakhile-nkob.com) at the eastern exit of the town. There are two categories of room. Its 10 double rooms in the 'auberge' cost 95dh with breakfast or 160dh half-board (communal bathrooms), whilst the five in the 'kasbah' cost 190dh with breakfast or 250dh half-board (en suite, with balconies). A *menu complet* is served at lunchtime for 70dh. Views over the palmery from the hotel terrace are beautiful. The management can organise 4- to 6-day treks across Jbel Sahro for 400dh per person per day, as well as outings to the prehistoric rock carvings at Aït Ouaazik (see opposite). Car rental can also be arranged. If you stay here, make a point of studying the Aït Atta family tree etched on a wall in the restaurant and ask to see the rifle used by the owner's grandfather to fight against French colonialism in 1933.

If you would prefer to **camp**, ***Auberge Ouadjou*** (☎ 0524-83 93 14; 💻 www.ouadjou.com), which is before the town on the western approach from Ouarzazate, charges 60dh for two people sharing their own tent or 100dh if you would like to stay in one of their pre-erected 'nomad' tents. A caravan spot, including use of electricity, costs 70dh for two. Use of communal toilets and showers, the cleanest I have ever seen on a campsite, is included. Alternatively, six simple double rooms (130dh) are available inside the pleasant auberge where breakfast (30dh) and meals (70dh) can be taken.

On the road leaving town to the north are two fine hotels. Both are restored old kasbahs and with furnishings and fittings in keeping with Berber traditions. ***Kasbah Imdoukal*** (☎ 0524-83 97 98; GSM ☎ 0661-13 69 32; 💻 www.kasbah-imdoukal.com) provides double, triple and quadruple rooms from €70/90/100, including breakfast. All rooms have air-conditioning and heating systems. A three-course lunch or dinner is 120dh. The hotel offers the benefit of a small pool in its central courtyard and fascinating views across the old town from its roof terrace. Excursions with a camel, mule or 4x4 can be organised.

Continue a little further along the road leaving town to the north, then turn off to the right to find the eco-friendly ***Kasbah Baha Baha*** (☎ 0524-83 97 63; 💻 www.kasbahabaha.com). Ironically, the two more expensive en suite ground-floor rooms (€38/50/69) are somewhat dark and less appealing than the eight rooms on the first and second floors (€25/37/50/61) which, however, require the use of a communal bathroom across the hotel gardens. There is also the option of sleeping amidst the orange groves in these gardens in a pre-erected 'nomad' tent (€10/19/26/34). Breakfast is served for 30dh; lunch and dinner, prepared with home-grown organic food, can be selected from a modestly priced, extensive menu. The hotel has a small outdoor pool by the side of which drinks can be served while you relax under the shade of traditional goat-hair awnings. Views from the roof terrace, both across the old town and the palmery, are something to savour. The hotel has a small on-site **museum** dedicated to Berber history and anthropology (entrance: 5dh). Excursions with a camel, mule or 4x4 can be organised, as can paragliding from the nearby hills south of Nkoub.

The most up-market hotel in striking distance of Nkoub is ***Ksar Jenna*** (☎ 0524-83 97 90; GSM ☎ 0667-96 32 48; 💻 www.ksarjenna.com). Four kilometres from the centre of town along the road to Ouarzazate, it stands alone facing the village of **Aït Ouzzine** (meaning 'beautiful people'). Despite the prevalence of old kasbahs in Nkoub itself, Ksar Jenna is a very new building, the beautiful creation of a Moroccan-Italian couple. *Tadlekt* walls, *bejmat* floors, Berber carpets and high-beamed ceilings are all found here. The six rooms, some of which are en suite, are all 550/1100/1650dh, including compulsory half-board. The hotel also boasts a beautiful shaded garden; being woken daily at dawn by resident singing nightingales is but a small price to pay.

Where to eat

There are only a handful of café-restaurants in Nkoub, for the most part clustered around the area between the very western end of town and the souk. The best include ***Café Restaurant Enarb***, ***Café Restaurant Id Bab n'Ali***, which offers the benefit of a first floor terrace, and ***Café Restaurant Merzouga***. All three serve staple Moroccan fare at standard café-restaurant prices.

If you are looking for anything better, all five hotels listed above would happily cater for you, although some advance notice is appreciated.

What to see

There are at least two sites in the vicinity of Nkoub where **prehistoric rock carvings** (*gravures rupestres*) can be found. Dating back to the Neolithic period, a time when the Sahara was still a fertile savannah and host to an array of birds and large mammals (see p44), a high concentration of rocks display a staggering range of beautiful and bold etchings. Some are of birds and animals, others are more abstract. Although you will not be able to find these without some local help, your efforts will be well repaid. Quite apart from the carvings, the adventure of getting there and back will lead you through a wonderful landscape and provide you with an insight into the beautiful wilderness that awaits you on your trek.

The best carvings are located 52km from Nkoub beyond Tazzarine, near the isolated village of **Aït Ouaazik**. Ask your driver to return via the village of Zenou and the Tamalalt Valley for spectacular views back down on Nkoub. Alternatively, more conveniently situated, though less impressive, are the rock carvings at **Im'n Oudraz**, just 7km from Nkoub.

JBEL SAHRO TRAVERSE

Nkoub–Hanedour–Tifdassine [Map 30, p208; Map 31, p210]

This first stage for the most part consists of a gentle day's level walking. However, from the trailhead you will pass through a series of villages to a camp which will leave you with the unmistakable feeling that you have truly left urban life behind and arrived in Jbel Sahro.

> **JBEL SAHRO TRAVERSE**
> - **Level of difficulty** Moderate
> - **Duration** 4-5 days
> - **Maps** *Tazzarine* (1:100,000), *Boumalne* (1:100,000), and *Qalaa't Mgouna* (1:100,000) Division de la Carte, Morocco Survey, or *Kultur-Trekking im Dschebel Saghro* (1:100,000) German-language trekking map.

Follow the piste which initially runs north-north-east from opposite the **post office** at the western entrance to Nkoub past Kasbah Imdoukal and Kasbah Baha Baha (see map p205). The piste quickly turns north and then north-north-west across a vast expanse of flat flood plain, once caused by waters flowing south from Jbel Sahro, and goes through occasional cassia trees. After 60 minutes pass straight through the small village of **Timharine** (not marked on the 1:100,000 maps) and 90 minutes from Nkoub meet a few more houses grouped together. Here the piste divides and you see the scattered village of **Tafroukht**

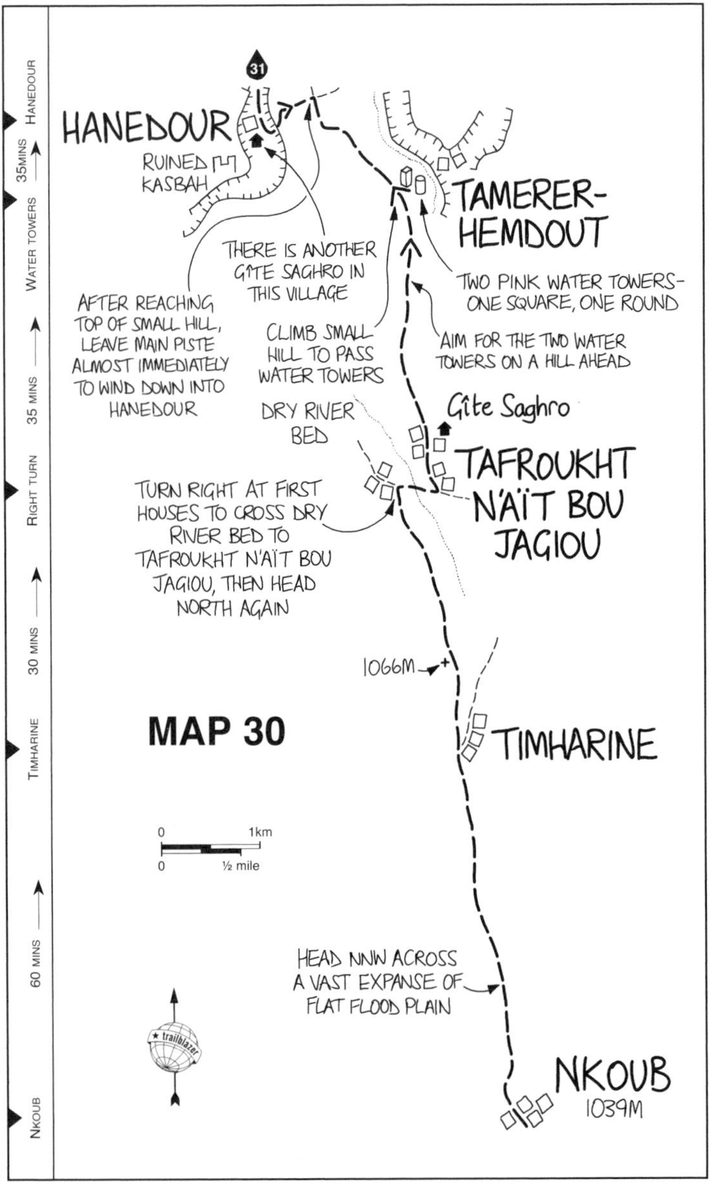

HANEDOUR

35MINS

WATER TOWERS

35 MINS

RIGHT TURN

30 MINS

TIMHARINE

60 MINS

NKOUB

31

HANEDOUR

RUINED KASBAH

THERE IS ANOTHER GÎTE SAGHRO IN THIS VILLAGE

AFTER REACHING TOP OF SMALL HILL, LEAVE MAIN PISTE ALMOST IMMEDIATELY TO WIND DOWN INTO HANEDOUR

TAMERER-HEMDOUT

TWO PINK WATER TOWERS- ONE SQUARE, ONE ROUND

CLIMB SMALL HILL TO PASS WATER TOWERS

AIM FOR THE TWO WATER TOWERS ON A HILL AHEAD

DRY RIVER BED

Gîte Saghro

TAFROUKHT N'AÏT BOU JAGIOU

TURN RIGHT AT FIRST HOUSES TO CROSS DRY RIVER BED TO TAFROUKHT N'AÏT BOU JAGIOU, THEN HEAD NORTH AGAIN

1066M

MAP 30

TIMHARINE

0 1km

0 ½ mile

HEAD NNW ACROSS A VAST EXPANSE OF FLAT FLOOD PLAIN

trailblazer

NKOUB
1039M

n'Aït bou Jagiou ahead and slightly to the right. Take the right turn, crossing the dry valley floor to reach the first outlying houses 10 minutes later. The piste leads through the village and then turns northwards again through the last of its houses. Almost the last building in Tafroukht is ***Gîte Saghro***, reached 15 minutes after the first. Expect to pay no more than 50dh for a bed here.

Head towards the twin **pink water towers**, one round and one square, on a small hill now directly ahead, climbing to reach them 10 minutes later. Pass to their left and under electricity pylons immediately afterwards, 125 minutes from Nkoub. As you ascend, the view into a valley to the right opens up; on the 1:100,000 maps the village in this valley is named **Tamererhemdout**, although my guide insisted that it is called Alminewakta.

Reach the **crest of the hill** five minutes later and then almost immediately, on the far side, leave the main piste by taking another which branches left and which in 30 minutes winds down into the picturesque village of **Hanedour**, nestling in the Assif Hanedour Valley. You will see its ruined kasbah perched on a bluff on the far side of the valley, black basalt rocks lining its sides, before you see either the village or even its fertile fields dotted with palm trees. In the village is another ***Gîte Saghro***, owned by Boaza, at which you might choose to stop for lunch. Should you arrive late in the day it would make a pleasant place to stay. There are four rooms; expect to pay no more than the standard gîte rates here of 50dh for a bed, 20dh for breakfast and 50dh for other meals.

From the village, descend to the bottom of the narrow Hanedour Valley and head north-north-west. Pass walled gardens to both the left and right on the inner side of the valley's meanders; in each place sufficient silt has been deposited to support cultivation. Cross to the left of the valley after five minutes and then switch back to the right as you approach the first houses in the village of **Igui n'Ouarraou** 45 minutes from Hanedour.

By now the valley has gradually widened and lightened, the black basalt giving way to yellow. Five minutes later, cross back to the left bank and make your way up the gentle valley side to the first houses there, reaching them 60 minutes from Hanedour. Rather confusingly, these houses also form part of the village of Igui n'Ouarraou. As you enter this second part of the village, there is a small **shop**. It is marked with a sign written in Arabic, but choose carefully: opposite is another building with its own sign in Arabic offering a corn-grinding service. This linear, spaced out village continues along the valley side for the next 50 minutes. **Jbel Amlal** (2447m/8028ft) is by now clearly visible due north in the distance. On this mountain for one day and one night only in the month of May, Berbers gather for a popular moussem as they move their flocks northwards, from the increasing heat of the south, towards the cool of the High Atlas Mountains.

Continue north-north-west along the left-hand side of the Hanedour Valley. Almost at the end of the village the path turns and climbs to join a piste to the left above the line of houses and then continues to trace the side of the valley once again. Pass the picturesque village of **Bou Tigguit n'Oualtkit** on the far (eastern) side of the valley, tucked up against its steep sides.

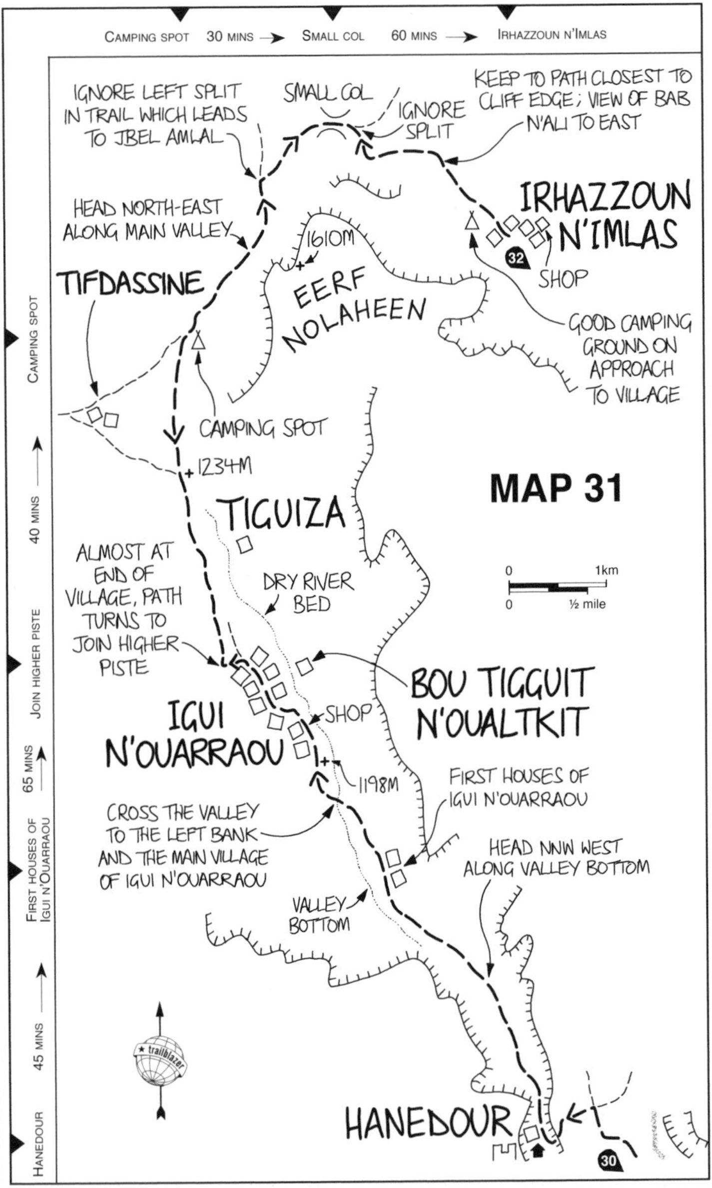

Camping spot 30 mins → Small col 60 mins → Irhazzoun n'Imlas

Hanedour 45 mins → First houses of Igui n'Ouarraou 65 mins → Join higher piste 40 mins → Camping spot

MAP 31

IGNORE LEFT SPLIT IN TRAIL WHICH LEADS TO JBEL AMLAL

SMALL COL

IGNORE SPLIT

KEEP TO PATH CLOSEST TO CLIFF EDGE; VIEW OF BAB N'ALI TO EAST

IRHAZZOUN N'IMLAS

SHOP

32

HEAD NORTH-EAST ALONG MAIN VALLEY

1610M

TIFDASSINE

EERF NOLAHEEN

GOOD CAMPING GROUND ON APPROACH TO VILLAGE

CAMPING SPOT

1234M

TIGUIZA

0 1km

0 ½ mile

ALMOST AT END OF VILLAGE, PATH TURNS TO JOIN HIGHER PISTE

DRY RIVER BED

BOU TIGGUIT N'OUALTKIT

IGUI N'OUARRAOU

SHOP

1198M

FIRST HOUSES OF IGUI N'OUARRAOU

CROSS THE VALLEY TO THE LEFT BANK AND THE MAIN VILLAGE OF IGUI N'OUARRAOU

HEAD NNW WEST ALONG VALLEY BOTTOM

VALLEY BOTTOM

trailblazer

HANEDOUR

30

After 120 minutes from Hanedour pass a sign, so very rare in Sahro, indicating the village of Tiguiza is on the right lower down the valley, but keep heading straight. Finally, in about 30 minutes, you arrive at a good **camping** ground; this is where the Hanedour Valley meets a major valley running across, south-west to north-east, and is just before the first houses of **Tifdassine**, the village lying in the main valley to the left (west). This village is not marked on either of the current 1:100,000 maps and was wrongly placed (in the adjacent Taoudacht Valley to the east) on a previous edition of the Boumalne map.

Tifdassine–Irhazzoun n'Imlas–Boilouz [Map 31; Map 32, p212]

This second stage, a little more demanding than the first, includes walks through two beautiful gorges: the Amguis Gorge in the first half of the day and later the Oufouarar Gorge. Between the two, the route involves a moderate climb up to the striking natural rock formation of Bab n'Ali, held by many to be the jewel of Jbel Sahro.

Head north-east along the main valley. The path soon divides. The branch on the left heads towards Jbel Amlal, that on the right towards the village of Irhazzoun n'Imlas. Take this right-hand path which gradually ascends to a small **col** (30 minutes) directly below the dramatic rock face of **Eerf Nolaheen** ('head beard', 1610m/5282ft). From the col, there are wonderful views back to your first night's camp at Tifdassine and to Berkik, beyond.

On the descent on the far side of the col, the path swings first east and then south-east. Further to the east, and still some way ahead, Bab n'Ali comes into view against the skyline. The path soon divides again. Once more, the left branch heads for Jbel Amlal but you should take the right-hand path. It follows the right side of the main valley, below sheer, beautiful yellow cliffs, to reach the green village of **Irhazzoun n'Imlas** one hour after leaving the pass. The name attributed to the village is derived from the Berber word for 'shearing', on account of the tradition to break the journey here to shear animals on the way to the moussem on Jbel Amlal. There are good ***camping*** places both on the immediate approach to the village and along the route afterwards within the Amguis Gorge described below. Between the two, at the top of the village is a small **shop** beside which I have previously pitched for the night.

At the eastern exit to the village do not follow the wide piste which climbs slightly to the right (north-east). Instead drop into a narrow, fertile **gorge** to the left, reached in 15 minutes, which runs more or less parallel to the piste. A house and gardens stand at its entrance along with a few palm trees. Thirty minutes into the gorge, pass an **azib**, deserted in winter, under the rockface on the right and then clamber over a few scattered rocks, through which a stream, the Assif n'Amguis, may be flowing; the gorge turns slightly right (east) here. Soon you will pass through **Amguis**, no more than a scattering of isolated houses and fields (55 minutes).

Continue through this very pleasant gorge, which from Amguis begins to widen, until, just by the first house you meet on the right (60 minutes), a path leads right (south) up the right-hand valley side for five minutes until above the house. It then continues to follow the right-hand side of the valley eastwards but

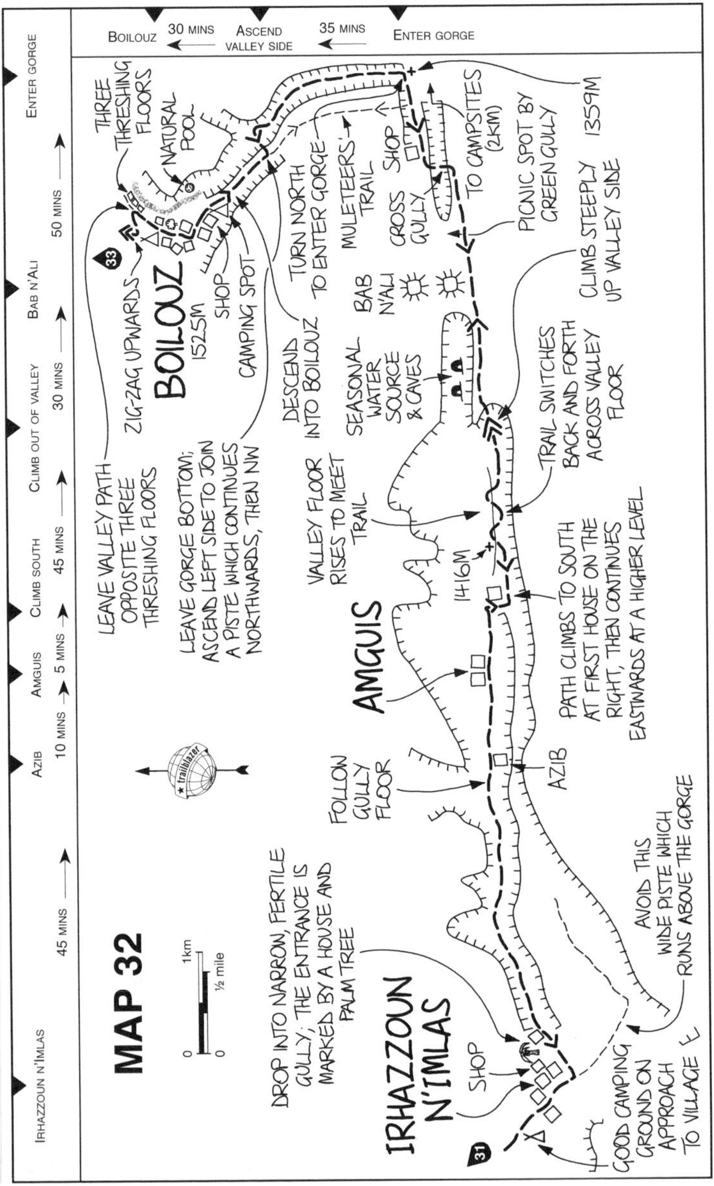

Irhazzoun n'Imlas
45 mins →
Azib
10 mins →
Amguis
5 mins →
Climb south
45 mins →
Climb out of valley
30 mins →
Bab n'Ali
50 mins →
Enter gorge
Enter gorge
35 mins ←
Ascend valley side
30 mins ←
Boilouz
MAP 32
0 1km
0 ½ mile
trailblazer
LEAVE VALLEY PATH OPPOSITE THREE THRESHING FLOORS
33
ZIG-ZAG UPWARDS
THREE THRESHING FLOORS
BOILOUZ
1525M
NATURAL POOL
LEAVE GORGE BOTTOM; ASCEND LEFT SIDE TO JOIN A PISTE WHICH CONTINUES NORTHWARDS, THEN NW
SHOP
CAMPING SPOT
DROP INTO NARROW, FERTILE GULLY; THE ENTRANCE IS MARKED BY A HOUSE AND PALM TREE
DESCEND INTO BOILOUZ
TURN NORTH TO ENTER GORGE
VALLEY FLOOR RISES TO MEET TRAIL
FOLLOW GULLY FLOOR
AMGUIS
SEASONAL WATER SOURCE & CAVES
BAB N'ALI
MULETEERS' TRAIL
IRHAZZOUN N'IMLAS
CROSS GULLY
SHOP
31
SHOP
1416M
TO CAMPSITES (2KM)
AZIB
PICNIC SPOT BY GREEN GULLY
TRAIL SWITCHES BACK AND FORTH ACROSS VALLEY FLOOR
PATH CLIMBS TO SOUTH AT FIRST HOUSE ON THE RIGHT, THEN CONTINUES EASTWARDS AT A HIGHER LEVEL
CLIMB STEEPLY UP VALLEY SIDE
1359M
GOOD CAMPING GROUND ON APPROACH TO VILLAGE
AVOID THIS WIDE PISTE WHICH RUNS ABOVE THE GORGE

at a higher level. This path will give you a different perspective on the dramatic rock towers which are looming up behind the far (northern) valley side.

Soon the trail ducks down again and meets the rising valley floor (75 minutes). Cross the **valley floor** to its left bank and pick your way through boulders and gorse. Continue to follow the valley, switching back to the left bank (80 minutes), the right bank (85 minutes) and then double switching (105 minutes) so that you are eventually back on the right bank. At this point, for the first time today, the trail climbs steeply, even zig-zagging for a while, up the valley side, reaching the top 120 minutes from Irhazzoun n'Imlas.

You will emerge onto a plain and be rewarded with impressive views of the magnificent twin conglomerate towers of **Bab n'Ali** appearing straight ahead, further to the east. Just below the trail and out of view, two minutes to the left, are small **caves**, which could provide shelter, and a seasonal **water source**. The path, however, leads straight towards Bab n'Ali (135 minutes). Immediately afterwards, continuing eastwards into a very wide valley, a short descent brings you to a good lunch spot alongside the head of a very narrow **small green gully** in which palm trees grow (150 minutes). From here the views ahead across the eastern reaches of Jbel Sahro are uninterrupted, while Bab n'Ali towers above you.

The path runs to the right of the gully for 15 minutes, then crosses to the left. Pass a single house and stone hut that serves as a **shop** (20 minutes) before arriving at the beautiful **Oufourar Gorge**, which enters the main valley from the north (35 minutes).

There are two **campsites** about two kilometres from here. One is behind the school, almost straight ahead and slightly to the right (east-south-east) on the far side of the Akka n'Ousdidene. The other is further to the right at the entrance to the narrower section of the Akka n'Ousdidene Valley. Both sites are equipped with toilets and showers and can provide hot meals.

The first part of the Oufourar Gorge would be impossible for your mule. Your muleteer will need to take the trail left (north) which climbs up the main valley side five minutes before the gorge. He will then cross over the headland at the top before dropping into the gorge from the west, enabling him to rejoin your trail. You, meanwhile, will enter the gorge, scrambling over fallen boulders and jumping over errant streams. The path becomes very unclear being subject to frequent shifts caused by rains and fresh avalanches. Even so, you cannot lose the way as you have no choice but to continue first north and then north-west within the confines of the impressive sheer gorge walls.

Thirty-five minutes into the gorge you must decide whether to continue along the gorge bottom, which around this point begins to open out, or to ascend its left-hand side via a thin but clear trail to meet a piste, along which your muleteer should have already passed. The piste, cut high into the valley side, continues to lead north-west through the gorge, eventually descending to the village of **Boilouz** (not marked on the 1:100,000 maps) 65 minutes after entering the gorge.

The accepted **camp spot** in Boilouz (meaning 'almonds') is on the level space in front of the **shop** at the entrance to the village. If this does not appeal, walk through the village to the far side (as described below) to find alternative possibilities. There is no natural water source in the village, but there are several **wells**: ask for directions.

Boilouz–Igli–Tizi n'Ouarg [Map 33]

This stage involves the highest walking on the route, including the crossing of Tizi Igli, and culminates in a scramble to the top of Kouaouch for panoramic 360° views across the whole of Jbel Sahro. Despite the final descent to Tizi n'Ouarg (2200m/7218ft) at the end of the day, you still need to pitch your tent at a higher level than on any other occasion during this trek. There are those who feel that the natural rock formations of Tassigdelt are even more impressive than those of Bab n'Ali (see p213). If you agree, this will be the most memorable of stages, especially as the day also includes views of a number of other quite special rock formations.

From the camping spot in front of the shop at Boilouz, cross the stream entering the main Oufourar Valley from the west and pick up the thin but clear trail which briefly climbs back up the valley side and then, just as quickly, descends once more to the valley bottom. Here it runs westwards alongside neat gardens which separate you from the river's edge. Within 20 minutes you reach the far (western) edge of the village where there are further **camping** possibilities.

Follow the meander in the river past the last house in the village and its outbuildings on your left, sitting at the entrance to a side valley, until you meet three threshing floors five minutes later on your right between the track and the main river. Leave the valley path and **zig-zag steeply upwards** north-west for 20 minutes between the side valley and the main valley. At the top are views straight ahead of **La Tête du Dromadaire** (The Camel's Head) and the sheer rock-face of Tassigdelt to its right. La Tête du Dromadaire is an amazing natural rock formation: looked at one way, it resembles the profile of a whole camel lying down and facing right; looked at another way, it could be the face of a camel looking directly at you with its humps behind.

Head north-west straight towards it across stony, level ground. There are valleys below you to both left and right. Forty minutes later the track briefly dips. Look to your left: on the horizon is the isolated rock formation, **Le Coeur** (The Heart). After another 20 minutes the trail dips again causing La Tête du Dromadaire to disappear from view for 10 minutes, but simply keep heading north-west. Fifteen minutes later the trail drops into a vale in which sits the picturesque green hamlet of **Igli**. Here a small unofficial ***gîte***, equipped with toilets and showers, can provide you with tea or even, with patience, a meal. There is also a small **shop**. Meanwhile from this angle, Le Coeur has magically transformed into L'Éléphant.

Mighty Tassigdelt now towers above you to the right (north) and the pass towards which you must now climb, Tizi Igli (not named on the 1:100,000 maps), is obvious between its two magnificent yellow conglomerate faces. Head due north from Igli and within a few minutes begin a steep climb which will continue for much of the rest of the day. Ten minutes from Igli you will pass a piped **water source** and after 45 minutes you will be below the right-hand rock

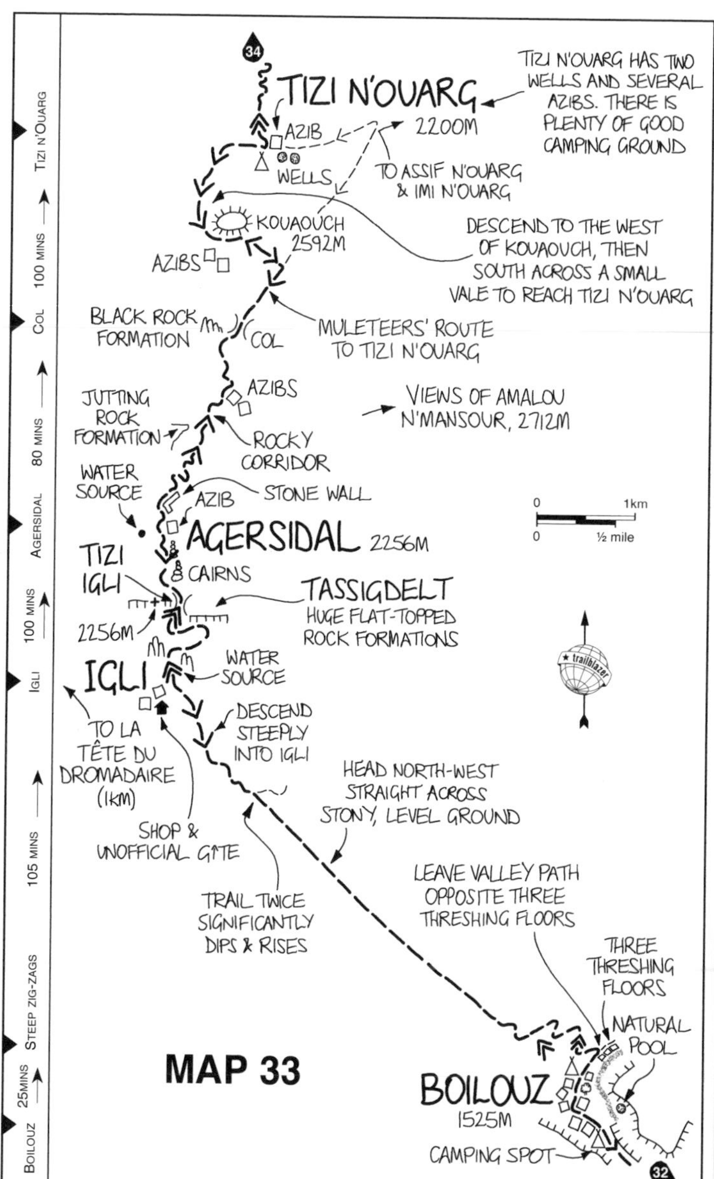
TIZI N'OUARG
2200M
TIZI N'OUARG HAS TWO WELLS AND SEVERAL AZIBS. THERE IS PLENTY OF GOOD CAMPING GROUND
AZIB
WELLS
TO ASSIF N'OUARG & IMI N'OUARG
KOUAOUCH
2592M
DESCEND TO THE WEST OF KOUAOUCH, THEN SOUTH ACROSS A SMALL VALE TO REACH TIZI N'OUARG
AZIBS
BLACK ROCK FORMATION
COL
MULETEERS' ROUTE TO TIZI N'OUARG
AZIBS
JUTTING ROCK FORMATION
VIEWS OF AMALOU N'MANSOUR, 2712M
ROCKY CORRIDOR
WATER SOURCE
STONE WALL
AZIB
AGERSIDAL 2256M
0 1km
0 ½ mile
TIZI IGLI
CAIRNS
TASSIGDELT
HUGE FLAT-TOPPED ROCK FORMATIONS
2256M
IGLI
WATER SOURCE
DESCEND STEEPLY INTO IGLI
TO LA TÊTE DU DROMADAIRE (1KM)
HEAD NORTH-WEST STRAIGHT ACROSS STONY, LEVEL GROUND
SHOP & UNOFFICIAL GITE
TRAIL TWICE SIGNIFICANTLY DIPS & RISES
LEAVE VALLEY PATH OPPOSITE THREE THRESHING FLOORS
THREE THRESHING FLOORS
NATURAL POOL
BOILOUZ
1525M
CAMPING SPOT
MAP 33
Boilouz
25MINS
Steep zig-zags
105 MINS
Igli
100 MINS
Agersidal
80 MINS
Col
100 MINS
Tizi n'Ouarg
trailblazer
34
32

face of **Tassigdelt**. Follow the clear path around to the left of it and then resume heading north towards Tizi Igli, which you will reach 90 minutes from Igli.

From the pass is a terrific panoramic view to the south all the way back to Eerf Nolaheen, which you passed on Day 1, and beyond. On the far (northern) side of the pass, just 10 minutes later, is a pleasant hollow, **Agersidal**: a good lunch spot. There is a **water source** to the left and an azib to the right which, although it has no roof, could provide some shelter. If you have time, you may choose to climb onto the pastures on the flat top of Tassigdelt which you have spent so much time looking up to today. Tassigdelt means 'lid', although only now will you gain the perspective to understand why it has attracted this particular name.

From Agersidal head north-north-east, almost straight, through a corridor of rocks ahead. The climb continues over rocky ground for the next 80 minutes and is fairly unrelenting. It includes, after 30 minutes, almost a scramble through a second short but very narrow **rocky corridor**. You will be inspired throughout this ascent by fabulous views opening up back south as far as the Bani Mountains in the vicinity of M'hamid. Breathe in also the staggering views of the eastern Jbel Sahro, including that of **Amalou n'Mansour** (2712m/8898ft), the highest peak in the entire Sahro range.

From the **col**, which you reach at the end of this climb, the land falls away in all directions. It would be possible to descend straight ahead (north-east) along the Assif n'Ouarg; if you hit bad weather at this point you should seriously consider doing this. There are several villages in this valley, the largest of which is **Imi n'Ouarg**, where shelter would be available. In all eventualities, your muleteer will need to drop into this valley and then ascend south-west to meet you at Tizi n'Ouarg (2200m/7218ft).

Your path from the col to Tizi n'Ouarg heads north-west. First descend gently with your muleteer towards Assif n'Ouarg for just five minutes before turning away and ascending the steep slopes on your left to the base of **Kouaouch** in a further 10 minutes. This fantastic rock tower (2592m/8504m) completely dominates the surrounding landscape. Leave your bag at the base and climb the tower (about five minutes) for staggering views in all directions. Those who have already completed the Jbel Sahro circular trek will particularly enjoy the views from here of Tine Ouaiyour to the south-west.

The final descent to Tizi n'Ouarg will take about 80 minutes from the top of Kouaouch. You will need to take a somewhat circuitous route on account of some intervening precipitous rocks, initially heading west before turning back north, then crossing over a small vale and finally arriving at your camp. Despite its name, **Tizi n'Ouarg** is not a pass at all but a flat pasture which provides a scenic ***camping*** ground. There are a few **azibs** at the eastern end of the pasture. Close by, a newly constructed **well**, alongside one that is clearly older and in decline, guarantees a good water supply.

Although we camped here in February, my guide considered this to be only just acceptable, warning against staying here in December and January which he believes to be too cold at this altitude. He recounted tales of previous years when he had to release his mules from here and wade through thigh-deep snow. Even in February, we awoke to find our tent frozen solid and as taut as a drum skin.

Tizi n'Ouarg to Tarbelout Neeloman [Map 34, p218]

This stage begins with a moderate ascent but, for the most part, the day is spent descending from the mountains to the Dades plain which comes into view during the course of the morning. Some will choose to end their trek once they reach Tarbelout Neeloman rather than cross the expansive Dades plain on foot.

Head due north by climbing the rocky path which leads past the azibs and the wells and wind your way up to a small, rounded crest (20 minutes). Drop into the small green vale of **Iffat** (meaning 'gutter', 2400m/7874ft) straight ahead. There is a **spring** here down to the left (west) in winter.

Cross over the vale and climb straight ahead, still due north, towards the prominent rocky peaks on the skyline. The path will deviate to the right of them as you ascend. After 45 minutes, views suddenly open across mountains to the right (east) including the distinctive Isk n'Alla (meaning 'Horn of Alla', 2569m/8428ft). Keep climbing and reach a second crest (50 minutes) which leads onto a **plateau** sprinkled with juniper woodland. The path leads north-west across it and within moments views of the Central High Atlas, including Ighil Mgoun, are revealed far away across the Dades plain.

At the far end of the plateau (55 minutes) follow the path as it heads west-wards over the edge into a narrow valley running north-west to south-east; this gradually narrows to the point of almost becoming a small **gorge**. The path follows the valley's right-hand (eastern) side, gradually descending through more juniper trees to the **valley bottom** (80 minutes). Continue straight ahead (north-west) along the valley bottom for a further 25 minutes until the trail rises again (105 minutes) climbing back up the valley side for 10 minutes, bringing you far-reaching views ahead towards Tagdilt and again across the Dades plain.

The path now continues almost straight ahead (north) along a snout formed by the merging of the side of the valley you have just been following and that of a parallel valley entering from the right. Descend the snout to arrive at the confluence of these two valleys in 20 minutes. This is **Tislit n'Ouzarzam**. Switch to the right bank of the right-hand valley and then, five minutes later, cross to the left bank of the unified valley. Gradually ascend the left bank and once again achieve good views of Tagdilt ahead. From here, pass a **farm** on your left with gardens, an orchard and a concrete pool (30 minutes) and then join the piste (40 minutes) that serves it before arriving at **Tarbelout Neeloman** ('spring of meeting camels'). The **water source** here might tempt you to stop for lunch.

Now that the mountains are behind, some trekkers might even choose to end their walk here having pre-arranged transport to pick them up at this point. Some, however, will continue as far as Tagdilt, whilst others will prefer the sense of achievement of continuing further still to cross the full width of the Dades plain by reaching either Boumalne du Dades or Qalaa't Mgouna via Tagdilt and Aït Hamt (not marked on the 1:100,000 maps) on foot. Route descriptions for these options follow overleaf.

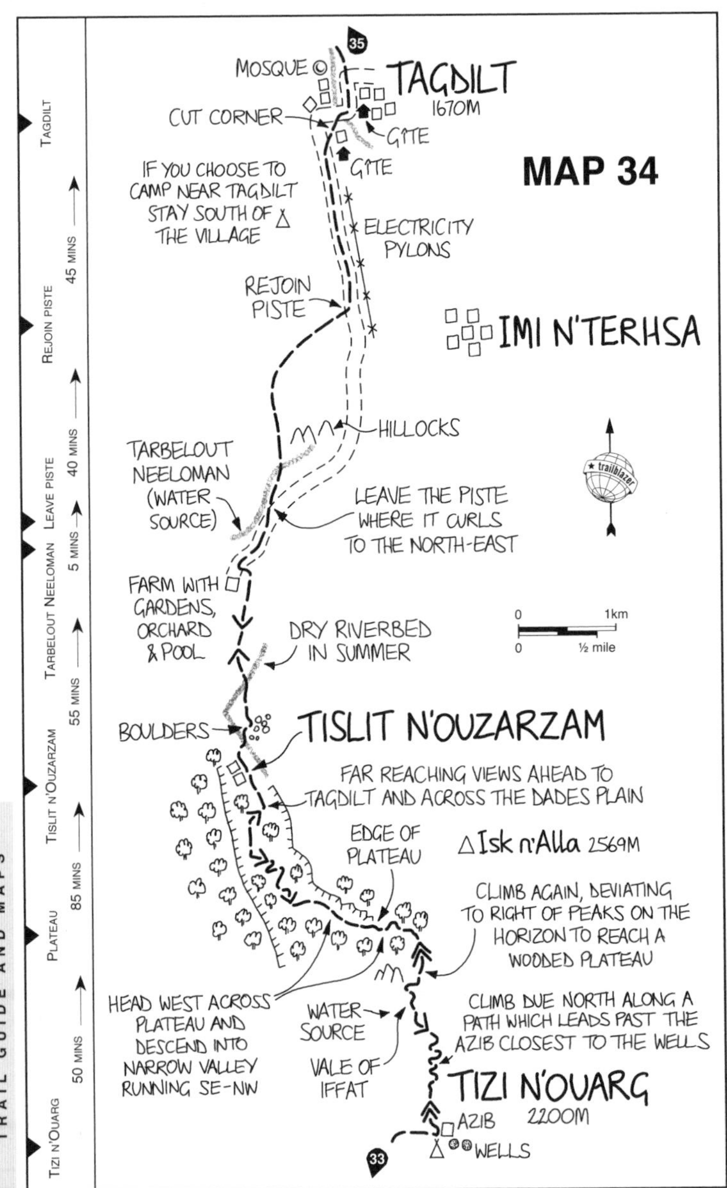
MAP 34
TAGDILT
1670M
MOSQUE
CUT CORNER
GîTE
GîTE
IF YOU CHOOSE TO CAMP NEAR TAGDILT STAY SOUTH OF THE VILLAGE
ELECTRICITY PYLONS
REJOIN PISTE
IMI N'TERHSA
HILLOCKS
TARBELOUT NEELOMAN (WATER SOURCE)
LEAVE THE PISTE WHERE IT CURLS TO THE NORTH-EAST
FARM WITH GARDENS, ORCHARD & POOL
DRY RIVERBED IN SUMMER
0 1km
0 ½ mile
BOULDERS
TISLIT N'OUZARZAM
FAR REACHING VIEWS AHEAD TO TAGDILT AND ACROSS THE DADES PLAIN
EDGE OF PLATEAU
Isk n'Alla 2569M
CLIMB AGAIN, DEVIATING TO RIGHT OF PEAKS ON THE HORIZON TO REACH A WOODED PLATEAU
HEAD WEST ACROSS PLATEAU AND DESCEND INTO NARROW VALLEY RUNNING SE-NW
WATER SOURCE
VALE OF IFFAT
CLIMB DUE NORTH ALONG A PATH WHICH LEADS PAST THE AZIB CLOSEST TO THE WELLS
TIZI N'OUARG
2200M
AZIB
WELLS
35
33
TAGDILT
45 MINS
REJOIN PISTE
40 MINS
LEAVE PISTE
5 MINS
TARBELOUT NEELOMAN
55 MINS
TISLIT N'OUZARZAM
85 MINS
PLATEAU
50 MINS
TIZI N'OUARG

Tarbelout Neeloman to Tagdilt

[Map 34, p218]

It is possible to follow the piste all the way from Tarbelout Neeloman to Tagdilt in around 90 minutes. There are, however, opportunities to cut corners. The first, after just five minutes, involves leaving the piste where it curls around to the north-east. From here, follow a dry **river bed** on the left for five minutes before crossing to its far, left bank and then head left again (north) behind hillocks.

Rejoin the piste at the point where **electricity pylons** begin to run alongside it. The piste by now is running due north. On the far side (east) of the pylons are a series of gardens which run all the way to Tagdilt. Increasingly, villagers are building their houses alongside them to remove the need to travel out from Tagdilt every day to work on them.

By now Tagdilt itself is clearly visible ahead: simply follow the piste through the wide open countryside, cutting off one more corner just before the village. **Tagdilt** is a popular starting point for those interested in bird-watching tours in the Valley of the Birds (*La Vallée des Oiseaux*). There are two ***gîtes*** here. The first is found immediately before the first houses on the approach to the village. The second is near the village centre. If you plan to **camp**, however, this is best done just before the village on the approach from the south.

Tagdilt to Aït Hamt

[Map 35, p220]

Follow the thin but clear trail which heads north-west from the village past the **mosque**, almost immediately crossing an irrigation channel. This rather beautiful route to Aït Hamt provides an interesting insight into isolated, rural life on the edge of the Dades plain. Enclosed, cultivated fields lie to your right, open land to your left. Deviate around a small **copse** (10 minutes) and then resume north-west, crossing two successive dry rivers (15 minutes). Soon the trail leads straight past the front door of an isolated house to reach fields bordered by small trees (25 minutes).

After 30 minutes the trail kicks slightly left and climbs very gently to meet a **piste** which in turn winds through open, cultivated fields. When the piste veers away to the north-east keep heading north-west towards the small brown hills in the mid-distance and the very apparent cleft, on the same level as the trail, which runs through them.

At this point Jbel Sahro lies over your left shoulder whilst the High Atlas Mountains are clearly seen ahead, behind these brown hills. Pass through the **cleft** (40 minutes) and continue along a soft piste which leads westwards, crossing three dry river beds in the next 10 minutes, after which it turns and leads back to the north-west. The valley gradually opens out into a flat plain as you head towards the Tiounouine Mountains.

Leave the piste at the point where it swings to the right (north-east) to follow another thin but clear trail which veers left (north-west) of the mountains into a very wide and very beautiful, flat-bottomed valley. The first houses of the dispersed village of Aït Hamt now lie straight ahead. Directly behind them, framed by the wide valley sides and seemingly nestling against the backdrop of the High Atlas Mountains, is the distant town of Boumalne du Dades. Jbel Sahro is now directly behind you. Reach the first three houses of **Aït Hamt** and

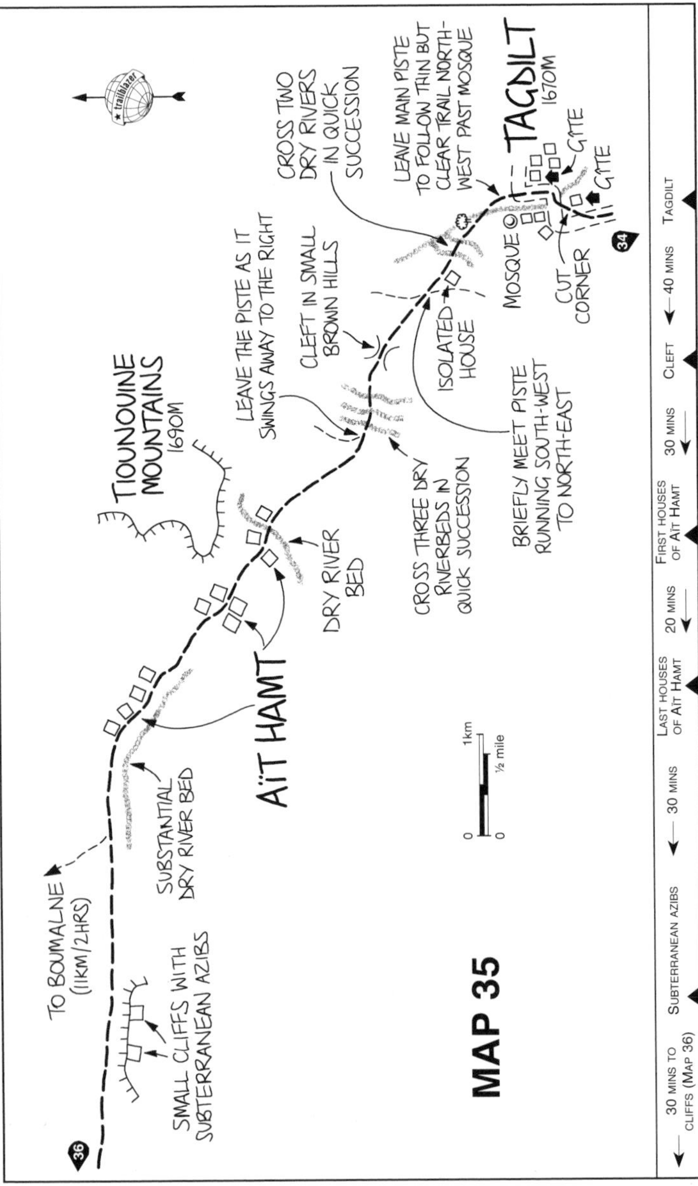
MAP 35
TAGDILT
1670M
GATE
GATE
MOSQUE
CUT CORNER
LEAVE MAIN PISTE TO FOLLOW THIN BUT CLEAR TRAIL NORTH-WEST PAST MOSQUE
CROSS TWO DRY RIVERS IN QUICK SUCCESSION
ISOLATED HOUSE
BRIEFLY MEET PISTE RUNNING SOUTH-WEST TO NORTH-EAST
CLEFT IN SMALL BROWN HILLS
LEAVE THE PISTE AS IT SWINGS AWAY TO THE RIGHT
CROSS THREE DRY RIVERBEDS IN QUICK SUCCESSION
TIOUNOUINE MOUNTAINS
1690M
DRY RIVER BED
AÏT HAMT
SUBSTANTIAL DRY RIVER BED
TO BOUMALNE (11KM/2HRS)
SMALL CLIFFS WITH SUBTERRANEAN AZIBS
1km
½ mile
0
0
34
36
30 MINS TO CLIFFS (MAP 36)
SUBTERRANEAN AZIBS
30 MINS
LAST HOUSES OF AÏT HAMT
20 MINS
FIRST HOUSES OF AÏT HAMT
30 MINS
CLEFT
40 MINS
TAGDILT

their small gardens, crossing the dry valley which runs between them (70 minutes). Continuing north-west, a second cluster of houses, seemingly a little more affluent than the first, is soon reached, and then a third, bordered on its southern edge by a substantial dry river. It would be possible to **camp** almost anywhere in the vicinity of Aït Hamt.

Aït Hamt–Boumalne or Qalaa't Mgouna [Map 35; Maps 36, 37, p222]

Those who have come this far are now presented with a choice: either to head north-west to Boumalne, visible straight across the Dades plain, or else to cut a longer trail across the Dades plain westwards to Qalaa't Mgouna, still a long way out of sight. For the first part of the morning, the route is the same: head west from Aït Hamt. Soon, far ahead on the horizon, you will see a round orange-pink **water tower**, associated with the unseen village of Sarveen (not marked on the 1:100,000 maps), set on a raised plateau above cliffs.

For Boumalne If your aim is Boumalne pick up a faint trail on your right just a few minutes after leaving Aït Hamt; this heads north-west straight to your final destination. Do not be unduly concerned if you have trouble finding it: simply strike out across the flat, stony **flood plain** in the direction of Boumalne and expect to cover the 11km in around two hours.

For Qalaa't Mgouna If you are set for Qalaa't Mgouna, you will soon be able to use the water tower to fix your direction. However, begin by continuing to head west along trails which at times will broaden into pistes, crossed over by many others. It is, however, impossible to lose the direction now. Within 30 minutes you will pass small cliffs on your left (south) into which are built subterranean azibs. As you at last reach the first cliffs of **Sarveen** (60 minutes) your path will remain on the flood plain, veering away to the south-west, passing to the left (south) of the cliffs.

Once you pass the **water tower** (75 minutes), look ahead, further south-west, to see the distant buildings and minarets of a string of settlements for which you are now clearly heading. As you round the cliffs look out for azibs cut into the sheer rock-face. After 150 minutes, as you pass large cultivated gardens to the left (south), look for a pisé **lookout tower** crumbling on the edge of the cliffs above you; this is associated with the ancient village of Sarveen. From here the track becomes a more substantial piste.

After 180 minutes you will reach **Aït Yassine**. It would be easy to arrange to be picked up from here. Alternatively, a walk through the village would bring you to the main road and frequent public transport both to Qalaa't Mgouna and Boumalne. For those intent on walking further, there is a solid piste all the way back to **Tassouit** (270 minutes), from where the Jbel Sahro Circular Trek starts (see p226).

From Tassouit, allow another hour to wind your way along quiet lanes, passing through traditional villages and cultivated fields to reach Qalaa't Mgouna, 5km to the north-west. Unfortunately, the final approach to the town, with the rapid advance of concrete houses and tarmac roads, has become rather disappointing. This should not, however, detract from your sense of achievement.

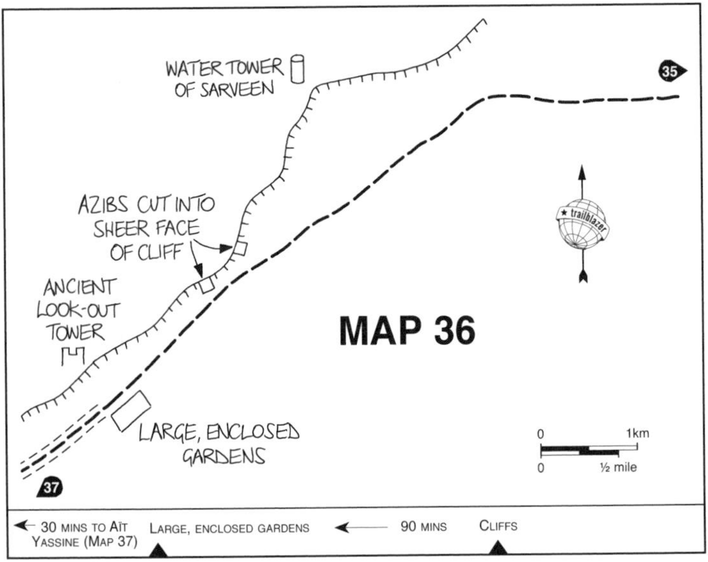
WATER TOWER
OF SARVEEN
AZIBS CUT INTO
SHEER FACE
OF CLIFF
ANCIENT
LOOK-OUT
TOWER
LARGE, ENCLOSED
GARDENS
MAP 36
35
37
0
1km
0
½ mile
trailblazer
← 30 MINS TO AÏT YASSINE (MAP 37)
LARGE, ENCLOSED GARDENS
← 90 MINS
CLIFFS

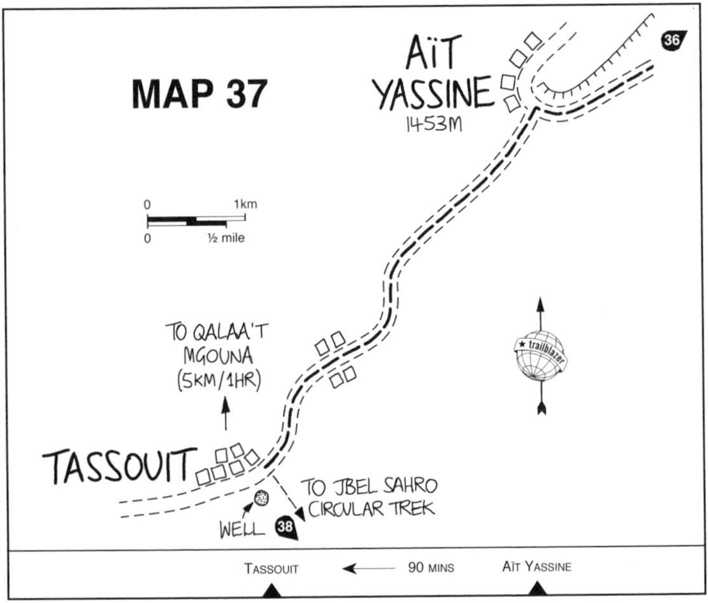
MAP 37
AÏT
YASSINE
1453M
36
0
1km
0
½ mile
TO QALAA'T
MGOUNA
(5KM/1HR)
TASSOUIT
TO JBEL SAHRO
CIRCULAR TREK
WELL
38
trailblazer
TASSOUIT
← 90 MINS
AÏT YASSINE

QALAA'T MGOUNA/EL KELAA M'GOUNA

There is little doubt that the best time to visit Qalaa't Mgouna is during the three days of the town's moussem, its annual **rose festival**, staged to celebrate the success of each year's rose harvest. Always held during the first weekend of May, the influx of villagers from the surrounding mountains, who bring with them their musical instruments and their enthusiasm for dance, lights up the town. Although the damask rose (*Rosa damascene*) is not even the principle crop of the region – that distinction belongs to the staple wheat – it is this rose that provides the town with its identity and so much of its spirit.

It has been estimated that there are over 2000km of rose hedges flourishing between the Mgoun and the Dades valleys. These hedges, which border, demark and offer protection to the wheat fields of Qalaa't Mgouna, are able to generate an astonishing 2000 tonnes of flowers. Yet such an enormous quantity is necessary, as no fewer than four tonnes of petals are required to obtain just 1kg of distilled rose oil and 400kg of petals to obtain just 1kg of rose concrete.

The process of distillation takes place at the **Capp and Florale factory**, founded in 1938 and built in the form of a huge kasbah, at the eastern end of the main street. It opens its doors to visitors, although sadly the opportunities for visits are limited to the brief period immediately after the harvest. This is the time when the rose-distillation process is quickly conducted, while the petals still remain fresh. There is no danger, however, of missing the importance of the rose to Qalaa't Mgouna at any other time of the year: within every few paces taken along its main street you will pass a shop dedicated to selling the factory's products.

Beyond May, on the surface, this small, dusty town would not appear to hold much of interest, and certainly there might not be much to immediately persuade anyone emerging from his taxi after a long journey over the Atlas Mountains or along the Dades Valley to stay long, but stay a while and this town can grow on you. More importantly for the trekker, Qalaa't Mgouna performs its role as a trailhead well.

Arrival and local transport

Regular long-distance **buses** head both east and west from Qalaa't Mgouna every day. The bus ticket office is found towards the western end of avenue Mohammed V. For an indication of destinations, frequencies and prices, consult the listings given in the Boumalne du Dades town description (see p243) and allow a difference of about half an hour when calculating timings.

Alternatively, the **taxi** stand is located in the very centre of town. A single seat for the 24km ride to Boumalne in a grand taxi costs 7dh and is covered in about half an hour, while the 90-minute journey to Ouarzazate costs 30dh. Further means of reaching Boumalne from Qalaa't Mgouna include regular **minibuses** (6dh) and, to be taken only if you really feel the need to save a dirham, the white **shuttle bus** (5dh) that stops everywhere en route and takes for ever to reach its destination.

Orientation

There is only one major street in Qalaa't Mgouna, avenue Mohammed V, making orientation straightforward. This main road, hemmed in by the Atlas Mountains to the north and the Dades River to the south, inevitably runs east–west.

The only other road of significance is that which heads north along the Valley of the Roses (La Vallée des Roses) from the centre of town to the village of Boutaghrare in the Atlas Mountains.

Services

There are three **banks** in the centre of town; Crédit Agricole has an **ATM** but Banque Populaire and Attijariwafa do not. All three are on the main road, avenue Mohammed V, close to the taxi rank. A Moneygram is found a short distance to the north-east.

A **pharmacy**, a **téléboutique** and a **photolab** are all within a stone's throw of the taxi rank and similar facilities are dotted along the length of this street to the south-west.

The Valley of the Roses/*La Vallée des Roses*

One of the more beautiful areas of the Central High Atlas Mountains, as yet relatively undeveloped, is the Mgoun Valley, popularly referred to as La Vallée des Roses. Running south from close to Ighil Mgoun, the Mgoun River flows into the Dades just south of Qalaa't Mgouna. Increasingly it is becoming a focus for trekking groups, notably for those wishing to complete a crossing of the High Atlas Mountains from Tabant and the Bou Guemez Valley (see p171) to the edge of Jbel Sahro. There are also growing numbers of visitors who simply wish to experience the valley for the peace and tranquillity it brings. Consequently, a number of small hotels have been built in the valley to complement longer-standing accommodation; all are within easy reach of Qalaa't Mgouna. La Vallée des Roses would provide a good base in which either to acclimatise on your arrival in Morocco or to rest after the exertions of your trek.

The accommodation below is selected because of its close proximity to Qalaa't Mgouna, although there are numerous other, equally appealing, possibilities further up the valley. For instance, if you feel like exploring and have transport, you might want to try visiting picturesque villages as far as Boutaghrare and even beyond.

Where to stay

Kasbah Tassourte (☎/🖷 0524-83 70 70; GSM ☎ 0615-93 37 30; 🖳 ab.aupa@gmail.com) just before the historic village of Aït Khigar, 3km north of Qalaa't Mgouna, has 15 rooms. Newly built, with many authentic Berber features, this hotel directly overlooks the Mgoun River. Double rooms cost 500dh or 300dh (with/without showers), half-board. ***Kasbah Assafar*** (☎/🖷 0524-83 65 77; GSM ☎ 0662-13 21 92; 🖳 www.kasbahassafar.com) is a family-run hotel, located in the centre of Aït Khigar. The style is also Berber, but with quite a lot of bright paint, apparently to appeal to Spanish visitors. Here the cooking is provided by the sisters of the manager, Abdulaziz Boullouz, who is himself an official mountain guide. Rooms are priced at 200dh per person (for rooms with views of the garden) or 191dh (without). These prices include breakfast; lunch or dinner can also be provided for a further 90dh.

Gîte d'étape Aflafal (GSM ☎ 0672-04 58 64) in the village of Tamalout offers the opportunity to experience everyday Berber life at close quarters with the Olkha Brahime family in their very simple home. Places in one of the four rooms cost 30dh plus 10dh for use of the shower. There is free use of the kitchen, or you can ask for breakfast (20dh) and meals (70dh) to be prepared for you. Another place to consider is ***Kasbah Itran*** (see opposite).

The managers at all of these establishments would be willing to collect you from Qalaa't Mgouna if you were to telephone them and ask; advance notice would be appreciated. Alternatively, take a seat in a shared taxi heading for Boutaghrare.

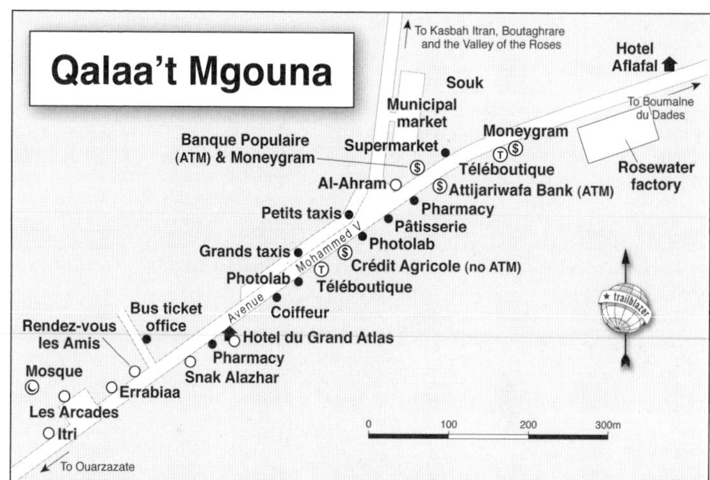

Should you need to stock up on food supplies, there is a small **supermarket** on avenue Mohammed V just north-east of the taxi rank and the municipal **market** is through a doorway about 100m along the road to Boutaghrare, on the right-hand side.

Trekking agencies and guides

- **Mohamed Abouhssen** (GSM ☎ 0668-44 62 78; 💻 guide_atlas@hotmail.com/abouhssen@gmail.com), Ilouahen, Qalaa't Mgouna
- **Youssef Alami** (GSM ☎ 0677-83 82 94; 💻 baalamyf@hotmail.com)
- **Abdulaziz Boullouz** contact via Kasbah Assafar (see box opposite)
- **Kasbah Itran** see Where to Stay.

Where to stay

There are just two hotels in Qalaa't Mgouna. Although quite basic, by far the better option is ***Hotel Aflafal*** (☎ 0524-83 68 00). Simple rooms cost from 70/130dh with access to a communal bathroom, while rooms with baths cost from 120/150dh. The hotel has a bar and a restaurant that serves breakfast.

The alternative is ***Hotel du Grand Atlas*** (☎ 0524-83 68 38; GSM ☎ 070-31 96 10; 💻 kelaa-m@hotmail.com) which represents a dramatic step down in standards. Nonetheless, should you get stuck with no other option, rooms cost 50/100/150dh, including use of communal showers. The hotel also has a dubious hammam on site (15dh, bring your own towel) and offers a massage service (200dh including oils). The management assure me that they have a mountain guide who can be contacted through the hotel, *tarif pas fixé*.

By far the best local hotel is ***Kasbah Itran*** (☎/📠 0524-83 71 03; GSM ☎ 0662-62 22 03; 💻 www.kasbahitran.com; PO Box 124, 45200 El Kelâa Mgouna, Ouarzazate), 4km north of Qalaa't Mgouna along the road to Boutaghrare. Set on a rocky promontory overlooking La Vallée des Roses, this modern hotel, built in traditional Berber style, is beautifully run by inspirational manager Mohamed Taghda and his wonderful brothers. To describe them as extremely hospitable is to do them less than justice. Moreover, the views from the hotel, not only down into the Mgoun Valley, but also north to the Atlas Mountains and even south across the Dades Valley to Jbel Sahro, are something to behold. To enjoy them while breakfast is served on the terrace, as the sun rises over Sahro, makes them special beyond words. Set meals are served in a traditional Berber salon after which you can expect the *tam-tams* to appear. If you arrive in Qalaa't Mgouna without transport, simply phone Mohamed and he will come and collect you. The Kasbah specialises in organising treks for individuals or groups along with many other activities related to raising environmental awareness and knowledge of Berber culture, including Berber language classes.

Simple rooms cost 150/210dh, while en suite rooms with balcony cost 300/360dh. Prices include breakfast, while lunch and dinner are served for an additional 70dh.

Should your penchant for out-of-the-way places not have deserted you after your trek, you might also want to consider one of a growing number of small hotels further into La Vallée des Roses (see box p224).

Where to eat

There are numerous functional café-restaurants along avenue Mohammed V. Try the centrally located ***Café Restaurant Al-Ahram*** for roast chicken while sitting on its front terrace and watching the world go by. Otherwise there is a cluster of slightly superior establishments both towards the western end of the main thoroughfare, including ***Itri***, ***Les Arcades***, ***Errabiaa***, ***Rendez-vous les Amis***, ***Snak Alazhar***, and also along the road which heads north to Boutaghrare from the centre of town, all of which do traditional Moroccan fare.

Hotel du Grand Atlas has its own adjacent restaurant, ***Restaurant du Grand Atlas***, which is open to non residents.

By far the best place to eat locally is ***Kasbah Itran*** (see p225).

What to see

The area around Qalaa't Mgouna is studded with **ancient kasbahs**. Two of the more interesting, both crumbling structures set amongst living villages, lie just three or four kilometres north of Qalaa't Mgouna in the lower part of La Vallée des Roses. Views of the first, **Talmout**, can be enjoyed from the terraces of Kasbah Itran (see Where to stay) while the second, **Tigharmet** is but a few minutes' walk further up the valley. If you are here at the right time of year visit the **Capp and Florale factory** (see p223).

JBEL SAHRO CIRCULAR TREK

Although this route is described as a circular trek, it begins in the village of Tassouit and ends in Boumalne du Dades, 24km away to the north-east. The trailhead for the trek is Qalaa't Mgouna (p223). It would be an easy and pleasant 5km walk to cross the River Dades from Qalaa't Mgouna to Tassouit, although you may prefer to organise transport. At the end of your trek, very good public transport links make a return to Qalaa't Mgouna from Boumalne easy to arrange (see p243).

JBEL SAHRO CIRCULAR
- **Level of difficulty** Moderate
- **Duration** 5-6 days
- **Maps** *Qalaa't Mgouna* (1:100,000) and *Boumalne* (1:100,000), Division de la Carte, Morocco Survey or *Kultur-Trekking im Dschebel Saghro* (1:100,000) German-language trekking map.

The route description is organised as for a five-day trek. However, as the second stage is very long, some trekkers will prefer to break at Tagmout and complete the route in six days.

Tassouit–Tikktarine [Map 38, p228]

On this first day, the trail is largely level with two small climbs. The walk is not especially physically challenging, but it crosses a largely barren landscape with infrequent landmarks. It would be very easy to lose the trail here and readers are reminded of the advice offered at the beginning of the Jbel Sahro section about the employment of guides and compasses (see p204).

Walk out to the southern end of Tassouit and meet the road which runs south-west to north-east and broadly parallel with the south bank of the Oued Dades. Follow the road briefly to the left (north-east) in the direction of the village of Aït Yassine but almost immediately turn off at the point where you pass a well on the right at which local women and children may be washing clothes (10 minutes).

A clear stony path leads right past the **well** at right-angles (south-east) along a very shallow, dry valley bed, **Issil n'Sidi Aqba** (not named on the 1:100,000 maps), through a barren landscape seemingly heading directly for the tallest peak that you can see on the distant horizon. This is in fact one of the peaks on the far, western side of the Issil Bou Izargane, the valley into which you will later drop and possibly pause for lunch.

Follow the shallow valley floor, for about 30 minutes before climbing onto its low right-hand (western) bank. While now maintaining a generally south-south-easterly direction, the trail soon begins to cut across successive sizeable deposits of alluvial moraine, separating one very shallow, dry tributary branch of the same main river bed from another; all run slightly south of south-east and more or less parallel to each other.

Sixty minutes later, having reached the true far right bank of the river, passing several azibs, occasional cave shelters and an abandoned, rusting car to your right, climb to the right again for 10 minutes, this time more steeply, to find the isolated azib **Tafza Melouln** (small white mountain). Close by, on the far (southern) side of the azib, is a **well** providing a good source of water. Immediately afterwards the trail briefly descends but then, five minutes later, climbs again, as it once more turns further to the right (west). Follow the trail quite steeply upwards until, 15 minutes later, it levels out and meets a piste coming in from the right (north-west).

The view all around from this elevated position is of bare hills as far as the eye can see. Follow the piste for five minutes only, for as long as it allows you to keep heading westwards, and then, as it turns away towards the south-east, follow a trail straight ahead and descend (in 20 minutes) into the main, flat-bottomed valley opening before you, **Issil Bou Izargane**. (Bou Izargane means 'the people who make mill stones'.)

As you descend, you will see the small village of **Bou Oudardour** to your right (north-west). The people of this village are famous not only for making mill stones but also for their flour production. You might choose either the village itself or the copse of mixed fig and almond trees, straight ahead on the valley bottom close to a small reservoir, as the place to have your lunch break.

Continue south-east along the dry river bed of Issil Bou Izargane. After ten minutes you will pass between two huge **rock buttresses**; these flank the valley sides like two enormous gate posts and form part of the impressive length of Tasfalout-n-Ougourram, a huge strata of rock running from east-north-east to west-south-west. In this area the rock is cut through by a series of rivers includ-

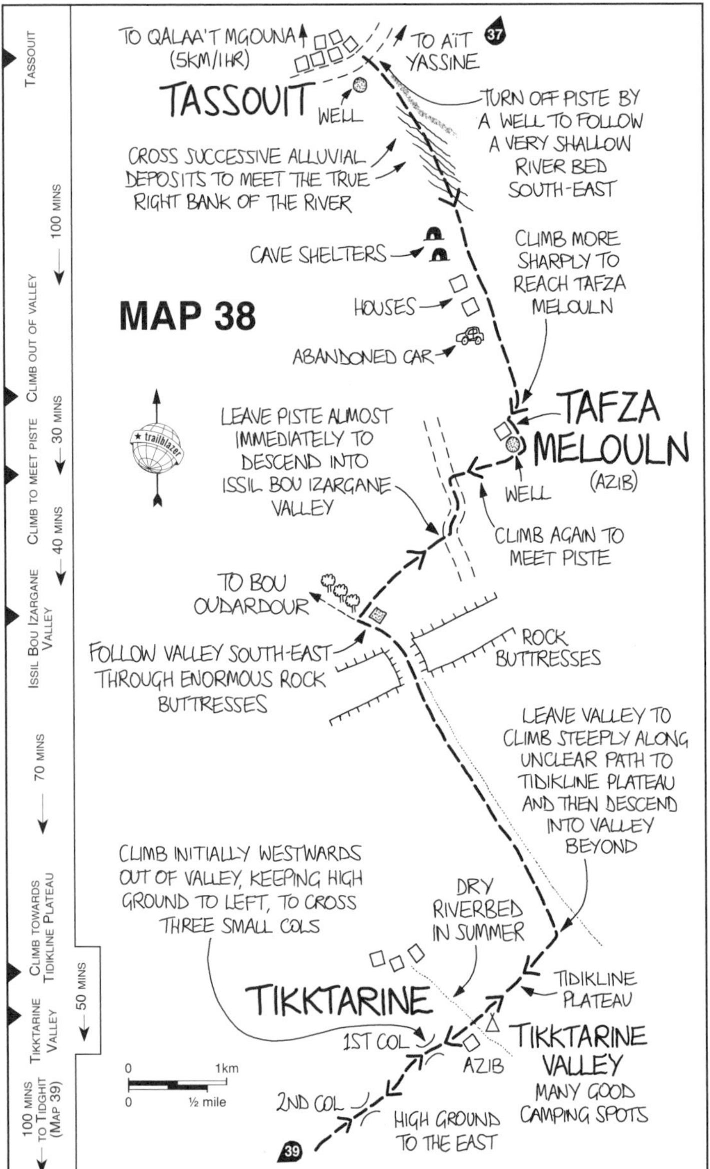

TASSOUIT

100 MINS

CLIMB OUT OF VALLEY

30 MINS

CLIMB TO MEET PISTE

40 MINS

ISSIL BOU IZARGANE VALLEY

70 MINS

CLIMB TOWARDS TIDIKLINE PLATEAU

50 MINS

TIKKTARINE VALLEY

100 MINS TO TIDGHIT (MAP 39)

TO QALAA'T MGOUNA (5KM/1HR)

TO AÏT YASSINE

37

TASSOUIT

WELL

TURN OFF PISTE BY A WELL TO FOLLOW A VERY SHALLOW RIVER BED SOUTH-EAST

CROSS SUCCESSIVE ALLUVIAL DEPOSITS TO MEET THE TRUE RIGHT BANK OF THE RIVER

CAVE SHELTERS

CLIMB MORE SHARPLY TO REACH TAFZA MELOULN

MAP 38

HOUSES

ABANDONED CAR

TAFZA MELOULN

(AZIB)

trailblazer

LEAVE PISTE ALMOST IMMEDIATELY TO DESCEND INTO ISSIL BOU IZARGANE VALLEY

WELL

CLIMB AGAIN TO MEET PISTE

TO BOU OUDARDOUR

FOLLOW VALLEY SOUTH-EAST THROUGH ENORMOUS ROCK BUTTRESSES

ROCK BUTTRESSES

LEAVE VALLEY TO CLIMB STEEPLY ALONG UNCLEAR PATH TO TIDIKLINE PLATEAU AND THEN DESCEND INTO VALLEY BEYOND

CLIMB INITIALLY WESTWARDS OUT OF VALLEY, KEEPING HIGH GROUND TO LEFT, TO CROSS THREE SMALL COLS

DRY RIVERBED IN SUMMER

TIKKTARINE

TIDIKLINE PLATEAU

1ST COL

AZIB

TIKKTARINE VALLEY

MANY GOOD CAMPING SPOTS

0 1km

0 ½ mile

2ND COL

HIGH GROUND TO THE EAST

39

ing Issil Bou Izargane. Its scale is best appreciated by looking behind once you have passed through the rock buttresses.

This next section of the same valley is simply called **Taghia n'Sa'ada** (taghia meaning 'valley'); it is inhabited by Aït Atta tribesmen who farm sheep and goats. Some of their isolated homesteads can be seen at a distance on the far north-east side of the valley.

The trail graduates from the middle of the dry river bottom towards the right (south-west) bank and then, 70 minutes from the copse by the small reservoir, suddenly climbs steeply to the right, up the valley side. There is no clear landmark to signpost this departure. The path, however, is clear and leaves the valley floor just as the valley sides become steeper, yet before you reach the small mountains which begin to rear up on the right-hand side of the valley, just ahead.

Climb for 20 minutes until you reach the hollowed plateau of **Tidikline** (meaning 'palm of the hand') and then continue westwards across it for 20 minutes before descending into the fertile Tikktarine Valley (Tikktarine meaning 'water drops', referring to the numerous water sources to be found here). Neither the plateau nor the valley is named on the 1:100,000 maps. The village of **Tikktarine**, with its pink school building, just out of sight around a bend in the river 1km to the north, isn't marked either.

There are many places in this valley where you might pitch your tent for the night. You may, of course, wish to **camp** near one of the water sources: simply look for a splash of green associated with one of the isolated houses, but always remember, as a courtesy, to ask permission first.

Tikktarine–Assaka-n-Aït Ouzzine

[Map 38; Map 39, p230, Map 40, p232]

This route is both much clearer and much more physically challenging, culminating in the ascent to the pastures of Tafoughalt and the crossing of the Tizi-n-Tagmout (1800m/5905ft). Highlights, such as the pretty village of Tidghit and the gorges on the approach to Assaka-n-Aït Ouzzine, offer encouragement, but this is a very long stage and some trekkers will elect to break their journey, even to spend the night, at the atmospheric village of Tagmout.

Cross to the far (western) bank of the Tikktarine Valley and gently climb south-westwards straight up the right-hand side of the pretty side valley which lies almost directly opposite. Within five minutes pass a well-maintained **azib** that was clearly visible from your camp, then pass its beehives, arranged on either side of the path, before reaching a small **col** at the head of the side valley after just 15 minutes.

Cross this col and follow the trail onwards, first along the left bank of the small ravine which appears on its far side. Although the path then quickly leaves the ravine and turns slowly away to the south-west, the key for this section of the trek is simply to keep the high ground immediately to your left all the way to the village of Tidghit (not marked on the 1:100,000 map).

The trail, undulating all the while, crosses a series of very small dry streams, and turns gradually more towards the south until, 25 minutes after the first col, the trail rises to a second. From here there are panoramic views of the High Atlas

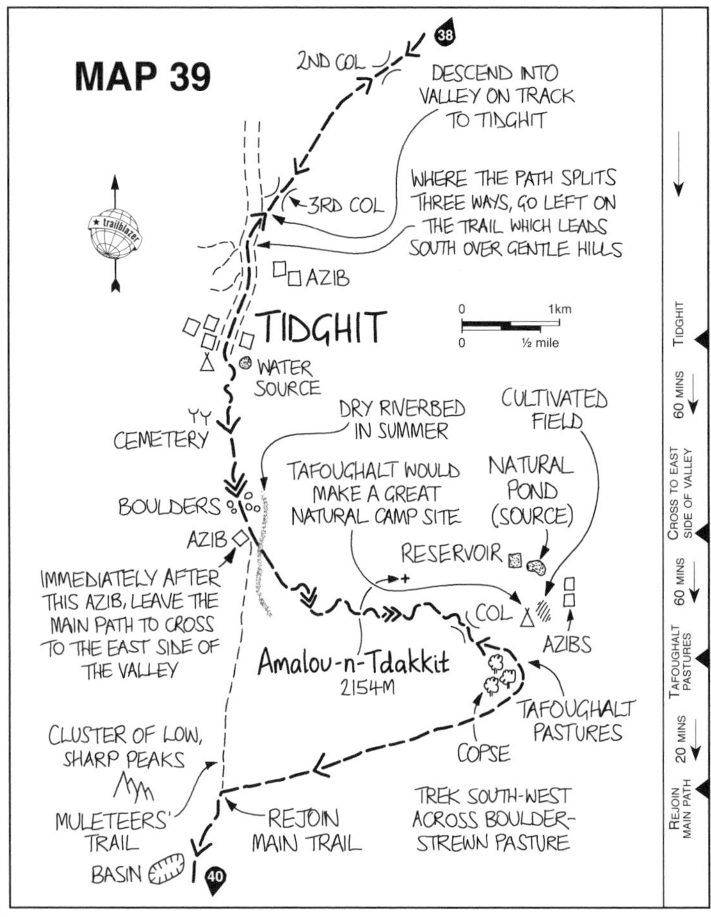

Mountains, including Ighil Mgoun, away to your right (north). The path then continues to undulate before rising to a third small **col** about 30 minutes after the second. From here the first outlying terraced fields of the village of Tidghit come into view ahead in the Tizi-n-Tagmout Valley, although it will take another 30 minutes to reach the picturesque village itself. Drop into the valley and continue to bear left. Should you choose to break your journey in **Tidghit** (meaning 'clay', which is found in abundance here), there are good tree-shaded **camping** spots and a **water source** a little to the left of the track.

From Tidghit, the trail onwards to Tafoughalt Pastures is straightforward. Simply head directly south up the Tizi-n-Tagmout Valley, initially keeping to its left-hand (eastern) bank. After 10 minutes, pass the village **cemetery** lying on your right (west) between the track and the river. Continue to climb, sometimes quite steeply but for the most part quite gently, until, 60 minutes from Tidghit, arrive at a large **azib** immediately to the right of the track. Here you are likely to meet a squatting Berber woman selling small artefacts.

From this point your muleteer will continue straight up the valley (south) which leads directly to Tizi-n-Tagmout itself. You, however, will follow the trail that turns left (east), immediately after the azib, to cross the valley bottom and continue on the far (eastern) side. Take care not to continue into the side valley which enters the main valley here from the east. Instead, immediately cross in front of it and begin to climb a steep path which zig-zags sharply up the rocky flanks of Amalou-n-Tdakkit (2154m/7067ft, not named on the 1:100,000 maps), which rises between the side valley and the main valley. Sometimes the trail seems to be either on the point of heading back into the side valley or into the main valley. During the ascent there are further lovely views of the High Atlas Mountains to the north behind you.

After 45 minutes of unrelenting climb, your path reaches a **col**. The beauty of the high level pastures of Tafoughalt slowly opens up before you during a 15-minute descent which leads between two rock-faces on the far side. Aim for the **copse** of poplar trees which you see on the plateau below. High above, and for now out of view to your left, rear the lofty peaks of Amalou-n-Tdakkit.

Once you have descended to **Tafoughalt Pastures**, your first impression may be that you have entered an open amphitheatre, bound by a far-flung ring of mountains. If, however, you were to wander to your left (north-east) for five minutes you would see that you are in a wide valley which curls away to the north. At this point, hidden amongst a series of rocks that rise out of the pasture, you can find a series of man-made reservoirs and channels which could be used for bathing, as well as a small natural **pond** reliably offering source water.

Tafoughalt Pastures are studded with isolated **azibs**. Quiet for much of the year, it is here, between March and May, just as colourful spring flowers are emerging, that a great reunion of Berber goatherds and shepherds takes place. Ostensibly to make the most of the summer pastures, this gathering effectively turns into a small annual music festival.

To leave Tafoughalt Pastures and rejoin the direct trail in the Tizi-n-Tagmout Valley to Tizi-n-Tagmout, find a path that leads across the boulder-strewn pasture, first south and then south-west, working around the huge outcrop of black basalt to the south of the copse. Tizi-n-Tagmout can be seen some way ahead. After 20 minutes you will rejoin the trail in the Tizi-n-Tagmout Valley. Follow it to the left (south), rising only gradually at this point, but soon climbing much more steeply, towards the col. Wonderful views open up back north, even as far as the Dades Valley, as well as good views once again of the High Atlas Mountains, emerging to the west.

You will reach **Tizi-n-Tagmout** 50 minutes after leaving Tafoughalt. From the col, follow the left (east) bank of the **gully** which greets you, continuing to head due south. The path undulates a little at first but is, of course, generally

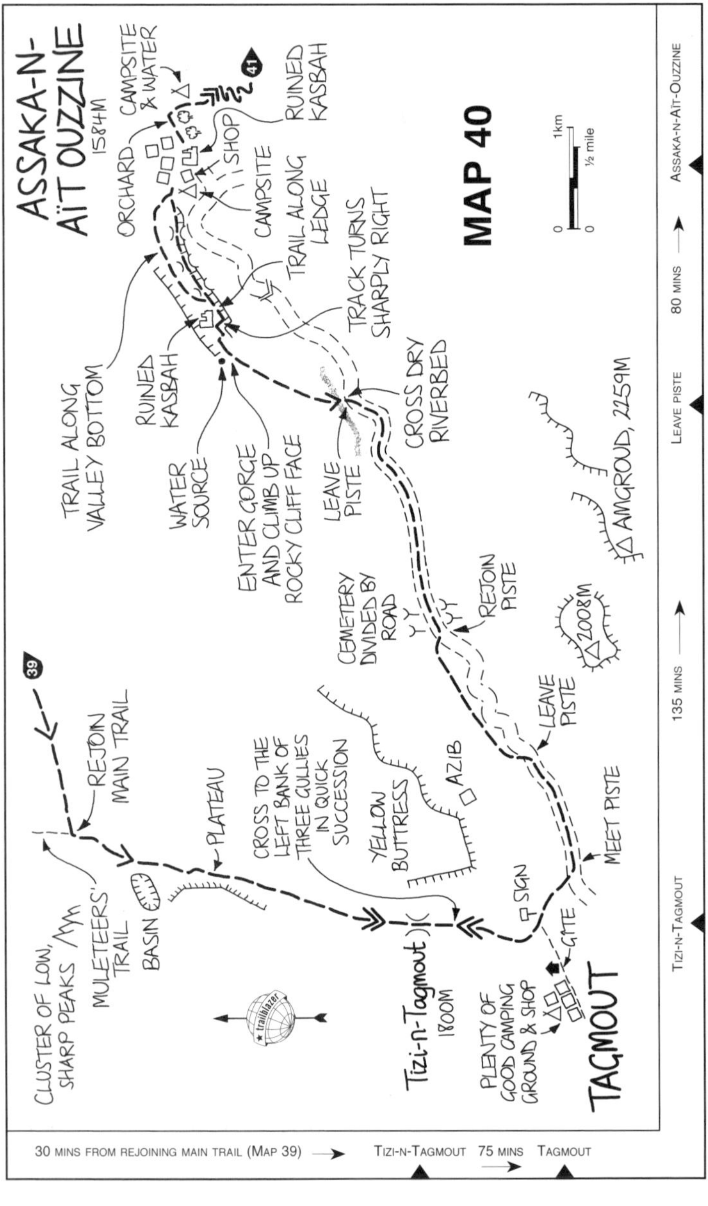

ASSAKA-N-
AÏT OUZZINE
1584M

MAP 40

30 MINS FROM REJOINING MAIN TRAIL (MAP 39) →
TIZI-N-TAGMOUT 75 MINS → TAGMOUT

CLUSTER OF LOW, SHARP PEAKS
MULETEERS' TRAIL
REJOIN MAIN TRAIL
BASIN
PLATEAU
CROSS TO THE LEFT BANK OF THREE GULLIES IN QUICK SUCCESSION
YELLOW BUTTRESS
AZIB
Tizi-n-Tagmout
1800M
PLENTY OF GOOD CAMPING GROUND & SHOP
SIGN
GÎTE
TAGMOUT
MEET PISTE
LEAVE PISTE
2008M
AMGROUD, 2259M
REJOIN PISTE
CEMETERY DIVIDED BY ROAD
CROSS DRY RIVERBED
LEAVE PISTE
TRACK TURNS SHARPLY RIGHT
ENTER GORGE AND CLIMB UP ROCKY CLIFF FACE
WATER SOURCE
RUINED KASBAH
TRAIL ALONG VALLEY BOTTOM
TRAIL ALONG LEDGE
CAMPSITE
SHOP
RUINED KASBAH
ORCHARD
CAMPSITE & WATER

0 1km
0 ½ mile

TIZI-N-TAGMOUT 135 MINS → LEAVE PISTE 80 MINS → ASSAKA-N-AÏT-OUZZINE heading downwards towards the expansive, flat-bottomed, main Tagmout Valley running east to west before you. Keep your eyes open for a huge yellow basalt **buttress** ahead to your left (east) on the main valley floor as your path will steadily work its way down towards it.

Twenty minutes after the col, ascend to the top of the left bank of the gully you are following and continue southwards along its ridge. A second parallel gully comes in to view immediately to your left so that there are now drops both to left and right. After five minutes descend into the second gully on your left and then immediately cross to its far left (eastern) bank before again continuing southwards. Five minutes later, the path turns sharply 90° to the left (east) towards a third parallel gully. After five more minutes, drop into this third parallel gully and immediately cross to its far (eastern) bank.

By now you have almost reached the Tagmout Valley floor and the huge yellow basalt buttress towers high above you. Continue southwards. Thirty minutes later a sign on the left-hand side of the path indicates the trail on your right to ***Am Groud*** (50dh including breakfast, shower 10dh, meals 60dh), the pleasant **gîte d'étape** in Tagmout that is five minutes away. It has three sizeable rooms built around a simple central courtyard.

The hospitable village itself is clearly visible five minutes beyond the gîte, right on the Tagmout Valley floor. It offers plenty of good **camping** opportunities. With still around 2½ hours before Assaka-n-Aït Ouzzine, you might decide to end the day here. A group of girls might even be waiting to serve you tea and bread and, in bad weather, the villagers may allow you to camp right up to their doors to receive the protection of their houses. There is a small **shop** selling basic items including water and soft drinks. To find it, follow a trail behind the gîte to an attractive house, five minutes to the north, partly shielded from view by its own small orchard. Mind the rabbit traps as you cross the intervening fields.

Otherwise keep straight ahead (southwards) until, just a few minutes later, having finally almost reached the main valley floor, your trail veers away to the left (south-east) and joins a piste which itself turns further left towards the east. The beautiful rock-faces of **Amgroud** (2259m/7411ft) now lie straight ahead. The piste continues to turn left, all the while skirting around the base of the yellow basalt buttress, until it faces north-east and begins to head into the wide Tafrout n'Ifran Valley ('tafrout' meaning 'water source' and 'ifran' meaning 'caves'). This valley leads directly to the village of Assaka-n-Aït Ouzzine.

After 20 minutes there is a chance to leave the piste as a path veers away to the left, although you will rejoin it after a further 40 minutes. At this point, small children from the lone **azib**, to the left, under the slopes of Tadaout-n-Aït Ouzzine, may well rush to greet you, hoping to sell you simple Berber tassles.

Almost immediately after rejoining the piste, you will pass through a small, basic **cemetery** which marks an ancient tribal border. On the one side lie the deceased of the Aït Atta, on the other the deceased of the rival Aït Seddrat. The days of these feuds have clearly long passed: my guide was of the Aït Atta tribe, my cuisinier of the Aït Seddrat, but they could not so much as remember whose cemetery lay on which side.

After 15 minutes the piste swings away markedly to the right to work its way around a small **ravine** and five minutes later does so for a second time, though less markedly. If you are in a hurry, you could continue north-east along the piste, which begins to move steadily over to the right side of the valley, to reach Assaka-n-Aït Ouzzine in about an hour.

A better option is to drop off the piste to the left and pick up a thin trail straight ahead which steadily veers left towards the bottom of the main valley and through a beautiful gorge. Join this trail at the point where the piste swings right for the second time. Look out for a small tree on the left, just below the piste, as this marks the beginning of the trail.

The trail gradually leads you further away from the piste and across a shallow, **dry river bed** to climb to its far (north-western) bank across exposed conglomerate rock while continuing to head north-east. Pass a large outcrop of yellow basalt on your left. Meanwhile, the piste which you have just left can be seen still broadly running parallel with your track, but by now receding into the mid-distance.

Twenty-five minutes after leaving the piste, traverse a large slab of black basalt rock. By now, if not before, you will have a clear view, ahead and slightly to your left (north-west), of the narrow gorge into which you are heading. The piste which you left swings away further to the right (east) and out of view behind other hills. Forty-five minutes from the piste enter the **gorge** at the bottom of which, at this near, narrower end, there is a **water source**. Despite the apparent isolation of this location, you might find that its beauty has attracted other trekkers.

The gorge is known simply as **Ifran** (meaning 'caves'). Climb up to the rocky **cliff-face** on its right (south-eastern) side and follow the track along its ledge. After five minutes both the cliff-face and the track turn sharply right where there are spectacular views of the valley straight ahead. On the far, left side of the valley bottom sits a picturesque **ruined kasbah**. The track descends almost to the floor of the gorge while continuing to keep to the right bank.

After 15 minutes the track divides and there is a choice of either walking along the valley bottom directly to Assaka-n-Aït Ouzzine or to climb again and follow a clear ledge along the rock-face, still on the right side of the valley. It would be impossible to lose either path. The ledge gently rises and falls to meet **three small cols** in the next 15 minutes. For much of this route, sheer cliffs rise above you to your right while the river runs below through the gorge to your left. Only after the third col does the dry river briefly disappear from view. This is when the trail turns away from the gorge to kiss the **piste**, which unexpectedly emerges from the right.

Leave the piste immediately, however, by following a small dry stream bed on your left down into **Assaka-n-Aït Ouzzine** (meaning 'people of the beautiful ford'). Reach the village just five minutes after passing the third col.

There are plenty of good **camping** spots here. One is on the football pitch close down by the river. Others are found higher up at both the entrance and the exit to the village. There is a small **shop** selling basic provisions and at least one

house which, while not an officially registered gîte, actively seeks to accommodate guests. Look out for the Islamic blessing painted above its blue front door or ask for Mohammed. Failing that, there is also the possibility of the village school rooms which the English-speaking teacher will probably happily open for you.

Assaka-n-Aït Ouzzine–Irhissi [Map 41, p236]

This stage is short and gentle which you may feel important if you completed the whole of yesterday's stage in a day. The day is dominated by the approach of the imposing Tine Ouaiyour. It is followed by a descent through the surreal Irhissi Gorge and rounded off with an exotic evening camp within the shell of the ancient agadir at Irhissi itself.

Leave Assaka-n-Aït Ouzzine by the trail that leads north-east out of the village past its abandoned kasbah into a lightly **wooded valley**. After five minutes, where a walled almond orchard ends, turn immediately right to cross the dry river bed, and zig-zag steeply for 10 minutes up the right-hand bank of the valley. The path levels out and turns towards the east about two-thirds of the way up the valley side, before rising again to meet a small **col** after 15 minutes. From here there are good views back to Assaka-n-Aït Ouzzine.

The path then gently falls and rises to a second small col after 30 minutes. Although the conglomerate rock you cross is completely barren at this point, there is compensation first in the splash of cultivated fields which can be seen on the valley floor below to the left and then in the walled terraced orchard close by, again on the left, just as the trail rises to a third small col after 45 minutes.

This third **col** marks the boundary between the first section of the valley from Assaka-n-Aït Ouzzine, called Bou Omarsit, and the following section, called Izggwarn, meaning 'red' on account of the natural reddish colour of the rocks found from here on. The nature of the landscape now becomes much softer and the cliffs, which had previously towered above immediately to the right, now fade away. Nevertheless, from this third col, the distinctive and dramatic rock of **Tine Ouaiyour** (2129m/6985ft) meaning 'Place of the Moon', the focal point of the next section of the trek, comes into view.

Simply follow the clear trail ahead as it gradually turns to lead towards the north-east. After five minutes you will cross from the right (south) side of the small dry valley running alongside the path to the left (north) side. The key is simply to keep aiming to pass close by the right-hand side of Tine Ouaiyour.

After 15 minutes you will notice **caves** in the mountains of Waslalaf away to the left (north). After 20 minutes you will drop into a shallow valley, skirt around cultivated, walled fields associated with a pretty azib, **Aït Amer**, to your left, and cross the dry river bed to climb its far (north-eastern) bank. You will emerge onto a wide open, shrub-covered plain.

The path climbs gently again to reach another small **col** after a further 15 minutes by which time Tine Ouaiyour will feel close by on your left. Head faintly right from the col for 10 minutes towards a small, dry gully which lies ahead. You will cross four successive small dry streams which flow down into it from Tine Ouaiyour, before dropping into the **gully** yourself. Follow its dry

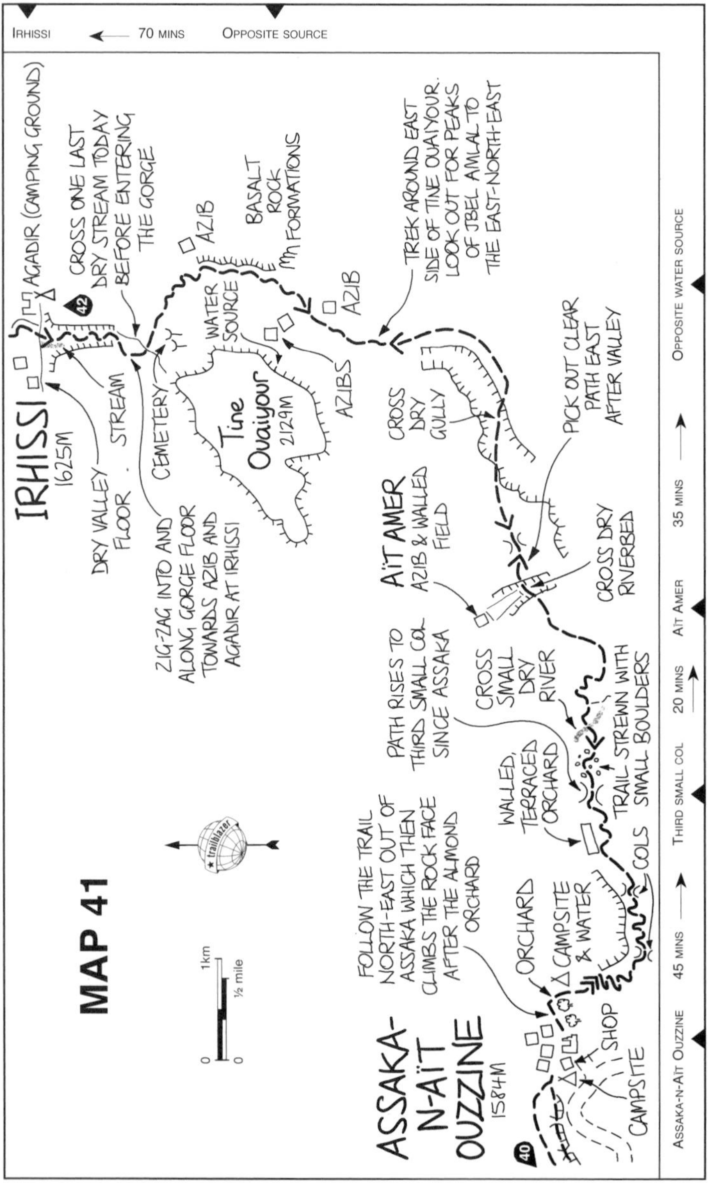

MAP 41

IRHISSI
1625M
AGADIR (CAMPING GROUND)
CROSS ONE LAST DRY STREAM TODAY BEFORE ENTERING THE GORGE
DRY VALLEY FLOOR
STREAM
ZIG-ZAG INTO AND ALONG GORGE FLOOR TOWARDS AZIB AND AGADIR AT IRHISSI
CEMETERY
AZIB
WATER SOURCE
Tine Ouaiyour
2129M
BASALT ROCK FORMATIONS
AZIBS
AZIB
0 1km
0 ½ mile
trailblazer
ASSAKA-N-AÏT OUZZINE
1584M
FOLLOW THE TRAIL NORTH-EAST OUT OF ASSAKA WHICH THEN CLIMBS THE ROCK FACE AFTER THE ALMOND ORCHARD
PATH RISES TO THIRD SMALL COL SINCE ASSAKA
AÏT AMER
AZIB & WALLED FIELD
CROSS DRY GULLY
TREK AROUND EAST SIDE OF TINE OUAIYOUR. LOOK OUT FOR PEAKS OF JBEL AMLAL TO THE EAST-NORTH-EAST
ORCHARD
CAMPSITE & WATER
WALLED, TERRACED ORCHARD
CROSS SMALL DRY RIVER
SHOP
CAMPSITE
COLS
TRAIL STREWN WITH SMALL BOULDERS
CROSS DRY RIVERBED
PICK OUT CLEAR PATH EAST AFTER VALLEY

IRHISSI ← 70 MINS OPPOSITE SOURCE

ASSAKA-N-AÏT OUZZINE 45 MINS → THIRD SMALL COL 20 MINS → AÏT AMER 35 MINS → OPPOSITE WATER SOURCE bed for just two minutes, cross to its far right bank and then climb quite steeply out of the gully and onto a **low ridge**. Follow the ridge to reach a small crest 10 minutes later. From here, only five minutes off the track, away to your left and out of sight, at the base of Tine Ouaiyour, is a good **water source**, protected by a small stone structure, with an adjacent animal trough.

Meanwhile, the trail continues to skirt around Tine Ouaiyour; its base, from now until the Irhissi Gorge, will remain about five minutes' walk away to your left. Soon you are heading due north. Straight ahead, mountains on the far (north) side of the Akka n'Imersidene Valley come into view, including Jbel Amlal (see p209).

After 35 minutes, shortly after passing an azib set right against the base of Tine Ouaiyour, the trail again swings to the left so that you now head north-west. Before long you can look to your right (east) down a side valley directly into Akka n'Imersidene Valley; another azib in the foreground offers you an opportunity to compose a dramatic photograph.

Still the path continues to curl to the left. After 45 minutes it passes a **cemetery** on the left. An adjacent stone structure covers a well, built to facilitate the customary Muslim practice of washing the bodies of the deceased before burial.

By now you are looking directly into the **Irhissi Gorge** (not named on the 1:100,000 maps) which, although close at hand, at this point looks little more than a gash in the rocks. For the moment continue turning left and cross over one final small, dry stream, the source of the gorge. Immediately, on its far side, the track divides. Take the right-hand, lower track which clearly leads down into the narrow gorge.

Allow 20 minutes for the descent to Irhissi. Do not hurry: the scenery is truly stunning. First, at its head, to your left, is a huge wall of yellow basalt, sculpted by the wind. Once inside the gorge, the contrasts of scattered red and green rocks, of different shapes and sizes, and rich, green plant life, of the bright blue sky above and a carpet of green shingle below, provide the substance of fantasy. As sheer rock-faces tower above you, to both left and right, your guide may well choose to demonstrate the gorge's propensity for producing high-quality echoes.

Once through the gorge, the trail emerges into the wide open space of the Irhissi Valley (irhissi meaning 'hole'). Take the path which works its way down to the dry **valley floor**. Cross to the far (north) side to enter the shell of an ancient pisé agadir, guarded by a couple of swaying palm trees, which provides a most picturesque **camping** ground. Water flows in the **stream** behind the agadir; for **source water**, however, respectfully approach any of the homesteads which are dotted about the valley. Should you be in need of fresh bread, it is quite likely that the small boys who gather at your tent door will be able to organise this.

Irhissi–Imi n'el Louh [Map 42, p239; Map 43, p240]

The key feature of this day is the climb to two cols, Tizi n'Tmirhcht (2378m/7799ft) and Tizi n'Irhioui (1954m/6409ft) although only the first presents anything like a strenuous challenge. Both passes offer distant views of the approaching Dades plain, thereby creating a sense of leaving the mountains and nearing the end of the trek.

Walk immediately behind the agadir to find a trail and gully running north towards Tizi n'Tmirhcht. At times the path is a little unclear as it switches back and forth across the valley floor of the **Assif Ouringgui**, but all the while it is gradually ascending northwards through boulder-strewn terrain. For now, keep your eye on the tall, craggy peaks directly ahead, for Tizi n'Tmirhcht lies amongst them. Each time the path bifurcates, continue to head north.

After about 30 minutes the trail swings to the right (east) away from the valley floor and soon begins to **zig-zag** very steeply up to the col. After 70 minutes a more substantial-looking trail heads off into the valley to the right (east) towards Tizi Ouringgui and Jbel Amlal, but you should ignore it and keep ascending northwards. After 80 minutes the trail briefly dips, descending into the right side of the gully that leads up to the col. It nevertheless remains apparent that the trail is still heading for the **Tizi n'Tmirhcht**.

The views in the last few minutes before you reach the col are quite spectacular. Not only can you look back towards Tine Ouaiyour and far beyond to the south, but also towards the east and south-east in the direction of the Sahro Traverse trek.

You will reach the **col** about 120 minutes after leaving Irhissi. A small cairn confirms the very distinct summit and, more usefully, a small stone wall offers protection from any strong winds. To the far north, still far below, two thin green ribbons of agricultural prosperity can clearly be seen, one running either side of the Oued Dades, cutting boldly across its parched brown plain.

The descent north-north-west from the col is rapid and straightforward although once you have reached the valley floor you will switch back and forward from the right bank to the left perhaps six times before you finally switch to the right one more time. You then climb over a small rocky outcrop and drop into the fertile **valley of Bouynoksa**, found at the southern foot of Tizi n'Irhioui. You will notice several **houses** to the left (west) and a walled garden that has a **well** with a water pump. From here, the gentle ascent to **Tizi n'Irhioui** takes only 10 minutes. The large settlement that can be seen in the distance from this second col is Qalaa't Mgouna.

Again, the descent north-north-west from the col is rapid and straightforward. Ten minutes after the col there is a **water source** immediately to the right of the path, protected by a brick structure. After five more minutes the trail is joined by a rocky piste which very quickly divides. Take the left (more westerly) branch, somewhat unpleasant underfoot, which leads down to and then across the dry stream to its left (west) bank.

As you begin to descend from the mountains, so settled agriculture becomes more prominent. Pass a large **farm** on your right, then successive large cultivated fields before arriving at the village **Imi n'el Louh** (not named on the 1:100,000 maps, although the road running through the village appears to be marked with this name), 50 minutes from the col. As you enter the centre of the

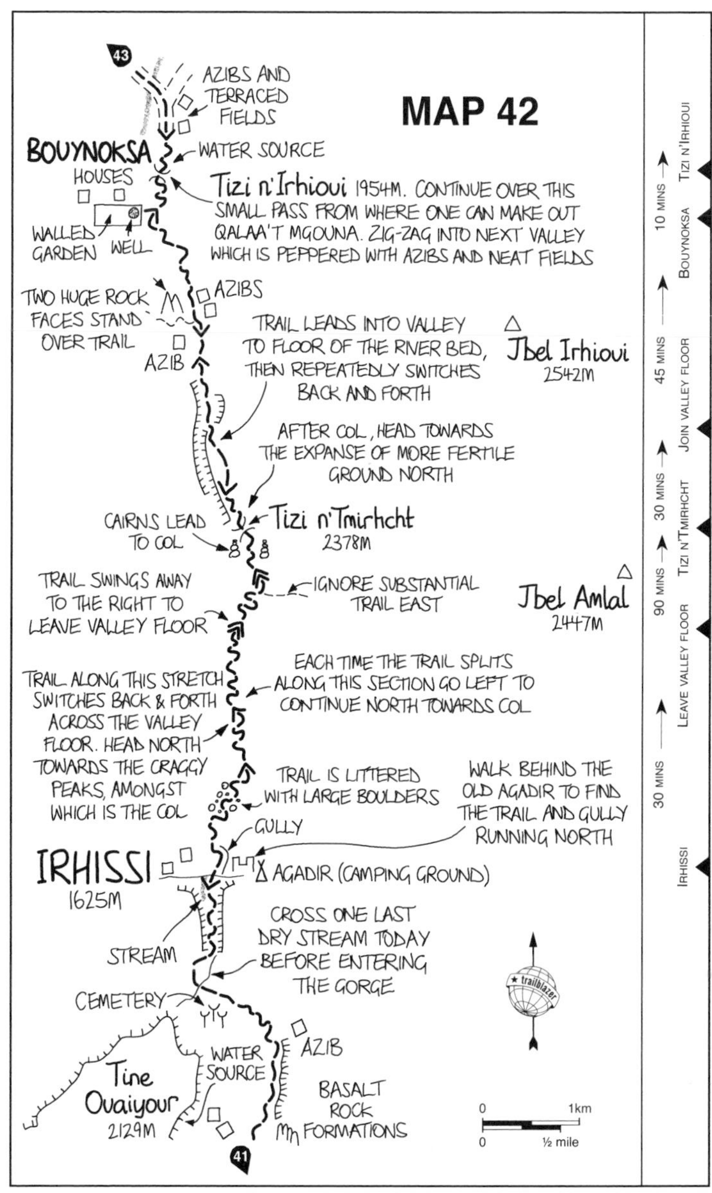
MAP 42
43
AZIBS AND TERRACED FIELDS
BOUYNOKSA
WATER SOURCE
HOUSES
Tizi n'Irhioui 1954M. CONTINUE OVER THIS SMALL PASS FROM WHERE ONE CAN MAKE OUT QALAA'T MGOUNA. ZIG-ZAG INTO NEXT VALLEY WHICH IS PEPPERED WITH AZIBS AND NEAT FIELDS
WALLED GARDEN
WELL
TWO HUGE ROCK FACES STAND OVER TRAIL
AZIBS
AZIB
TRAIL LEADS INTO VALLEY TO FLOOR OF THE RIVER BED, THEN REPEATEDLY SWITCHES BACK AND FORTH
Jbel Irhioui 2542M
AFTER COL, HEAD TOWARDS THE EXPANSE OF MORE FERTILE GROUND NORTH
CAIRNS LEAD TO COL
Tizi n'Tmirhcht 2378M
TRAIL SWINGS AWAY TO THE RIGHT TO LEAVE VALLEY FLOOR
IGNORE SUBSTANTIAL TRAIL EAST
Jbel Amlal 2447M
TRAIL ALONG THIS STRETCH SWITCHES BACK & FORTH ACROSS THE VALLEY FLOOR. HEAD NORTH TOWARDS THE CRAGGY PEAKS, AMONGST WHICH IS THE COL
EACH TIME THE TRAIL SPLITS ALONG THIS SECTION GO LEFT TO CONTINUE NORTH TOWARDS COL
TRAIL IS LITTERED WITH LARGE BOULDERS
WALK BEHIND THE OLD AGADIR TO FIND THE TRAIL AND GULLY RUNNING NORTH
GULLY
IRHISSI 1625M
AGADIR (CAMPING GROUND)
STREAM
CROSS ONE LAST DRY STREAM TODAY BEFORE ENTERING THE GORGE
CEMETERY
trailblazer
AZIB
WATER SOURCE
Tine Ouaiyour 2129M
BASALT ROCK FORMATIONS
41
0 1km
0 ½ mile
IRHISSI
30 MINS
LEAVE VALLEY FLOOR
90 MINS
TIZI N'TMIRHCHT
30 MINS
JOIN VALLEY FLOOR
45 MINS
BOUYNOKSA
10 MINS
TIZI N'IRHIOUI

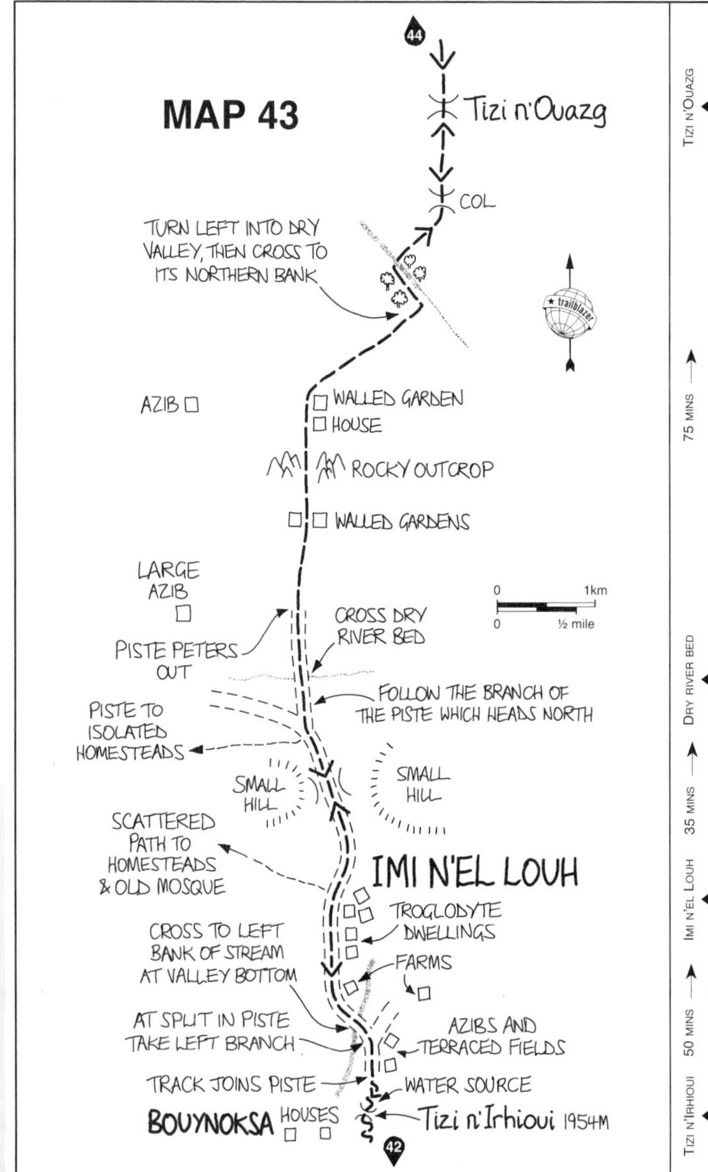
MAP 43
44
Tizi n'Ouazg
COL
TURN LEFT INTO DRY VALLEY, THEN CROSS TO ITS NORTHERN BANK
trailblazer
AZIB
WALLED GARDEN
HOUSE
ROCKY OUTCROP
WALLED GARDENS
LARGE AZIB
0 1km
0 ½ mile
CROSS DRY RIVER BED
PISTE PETERS OUT
FOLLOW THE BRANCH OF THE PISTE WHICH HEADS NORTH
PISTE TO ISOLATED HOMESTEADS
SMALL HILL
SMALL HILL
SCATTERED PATH TO HOMESTEADS & OLD MOSQUE
IMI N'EL LOUH
TROGLODYTE DWELLINGS
CROSS TO LEFT BANK OF STREAM AT VALLEY BOTTOM
FARMS
AT SPLIT IN PISTE TAKE LEFT BRANCH
AZIBS AND TERRACED FIELDS
TRACK JOINS PISTE
WATER SOURCE
BOUYNOKSA
HOUSES
Tizi n'Irhioui 1954M
42
TIZI N'OUAZG
75 MINS
DRY RIVER BED
35 MINS
IMI N'EL LOUH
50 MINS
TIZI N'IRHIOUI

village, to the right, cut into the rock-face, there are **troglodyte dwellings** with fields above acting as their roofs.

Although there is no official gîte here, the locals appear used to people arriving in the village in need of **shelter**. If in need yourself, you should certainly ask around. Just north of the village centre, before the first small hills ahead, a trail leads to the left (west) where, out of sight from the piste, are many more scattered homesteads. There it is sometimes possible to receive shelter in the old **mosque** alongside which another has recently been built.

Imi n'el Louh–Boumalne du Dades [Map 43; Map 44, p242]

This final stage, just like the first, consists of much walking across wide open terrain with a dearth of significant landmarks to offer guidance. Nonetheless, the early ascent of two cols in quick succession offers tantalising views of the Dades flood plain ahead and the final long march into Boumalne du Dades affords plenty of opportunity to reflect upon the previous four days' achievement.

Briefly return to the piste that leads out of Imi n'el Louh and follow it to the north-west away from the village and over a small outlying hill after 20 minutes, before quickly dropping to the vast expanse of dry plain which opens up before you. The **piste divides** here. One branch leads left (west) towards the isolated homesteads and mosques previously mentioned. You, however, should take the right branch which leads north and set your sights straight ahead on the col which leads through the mountains on the horizon. Although you will eventually cross these mountains via a second col to the right (east) of the one you can presently see, you will head towards this first col for some time.

Ten minutes after the piste divides, cross over a dry **river bed** where a large azib stands away to the left. The piste peters out quickly and is lost as you cross raised flat rock, bare but for a thin covering of sand. Nevertheless, aim to pass between the two large **walled gardens** just beyond, both with trees, and then, immediately afterwards, between two isolated 20m-high rocky outcrops. Once past the outcrops, you will reach a house with solar panels on the right side of the trail while another azib appears away to the left.

Immediately after this house, there appears another large walled garden, again on the right. Follow the trail around its edge to the north-east until, 20 minutes beyond, it meets a wide, dry river valley running south-east to north-west.

Turn left (north-west) into the valley and follow its left bank. Suddenly, as a little water appears in the valley bottom, trees immediately start to line both banks. After 10 minutes, cross to the far, right bank of the valley and immediately begin to climb up to a small **col** to the north, clearly visible from below, which you will meet 20 minutes later. The views north from here are disappointingly obscured by the bluff of a large mountain to the right.

Descend into a valley on the far side of the col, but do not lose too much altitude, keeping to the trail along its right bank. Quickly cross a small **dry ravine** and follow the trail over the bluff that obscured your view from the col, before the trail briefly dips and then climbs again to meet a second, higher col,

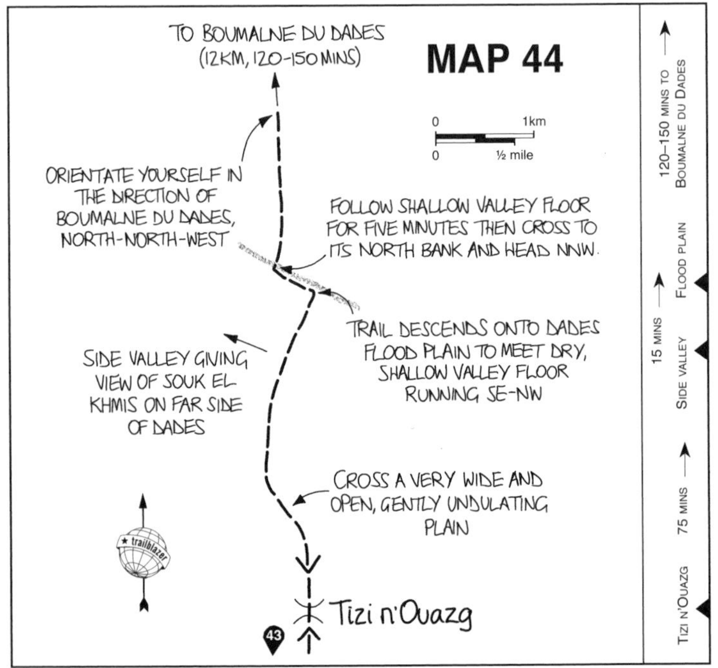

Tizi n'Ouazg (not named on the 1:100,000 maps), just 10 minutes after you began your descent from the first. This time you will be rewarded with far-reaching views stretching northwards across the Dades Valley to the High Atlas Mountains beyond.

Begin the gentle descent from Tizi n'Ouazg across a very wide and open, gently undulating plain of orange sand and stone. The trail veers to the left of the plain and keeps relatively close to the mountains on that side, but otherwise distinctive landmarks, by which this route might be described, are very scarce. Seventy-five minutes after crossing Tizi n'Ouazg a **side valley** opens up to the left of the trail. Look down into it to enjoy a beautiful view of the town of Souk el Khmis ('Thursday market') on the far side of the River Dades, with Ighil Mgoun majestically rising directly behind it.

Just 15 minutes later, the trail descends onto the vast **Dades flood plain** and immediately meets a wide and shallow, dry valley floor running south-east to north-west. Boumalne du Dades, for the moment, comes clearly into view, close to the horizon and against the backdrop of the Central High Atlas Mountains. It is very important to orientate yourself at this point and to be clear of the direction of Boumalne du Dades, about 12km away. Your final destination will take about another 120 to 150 minutes to reach. During this time you will occasionally lose sight of the town as the trail crosses very gently undulating terrain. What is more, although at times your route is along sections of clear piste, at others the trail peters out altogether.

Follow the near (western) valley side to the left for five minutes before crossing to its far (eastern) side. Pick up a trail here which at this stage appears to be heading straight for Boumalne du Dades, knowing that you will not be able to rely upon it for very long. Keep walking to the north-north-west as straight as you can.

BOUMALNE DU DADES

Although much expanded through the development of suburbs in recent years, it is the old town centre which is likely to be of most interest to trekkers completing the Jbel Sahro Traverse or Circular Trek.

Against the backdrop of the Dades Valley and the Central High Atlas Mountains, Boumalne is a pleasant town in which to arrive after days in the mountains, although in truth the single, simple street of the old town, avenue Mohammed V, holds nothing of special interest. The best day to be here would be a Wednesday, the day of the weekly souk.

Arrival and departure

Buses regularly pass through Boumalne heading both east and west following the Dades along the P32.

Two private bus line ticket offices are situated on the south side of the main street opposite the central mosque. Trans Gazala (90dh) and Supratours (110dh), operating from the first office, each run a daily bus to **Marrakech** departing at 6pm and 6am respectively, arriving in Marrakech 6½ hours later at 12.30am and 12.30pm.

The second office offers the following services: **Errachidia** 5am, 10.45am, 1pm, 2pm, 4pm; 3½hrs; 53.30dh; **Marrakech** 6am, 7am, 8.30am, 4pm; 6hrs; 99.10dh; **Casablanca** 4pm; 10hrs; 120dh; **Rabat** 7.30pm; 11hrs; 130dh; **Fes** 4.30pm; 10hrs; 118dh/161.90dh; **Khenifa** 10.45am; 10hrs; 90dh; **Erfoud** 7.30am, 2.30pm; 4-6hrs; 50dh/60dh; **Zagora** 2pm; 6hrs; 60dh; **Ouarzazate** Very frequently from 4am until 10pm; 2hrs; 25dh/30dh.

Local transport

The taxi and minibus stand is found right by the central mosque. A place in a shared **taxi** to Qalaa't Mgouna (24km/30mins) costs 7dh, or 5dh in a **minibus**. There is also a larger white bus which heads back and forth between Tinerhir and Qalaa't Mgouna which also charges 5dh but which stops anywhere along the way to pick up anyone who puts out a hand: only take this bus if you have a lot of time to spare. **Bicycles** can be rented from a small shop in the market square.

Orientation

Approaching Boumalne across the plains from the south at the end of your trek, first skirt around the left-hand side of the military barracks and then descend into Boumalne Old Town by the only road which heads down to the River Dades. Most of the services you will need along the stretch of road between the central mosque and the bridge across to the north bank of the Dades. The **market square**, which serves also as the site of the weekly souk, is off the south side of the main street, almost directly opposite the central mosque.

Services

Banks are represented by Atttijariwafa and Crédit Agricole near the bridge over the Dades, both with **ATMs**, and by Banque Populaire higher up avenue Mohammed V,

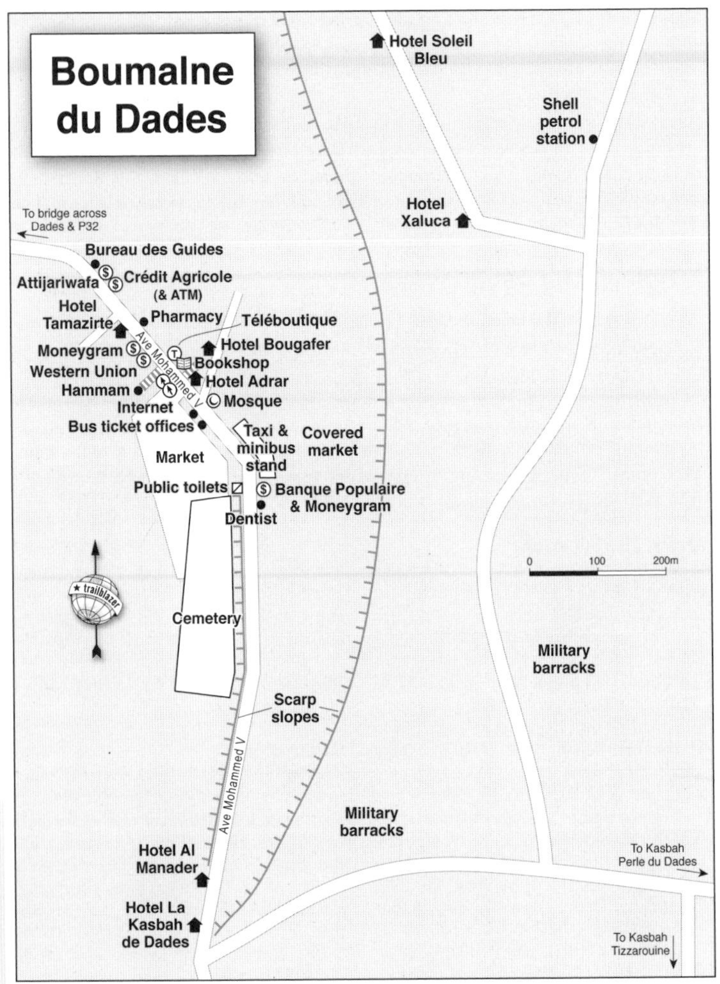

just above the taxi stand. There are also Western Union and Moneygram exchange facilities dotted about the old town, as well as a couple of **pharmacies**, **téléboutiques** and **internet cafés**.

Boumalne has a small, centrally located **bookshop**, with occasional publications in French, while there is a **dentist** (☎ 0644-83 11 08) a little higher up on the main street, just beyond Banque Populaire. A **Bureau des Guides**, through which the experienced and dependable Hamou aït L'hou can be contacted (see Trekking Guides, opposite), is found towards the bridge over the Dades near the bottom of town.

For **petrol**, try either the Shell station back up in the newer part of town near Hotel Xaluca, or head across the bridge over the Dades to the river's north bank.

A reasonable **hammam** (10dh, soap available, but bring your own towel), down a set of steps on the southern side of the main street, just below the market square, offers a massage service (40dh). The initial delight at finding public lavatories on avenue Mohammed V may be tempered by the reality within: enter at your own peril.

Trekking guides

It is very easy to make contact with guides in Boumalne. All the hotels listed in Where to stay below seem to have a guide that they can recommend. However, having met the following official guides, they can be listed with confidence:

- **Hamou aït L'hou** (GSM ☎ 0667-59 32 92; 💻 Hamou57@voila.fr), Bureau des Guides. Hamou can also offer accommodation in his very large and pleasant modern house, just outside Boumalne, to both individuals and groups choosing to trek with him.
- **Lachen Bahda** Contact via Hotel Bougafer (see column opposite).
- **Mustapha Naji** Contact via Hotel Soleil Bleu (see Where to stay p246); specialises in birdwatching tours.

All these gentlemen would offer their services simply as a guide. Alternatively, they can arrange your whole trekking expedition, *tout compris*, to include mule, muleteer, cuisinier, food, cooking equipment and tent. Prices are not fixed but expect to pay around 300dh per day for the services of a guide only. For a full trekking expedition, count on paying from about 500dh per person per day in the low season (Nov to Feb and Jun to Aug) or about 700dh in the high season (Mar to May and Sep to Oct). Naturally, these prices fall per head if more than a couple of trekkers join your group.

Where to stay

Given the small scale of the town centre, Boumalne has a generous number of satisfactory and better places to stay. Three of the simpler hotels are all on, or immediately off, the lower half of the main street, closest to the Dades River.

First is the 11-roomed ***Hotel Tamazirte*** (☎ 0524-83 03 33; GSM ☎ 0668-88 65 64), which, with prices starting at 50dh per person (room only, communal shower and toilet), offers rooms as cheaply as you will find in Boumalne; for 10dh more you will be provided with an attached bathroom and half-board is available for 160dh. Terraces to the front and rear offer a view over the main street and across the Dades Valley respectively.

Climbing the main street away from the Dades, ***Hotel Adrar*** (☎ 0524-83 07 29), overlooking the central mosque, also offers simple rooms for 50dh. Breakfast can be bought in the restaurant downstairs where you may wish to make contact with the restaurant manager, Lhoussain Ouftir, who will be happy to discuss, in excellent English, his experience as an unofficial mountain guide.

Just around the corner, off the main street, ***Hotel Bougafer*** (☎ 0524-83 13 07; GSM ☎ 0668-16 77 57) again offers small, traditional, simple rooms for 50dh, or half-board for just 120dh. For this you also gain access to a salon, heated in winter, and a roof terrace shaded by an overhead trellis of vines.

Rising further out of Old Boumalne, in quality and in price, ***Hotel Restaurant Al Manader*** (☎ 0524-83 01 72; 💻 aubergealmanader@hotmail.com) has wonderful views from its rear terrace, enhanced by its elevated position, over the Dades and beyond to Ighil Mgoun and the High Central Atlas Mountains. Indeed, as all rooms, which are clean, modern and spacious, have a balcony, it would be well worth asking for one at the rear of the hotel to enjoy the views to their maximum. Rooms cost 130dh/180dh, 140/190dh with breakfast, or 230/380dh half-board. The hotel has a pleasant, sizeable restaurant in which traditional musicians play nightly. An unofficial guide can be provided for 300dh per day for two people.

Next door, rising in quality once again, ***Hotel Restaurant La Kasbah de Dades*** (formerly Hotel Chems; ☎ 0524-83 00 41; GSM ☎ 0661-37 30 25; 🖳 www.kasbahdedades.com) has a total of 30 rooms charged at 280dh/450dh for half-board or at 360/560dh if you would like one of its six rooms with air-conditioning. The large, freshly decorated restaurant at the rear of the hotel has a big chimney at either end, providing heating in winter, and fabulous views from its terrace to match those of its neighbour, Al Manader.

Rising out of Old Boumalne altogether, onto the plain that stretches all the way back to Jbel Sahro, are a number of very large, modern hotels aimed at the international market. As a lot of new breeze-block buildings have recently been constructed here, you might decide that this part of town will not serve as the oriental haven you are seeking at the end of your trek. Take, for example, the soulless tourist complex of ***Kasbah Tizzarouine*** (☎ 0524-83 06 90/91; 🖳 kasbah.tizzarouine@menara.ma) which, while clearly built with Berber traditions much in mind, sadly offers, on approach, only the charm of an austere fortress. Once within its high walls, it does, however, offer the benefit of a swimming pool, a large restaurant and the facility to pay by credit card. In the high season (end of March to June) classic rooms cost 450dh per person for half-board and suites 500dh, both falling to 350dh in the low season. There are also so-called 'troglodyte' rooms, priced similarly to the classic rooms, which are actually modern holes cut into the cliff-side during the construction of the hotel.

Of quite a different class altogether is the delightful ***Hotel Soleil Bleu*** (☎ 0524-83 01 63; 🖳 www.hotelsoleilbleu.com) run by the passionate and hospitable Mustpha Naji and his brothers. A little cut off from the old centre of Boumalne by the large scarp slope above the town, it can be found by first following the road signs round to the modern Hotel Xaluca, popular with touring coach groups, and then continuing northwards, a little beyond. Once you understand the lie of the land a little better, you will be able to find a much more direct way to town on foot over the scarp slope.

Rooms, most of which are perhaps best described as Berber with a modern twist, cost 300/500dh for half-board in the high season and 200/350dh in the low season. There is also a small hard-surfaced **camping** area adjacent to the hotel available for 10dh per person in a tent or 40dh per person in a caravan, including free access to the **internet** but with extra charges for hot showers (10dh) and electricity (20dh). Alternatively, visitors are invited to sleep on the **hotel terrace** for 35dh or even in the lounge for 40dh.

If, however, you prefer to be totally away from the centre of Boumalne, you may wish to try ***Kasbah Perle du Dades*** (GSM ☎ 0677-78 10 75/20 26 77; 🖳 www.laperledudades.com), the most up-market hotel locally. Seven kilometres south of town, it benefits from having its own pleasant, green gardens. Created through the reconstruction and renovation of an ancient kasbah, the hotel's modern facilities include a 15m by 8m swimming pool, a small cinema and a games room with a table tennis table. Its eight double rooms, most with air-conditioning, start at €55 and its four suites at €87, breakfast included; there is a 20% reduction for single occupancy and children under two years of age are not charged. Meals are served in the hotel restaurant for €12.

Where to eat

There is a wide range of eating possibilities in Boumalne. As with the town's hotels, the cheapest options are to be found towards the river at the lower end of the old quarter, particularly around the market square, but all the hotels listed under Where to stay have restaurants which are open to non residents. Quite simply, the better the class of hotel you choose, the better the class of restaurant you will enjoy.

APPENDIX A: ARABIC, FRENCH & BERBER

ARABIC

Basic words and phrases are given here but if you plan to take your Arabic beyond the 'hello' and 'goodbye' stage, you should take a phrasebook with you. Lonely Planet's *Moroccan Arabic* phrasebook is recommended.

Pronunciation

Moroccan Arabic is a spoken language which is not often written; as a dialect of Modern Standard Arabic, which developed from the Arabic of the Qur'an, it is considered to have no proper written form. This makes writing Arabic words in Roman letters particularly difficult and inexact. Pronunciation is tricky for most Westerners but Moroccans do tend to make an effort to understand anyone trying to speak Moroccan Arabic; they appreciate the effort.

The most difficult sound in Arabic is the **glottal stop** ('), which is produced by tightening the back of the throat as in a hiccup. Note also:

ai as in 'eye'
ay as in 'pay'
g hard 'g', like 'go'
gh low rolled 'r'
kh as above but harsher and shorter
q like 'k'
r high, rolled 'r'
zh 's' as in 'pleasure'

Pleasantries

Hello	*Salam a'laykum* (lit 'peace be upon you')
(Response)	*Walaykum salam*
Goodbye	*M'a-ssalama*
Please	*'afakum*
Thank you	*Shokran*
How are you?	*Labas?*
I'm fine, thank you	*Labas, barak*
God willing!	*Inshallah!*
Excuse me	*Smeh leeya*

Basic conversations

I	*ana*
you	*nta/ntee(m/f)*
we	*hoona*
they	*hma*
why?	*'lash*
when?	*eemta*
open	*mehlool*
closed	*mesdood*
I don't speak much Arabic	*makan'refsh l'arbeeya*
Do you speak English?	*wash kat'ref negleezeeya*
Could you repeat that please?	*ash gulltee?*
I don't understand	*mafhemtsh*
What's your name?	*asmeetek*
My name is ...	*smeetee ...*
I'm from ...	*ana men...*
I'm here on holiday	*zheet l Imaghreeb fe fel 'ohla*

Basic conversations ***(cont'd)***

I'm married	*ana mzhoowzh/a* (m/f)
I'm single	*ana mamzhoowzhsh/ash* (m/f)
How old are you?	*shhal f'merek?*
I'm ...	*'andee* .... (see Numbers p250)

Problems and emergencies

Help!	*'ateqnee!*
Fire!	*l'afiya!*
Thief!	*sheffar!*
Help me	*'awennee 'afak*
I've been attacked	*thzhem 'leeya*
I've been raped	*thzhem ghtasabunee*
There's been an accident	*ooq'at kseeda*
Please call the police/an ambulance	*'ayyet 'la lbolees/'la ssayyara del'as'af*
My .... was stolen	*tesreq leeya .... dyalee*
I need to make a phone call	*wakha nsta'mel ttoleefoon*
I'm very sorry, forgive me	*smeh leeya*

Trekking terms

How many kilometres is the walk?	*shhal dyal lweqt kayn f had ddohra?*
I'm lost	*tweddert*
Please show me on the map	*werri liya men l kharita 'afak*
col	*tizi*
compass	*bawsala*
lake	*daya*
map	*khareeta*
mountain	*zhbel/jbel*
path	*triq sgheer*
river	*wad*
summit	*ras*
trek	*temsha 'ls rezhleen* (v)
valley	*sehl*

Travel and directions

How do I get to ....?	*keefesh ghadee nuwsul l ....?*
Is it far?	*wash b'ad?*
opposite	*quddem*
next to	*hedda*
near to	*qreeb*
left	*leeser*
right	*eemen*
straight on	*seer neeshan*

Shopping

Where can I buy ......?	*fin ghadee neshree ......?*
How much?	*bshhal?*
It's too expensive for me	*bezzaf'liya*
That's my final price!	*akheer ttaman dyalee heewa hada*
Is there a market?	*fin kayn ssooq*

Accommodation

hotel	*shee ootayl*
camp-site	*shee mukheyyem*

Please take me to a hotel	*wesselnee l shee ootayl 'afak*
Do you have any vacancies?	*wash kayn shee beet khawtya?*
We'd like to stay .... nights	*ghadee ngles* ..... (see Numbers p250)
full (no vacancies)	*'amer*

Food and drink

The menu, please	*'afak zheeblee lmeenoo*
Do you have ....?	*wash 'endkem .....?*
What is in this?	*ash kayn f hada?*
The bill, please	*'afak zheeblee lhsab*
beer	*beera*
bread	*khobz*
breakfast	*ftur*
cheese	*frumazh*
coffee	*qehwa*
dinner	*'sha*
egg	*bayd*
fish	*hoht*
fruit	*fakeeya*
lunch	*ghda*
meat	*lhem*
milk	*hleeb*
salad	*shlada*
tea	*atay*
water	*lma*
wine	*shrab*
vegetables	*khdra*

Days, months and seasons

Monday	*nhar letneen*
Tuesday	*nhar ttla*
Wednesday	*nhar larb'*
Thursday	*nhar lekhmees*
Friday	*nhar zhzhhem'a*
Saturday	*nhar ssebt*
Sunday	*nhar lhedd*
January	*zhanveeyeh*
February	*fevreeyeh*
March	*mars*
April	*abreel*
May	*mayyoo*
June	*yoonyoo*
July	*yoolyooz*
August	*ghoosht*
September	*sebtamber*
October	*'ooktoober*
November	*noovamber*
December	*deesamber*
autumn	*khreef*
winter	*shta*
spring	*rbee'*
summer	*sseef*

Numbers

one	*wahed*	twenty	*'ashreen*
two	*zhoozh*	thirty	*tlateen*
three	*tlata*	forty	*reb'een*
four	*reb'a*	fifty	*khamseen*
five	*khamsa*	sixty	*setteen*
six	*setta*	seventy	*seb'een*
seven	*seb'a*	eighty	*tmaneen*
eight	*tmenya*	ninety	*tes'een*
nine	*tes'ud*	one hundred	*mya*
ten	*'ashra*	one thousand	*alf*

❑ Berber terms

Below is a selection of Berber words most likely to be of use to trekkers. As Berber was not originally written using the Roman alphabet, words given here are spelled phonetically.

Berber person	*amazigh* (pl *imazighen*)
bread	*aroum*
col	*tizi*
food	*teremt*
gateway	*imi*
goodbye	*akayoon arbey/b'slama*
gorge	*aqqa*
hello	*la bas darik/darim* (m/f)
hello (in response)	*la bas*
house	*taddert*
in the name of God	*Bismillah*
lake	*aguelmann*
left	*fozzelmed*
moon	*ayyour*
mountain	*adrar*
mule	*asseerdoun* (m)
no	*oho*
please	*barakalaufik*
rain	*anzar*
right	*ffaseenik*
river	*assif*
snow	*adfel*
star	*itran*
thank you	*barakalaufik/sa-ha*
village	*douar*
water	*amen*
well	*anu*
yes	*eyeh*

FRENCH

Pleasantries

Hello	*Bonjour*
Goodbye	*Au revoir*
Please	*S'il vous plaît*
Thank you	*Merci*
How are you?	*Comment allez-vous/comment ça va?* (formal/informal)
I'm fine, thank you	*bien, merci*
Excuse me	*Excusez-moi/pardon*

Basic conversations

I	*je*
you	*vous/tu* (formal/informal)
we	*nous*
they	*ils/elles* (m/f)
Why?	*pourquoi?*
When?	*quand?*
Is there .....?	*Est-ce qu'il y a .....?*
open	*ouvert*
closed	*fermé*
I don't speak much French	*Je parle peu de français*
Do you speak English?	*Parlez-vous anglais?*
Would you repeat that, please?	*Voulez-vous répéter, s'il vous plaît?*
I don't understand	*Je ne comprends pas*
What's your name?	*Quel est votre/ton* (formal/informal) *nom?*
My name is	*Je m'appelle ......*
I'm from	*J'habite à ......*
I'm here on holiday	*Je suis ici en vacances*
I'm married	*Je suis marié(e)*
I'm single	*Je suis célibataire*
I have ...... children	*J'ai .... enfants* (see Numbers pp253-4)
How old are you?	*Quel âge avez-vous/as-tu?*
I'm ..... years old	*J'ai ...... ans* (see Numbers pp253-4)

Problems and emergencies

Help!	*Au secours!*
Fire!	*Au feu!*
Thief!	*Au velour!*
Can you help me?	*Pouvez-vous m'aider?*
I've been attacked	*On m'a attaqué*
I've been raped	*On m'a violée*
There's been an accident	*Il y a eu un accident*
Please call the police/an ambulance	*S'il vous plaît, appelez la police/une ambulance*
Someone's stolen	*On m'a volé ......*
I need to make a phone call	*Il me faut téléphoner*
I'm very sorry, officer	*Je suis vraiment désolé(e), monsieur l'agent*

Trekking terms

How many kilometres is the walk?	*La promenade fait combien de kilomètres?*
How long will it take?	*Ça prendra combien de temps?*
Can you show me where .... is on the map?	*Pouvez-vous m'indiquer où est .... sur la carte?*

Trekking terms *(cont'd)*

circular trek	*boucle* (f)
col	*col* (m)
compass	*boussole* (m)
lake	*lac* (m)
map	*carte* (f)
mountain	*montagne* (f)
mountain guide	*guide de montagnes* (m)
path	*chemin* (m)
river	*rivière* (f)
shelter	*abri* (m)
summit	*sommet* (m)
trek	*randonnée* (f)
valley	*vallée* (f)

Travel and directions

How do I get to .....?	*Pour aller à .....?*
Is it far?	*C'est loin?*
Is this the right way to..?	*C'est la bonne direction pour .....?*
opposite	*en face de*
next to	*à côte dé*
near to	*près de*
left	*à gauche*
right	*à droite*
straight on	*tout droit*
left-luggage office	*consigne*
train station	*gare ferroviaire*
bus station	*gare routière*

Shopping

Where can I buy .....?	*Où est-ce qu'on peut acheter .....?*
How much?	*Combien?*
It's too expensive for me	*C'est trop cher pour moi*
Do you have anything else?	*Vous n'avez rien d'autre?*
Is there a market?	*Est-ce qu'il y a un marché?*
Which day?	*Quel jour?*

Accommodation

hotel	*hôtel*
lodging	*gîte d'étape*
camp-site	*camping*
Do you have a list of hotels?	*Est-ce que vous avez une liste des hôtels?*
Is there a hotel here?	*Il y a un hôtel ici?*
Do you have any vacancies?	*Vous avez des chambres?*
We'd like to stay ..... nights	*On voudrait rester ..... nuits* (see Numbers opposite)
full (no vacancies)	*complet*

Food and drink

Where can we eat?	*Où est-ce qu'on peut manger?*
The menu, please	*Le menu, s'il vous plaît*
Do you have .....?	*Avez-vous .....?*
What is in this?	*Qu'est-ce qu'il y a dedans?*
more	*encore de ......*
The bill, please	*L'addition, s'il vous plaît*

beer	*bière* (f)
bread	*pain* (m)
breakfast	*petit déjeuner* (m)
cheese	*fromage* (m)
coffee	*café* (m)
dinner	*dîner* (m)
egg	*oeuf* (m)
fish	*poisson* (m)
fruit	*fruit* (m)
kebab	*brochette* (f)
lunch	*déjeuner* (m)
meat	*viande* (f)
milk	*lait* (m)
salad	*salade* (m)
tea	*thé* (m)
water	*eau* (f)
wine	*vin* (m)
vegetables	*légumes* (m)

Days, months and seasons

Monday	*lundi*
Tuesday	*mardi*
Wednesday	*mercredi*
Thursday	*jeudi*
Friday	*vendredi*
Saturday	*samedi*
Sunday	*dimanche*

January	*janvier*
February	*février*
March	*mars*
April	*avril*
May	*mai*
June	*juin*
July	*juillet*
August	*août*
September	*septembre*
October	*octobre*
November	*novembre*
December	*décembre*
autumn	*l'automne*
winter	*l'hiver*
spring	*le printemps*
summer	*l'été*

Numbers

one	*un*
two	*deux*
three	*trois*
four	*quatre*
five	*cinq*
six	*six*
seven	*sept*
eight	*huit*

Numbers *(cont'd)*

nine	*neuf*
ten	*dix*
twenty	*vingt*
thirty	*trente*
forty	*quarante*
fifty	*cinquante*
sixty	*soixante*
seventy	*soixante-dix*
eighty	*quatre-vingts*
ninety	*quatre-vingt-dix*
one hundred	*cent*
one thousand	*mille*

APPENDIX B: GLOSSARY

adrar (pl *adraren*)	mountain
afella	summit
agadir	fortified granary, often communal
aghbalou	water source/spring
aguelmann	lake
aïn	water source/spring
aït	sons of; tribe
Alaouite	current ruling dynasty, founded in 1665
Almohad	dynasty which ruled from 1145 to 1248
Almoravid	dynasty which lasted from 1062 to 1145
almou	plateau
amen	water
anu	well
aqqa	gorge
ararras	path
asseerdoun	mule
assif	stream/mountain river
attar	herbalist
azaghar	plateau
azib	summer shelter for shepherds or goatherds
bab	gate/gateway (often in city wall)
bejmat	small, natural terracotta-coloured tiles
bergerie	goat or sheep pen
boucle	circular route or trek
brochette	kebab
burnous	hooded smock for men
caid	Berber leader or official
calèche	horse-drawn carriage
camion	lorry
caravanserai	lodgings for travellers on a caravan route
couscous	semolina steamed in a pot (a couscoussier) over a stew
cuisinier	cook
dar	building or house

djemaa / jemaa	assembly or meeting place
djinn	mischievous spirit appearing in human or animal form
douar	village, hamlet or small settlement
ensemble artisanal	government-run craft market
erg	desert sand dunes
Fatima	daughter of the Prophet
faux guide	unofficial guide, conman
fêtes nationales	public holidays
gardien	refuge keeper, parking attendant
gare ferroviaire	train station
gare routière	bus station
gîte d'étape	lodging
Gnaoua	an ethnic group largely descended from slaves from sub-Saharan Africa and others who migrated to Morocco through following the trans-Saharan trade caravans
grand taxi	taxi for up to six passengers, usually for longer journeys
haik	cloth worn by women to conceal themselves
hajj	pilgrimage to Mecca or the title bestowed on a man who has fulfilled this pilgrimage
Hamdullah	Praise be to God
hammam	communal steam bath
hanbel	carpet designed for domestic rather than ornamental purposes
harem	women of a Muslim household; their living quarters
harira	thick soup made with spices, chick peas, lamb and tomatoes
harissa	sauce made from chillies and garlic used to flavour dishes
ifri (pl *ifran*)	cave
ighzer	ravine
imam	religious leader
imi	river mouth or gate
imouzzer	waterfall
irhil/ighil	mountain massif
jallabah	large hooded smock with sleeves
jbel / jebel / djebel	mountain
jihad	holy war
kanun	Berber laws
kasbah	citadel, fortress, fortified house
kif	marijuana
kilim	woven rug
koubba	dome-shaped structure over a holy site
ksar (pl *ksours*)	fortified village
kufic	stylised Arabic script often used in engravings
mechoui	whole lamb roasted slowly in a sealed clay oven
Maghreb	the 'land of the furthest West': Morocco, Algeria and Tunisia
marabout	tomb or shrine of a holy man; can also mean the holy man himself
mashreq	eastern Arab world
mechoui / m'choui	roast mutton
medersa	university for religious study
medina	the old part of a city, often walled
mellah	Jewish Quarter
menzeh	summer pavilion
Merenid	dynasty in power between 1248 and 1465
merlons	squared battlements
miâara	Jewish cemetery

minaret	mosque tower
mirhab	alcove in mosque which points to Mecca
mouflon	Barbary sheep
moussem	seasonal festival, often religious
mudawana	new family code introduced by Mohammed VI
muezzin	one who calls the faithful to prayer; the call to prayer
oued	river
pastilla	sweet pigeon pie made with light pastry
pbuh	'peace be upon him' – words written or spoken immediately after the Prophet Mohammed's name as an indication of respect towards him
petit taxi	taxi used for short, local trips
pisé	mud wedged between wooden boards for building
piste	dirt or loose stone road
quatre-quatre	4WD vehicle / 4x4
Ramadan	holy month during which Muslims fast from sunrise to sunset
ribat	fortified monastery
Saadian	dynasty which lasted from 1554 to 1669
Shahada	profession of belief in the Muslim faith
Sharia	Muslim law
sidi	saint, honoured person
souk / souq	market, often named after the day of the week on which it is held: Tnine (Monday), Tleta (Tuesday), Arba (Wednesday), Khemis (Thursday), Sebt (Saturday), Had (Sunday). Souks are not normally open on a Friday.
Sufi	Muslim mystic or mystical brotherhood
taddart	house
tadlekt	A traditional, polished, lime-based, near-waterproof wall plaster
taghia	valley or gorge
tagine	earthenware pot with a chimney in which meat or vegetable stews are prepared; the stew cooked in such a pot
tamda	lake
tam-tam	a small hand drum, similar to a bongo, usually made with wood but sometimes with brightly painted ceramic, and normally with a goat-skin drumhead
talat	ravine
Tamazight / Tarafit	Berber dialect spoken in central Morocco / north Morocco
Tashelhit	Berber dialect spoken in the High Atlas, Anti-Atlas and Sous
téléboutique	privately run payphone kiosk
tichka	common pasture
tighremt	fortified store or house
tizgui	forest
tizi	col/mountain pass
vale	wide flat valley
vizier	high-ranking political adviser or minister
wadi	water-course, dry in summer
Wattasid	dynasty in power between 1465 and 1554
zakat	Muslim alms
zellij	geometrical mosaic pattern used in traditional décor
ziouvani	bright lemon-yellow colour leather, popular in babouches, traditionally achieved using milled pomegranate bark

(Opposite) Self-explanatory pictorial signboards.

BIENVENUE AUX VOYAGEURS
WELCOME
مرحبا بالمسافرين
ماء الورد

بائع الدجاج
والفواكه
خدمات مقهى
احتوش
SERVICES.CAFE.OUHATOUCH

صانع الأسنان
DENTISTE
حلاق
COIFFEUR

CAFE
DES AMIS

OMO

مقهى ادازن
ترحب بالجميع
CAFE
ADAZEN

مجزرة
BOUCHRIE

APPENDIX C: HEALTH

REDUCING THE RISKS OF GETTING ILL

Any journey will expose the traveller to a different set of risks than he or she might experience at home. Trekking, of course, creates its own dangers, as does travelling in a developing country like Morocco. Disease is more prevalent, standards of hygiene are low and the quality of medical provision is variable. However, while it's important to be aware of the dangers, one should not be intimidated by the prospect of an Atlas trek. Simply take your health seriously to significantly reduce the risk of any major problems.

Before you arrive in Morocco

- Take out medical insurance (see Insurance, p42).
- Have your inoculations in good time (see Inoculations, p42).
- Visit the dentist.
- Consult your doctor if you suffer from any ongoing medical difficulties and take appropriate medicines with you. Ask your doctor for a letter explaining your condition and have it translated into French and Arabic, if possible.
- Prepare medical and first-aid kits (see Medical and first aid kits, p34).
- Check that your equipment, particularly footwear, is fit for purpose and comfortable (see Footwear and footcare, pp31-2).
- Take steps to ensure that you are reasonably healthy.

In Morocco

- Drink plenty of liquids, whether water, well-known brands of soft drinks, or hot drinks such as tea or coffee. Your chances of drinking sufficient quantities of liquid are enhanced if you have an efficient means to purify water. See the box about water purification on p29.
- Avoid salads and raw vegetables if they have not been freshly made or if there is any chance that they have been prepared with contaminated water (see p111).
- Eat hot food which has just been cooked or fruit which you can peel yourself.
- Eat plenty of carbohydrates and protein, even if you're not hungry, to keep your strength up.
- Follow the advice given in the box on Acute Mountain Sickness (AMS) on pp258-9.
- Look after your feet (see p260).
- Be very careful when mules pass you on the trail; stand on the mountain side of the path to make sure that the mule does not knock you off.
- Don't hurry on the trail and avoid trekking in bad light.
- Avoid trekking alone.

> ❑ **Normal health in adults**
> **Body temperature:** 37°C or 98.4°F
> **Pulse rate:** 60-100 per minute
> **Breathing:** 12-20 breaths per minute

HEALTH CARE IN THE ATLAS REGION

Standards of health care in Morocco can vary considerably from one doctor or hospital to the next. In the case of serious illness, contact your embassy or consulate for advice (see p71). It might be that your best course of action is to arrange a prompt flight home. There are hospitals in Azilal, Ouarzazate and Marrakech. Most CAF huts have a first-aid kit and stretcher and all official mountain guides have had some basic training in first-aid. See p41 for information about mountain rescue.

(Opposite) For some post-trek ideas see pp26-7. To Erg Chegaga by camel is just one option (**top**). With beautiful fabrics, rugs and ceramics in local designs (**bottom**), you'll be spoilt for choice when it comes to souvenir shopping.

AIDS

While both HIV and AIDS (*SIDA* in French), remain far from widespread in Morocco, both are on the increase. According to the Moroccan Health Ministry (December 2009), the total number of people in Morocco who have been officially registered with AIDS since 1986 has risen to 3198. The government currently spends 18dh million per year fighting the disease and has recently launched a series of awareness-raising campaigns to help people understand its dangers and the means of avoiding the HIV virus. Meanwhile, however, public awareness remains very low. Any exposure to blood or body fluids could be dangerous. Most visitors will be aware that unprotected sex or intravenous drug use might expose an individual to HIV but the disease can just as easily be passed on through piercing, vaccinations or even blood transfusions. If you need an injection, make sure you see that the needle is removed from a sealed wrapper. Better still, carry your own sterile needles (although be prepared for some fast-talking if a customs official finds them in your bag). Best of all, be

❑ ACUTE MOUNTAIN SICKNESS (AMS)

The higher you climb, the less oxygen is available to you. So, whereas at 1000m/3280ft there remains 89% of the oxygen that is available at sea level, this is reduced to 79% at 2000m/6561ft and to just 70% at 3000m/9842ft. AMS is caused by a lack of oxygen reaching your lungs, muscles and brain. This is extremely dangerous and can even be fatal.

Many trekkers are surprised to find that it is possible to suffer from AMS at relatively low altitudes. The key point to remember, however, is that it **is not so much your altitude as your rate of ascent which ultimately causes AMS**. It is important to give your body time to adjust to the change in oxygen levels as you climb.

'Altitude starts to have an effect around 1500-2000m. The body starts to behave slightly differently as it tries to make up for the change in oxygen levels. Go up too fast to about 2500m and altitude illnesses are common.' **Medex** (www.medex.org.uk)

Since most of the treks in this guide rise to over 2500m, and the highest peaks are over 4000m, trekkers should read this section very carefully. Although some people are more susceptible to AMS than others, fitness appears to make no difference. In nearly all cases, however, AMS is relatively easy to avoid.

Particular care should be taken with children: *'Children have the same problems at high altitude as adults, but it is more difficult to tell when they are having these problems. It is essential to climb slowly to allow children time to acclimatise. Young children can't tell you how they feel. The carer should be guided by the child's fussiness, eating, sleeping and playing. If these are worse than usual the child should be assumed to have altitude illness and stay at the same altitude or descend until they are better. Older children can describe the symptoms of AMS, which are the same as for adults. Assume symptoms are caused by altitude and stay at the same altitude or descend until they are better.'* **Medex** (www.medex.org.uk)

Prevention

- **Don't exceed the recommended rate of ascent** Your body must have time to acclimatise to altitude. Take two or more days to reach 3000m (10,000ft) and spend subsequent nights at no more than 300m (1000ft) higher than the previous night. It's also a good idea to sleep a little lower than the highest point reached that day. Spend a rest day after each 900m (3000ft) gained over 3000m (10,000ft).
- **Drink lots of fluids** Drink at least six litres of water each day. If your urine is dark, you need to drink more water.
- **Eat well** Keep eating plenty of carbohydrates even if you have lost your appetite.

prepared to buy your own needle should you need one. When I had stitches removed in Taliwine, the local doctor actually asked me to pop out from his clinic to buy my own sealed blade from the pharmacist across the street.

Do not refuse a transfusion through fear of contracting HIV; the better Moroccan hospitals screen blood and the chance of picking up the disease in this way is minimal.

BILHARZIA

Bilharzia is a disease caused by parasitic worms called schistosomes. Bilharzia worms are thought to be present in some still pools and slow-moving streams in the south and, perhaps, the lower parts of the High Atlas. The higher you go, the less chance of catching bilharzia worms. They grow in snails which inhabit the edges of lakes and streams, bore into humans and live in their intestines. The effects can be painful and debilitating but there is a cure. Avoid bathing in any water which you think might harbour the worms; in particular avoid the

- **Avoid alcohol and sedatives** Drinking alcohol at altitude can lead to dehydration.
- **Don't rush** Ascend steep inclines slowly, allowing yourself plenty of rests. The faster you gain height, the higher the chance of suffering AMS.
- **Look out for symptoms** Read the section below and look out for symptoms of AMS. Since one symptom is confusion and delirium, you should keep an eye on your fellow trekkers and they should do the same for you.
- **Diamox** You should consult your doctor before using Diamox. Some doctors believe it is dangerous because it hides the symptoms of AMS. Do not take Diamox to prevent AMS, only to help you cope with early symptoms. Should symptoms of AMS develop, descend as quickly as is safely possible.

'Acetazolamide (Diamox) can be used to help prevent mountain sickness when a gradual ascent cannot be guaranteed. It should NOT be used as an alternative to a gradual ascent. It acts on acid-base balance and stimulates respiration. It should be combined with a good fluid intake. It should not normally be used in young children except under close medical supervision. Dose: 125mg to 250mg twice daily for adults. It should be started 24 hours before ascent and continued only for the first two days at high altitude while acclimatisation occurs.' **NHS** (Scotland)

Symptoms and treatment

- **Mild AMS** Early signs of AMS include headache, nausea, difficulty sleeping, loss of appetite and dizziness. If you experience these symptoms, and can't attribute them with certainty to some other problem, stop ascending. Rest until you feel better before moving higher or, if the symptoms persist, descend at least 500m and ideally 1000m.
- **Acute AMS** Symptoms of advanced AMS include extreme tiredness, loss of co-ordination, delirium, vertigo, headache, vomiting, cyanosis (blue lips), coughing attacks producing pink or brown sputum, bubbling breath, rapid heartbeats at rest and eventual coma. The sufferer must descend immediately. Acute AMS can be fatal.
- **High Altitude Cerebral Edema (HACE)** Believed to be an acute form of altitude sickness caused by a build up of fluid on the brain, HACE can, in worst cases, kill in just a few hours. Symptoms include severe headache, vomiting and lethargy progressing to unsteadiness, confusion, drowsiness and ultimately coma. Although the lowest reported case of HACE is at 2100m, it is nonetheless experienced by 1% of people who ascend to above 3000m/9842ft (💻 www.altitude.org). Once again, the likelihood of suffering from HACE increases through rapid ascent and the only effective treatment is rapid descent.

water's edge. Since the worms often bore into the soles of feet, wear rafting sandals to paddle. Early symptoms include a rash where the worm entered and, later, a high fever. Later still, blood might appear in your urine. If left untreated, the problems could recur for 30 years.

DIARRHOEA

Travellers to Morocco commonly experience diarrhoea. In the Atlas Mountains, of course, where proper lavatories are few and far between, this can be a particularly unpleasant state of affairs. Diarrhoea is almost always caused by food poisoning or drinking dirty water (see box on water purification, p29). Take great care over what you eat and drink (see p111) and follow a strict personal hygiene regime to reduce your chances of getting ill. Certainly, always wash your hands carefully before eating. It's generally best to avoid taking treatments like 'Imodium' or 'Arret' which simply block up your bowels but don't treat the infection. These treatments are, however, gifts from Allah when it comes to long bus or train journeys. The three main ways to combat diarrhoea are to rest, to drink plenty of fluids, and to replace salts with rehydration mixtures such as Dialoryte.

- **Traveller's diarrhoea (bacterial)** This most common form of diarrhoea can be brought on simply by a change of diet. Bacterial diarrhoea will normally clear up on its own after a few days so take no treatment at first except rest, fluids and rehydration preparations.
- **Amoebic dysentery (amoebiasis)** This is an infection of the intestine (gut) caused by an amoeba called *entamoeba histolytica*. This can be rather more serious than traveller's diarrhoea. Symptoms include frequent and sometimes bloody diarrhoea which recurs in cycles every few days or so. It might be accompanied by vomiting and abdominal cramps. Seek medical advice where possible. If this is not possible, amoebic dysentery can be treated with metronidazole (such as Flagyl tablets). Normally two 400mg tablets are taken three times a day for five days although this would be inappropriate for anyone who is either pregnant or breastfeeding. It is important to avoid drinking alcohol during treatment. Always see a doctor as soon as possible to ensure that the treatment has been effective. As metronidazole requires a prescription, you could ask your own doctor to write a prescription in advance as you know that you will be travelling to a remote area where access to a doctor or hospital is likely to be difficult.
- **Giardia (giardiasis)** A particularly unpleasant form of diarrhoea caused by parasites in contaminated water. The effects might not appear for weeks. Symptoms are a few loose stools every day, nausea, abdominal pain and heinous wind. Treatment is as for amoebic dysentery, above.

CARE OF FEET, ANKLES AND KNEES

A simple blister or sprain could ruin your trek so take great care to look after your feet, ankles and knees.

- **Blisters** Prevention is better than cure. See Footwear and footcare, pp31-2.
- **Sprains** Good boots will help (see p31). Watch where you walk, particularly when you are tired, and always try to avoid trekking in bad light. Don't carry too heavy a load and don't rush. If you do suffer a sprain, keep it cool, firmly bandaged, raised and rested for a while. A mountain stream would be the best place to cool the swelling.
- **Knee problems** On your descent, bend your knees slightly to avoid jarring them. Use knee supports if you have had trouble before. Deep Heat or Tiger Balm might help at the end of the day.

INFECTIOUS HEPATITIS

There are two types of infectious hepatitis, A and B, and both are fairly common across North Africa. See also Inoculations, p42.

- **Hepatitis A** is the less serious. It is an infectious disease of the liver with an incubation period of two to six weeks. Early symptoms can be mistaken for influenza although some sufferers, particularly children, show no symptoms at all. Symptoms, which can return over the following six to nine weeks, include stomach cramps, nausea, fatigue, depression, jaundice (yellowness of the skin or eyes), appetite loss and weight loss. Hepatitis A can be picked up from contaminated food, polluted water or bad sanitary hygiene. A gamma globulin injection prior to departure helps to prevent the disease.

• **Hepatitis B** is the more serious. It is a virus of the liver leading to its inflammation with an incubation period of anything from four weeks to six months. Symptoms are broadly the same as for Hepatitis A although they can include, if only rarely, death.

Acute Hepatitis B does not usually require treatment as most adults clear the infection naturally. However, treatment for chronic Hepatitis B may be necessary to reduce the risk of cirrhosis or even eventual cancer of the liver. It can be picked up in the same way as AIDS: as a sexually transmitted disease, from contact with contaminated blood or body fluids, through needles or blood transfusions, or, most predominantly, from mother to baby at childbirth. There is no cure for Hepatitis B but infection is preventable by vaccine.

MALARIA

Malaria is a serious and sometimes fatal disease transmitted by mosquitoes. It is uncommon in Morocco and most of the country is considered low to no risk by the National Health Service (Scotland). A strip of Morocco stretching from north-east of Marrakech through Meknes to just beyond Fes is considered minimal risk although antimalarials are not usually recommended for any part of Morocco (see Inoculations, p42).

On the other hand, Algeria is considered to be a malaria risk and anyone considering heading towards the southern desert areas of Morocco, for example, after their trek should take advice from their doctor before departure. There is a very small risk of exclusively benign malaria from May to October in eastern parts of the country in rural valleys, west of the Atlas Mountains (Chefchaouen Province).

In all events, try to avoid getting bitten by mosquitoes. Use repellents and perhaps a mosquito net as well. Most bites are inflicted at dawn and dusk so wear socks, trousers and long-sleeved shirts at these times.

For more information see the malaria map on 💻 www.fitfor travel.nhs.uk.

OTHER HEALTH PROBLEMS

Bedbugs

There is a chance you will have difficulties with bedbugs if you sleep on old, dirty bedding. Better to sleep in your sleeping-bag even in gîtes. Bedbugs leave rows of itchy red bites which are best soothed with cool antiseptic cream.

Dehydration

In the Atlas temperatures can soar and you will lose a lot of fluid through sweating. This can lead to salt loss and heat-stroke and can be very serious. Drink as much clean water as you can while trekking, even when you are not thirsty. In order to maintain your sugar and salt levels, use rehydration mixtures regularly, both in the middle and at the end of each day. Failing this, unless you suffer from blood-pressure problems, add extra salt to your food and always make sure that there is plenty of sugar in your mint tea. The best way to look for dehydration is to monitor your urine. The darker the urine, the more advanced the dehydration.

Exposure (hypothermia)

This is unlikely to be a problem for summer trekkers but in winter at altitude it is a very real danger for the ill-equipped (see What to take pp28-33). Caused by a combination of inadequate food and clothing, dehydration, exhaustion and altitude change, the early symptoms are a lowering of the body temperature by as little as one degree, mild to strong shivering, quick, shallow breathing, fatigue and poor co-ordination. Often sufferers will pass through a stage of feeling warm and thinking that they are recovering but this is actually a sign of further deterioration. The victim will become pale and lips, ears, fingers and toes may all become blue. As the condition worsens, hallucinations may follow. Pulse and breathing rates will significantly drop whilst heart rates can quicken. Unconsciousness, failure of major organs and then death follow quickly.

Find shelter in the early stages if possible. If wet, dry and then gradually warm the patient's body but avoid rubbing. Blankets are useful but alone are insufficient to treat hypothermia. The most effective treatment is transfer of body heat and therefore you should strip and get into a sleeping bag with the naked patient, piling extra bedding underneath and around you. Put in a hot water bottle (your drinking bottle will do). It is critical that the centre of the body is warmed first, therefore, where possible, encourage the patient to drink warm, sweet liquids. However, if the patient's condition becomes moderate or severe, evacuate to hospital immediately.

Frostbite

Caused chiefly by extremely cold temperatures and wet clothes, like hypothermia, in Morocco this is likely to be a potential threat only at altitude in winter. In the early stages, often called frostnip, blood circulation to the extremities decreases, and toes and fingers become very cold, numb, white and painful. The sensation can be that of tingling or burning. Warm the affected parts against your body. Actual frostbite occurs when a body part becomes frozen. Nerves become damaged due to lack of oxygen to the affected areas while the skin will turn purple at first and then black. If not treated immediately the damage will become permanent and amputation may be necessary. Treat the affected area in warm, but not hot, water. Do not rub or slap the affected body parts as further damage will be caused by the ice crystals forming in the damaged skin. Once warm, do not allow the patient to become cold again as refreezing following thawing worsens the damage. Seek help.

Gynaecological problems

Dietary change, travel or strenuous exercise can make periods irregular or even stop them altogether but this is no cause for alarm. However, during acclimatisation the body increases its iron rich blood cells so a woman who normally experiences heavy periods might discuss with her doctor taking iron supplements prior to departure for Morocco.

Although there may be some increased risk of blood clots in the legs when taking the combined contraceptive pill at altitude, this is only linked to stays at over 4000m for lengthy periods so should not be an issue in Morocco.

Haemorrhoids

Constipation is fairly common on treks and can lead to haemorrhoids. If you've suffered from this problem in the past, bring remedies with you just in case.

Miliaria (Prickly heat)

This is an uncomfortable skin disease appearing as an itchy rash caused by sweat glands becoming blocked by dead skin or bacteria which can follow sudden exposure to a hot climate. It is particularly common in children as their sweat glands have not fully developed. Bathe as often as possible and wear specialist trekking clothing with wicking properties or otherwise cool, loose clothing (see What to take, pp32-3). Unscented or baby talcum powder may help.

Rabies

Rabies is common in North Africa and is always fatal without treatment so, if you get bitten or if an open wound is licked by any animal which you think might have rabies, wash the wound immediately and abundantly with soap and water, apply an antiseptic such as iodine or alcohol and seek a vaccine from a doctor as soon as you can. In theory the offending animal should be captured for observation. In practice, however, this will probably lead to your getting bitten again. There is an anti-rabies pre-exposure vaccine which is sometimes advised for Morocco by NHS (Scotland), although not currently (June 2010). Even if you have this vaccine, you should still seek medical attention urgently if you suspect you have been exposed to rabies.

Snake bites

If you see a snake, leave it alone and avoid putting your hands or feet into a hole or crevice where there might be one. Even if there isn't a snake, there may well be a scorpion or a spider. The possibility of coming across a snake diminishes with altitude but, even should you be bitten, don't panic: more people die from shock than from snake bites and even the most venomous snakes do not always release venom when they bite. Don't cut or suck the wound. Immobilise the bitten limb and keep still to minimise the spreading of the poison. Identify the snake if you can but don't waste time trying to do so, since the right antivenene is likely to be available only at major hospitals which may take some time to reach.

The two snakes most likely to inflict a bite in Morocco are the lebetin viper (*Vipera lebetina*), and the horned viper or sand viper (*Cerastes cerastes*). The rather corpulent Vipera lebetina grows typically to 1.3m in length. Matt grey to brown in colour, it has three very small black spots on its head, and tends to move little, choosing to lie in and around small water pits awaiting birds to prey upon. The smaller Cerastes cerastes has a length of usually no more than between 30 and 60cm. It is best recognised by its horns, one above each eye, although these are not always present. Its colour tends to match that of the ground where it is found, varying from a yellow to grey to pink to pale brown. A series of dark blotches run along the length of its body. Its belly is white and its tail can have a black tip.

Sunburn and heat stroke

There is a real chance of being struck down by heat stroke in the Atlas Mountains. The sun can be frighteningly strong and its effects can be greater at altitude. Heatstroke can, in extreme cases, lead to death so its dangers must be taken seriously. Drink at least six litres of clean water a day to avoid dehydration and to enable you to sweat and dissipate your body's heat. Wear plenty of sunscreen and protect yourself from the sun with sunglasses, a neckerchief or a shirt with a high collar and a wide-brimmed hat (see What to take, p33). Rest regularly in the shade. Sometimes heat exhaustion may come on as a prelude to heat stroke. Symptoms of heat exhaustion include nausea, vomiting, fatigue, headache, aching muscles and dizziness.

Other people might suddenly exhibit symptoms of heat stroke. Symptoms of heat stroke can be quite varied and different from person to person but typically include a high body temperature accompanied by an absence of sweating, a rapid pulse, laboured breathing, confused behaviour including hallucinations, agitation, seizure and even coma. Immediate treatment involves removing the patient from the sun, stripping them and coating them in cool, wet towels. Fan the patient to induce sweating. Make sure the patient drinks lots of water for so long as they are conscious, ideally with added electrolytes such as dioralyte or, if unavailable, with added salt. In all cases, seek medical help.

AFTER YOUR TREK

If you want to leave unused medical supplies in Morocco, you should find someone in a position of responsibility, perhaps the mayor of an Atlas village. Avoid dispensing them to random people who you think might need them but who might not use them appropriately.

If you want to help with developments in Morocco after your return home, and if based in Britain, you might consider contacting the registered charity, The British Moroccan Society (💻 www.british-moroccansoc.org), Dartmouth House, Dartmouth Place, London W4 2RH.

ACKNOWLEDGEMENTS FOR QUOTATIONS

The author thanks the following publishers and authors for quotations used in the text from *The Voices of Marrakech* (Elias Canetti, translated by JA Underwood, Marion Boyars Publishers Ltd, 1967, 1st translated edition) on pp27, 65, 69, 113 and 118, by permission of Marion Boyars; from *Great Atlas Traverse Vols 1 and 2* (Michael Peyron, West Col, 1989 and 1990) on p30 and p139 (from Vol 1, 1989) and p151 (from Vol 1, 1989, and Vol 2, 1990) by permission of West Col Productions; from *The City in the 1960s* (Anthony Gladstone-Thompson, printed in *Marrakech, The Red City* ed Barnaby Rogerson and Stephen Lavington, Sickle Moon Books, 2003, 1st edition) on p49 by permission of the author; from *Morocco* (André Launay, Batsford, 1976, 1st edition) on p55 by permission of Batsford, an imprint of Anova Books Ltd; from *Couscous and Other Good Food from Morocco* (Paula Wolfert, Harper & Row, 1973, 1st edition) on p81 by permission of the author; from *A Moroccan Luncheon* by Colette, reprinted in *A Book of Travellers' Tales* by Eric Newby, Picador, 1985, 1st edition, by permission of MacMillan Publishers; from *The Mountains Look on Marrakech* (Hamish Brown, Whittles Publishing, 1st edition, 2007) on p142 and p157 by permission of the author; from www.Medex.org.uk on p258 by permission of Simon Currin; from *Mogreb-el-Acksa* (RB Cunninghame Graham) on pp10, 36, 38, 43, 48, 60, 69, 75, 91, 93, 98 and 114-15 from the Heinemann, 1898, 1st edition; from *Journal of a Tour in Marocco and the Great Atlas* (Joseph D Hooker and John Ball) on p28 from the Macmillan and Co, 1878, 1st edition; from *Peeps at Many Lands Morocco* (John Finnemore) on p119 from the 1st edition published by Adam & Charles Black, 1908; from *The Adventures of Thomas Pellow, of Penryn, Mariner: Three and Twenty Years in Captivity among the Moors* (Thomas Pellow) on p74 from the T Fisher Unwin, 1890, 1st edition; from *Travels in the Atlas and Southern Morocco* (Joseph Thomson), on p84, from the George Philip & Son, 1889; from *Moorish Lotos Leaves* (George D Cowan and RLN Johnston) on p122 reproduced from the Tinsley Brothers, 1883, 1st edition.

See p4 for further acknowledgements.

INDEX

Abbreviations: (A) Azilal, (BD) Boumalne du Dades, (I) Imlil, (M) Marrakech, (N) Nkoub, (O) Ouarzazate, (QM) Qalaa't Mgouna, (T) Tabant, (Ta) Taliwine

Page references in bold type refer to maps

MORE GUIDES FROM TRAILBLAZER
(see overleaf for full list)

Morocco Overland – from the Atlas to the Sahara
Chris Scott, 1st edition, £15.99, ISBN 978-1-905864-20-1
276pp, 40pp maps, 24 colour & 170 B&W photos
This is a guide to 49 routes through southern Morocco's spectacular landscape – from the snow-clad High Atlas to the dunes of the Sahara and right down to the Mauritanian border. With easy-to-follow routes for 4WDs, motorcycles and mountain bikes with hundreds of GPS waypoints, this comprehensive route and planning guide will appeal to both the seasoned adventurer and the first timer. Each route is reversible and is graded for suitability for mountain bikes. Includes fuel stations, restaurants and places to stay. With over 40pp of mapping. *'The bible for off-roading to and across this corner of North Africa'* Wanderlust Magazine

Kilimanjaro – the trekking guide to Africa's highest mountain *Henry Stedman*, 3rd edition, £12.99
ISBN 978-1-905864-24-9, 368pp, 40 maps, 30 photos
At 19,340ft the world's tallest freestanding mountain, Kilimanjaro is one of the most popular destinations for hikers visiting Africa. It's possible to walk up to the summit: no technical skills are necessary. Includes town guides to Nairobi and Dar-Es-Salaam, excursions in the region and a colour guide to flora and fauna. Includes Mount Meru.

Nepal Trekking and the Great Himalaya Trail
Robin Boustead, 1st edition, £14.99, ISBN 978-1-905864-31-7
320pp, 8pp colour maps, 40 colour photos
This guide includes the most popular routes in Nepal – the Everest, Annapurna and Langtang regions – as well as the newest trekking areas for true trailblazers. This is the first guide to chart The Great Himalaya Trail, the route which crosses Nepal from east to west. Extensive planning sections.

Trekking in the Everest Region
Jamie McGuinness, 5th edition, £12.99, ISBN 978-1-873756-99-7
320pp, 30 maps, 30 colour photos
Fifth edition of this popular guide to the Everest region, the world's most famous trekking region. Includes planning, preparation and getting to Nepal; detailed route guides – with 30 route maps and 50 village plans; Kathmandu city guide – where to stay, where to eat, what to see.

The Inca Trail, Cusco & Machu Picchu
Alexander Stewart, 4th edition, £12.99, ISBN 978-1-905864-15-7
352pp, 74 maps, 40 photos
The Inca Trail from Cusco to Machu Picchu, is South America's most popular trek. Practical guide including detailed trail maps, plans of Inca sites, plus guides to Cusco and Machu Picchu. Route guides to other trails in the area: the Santa Teresa Trek and the Choquequirao Trek as well as the Vilcabamba Trail plus the routes linking them. This entirely rewalked and rewritten fourth edition includes a new history of the Incas by Hugh Thomson.

Title list – www.trailblazer-guides.com

Adventure Cycle-Touring Handbook	2nd edn out now
Adventure Motorcycling Handbook	5th edn out now
Australia by Rail	5th edn out now
Australia's Great Ocean Road	1st edn out now
Azerbaijan	4th edn out now
Coast to Coast Path (British Walking Guide)	4th edn out now
Cornwall Coast Path (British Walking Guide)	3rd edn out now
Corsica Trekking – GR20	1st edn out now
Cotswold Way (British Walking Guide)	1st edn out now
Dolomites Trekking – AV1 & AV2	2nd edn out now
Inca Trail, Cusco & Machu Picchu	4th edn Dec 2010
Indian Rail Handbook	1st edn mid 2011
Hadrian's Wall Path (British Walking Guide)	2nd edn out now
Himalaya by Bike – a route and planning guide	1st edn out now
Japan by Rail	2nd edn out now
Kilimanjaro – the trekking guide (inc Mt Meru)	3rd edn out now
Mediterranean Handbook	1st edn out now
Morocco Overland (4WD/motorcycle/mountainbike)	1st edn out now
Moroccan Atlas – The Trekking Guide	1st edn out now
Nepal Mountaineering Guide	1st edn mid 2011
Nepal Trekking & The Great Himalaya Trail	1st edn Nov 2010
New Zealand – The Great Walks	2nd edn out now
North Downs Way (British Walking Guide)	1st edn out now
Norway's Arctic Highway	1st edn out now
Offa's Dyke Path (British Walking Guide)	2nd edn out now
Overlanders' Handbook – worldwide driving guide	1st edn Feb 2011
Peddars Way & Norfolk CP (British Walking Guide)	1st edn Jan 2011
Pembrokeshire Coast Path (British Walking Guide)	3rd edn out now
Pennine Way (British Walking Guide)	2nd edn out now
The Ridgeway (British Walking Guide)	2nd edn out now
The Silk Roads – a route and planning guide	3rd edn out now
Sahara Overland – a route and planning guide	2nd edn out now
Scottish Highlands – The Hillwalking Guide	2nd edn out now
South Downs Way (British Walking Guide)	3rd edn out now
Tour du Mont Blanc	1st edn out now
Trans-Canada Rail Guide	5th edn out now
Trans-Siberian Handbook	7th edn out now
Trekking in the Annapurna Region	5th edn Jan 2011
Trekking in the Everest Region	5th edn out now
Trekking in Ladakh	3rd edn out now
Trekking in the Pyrenees	3rd edn out now
Walker's Haute Route – Mont Blanc to Matterhorn	1st edn out now
West Highland Way (British Walking Guide)	4th edn out now

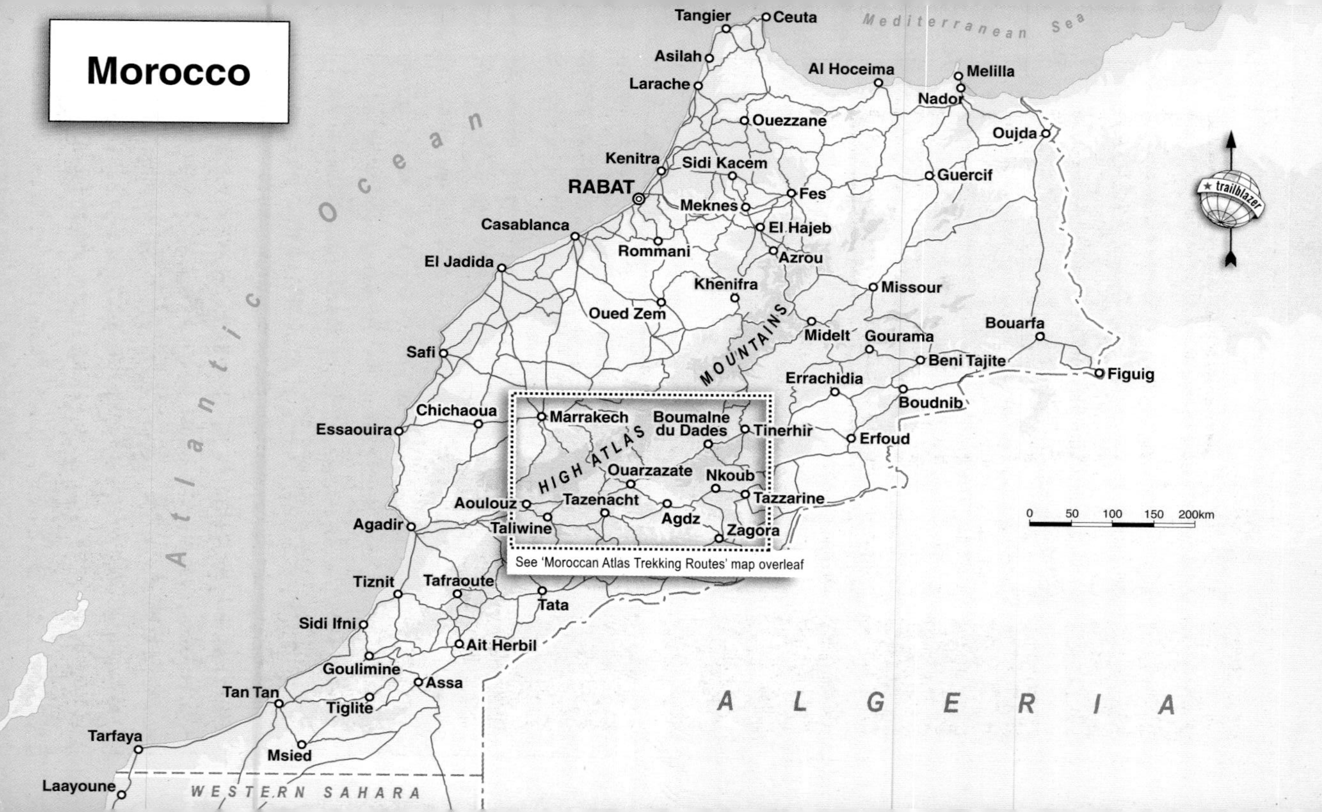
Morocco
Mediterranean Sea
Atlantic Ocean
Tangier
Ceuta
Asilah
Larache
Al Hoceima
Melilla
Nador
Ouezzane
Oujda
Kenitra
Sidi Kacem
Guercif
RABAT
Fes
Meknes
El Hajeb
Casablanca
Rommani
Azrou
El Jadida
Khenifra
Missour
Oued Zem
MOUNTAINS
Midelt
Gourama
Bouarfa
Safi
Beni Tajite
Figuig
Errachidia
Boudnib
Chichaoua
Marrakech
Boumalne
du Dades
Tinerhir
Essaouira
Erfoud
HIGH ATLAS
Ouarzazate
Nkoub
Tazzarine
Aoulouz
Tazenacht
Agdz
Agadir
Taliwine
Zagora
See 'Moroccan Atlas Trekking Routes' map overleaf
0
50
100
150
200km
trailblazer
Tiznit
Tafraoute
Tata
Sidi Ifni
Ait Herbil
Goulimine
Assa
Tan Tan
Tiglite
ALGERIA
Tarfaya
Msied
Laayoune
WESTERN SAHARA

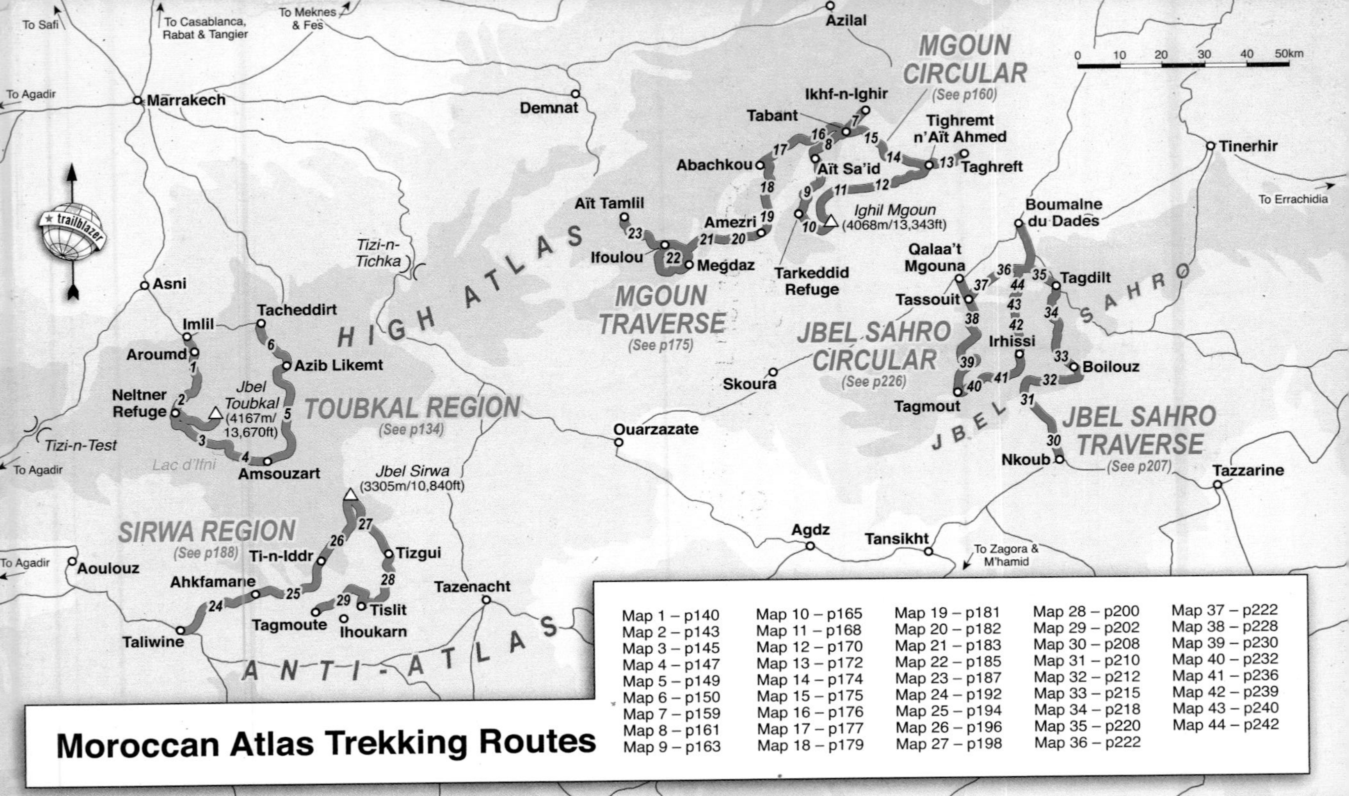

Moroccan Atlas Trekking Routes
Map 1 – p140
Map 2 – p143
Map 3 – p145
Map 4 – p147
Map 5 – p149
Map 6 – p150
Map 7 – p159
Map 8 – p161
Map 9 – p163
Map 10 – p165
Map 11 – p168
Map 12 – p170
Map 13 – p172
Map 14 – p174
Map 15 – p175
Map 16 – p176
Map 17 – p177
Map 18 – p179
Map 19 – p181
Map 20 – p182
Map 21 – p183
Map 22 – p185
Map 23 – p187
Map 24 – p192
Map 25 – p194
Map 26 – p196
Map 27 – p198
Map 28 – p200
Map 29 – p202
Map 30 – p208
Map 31 – p210
Map 32 – p212
Map 33 – p215
Map 34 – p218
Map 35 – p220
Map 36 – p222
Map 37 – p222
Map 38 – p228
Map 39 – p230
Map 40 – p232
Map 41 – p236
Map 42 – p239
Map 43 – p240
Map 44 – p242
MGOUN CIRCULAR
(See p160)
MGOUN TRAVERSE
(See p175)
JBEL SAHRO CIRCULAR
(See p226)
JBEL SAHRO TRAVERSE
(See p207)
TOUBKAL REGION
(See p134)
SIRWA REGION
(See p188)
HIGH ATLAS
ANTI-ATLAS
JBEL SAHRO
trailblazer
0 10 20 30 40 50km
To Safi
To Casablanca, Rabat & Tangier
To Meknes & Fes
To Agadir
To Errachidia
To Zagora & M'hamid
Marrakech
Asni
Imlil
Aroumd
Neltner Refuge
Tacheddirt
Azib Likemt
Jbel Toubkal (4167m/13,670ft)
Amsouzart
Lac d'Ifni
Tizi-n-Test
Tizi-n-Tichka
Demnat
Azilal
Aït Tamlil
Ifoulou
Megdaz
Amezri
Abachkou
Tabant
Ikhf-n-Ighir
Aït Sa'id
Tarkeddid Refuge
Ighil Mgoun (4068m/13,343ft)
Tighremt n'Aït Ahmed
Taghreft
Tinerhir
Boumalne du Dades
Qalaa't Mgouna
Tassouit
Tagdilt
Irhissi
Boilouz
Tagmout
Nkoub
Tazzarine
Skoura
Ouarzazate
Agdz
Tansikht
Jbel Sirwa (3305m/10,840ft)
Ti-n-Iddr
Tizgui
Tislit
Ihoukarn
Tagmoute
Ahkfamane
Taliwine
Aoulouz
Tazenacht